The Calvinist Roots of the Modern Era

The Calvinist Roots
of the Modern Era

Edited by

Aliki Barnstone
Michael Tomasek Manson
Carol J. Singley

University Press of New England / Hanover and London

University Press of New England, Hanover, NH 03755
© 1997 by University Press of New England
All rights reserved
Printed in the United States of America
5   4   3   2   1
CIP data appear at the end of the book

For our teachers,

MITCHELL ROBERT BREITWIESER

LINDA HAJEK

BARTON LEVI ST. ARMAND

Contents

PART TWO
"The Disturbed Eyes Rise / Furtive, Foiled, Dissatisfied"
The Rebellion Against Calvinism

PART THREE
"Nothing Fit Us"
Writers Who Claim Their Own Traditions

Acknowledgments

We thank Tony Barnstone, Willis Barnstone, Marianne Noble, Sarah Way Sherman, Timothy Spurgin, Susan Elizabeth Sweeney, and Kathryn Manson Tomasek for their thoughtful comments on the introduction; Deborah Cornatzer, Eric Van Gordon, Mary Abigail Rice, and Tina Tuminella for their help in spot-checking, in proofreading, and in assembling the Works Cited; and the staff at University Press of New England for expertly leading the book through production.

Excerpts from *Homage to Mistress Bradstreet* by John Berryman are reprinted by permission of Farrar, Straus & Giroux, Inc. and Faber & Faber Ltd. Copyright © 1956 by John Berryman. Copyright renewed © 1984 by Kate Berryman.

"Puritan Legacies of Masculinity: John Berryman's *Homage to Mistress Bradstreet*" by Ivy Schweitzer was originally published in *The Work of Self Representation: Lyric Poetry in Colonial New England* by Ivy Schweitzer. Copyright © 1991 by the University of North Carolina Press. Used by permission of the publisher.

"Calvinist Tortures in Edith Wharton's *Ethan Frome*" is adapted from a chapter entitled "Calvinist Tortures" in *Edith Wharton: Matters of Mind and Spirit* by Carol J. Singley. Copyright © 1995 by Cambridge University Press. Reprinted with permission.

"Un-Utterable Longing: The Discourse of Feminine Sexuality in *The Awakening*" by Cynthia Griffin Wolff originally appeared in *Studies in American Fiction 24*, no. 1 (Spring 1996). Reprinted here by permission of *Studies in American Fiction* and Northeastern University.

"*Apocalypse Now* and the New England Way" reprints material from *The Wars We Took to Storytelling* by Milton J. Bates. Copyright © 1996 by The Regents of the University of California. Used with the permission of University of California Press.

The poems "Behaving Like a Jew" and "Burying an Animal on the Way to New York" originally appeared in *Lucky Life* by Gerald Stern, published by Houghton Mifflin. © 1977 by Gerald Stern; reprinted by permission of HarperCollins Publishers.

"Traveling Through the Dark" copyright © 1977 William Stafford from *Stories That Could Be True* (Harper & Row). Reprinted by permission of the Estate of William Stafford.

Excerpts from "28" from *A Walk with Tom Jefferson* by Philip Levine. Copyright © 1988 by Philip Levine. Reprinted by permission of Alfred A. Knopf, Inc.

Experts from the poems of Gary Soto from *Home Course in Religion: New Poems*. Copyright © 1991 Gary Soto. Reprinted by permission of Chronicle Books.

"The Gift Outright" and "America is Hard to See" from *The Poetry of Robert Frost*, edited by Edward Connery Lathem. Copyright © 1942, 1952, 1962 by Robert Frost, © 1970 by Lesley Frost Ballantine, © 1969 by Henry Holt & Co. Reprinted by permission of Henry Holt & Co., Inc.

"Meditation at Lagunitas" from *Praise* by Robert Hass. Copyright © 1974, 1975, 1976, 1977, 1978, 1979 by Robert Hass. First published by The Ecco Press 1979. Reprinted by permission.

Excerpts from the work of Alfred Kreymborg are reprinted here with the permission of the International Publishers Company.

"Before the Hour" by Edwin Rolfe originally appeared in POETRY, May 1936. Copyright © 1936 by The Modern Poetry Association. Reprinted by permission of the editor of POETRY.

Introduction

CALVINISM'S INFLUENCE ON American literature and culture has long been recognized by critics, but studies of this legacy tend to focus on the nineteenth century and neglect important links between Calvinism and modernity.[1] *The Calvinist Roots of the Modern Era* is unique in bringing together new essays that focus on Calvinism's dynamic presence in twentieth-century American poetry, fiction, and film. The reader will find a wide range of essays in this collection, from single-author studies and close readings of texts to interdisciplinary and multicultural studies. We have been particularly interested in essays that look at aspects historically neglected or devalued, especially those relating to gender, ethnicity, and race. Many of the essays treat writers who are not Calvinist or even religious but who are nonetheless influenced by Calvinism's transformation from theological doctrine to secular ideology. In this century, Calvinism appears as a psychological construct, a cultural institution or artifact, a habit of mind, or a sociopolitical structure. Because Calvinism has had such a great cultural influence, Americans of all religions look back to and are affected by John Winthrop's "City Upon a Hill" ("Model" 91). For this reason, we include essays on a diversity of voices, such as Catholic, Jewish, and African American writers who, although not in direct lineage from the Puritans, engage Calvinism through their experience as Americans. By the same principle, this book also addresses popular culture — in particular, how the Vietnam war era produced its own distinct reaction to Calvinist precepts. With their broad range of views and methodologies, these essays open new areas of inquiry and will, we hope, inspire still more study of Calvinism's continuing and always shifting presence in the twentieth century.

Before summarizing the essays, we would like to suggest that twentieth-century writers have had three, frequently overlapping, relationships with the United States' Calvinist heritage: continuity, independence, and convergence. Continuity has primarily been expressed in the persistence of particular Calvinist beliefs (such as innate depravity and divine grace), in the Puritan legacy of antinomian rebellion, in the influence of Calvinism on romanticism and sentimentalism, and in immigrant repetition of generational patterns of Puritan settlement. Despite these continuities, independence from Calvinism formed the theme of many twentieth-century writers, particularly early in the century. Marx, Darwin, new technologies, and the growing independence of women each suggested that Calvinism was outdated, and the sexual license many found in Freud gave us the image of the dour Puritan, hardworking and repressed. Despite the era's anti-Calvinism, however, convergence appeared as writers often rediscovered the relevance of Calvinism, finding that many Puritan experiences (such as alienation and anxiety) offered a more suitable sensibility than nineteenth-century optimism. As we describe these three relationships in more detail, we also define Calvinism's central terms and sketch a history that has produced disparate images of the Puritan, making the Calvinist inheritance one of the United States' most contested legacies.

The first relationship into which many twentieth-century writers enter—continuity—has largely centered on the Puritan legacy of antinomian rebellion, the conviction that a person must follow his or her own conscience despite law or social convention. This rebellion formed an essential part of a paradox that shaped the Puritan experience in the New World: an insistence both on individual autonomy and on conformity to a communal interpretation of God's law. The Puritans left England because they believed that the church allowed plainly corrupt clergy and members of the congregation to prosper within it. This dispute over church membership was grounded in the Augustinian distinction between the invisible and visible church. The pure, invisible church included all those, living and dead, whom God has predestined for salvation, whereas the impure, visible church included those who declare their faith in Christianity but remain fallen because humanity is innately depraved. "Not every member of the visible church," Edmund Morgan explains, "was predestined for salvation, for not every man who professed belief would actually possess the true belief, the saving faith necessary for redemption. The visible church, operating in the world of time and of human corruption, must inevitably contain sinful men" (*Visible* 3). Despite this inevitability, Puritans wanted the visible church to approximate the invisible one. Distressed by the overt displays of sinfulness by clergymen and congregations, they even compiled a register of notorious and wicked clerics whom they alleged committed such sins as fornication, gambling, drunkenness, adultery. Their list included such evildoers as one "Mr. Ampleforth, vicar of Much Badow," who they claimed had a child with his own sister and was "suspected of poperie" and of falsifying the Scriptures (*Visible* 8–9).

Further, the Puritans contended that their own souls were jeopardized by the evil of the clergy in the visible church, for, as Morgan asks, "without good teachers to instruct them, how could Englishmen recover from the dark ages when Rome had kept them in ignorance of the Scriptures?"

(*Visible* 9). In contrast to Catholic Rome, which had confined Scripture to its Latin translation and had withheld it from all but the clergy, the Puritans widely distributed the Bible in English. Through understanding the Word, they hoped to be saved. Each person read the Bible for him or herself but still relied on good clergymen to guide them to its truth. From the beginning, then, the Puritans were concerned with Scripture and its teaching and with determining the moral character of their community; it was to establish a more disciplined visible church that they settled in New England.

This decision to make the visible church adhere as closely as possible to the invisible one led to the Puritan's paradoxical emphasis on both individualism and conformity. Puritan doctrine stressed autonomy—both of each congregation and of the individual within each congregation—and thus Puritan dissent in England was antihierarchical, opposing the power structure of the Church of England, whose bishops, as in the Roman church, assumed all disciplinary powers over the clergy and individual churches. The Puritans asserted the duty of congregations to elect their own ministers and to decide who could become members and whose behavior warranted excommunication. The autonomy of the individual believer was expressed in crisis conversion, an experience that created its own paradox. On the one hand, as Richard Slotkin explains, at the moment of conversion, "The Puritan could rely only on his own reading of Scripture and his own conscience for light," without the mediation of churches or ministers. On the other hand, "Only God himself could give the necessary light for a man to truly read the Bible or his conscience, since without God man's corrupted reason would lead him astray" (*Regeneration* 52). Since Calvinists believed the soul was innately sinful, the self and all its earthly attachments must be vanity. The sinner who would walk the straight and narrow path must rely on God's grace to annihilate the self. In Puritan eyes, human depravity was so complete that only God, a terrible deity, could give to his flock the requisite, but selective, mercy. A person could not "do anything," Slotkin notes, to "induce God to perform the miracle [of conversion], since man's understanding of God is totally incompetent and since God himself has no moral or other obligation to man" (52). Puritan individualism thus disempowered the very self it otherwise empowered as each person faced the judgment of God in terror of divine wrath and with a profound understanding of his or her own utter helplessness. As John Cotton (1584-1652) writes in *The Covenant of God's Free Grace*, "man is so cast down he cannot tell what to make of himself; but there he lieth, to see what the Lord will do with him, whether He will reach forth the hand of salvation unto him." Thoroughly alone, the sinner is left "utterly void" and passive before God (qtd. in Pettit 136).

Although the conversion experience promoted individualism, it also required conformity. Puritans feared that without some communal oversight both clergy and congregation would be infected by the same hypocrisy that had corrupted the Church of England. After the experience of crisis conversion, the believer was thus required to face the church elders, endure their interrogation about the sincerity of his or her faith, and display what Cotton called a "visible state of salvation." Describing this examination as a "pillar of purity and piety," Cotton insisted that "those who have the keys to the church should not open the doors" to would-be members until they "may be conceived to be received of God" (qtd. in Pettit 135). Although, as Amy Schrager Lang points out, Puritans realized that "certain knowledge of election was God's alone," they also wanted to render the "invisible virtually visible." The congregation thus granted membership only to those who could convince it that they had truly had a personal experience of conversion. Always keeping in mind human frailty, the congregation further examined the applicant for signs of visible sainthood, reasoning that "if the motion of grace is accompanied by the will to do good, a saint ought to be identifiable by his deeds." Trying to balance their conviction that only God could discern the elect with their desire to "uphold the special covenant between God and the New Israel (18–19), Puritans synthesized a powerful individualism with obedience to the community.

Nowhere do we see the struggle between the forces of individualism and conformity more dramatically than in the case of Anne Hutchinson (1591–1643), who was accused of antinomianism. Committing themselves to the principle that the soul must confront God alone, the Puritans dispensed with the kind of clerical authority that had typified both the Roman Catholic Church and the Church of England, but Hutchinson argued that the Puritan ministry itself still stood between God and the soul. Reminding them that good works could not reveal grace, Hutchinson accused the ministers of Boston of advocating a doctrine of works in their examinations for church membership. In other words, she charged the clergy with the heresy of Arminianism. Arminianism took its name from Jacobus Arminius (1560–1609), who "had rejected the doctrine of unconditional election and had asserted that man, by his own natural will, may assist in the work of salvation" (Pettit 125). A state of grace, he argued, could not be true unless a person's soul was affected, turning that state of grace outward to the world. Hutchinson argued that by examining potential church members for signs of sainthood, church elders had implied that Christians could will their salvation by doing the good deeds that marked their eligibility for church membership. Grace alone, she asserted, effected salvation.

Confronted with Hutchinson's accusation of Arminianism, the ministry in turn accused her of the antinomian heresy. Antinomianism (literally, "against the law") was formalized as a doctrine in 1525 by Johann Agricola

(1494–1566), who argued that grace had freed Christians from the Mosaic law or Ten Commandments, making obedience a mere legality that should be replaced by the inner prompting of the Holy Spirit. Or in Hutchinson's words, "The Law is no rule of life to a Christian" (qtd. in Gura 262). This position profoundly challenged the clergy, undermining not only their authority over their congregations but also any appeal they might make to Scripture. Hutchinson "hath very much abused" the people, Winthrop argued at her trial, "that they shall look for revelations and are not bound to the ministry of the word, but God will teach them by immediate revelations" (qtd. in Gura 260). Tried, banished to Rhode Island, and then excommunicated, Hutchinson moved to New York and was killed by Indians, a fate that proved her heretical nature to the clergy. When Anne Hutchinson challenged the ministers of Boston, American Puritanism rebelled against itself. She had affirmed the individual's direct and personal communication with God through the Holy Spirit, unmediated by clergy or even Scripture. At the heart of Calvinism, then, lay both protest against prevailing orthodoxy and intolerance of any deviation. Seventeenth-century Puritans had dissented from the English church, but their tradition of dissent produced still more rebellions against the very social order they desired. The path of protest thus repeatedly established new orthodoxies that attempted—and failed—to exclude further protest. The rebelliousness that continues to shape twentieth-century culture stems in part from Hutchinson's example and, indeed, from the Puritans themselves.

If modern writers inherit the paradox of individualism and conformity intrinsic to Calvinist theology, they also inherit the Calvinist paradox of terror and delight. Later generations' rejection of Calvinism has focused our attention on the Puritans' religious experience of terror, but their visionary experience also included joy. Early writers such as Anne Bradstreet (1612–1672), Edward Taylor (c. 1642–1729), and Jonathan Edwards (1703–1758) saw in nature God's beautiful design and signs of His love, and they found happiness there. As Edwards writes in "Beauty of the World": "How much a resemblance is there of every grace in the fields covered with plants and flowers, when the sun shines serenely and undisturbedly upon them. How a resemblance, I say, of every grace and beautiful disposition of mind; of an inferior towards a superior cause, preserver, benevolent benefactor and a fountain of happiness" (*Works* 6:305). The legacy of Edwards's delight can be seen in such nineteenth-century writers as Emily Dickinson, Ralph Waldo Emerson, Henry David Thoreau and Walt Whitman, as well as such twentieth-century writers as Elizabeth Bishop, Marianne Moore, and Gerald Stern. American literature has a tradition of enconium and ecstasy in nature whose origins lie within Calvinism.

Twentieth-century writers have been influenced not only by seventeenth-century beliefs and practices, but also by Calvinism's transformation in the nineteenth century at the hands of liberal theologians, romantics, and sentimentalists. As a result, Calvinism has influenced other Protestant denominations—and indeed all of American culture—into our century. Living in a new, democratic nation, late-eighteenth- and early-nineteenth-century liberal theologians rejected as elitist the Calvinist tenet of eternal damnation for the many and redemption for the few and de-emphasized sin as the crucial, tormenting spiritual concern of Christians, making the individual's relationship to God paramount. As Richard Forrer observes, "liberal theologians . . . argued that the sovereign God of Puritan orthodoxy is an amoral deity, an unjust tyrant, whose arbitrary disposition of human destinies denies people any reliable foundation for the moral life" (5). These theologians—including, among others, Emerson, William Ellery Channing, and Horace Bushnell—aligned the ideals of democracy with a revised and more all-embracing Protestant doctrine in which everyone had the potential to achieve grace and attain salvation. This democratization of Calvinist theology represented an internalization of Arminianism, both in its emphasis on good works and in its reliance on the freedom of will, whereby everyone can choose salvation.

As theologians reworked Calvinism, nineteenth-century writers transformed it into romanticism and sentimentalism, creating new continuities into the twentieth century. While many critics have considered modernism as a challenge to romanticism, the essays collected in this volume acknowledge that American romanticism itself responded to New England Calvinist theology. It is no accident that American romanticism emerged at the same time as a second wave of Calvinist revivalism in the 1830s and 1840s since both Calvinist and romantic cosmologies provided visionary alternatives to enlightenment rationalism. Any history of American romanticism must thus account for the influence of not only European romanticism but also Calvinism. We see this influence first in the antinomian rebellion of such romantics as Hawthorne, Melville, Whitman, and Dickinson, who doubted and revised Calvinist tenets and cultural norms in light of their own inner prompting.

A second Calvinist influence on romanticism is, as Roy Harvey Pearce describes, the "gradual but nonetheless revolutionary shift in the meaning of 'invention': from 'coming upon' something made and ordered by God, to 'making' and 'ordering'—transforming—something, anything, into that which manifests above all man's power to make and to order" (*Continuity* 41). "Invention" literally means to come upon or discover, and the Puritan writer sought to discover the truth of God's Word in all things. For example, the anagrammatic poems so popular with Puritans found meanings consonant with Scripture in the letters of a person's name. No matter how dedicated to God's Truth, however, poetry also reveals the individual style of the poet. Thus, as Puritan antinomianism grew from being censured (as Anne Hutchinson was by Boston ministers in the seventeenth century) to being celebrated (as self-reliance was by Emerson in the nineteenth century), invention became "the 'Romantic' drive to testify that one can really know only one's own power" (41). Turning writing from the discovery of God's Word to the creation of the self's own expressive words, antinomianism eventually inverted Puritan doctrine, producing a specifically American version of romanticism.

Also questioning the Puritan legacy through a Puritan tradition of dissent were the sentimentalists who, as Ann Douglas, David Reynolds, Jane Tompkins, and others have argued, presented a powerful alternative to orthodox Calvinist doctrine. While seventeenth-century Puritans and, later, Jonathan Edwards focused on the depravity and innate sinfulness of humanity, sentimental writers joined liberal theologians in portraying God not as a wrathful Father but as a feminized God of mercy. These writers, Douglas notes, "represented a shift from this basically paternal (or gubernatorial) and authoritarian view to a fundamentally maternal and affective one. God is no longer expressing hatred of sin in his sacrifice of his son but love of man" (146). The sentimentalists made sacred the loving family circle, especially maternal love, and they refigured God the father as the eternal unifier of the family who, through the salvific, compassionate love of his son, would vanquish death, allowing the family to dwell forever in its heavenly home.

Because liberals and sentimentalists succeeded so well in transforming Puritan antinomianism into a broader culture, studies that begin in the twentieth century, including many of the essays in this volume, treat Calvinism not as a theology in its seventeenth-century form but as a general Christian ethic emphasizing both individualism and a strict moral code. Although the twentieth century is known for its secularism, one need not look far to find "residual" Christianity (C. Brooks 129) in such writers as Ernest Hemingway, William Faulkner, and Robert Penn Warren. Chard Powers Smith even suggests that the young iconoclasts of the twenties were really the last, or next to last, wave of Puritans—despite their use of the term as the ultimate abuse (451-59). Perry Miller similarly compares these writers with the transcendentalists: both speak for the spirit rather than for materiality, and both belong to a series of revolts against what Miller calls "American Philistinism" (*Transcendentalists* 8). Calvinism's influence especially persisted in the literary talent that New England continued to produce and nurture. For example, Edwin Arlington Robinson, Robert Frost, Edna St. Vincent Millay, Conrad Aiken, e.e. cummings, Amy Lowell, Eugene O'Neill, and later, Robert Lowell, all positioned themselves as offspring, refugees, or mediators of the New England experience. Like many writers who preceded them, they viewed Calvinism as central to American identity.

The Puritan legacy remains a continuity in American literature even when the writer's heritage does not directly descend from New England, because both Puritan and twentieth-century texts share a particular search for identity, destiny, and promised regeneration. As Andrew Delbanco argues, the immigrant experience parallels the Puritan: history recurs as new groups arrive on American shores. Like the first Puritans, successive waves of immigrants must negotiate an initially alien, unwelcoming "wilderness," must reconcile their old culture with the new, and must contend with the fear that succeeding generations will dilute the meaning of their (often sacred) mission. Delbanco finds parallels with Puritanism especially strong for Jewish immigrants and less strong or nonexistent for African Americans, the only group whose arrival was fully involuntary and whose literature replaces a Puritan-derived narrative tradition of self-discovery through spiritual conversion with an exposure of the cost of enduring an alien and imposed identity (243-45). Twentieth-century writers, as the essays in this volume demonstrate, thus find a number of continuities with Calvinism, from following its theological beliefs to joining in its antinomian rebellion, and from drawing on romanticism and sentimentalism to reliving the experience of immigration.

Although many twentieth-century writers exhibit these continuities, others developed different relationships with Calvinism—independence and convergence. The idea that the history of the small colony on Massachusetts Bay was essential to the American character was the cultural work of much nineteenth-century literature, and the success of this view bred its own reaction, making the twentieth century the first to declare its independence from Calvinism. Often in the essays collected in this volume, Calvinism appears as the enemy of both art and modernity. "By the end of the [nineteenth] century," historian Warren Susman asserts, "almost every aspect of what was taken to be historic Puritanism was called upon as part of the bulwark of the prevailing order" (43), and consequently, those intellectuals, artists, and writers who wanted to transform American culture and make it modern often fought their battles on the ground of Puritanism. John Jay Chapman's essay on Emerson (1897) struck first, explaining that Puritanism limited Emerson's ability to feel human compassion. It was followed by Van Wyck Brooks's call for an end of Puritan provincialism in *The Wine of the Puritans* (1908); George Santayana's criticism of an attenuated, Puritan-derived "genteel tradition" (1911); H. L. Mencken's attack on Puritan repression and censorship in "Puritanism as a Literary Force" (1917); and Randolph Bourne's concern about a moral elite out of touch with social reality in "The Puritan's Will to Power" (1917).[2] Together, these works replaced the popular image of Puritan as originator of American democratic institutions and guarantor of personal moral rectitude with the image of the Puritan as theocratic killjoy who repressed the individual's ability to experience beauty and create art. These arguments were aided by a widespread portrayal of the Puritans as the root of Victorian sexual codes and of Freud as the enemy of repression and a proponent of free love. In 1927, at the height of this equation of modernity with anti-Calvinism, Vernon Parrington enjoyed much popular success when he attacked Puritanism as foreign (meaning British), elitist, and antidemocratic. Many of the authors discussed in *The Calvinist Roots of the Modern Era* grew up in such an atmosphere and found themselves looking for alternatives to Calvinist repression.

Female writers, in particular, experienced Calvinism as a potent, often forbidding legacy. Pauline doctrine, on which this faith is based, emphasized woman as man's spiritual equal but social subordinate. When he admonished women to be silent and obedient, Paul helped establish a tradition of female passivity. Inheriting but also subverting this tradition, nineteenth-century sentimentalists directed their creative energies into a religion of domesticity and found opportunity for literary expression within traditional feminine norms, which dictated that women write only out of a sacred duty or financial necessity and only for didactic purposes. But women like Emily Dickinson—who experienced neither crisis conversion, nor motherhood, nor suffered pressing economic need—found Calvinism a poor fit. In addition, as Margaret Thickstun explains, Calvinist theology frequently associated women with the flesh and men with the spirit. In literature, the spirituality of female characters was easily displaced by that of male characters, and female sexuality was often depicted negatively (19–21). So long as nineteenth-century codes of female chastity and subservience were in place, women sublimated their sensuality into ideals of motherhood and selfless service. But for women of the modern era who acknowledged their sexuality, such as Kate Chopin, Edith Wharton, and Ellen Glasgow, Calvinism could be an unwelcome censor. These writers experienced Calvinism as a restriction of their sensual and artistic selves.

These two relationships to Calvinism—the continuity created by American antinomianism and the rejection of Puritanism as central to American identity—are complicated by a third relation, which in a given writer's work frequently overlaps with the other two. That third relation is the rediscovery of those aspects of Calvinism that nineteenth-century theologians, romantics, and sentimentalists sought to replace. Many twentieth-century writers discovered a surprising similarity between their experience of the world and the Calvinists'. Both Calvinism and modernism emphasize an alienation of self from God and nature, whether through the Calvinist's apprehension of a fearsome, punishing deity or through the post-Darwinian skeptic's sense that God is distant or absent. Both Calvinism and modernism encourage introspection, a heightened self-consciousness that reflects anxiety over an inability either to affirm or alter one's place in the universe. A paralysis of will and a failure to act, especially for one's own well-being, may equally afflict the Calvinist and modernist. Indeed, one might argue that modernism is a kind of Calvinism manqué: it maintains Calvinism's harshness and despair without its visionary idealism, and its suffering without salvation.

This convergence of Calvinism and modernism can be seen in the characteristics shared by seventeenth-century Puritans and twentieth-century writers. Critic Henry May, for example, links the hardheaded realism of novelists such as Henry James to Calvinism and argues that, in an age of material expansion, many American writers still expressed concern over the relationship between the size of one's pocketbook and the state of one's soul. More particularly, Puritans and modernists share "a habit of agonized self-doubt, a deep suspicion of material appearances, a positive hatred of blandness and complacency, and above all a most intense and even painful seriousness about oneself, one's country, and its mission" (62-63). Perry Westbrook, noting the twisted wills and other "peculiarities" of characters in the post–Civil War novels and short stories of New England writers such as Mary Wilkins Freeman, explains that although the forces of Calvinist theology had waned, the roots of Calvinist character remain deep and recalcitrant (98-99).

With its wide range of perspectives, the collection as a whole serves as a sourcebook for readers of American literature, literary history, and culture. Its variety of approaches—historical, theoretical, and theological— enriches the study of individual writers as well as the religious and literary cultures from which they develop. We hope that by exploring and fostering an interplay of seemingly disparate forces, *The Calvinist Roots of the Modern Era* will spark new work on the connections between America's religious inheritances and its modern and contemporary literatures.

Calvinist influences—both direct and indirect, both resisted and reshaped by competing traditions—have guided our arrangement of this collection into three sections. Across these three sections run at least five different and frequently overlapping understandings of the continuity between Calvinism and the modern era. For such critics as Elsa Nettels and Carol J. Singley, Calvinism and modernism are united by a philosophic view of the universe as inscrutable and by a perception of continued spiritual and moral crisis. Other contributors—Mutlu Konuk Blasing and Loris Mirella —focus on Calvinist typology and its influence on modernist understandings of history. Others—Aliki Barnstone, Susan Goodman, George Monteiro, John J. Murphy, and Elisa New—explain how modernists update such religious experiences as election, introspection, grace, conversion, and wonder. For some contributors, Calvinism is a potent sociopolitical force. Jonathan Barron, Milton J. Bates, Jane Cocalis, Michael Tomasek Manson, and Rocco Marinaccio argue that the continuity of Calvinism lies in its placement of other peoples in an ideological "wilderness" that must be conquered in order to be seen as American. The social construction of gender also links Calvinism and modernism: Manson and Ivy Schweitzer describe how Calvinism shapes different versions of masculinity, while Jeredith Merrin argues for its liberating effect for women, and Barnstone, Goodman, Singley, and Cynthia Griffin Wolff describe it as a force from which women must liberate themselves. With these continuities in mind, then, the seventeen critics collected in this volume examine in new ways artists who either adapt Calvinism, rebel against it, or appeal to other traditions in order to create the modern.

"New Minted by Thy Stamp": *Calvinism's Extension into the Twentieth Century*

The first section takes its title from a line in Edward Taylor's "The Return" and considers modern writers from William Dean Howells to John Berryman who extend the reach of Calvinism into the twentieth century. Some of the writers in this section celebrate their Calvinist legacies; others hope that modernity means the end of Calvinism's hold on the United States even while they still work within or echo its terms. Willa Cather, Ernest Hemingway, Marianne Moore, and Elizabeth Bishop, for example, carry Calvinism deeply into their art, while Howells, Ezra Pound, T. S. Eliot, and Berryman adapt Calvinist forms.

Although Ezra Pound purports to share nothing with Calvinism, calling Calvin himself a "bigot" and placing him in the eighth circle of hell, in "Designs on History: Ezra Pound, the Puritans, and Self-Fulfilling Prophecies," Mutlu Konuk Blasing argues that Pound's modernism imitates the form, if not the substance, of Calvinism. Both Pound and the Puritans radically break from the present and return to "purer" origins through specific texts. Examining Canto I and the early poem "The Tree," Blasing defines and explores Pound's use of type and antitype, of translation and metalepsis. Like the Puritans, Pound finds typology appealing because it confirms a totalitarian, closed system of meaning that enfolds historical development. Ultimately, Blasing argues, both Pound and the Puritans repress rhetoric, ignoring poetry's necessary disturbance of any sealed system.

Loris Mirella gives new coherence to T. S. Eliot's career in his essay, "T. S. Eliot's Calvinist Modernism." Instead of dividing Eliot's work into two phases, modernist and religious, Mirella argues that Calvinism shapes all of Eliot's corpus, both thematically and structurally. Calvinism's radical break with Anglican practice informs Eliot's modernist desire to sweep away previous forms of expression. For both Calvinists and Eliot, this total break is accompanied by the appearance of a unified system that frames all endeavors, including poetry. This idea of a framework carries Eliot throughout his career, as Mirella demonstrates in readings of Eliot's essays, poems, and verse dramas.

In " 'Inherited Puritanism': The Legacy of Calvinism in the Fiction of William Dean Howells," Elsa Nettels argues that Howells represents the fundamental ideas and practices of Calvinism even though he explicitly refutes its doctrines. Making the legacy of Calvinism the subject of many of his novels, Howells criticizes romantic fiction for filling the vacuum left by Calvinist theology, giving many people—particularly women—false ideals and morbid scruples. As an alternative, Howells's realism offers male characters who believe in individual conscience and the existence of a just and merciful God. In extended readings of *The Son of Royal Langbrith*, *A Modern Instance*, and *The Shadow of a Dream*, Nettels demonstrates that Howells's modernism—evident in his unresolved debates, unanswered questions, and multiple readings of events—still retains a standard of judgment promulgated by the Puritans.

For John J. Murphy, Willa Cather's modernism lies in her use of surrealism to transform the seventeenth-century experience of salvation. In "The Modernist Conversion of Willa Cather's Professor," Murphy analyzes Godfrey St. Peter's crisis in the final book of *The Professor's House* in terms of conversion literature. Finding similarities between the professor's story and Leo Tolstoy's autobiographical *My Confession*, Murphy argues that St. Peter's conversion follows the pattern described both by Jonathan Edwards in "A Divine and Supernatural Light" and by William James in *The Varieties of Religious Experience*. Murphy explains how the surreal dimension of conversion, which James articulates philosophically and René Magritte visually, helps us to understand Cather's modernist treatment of religious conversion.

In his essay, "Grace, Good Works, and the Hemingway Ethic," George Monteiro proposes that, unlike other modernists who transform Christianity through myth, Hemingway transforms it through ethics. Elaborating on Max Weber's portrait of the interrelation of Calvinism and capitalism, Monteiro examines Bruce Barton's bestselling novel, *The Man Nobody Knows* (1925), for its description of Jesus's life as that of a good businessman — rugged, sociable, athletic, capable of building solid sales organizations like the Apostles. Barton was the son of Hemingway's pastor, and Monteiro argues that such works as "Today Is Friday," "A Clean Well-Lighted Place," "The Snows of Kilimanjaro," *Across the River and into the Trees*, and *The Old Man and the Sea* extend Barton's vision as much as they depart from it. Suggesting that sports, war, and writing potentiate the earning of grace, Hemingway, like Barton, focuses on calling, vocation, and the creation of a humanistic grace.

Jeredith Merrin's essay, "Sites of Struggle: Marianne Moore and American Calvinism," places Calvinism at the center of Moore's modernism and Moore herself at the center of American literary history. Describing in detail Moore's proud Presbyterian upbringing and her wordplay, Merrin explains that an ethos of Puritan struggle permeates the tropes and forms of her poetry. Readings of "The Fish" and "New York" as well as other poems demonstrate that Moore's Calvinist morality and formal modernity complement each other, creating a distinctly Puritan and, in some cases, distinctly American struggle between self-effacement and self-assertion. Merrin further argues that Moore's respect for individual character led to an active feminism that belies assumptions of an enmity between feminism and Calvinism.

Elisa New's essay, "Awe, Wonder, and Wit: Elizabeth Bishop and the Modernization of Calvinist Mood," finds in Calvinism a more appropriate, modernist, and American form of lyricism than that found in romanticism. If, for modernists, Calvinism is no longer relevant intellectually, neither is romanticism, which celebrates the will and labor that poets expend to discover the truth. More pertinent to modernists like Bishop is Calvinism's lyric habitation of lostness and its marriage of ego with the engulfing complexity of the universe. In readings of "In the Waiting Room," "The Fish," and "Filling Station," New finds descriptions of awe, wonder, and wit that are also found in Jonathan Edwards and Søren Kierkegaard. The lyric thus continues to reanimate the surprise of experience, Edwards's notion that beauty is created when being consents to itself.

In John Berryman's poetry, Ivy Schweitzer argues in her essay, "Puritan Legacies of Masculinity: John Berryman's *Homage to Mistress Bradstreet*," there is at work what Alice Jardine calls "gynesis" — "discourse *by, through, as* woman"(36) — and Schweitzer traces this gynesis both as an inheritance from Puritanism and as a prefiguration of postfeminism. While a Puritan man had to learn how to become simultaneously a masculine authority figure in the house and the bride of Christ in his soul, so too has the male postmodernist had to learn to speak as woman in order to deconstruct phallogocentrism. Schweitzer analyzes the stages of Berryman's romance with Bradstreet, exposing the imaginary body he creates as a locus both for his aggression and for the power he envies.

"*The Disturbed Eyes Rise / Furtive, Foiled, Dissatisfied*": *The Rebellion Against Calvinism*

The modern period has also seen writers who question or quarrel with their Calvinist inheritance. The title of the second section borrows lines from Robert Lowell's poem "Hawthorne." The essays in this section examine such artists as Emily Dickinson, Edith Wharton, Kate Chopin, Ellen Glasgow, and Francis Ford Coppola, whose personal or intellectual inheritance is Calvinist but whose rebellion against that legacy inaugurates a search for new forms and creeds. These artists reject Calvinist authoritarianism as well as what they perceive to be its preoccupation with guilt, sin, and violence.

Aliki Barnstone's essay, "Mastering the Master: Emily Dickinson's Appropriation of Crisis Conversion," explains how Dickinson's protomodernism results from a rebellion against Calvinism. In a discussion that centers on a delineation of Dickinson's poetic development, Barnstone argues that, before 1862, Dickinson was engaged in an externalized battle with God in which she satirized both him and conventional religious practice. Around 1862, Dickinson entered a second, culminating phase in her artistic development in which she internalizes the conflict. In this period, the poet appropriates the language of Calvinist crisis conversion in order to turn the self away from God and toward poetry. In close readings of "Me from Myself—to banish—," "There's a certain slant of light," and the second Master letter, Barnstone demonstrates that through her poetic innovation Dickinson subverts orthodoxy and levels a hierarchical relationship with a masculine deity.

Carol J. Singley's essay, "Calvinist Tortures in Edith Wharton's *Ethan Frome*," suggests that Wharton performs both a modernist cultural critique and a personal exorcism of the Calvinist demons that had tortured her. Despite an Episcopalian background, Wharton's sensibilities were decidedly Calvinist. However, her modernist techniques—including a narrative frame which permits subjective interpretation and indeterminacy—allow her to leave *Ethan Frome*'s bleak world behind. Wharton's novel, like Hawthorne's *The Scarlet Letter*, revisits Calvinism in order to reject it, but Wharton also refuses the catharsis of tragic heroism, accepting instead a more Manichean and more modern understanding of conflict.

In "Un-Utterable Longing: The Discourse of Feminine Sexuality in Kate Chopin's *The Awakening*," Cynthia Griffin Wolff reevaluates Chopin's modernism—the minimalism of her prose—arguing that textual absences point to that which cannot be spoken because it does not have a name. Edna Pontellier's unutterable longing is for a viable mode of expressing her sexuality. Late-nineteenth-century science, however, believed that women had no erotic inclinations and thus had nothing to say; Edna's Presbyterian Church similarly argued that women should not speak. The result is that when Edna and Léonce argue about their sexual needs, they do so without ever mentioning sex itself. Edna detaches herself from language, and her efforts to create a narrative of self-affirmation remain formulaic rather than truly assertive. That accomplishment is left to Chopin herself as she invents—through the novel—a powerful discourse about feminine sexuality.

Susan Goodman, in "The Fatherlode: Glasgow's Religious Inheritance," describes how Glasgow redefined Calvinism to include both the maternal and the aesthetic. In detailed readings of the autobiography *The Woman Within* and the novel *Barren Ground*, Goodman shows how the personal myth that Glasgow articulates in her memoir becomes in the later work of fiction a theory as well as an aesthetic of feminist self-determination. Although Glasgow focuses on Calvinist beliefs—particularly election, redemption, and irresistible grace—she also creates unholy and empowering alliances among Calvin, Emerson, and Darwin. Ultimately, her modernist linguistic experimentation allows her to live in a world of her own, not God's, making.

Milton J. Bates examines the Vietnam War as a secular crisis that has inspired a popular reassessment of Puritan influence in his essay "*Apocalypse Now* and the New England Way." Bates sees filmmaker Francis Ford Coppola's debt to Puritanism in his treatment of wild places and wild men and in his conception of history and community. Coppola suggests the bankruptcy of this legacy when he changes the ending of his film from a Puritan apocalypse to a Montagnard ritual that presents a more primitive, cyclic conception of history. Finding an unresolved and deep contradiction in both endings, Bates suggests that the Montagnard ritual also has an American genealogy in the Daniel Boone myth, a myth that informs not only Michael Cimino's *The Deer Hunter* and Michael Herr's *Dispatches* but also the countercultural resistance offered by Susan Sontag, Gary Snyder, and Robert Bly.

"Nothing Fit Us":
Writers Who Claim Their Own Traditions

The third section looks at writers who have argued for their own traditions despite pressure to follow Calvinist religious and cultural prescriptions. Its title comes from Gerald Stern's poem "Knowledge Forwards and Backwards," one of many in which the poet—like his counterparts in this section—imagines a "different" "language" and "dream," with "no hierarchy" and "no degradation." The work of such authors as Stern, Philip Levine, Toni Morrison, H. H. Lewis, and Gary Soto develops from non-Calvinist religious, political, and cultural roots, offering alternatives to the view that United States history centers on this early New England tradition. Each of these writers suggests different directions for literature of the United States by refusing to employ the literary strategies that have traditionally informed much of our canonical literature.

For Jonathan Barron, William Stafford's widely anthologized poem "Traveling Through the Dark" has attained such canonical status that Gerald Stern and Philip Levine have approached it much as Talmudic scholars approach the Torah, seeking first to expose and then to fill in the gaps in the biblical text. In "New Jerusalems: Contemporary Jewish American Poets and the Puritan Tradition," Barron argues that Stern, in the poems "Behaving Like a Jew" and "Burying an Animal on the Way to New York," and Levine, in the poem "28," apply midrashic techniques like mashal, and rules like binyan av from the legal code halacha, to Stafford's typologically Christian story of sacrifice. While Stern uses these Jewish exegetical techniques to explain how Stafford fails to respect the dead doe and her fawn, Levine writes his own midrash on Stern, suggesting that both Stafford and Stern err in placing faith in types and symbols. He instead points to America as a secular and benign social contract, treating the story of the dead animal as one of abandonment rather than of sacrifice or respect. Despite their differences, both Stern and Levine break with the traditional conflation of Calvinism with the American spirit.

In "The 'Dark and Abiding Presence' in Nathaniel Hawthorne's *The Scarlet Letter* and Toni Morrison's *Beloved*," Jane Cocalis explains how Morrison deliberately retraces and corrects a line of inquiry inaugurated by Hawthorne. Seeing a symbiotic relationship between Puritanism and slavery, Hawthorne inadvertently creates in Hester the possibility of a remarkable heroine who can denounce the societal codes that bind a minority to its confused self-image. While Hawthorne is ambivalent toward this figure, believing that redemption cannot come from "dusky grief," Morrison insists that a dark presence is an essential part of mortal being and that, through the agency of such women as Baby Suggs, Sethe, and Denver, redemption will come, not from some outside power, but from within the community itself.

In "Poetry and Masculinity on the Anglo/Chicano Border: Gary Soto, Robert Frost, and Robert Hass," Michael Tomasek Manson proposes that we replace the notion that the origins of U.S. literature lie in Puritanism with the idea that our literature is created by border conflicts and exchanges among many peoples. Through readings of Frost's "Mending Wall," "The Gift Outright," and "America Is Hard to See"; Hass's "Meditation at Lagunitas"; and Soto's *Home Course in Religion*, Manson explains the shaping influence of the Anglo/Chicano border on U.S. poetry in general and on conceptions of masculinity in particular. While Frost's verse sometimes reveals and more frequently represses its origins on the border, Soto's develops a Chicano Catholic sensibility that empowers his resistance to the dominant Anglo-Protestant understanding of masculinity and the self. That Soto's work is both Chicano and Catholic is seen when Hass's reveals its origins in both Catholicism and Puritanism.

Rocco Marinaccio's essay, " 'Communism is Twentieth-Century Americanism': Proletarian Poetry and the Puritan Tradition," examines the marginalized work of proletarian poets of the 1930s for its resistance to and participation in mainstream cultural practices. In close readings of poems by Alfred Kreymborg and Edwin Rolfe as well as criticism by Mike Gold, John Dos Passos, Granville Hicks, Alan Calmers, and Isidor Schneider, Marinaccio explains that these central figures in the proletarian movement still subscribe to the values of the dominant culture, values that derive from Puritanism and undermine the movement's professed radicalism. To find an alternative, Marinaccio turns to the virtually forgotten H. H. Lewis, whose poetry breaks with the symbol of America in order to create radical social analysis.

As the range of essays in this volume demonstrates, Calvinism's influence does not end in the nineteenth century, but continues to shape American literary history three hundred and fifty years after its introduction to these shores. Calvinism has not been a static but a dynamic force, as different writers redefine and restructure it to fit their purposes and beliefs.[3] The essays in this collection explore new territory by charting the intersection of Calvinism, modernism, and postmodernism—a confluence and often collision that has produced our era's complex cultural, literary, and religious aesthetics. Our contributors' vital perceptions begin the journey.

Notes

1. Studies of Calvinism's influence through the nineteenth century include those by Bercovitch (*American Jeremiad, Office, Puritan*), Chase, Elliott, Fiedler, Miller ("From Edwards," *Life*), Weber, and Winters. These critics describe Puritanism's symbolic, mythic, and rhetorical power to shape American consciousness.

2. Hoffman describes the work of these writers as scapegoating (314–27).

3. As Reising notes, "Puritan origins" theorists tend to view Puritanism as fixed or monolithic and to interpret it according to their own critical paradigms (50). Also see Ziff, who cautions about overemphasizing Calvinism's centrality in modern life (*Puritanism* xi), and Breen, David Hall, and Rutman, who all stress the differences within Puritan culture.

PART ONE

"New Minted by Thy Stamp"
Calvinism's Extension into the
Twentieth Century

Designs on History
Ezra Pound, the Puritans, and Self-Fulfilling Prophecies

TO PROPOSE ANY continuity between Ezra Pound's work and Calvinism may seem perverse, since Pound does not have one good word to say about the whole Judeo-Christian enterprise in general or Calvinism in particular. Calvin, the "bigot" (14:62)[1] from "Geneva the usurers' dunghill" (78:481), occupies the eighth circle of Pound's hell; "the original-sin racket . . . the hex-hoax" (97:679, original ellipsis) puts him in the company of frauds and falsifiers. Pound attacks Calvinism for ushering in a tolerance of usury, reducing religion to an oppressive moral code, and denying sensory experience. Calvinism is both too otherworldly in deferring "paradise" and too worldly in assuring capitalism's triumph, to the detriment of all arts, communities, and values.

Pound's thought is wholistic: social, political, economic, artistic, literary, and linguistic values are of a piece, and usury is a systemic disease. In terms of literary and linguistic health, usury translates as the erosion of clear terminology and distinctions, the forgetfulness of real values, the obfuscation of the true texts—in a word, "blackout." Above all, Calvinist "ignorantism" (*Selected Prose* 65) "forgets" the pagan-humanist tradition, which the Catholic Church had assimilated; that is why Christianity in Italy has not "degenerated into that pest, eccentricity, accompanied by oppressions, witch-burnings, that it has so often become in countries not built on a 'classic' basis" (*Guide* 141). The Latin language, the thread connecting classic and Christian traditions in Italy, has spared the Italian Church; "Latin is sacred," Pound writes, as "grain is sacred" (*Selected Prose* 317). Thus the reason that "Jimmy Stuart" is the "foulest" of all the "damned scoundrels" (107:758) is more than political. "That slobbering bugger Jim First / bitched our heritage" (757): "the hog-wash with King James / his 'version' / till in 1850 to unfashion the lingua latina; / to drive truth out of curricula" (760).

With Protestantism, not only are the classics forgotten, but certain "barbaric" texts are revived. "Nothing cd. be less civil, or more hostile to any degree of polite civilization than the tribal records of the hebrews," Pound writes, and "the revival of these barbarous texts in the time of Luther and Calvin has been an almost unmitigated curse to the occident" (*Guide* 330). The semitic offers a gross "system" of values "in which everything was good or bad without any graduation, but as taboo," for "the semitic is excess. The semitic is against ANY scale of values" (*Selected Prose* 151, 86).[2] The "Mediterranean paideuma," with its "sanity," "moderation," and "order," fell with the advent of Protestantism, when Christianity "flopped" back into "pre-Christian barbarisms"; for Pound, "civilisation consists in the establishment of an hierarchy of values, it cannot remain as a mere division between the damned and the saved" (*Selected Prose* 150, 90). Medieval civilization, whose "order" and refined gradation of values Pound relates to Confucianism, declined when "the brutal and savage mythology of the Hebrews was revived," and "the festering mind of Calvin, haeresiarchus, perditissimus, distilled a moral syphilis throughout the whole body of society. The grossening and fattening of European architecture was the contemporary imprint of his diseased condition." Eventually, Calvin's "disease" also "shows in England's versification. These things move parallel" (*Selected Prose* 265).

Given Pound's immoderate and unrelenting hostility to Calvinism, it would be hard to argue for any substantive continuity between his work and Puritan thought. But if we consider how Pound figures "continuity" itself, we see his strategic affinity with the Puritans. Curiously, he attacks Calvinism primarily for forgetting the continuous classical tradition and reviving texts of oriental "barbarism," "the rise of old-testament-olatry" (*Selected Prose* 265–66). And his attack is part and parcel of his own program to correct such a deviation by reviving the equally old texts of classical Greece, for example. Pound's modernism, in form though not in substance, deploys the very strategy he condemns in Protestantism: while they revive different "scriptures," to be sure, both appeal to the authority of older texts for leverage in their revolutionary breaks with the institutional practices that immediately precede them—whether the rituals of the Catholic and Anglican Churches that deform the Scriptures, or the institutionalized "iambics" of nineteenth-century English poetry that "deform thought" (98:687). The Puritans and Pound alike figure radical breaks with immediate precedents as returns to "purer" origins, which they think to access through certain texts. In the largest terms, then, Pound's modernist strategy of progress through recuperation is Calvinist.

Specifically, his brand of revivalism relies as much as the Calvinists' on a typological model of continuity, whether or not he was consciously influenced by his Presbyterian upbringing.[3] Typology, the quintessentially Puritan interpretive method, is a way of figuring continuity across temporal or historical discontinuities. To see how typology may be deployed to authorize historical breaks with precedent, I want to look first at the Christian beginning itself, the earliest use of figural typology. Discussing the etymology and history of *figura*, Erich Auerbach traces how the term, which meant "plastic form" or "image" in pagan antiquity, was appropriated for a different function in the Christian world, when "the strangely new meaning of *figura*" as a "prophecy or prefiguration" emerged ("*Figura*" 28–29). In Christian usage, *figura* came to mean "something real and historical which announces something else that is also real and historical" (29); in particular, figural interpretation aimed "to show that the persons and events of the Old Testament were prefigurations of the New Testament and its history of salvation" (30). This method of textual interpretation reads the Bible not symbolically or allegorically but literally or historically, taking biblical events as actual incidents that also show forth the divinely intended pattern of history.

The relation between the prefiguring event and its fulfillment, Auerbach writes, "is revealed by an accord or similarity" (29). Here, deploying a metaphor or a trope of similitude across historical time to link "before" and "after" makes for a type. As Mason Lowance puts it, "the most crucial distinction between the type and trope involved a concept of linear time. The trope was a Platonic representation of one thing by another, but the type by definition preceded the antitype in the context of time" (5). The interpreter who can see such relations in effect stands outside history and pierces the suprahistorical design. "Figural interpretation," Auerbach explains, "establishes a connection between two events or persons, the first of which signifies not only itself but also the second, while the second encompasses or fulfills the first." Although such interpretation deals with "real historical events, which have either happened in the incarnation of the Word, or will happen in the second coming," the "understanding of the two persons or events is a spiritual act" ("*Figura*" 53). In this way, *figura* moves from the realm of rhetoric into "a realm both real and spiritual, hence authentic, significant, and existential" (45).

Auerbach also addresses the origins of "figural phenomenal prophecy" in the Pauline epistles. It "had grown out of a definite historical situation, the Christian break with Judaism and the Christian mission among the Gentiles; it had a historical function" (56). Converting the Gentiles, then, was the rhetorical or persuasive function of typological readings of the Bible, and the complex time sense of figural interpretation made it particularly useful for such purposes. For it was at once "youthful and newborn as a purposive, creative, concrete interpretation of universal history" and "infinitely old as the late interpretation of a venerable text, charged with history, that had grown for hundreds of years" (58). Figural interpretation acknowledges the authority of a prior text in order to authorize an advance beyond it and to justify a historical new beginning; it tropes immediate historical discontinuity as a deeper figural continuity and thus both masters the past and lays claim to the future.

Similarly, the Puritans appealed to typology to read their historical break with precedent. After the Reformation, typological exegesis again becomes the dominant interpretational method, and Puritan typology also posits a providential history, wherein types both pattern "the horizontal plane of temporal life" and point to an "overarching redemptive design" (Rowe, *Saint* 2). While Pauline typology reads the Old Testament primarily as a book of prophecies of the New, however, the Reformation returns the Old Testament to the status of a history of the Jews (Auerbach, "*Figura*" 52–53). The American Puritans in particular read the Old Testament as the historical chronicle of a people, which serves as a type of the historical experience of another people. Here, purely intratextual continuities of before and after, of type and antitype, in the Bible modulate into extratextual continuities between biblical narratives and purely secular historical narratives, which now fulfill biblical prophecy.

The New England Puritans' contribution to Puritan typology, then, was to extend "to contemporary history the principle of reading one time in terms of another: biblical objects or events now might not only prefigure other biblical events or concepts but also the events of later history" (Paul Hunter, qtd. in Lowance 62). The Puritans used biblical patterns to "justify their errand into the New World and to defend their claim to national election," Karen Rowe writes (*Saint* 2). "Paradoxically, visions of America's destiny began with a retrospective appeal to biblical visions of Israel's journey out of Egypt into Canaan" (Rowe, "Prophetic" 47). Thus the New England Puritans' use of typology to oversee the traffic between scriptural and secular history also had a historical function. According to Sacvan Bercovitch, their idea of a "sacred history" saw them through a series of "betrayals" by history, beginning with the failure of the English Puritan Commonwealth. The Puritans, he writes, were never left "entirely alone" with America, for "the rhetoric they carried with them offered a ready means of compensation," allowing them "by scriptural precedent to *consecrate* their 'outcast,' 'exiled,' 'wilderness condition.' If they could not compel the Old World to yield to their vision, they could interpret the New in their own image" ("Ends" 179).

Thus, whether Pauline or Puritan, figural typology has designs on history. Typological interpretation in effect reverses and neutralizes the chronological, historical order of events within a divine design. In the biblical narrative sequence, for example, Israel historically precedes Christ; but, in the divine order of things, Christ precedes Israel. Kenneth Burke would call this a "confusion" of narrative-temporal precedence and logical precedence, which seems to be an element of religious rhetoric. In his example, the father precedes the son in the temporal order; in the logical order, however, they are "simultaneous," for there must be a son to confer the status of "father" (*Rhetoric* 31–32). When we bring secular history into such a pattern, sacred biblical history again temporally precedes secular events, but secular history fulfills and is logically simultaneous with its type. Typology enables a constant conversion of temporal-narrative sequences into logical terms, whereby temporality is both affirmed and neutralized from a higher perspective. In the two-way temporal pull of a typological sequence, each new development at once validates the past prophecy, affirming its prophetic or typal function, and surpasses it. In such an order, progress is authorized precisely by reinstituting the precedent as authoritative. Typological history is progressive history that keeps recapitulating the past; Rowe's nice term for this process is "the avant-garde development of recapitulative typology" (*Saint* 17).

Such a conservative avant-gardism also marks Pound's modernism. In his modernist refiguring of literary history, Pound justifies his revolutionary break with nineteenth-century English verse by appealing to essential figural continuities across historical divides.[4] Again, typology serves a historical function by representing a literary-historical rupture as a return to a truer tradition—if not, indeed, to the very origins of Western literature. Pound's modernism is a way of being at once radically old and radically new; his work is not merely a phase of a continuous, evolving enterprise. Standing at both the beginning and the end, he fulfills and abrogates the entire tradition.

Pound is certainly aware of the anachronism of his "pawing over the ancients" (*Literary* 11). For example, he admits, "Stage set à la Dante is *not* modern truth. It may be O.K. but *not* as modern man's"—"Aquinas *not* valid now" (*Selected Letters* 293, 323). Yet he repeatedly invokes Dante as a guide through his own dark thicket and quotes, alludes to, and imitates Dante so freely that the *Cantos* are unimaginable without him. For Pound, Dante is at once an authorizing precedent and irrelevant, for Pound's project annuls Dante's Christian project precisely by fulfilling it, essentially repeating Dante's use of Virgil as a pagan *figura* of the very Christian fulfillment that annuls him.[5] Pound's dilemma is how to figure literary continuity—which must exist in some sense for the literariness of his new work to be recognizable as such—at the juncture of a historical discontinuity, a new or "modern" historical condition to which literature nevertheless must respond adequately in order to be "modern." Thus his flaunting literary and compositional discontinuities in order to establish deeper continuities—those not affected by "surface" historical contingencies—represents his solution to what is, by his own admission, a historically contingent problem. It seems that the "modern" experience of discontinuity elicits Pound's universalizing strategy, his typological literary history.

Typology, by providing a metaphysical closure that can accommodate historical, experiential, and textual discontinuity, also offers a model of intratextual coherence that does not do violence to the *Cantos'* open form, where a "great disorder" and a "violent order" are indeed "one." Pound conceived of the *Cantos* as an open-ended work; he hoped the design of the poem would "happen" as it was written—that its form would be immanent in its history: "As to the *form* of *The Cantos*: All I can say or pray is: *wait* till it's there. . . . I haven't an Aquinas-map" (1939; *Selected Letters* 323). While Pound may lack an "Aquinas-map," his poem nevertheless appears capable of absorbing all kinds of unforeseen historical and biographical events—most important, his experiences at Pisa. Pound weaves even this cataclysm into the fabric of the *Cantos* and begins again by turning once more to typology.

Samuel Mather's distinction between type and antitype, which follows Calvin's, is useful for following Pound's design. For Mather, the type is a "Shadow"—"a dark and weak resemblance and representation of Things. But the very Image of the Things themselves, is a clearer and better Representation of them." The "Shadow is the first rude Draught: But the Image is a more lively and exact Representation. So the dark Shadow is ascribed to the *Law*. The more lively Image to the *Gospel*. The Things themselves are in Heaven" (qtd. in Rowe, *Saint* 44). Pound's idea of a three-part movement in the *Cantos* corresponds to this three-tiered scheme of "Shadow," "Image," and "Things themselves." Pound repeatedly argues for the *Cantos'* threefold design:

A. A. Live man goes down into world of Dead
C. B. The "repeat in history"
B. C. The "magic moment" or moment of metamorphosis, bust thru from quotidien into "divine or permanent world." Gods, etc. (1927; *Selected Letters* 210)

The poem is not a dualism of past against present. . . . If the reader wants three categories he can find them rather better in: permanent, recurrent and merely haphazard or casual. (1933; Cookson xvii)

A. Dominated by the emotions.
B. Constructive effort—Chinese Emperors and Adams, putting order into things.
C. The domination of benevolence. Theme in Canto 90. Cf. the thrones of Dante's "Paradiso." (*c.* 1955; Cookson xx)

a) What is there—permanent—the sea.
b) What is recurrent—the voyages.

c) What is trivial—the casual—Vasco's troops weary, stupid parts. (*c.* 1955; Cookson xx–xxi)

The middle term, which has to do with "order," involves recurrence or "repeats." The "casual" event correlates with the descent of one man into the world of the dead, whether Odysseus into Hades or Pound into post–World War I London. Either descent would be "haphazard," "trivial," or accidental unless advanced into the second category, the recurrent, by getting its repeat. By being repeated, the isolate event comes to function as a type: it receives its antitype, and both the original and the subsequent event are rescued from triviality. The significance of events depends on their entering a pattern of historical repeats—of foreshadowings and fulfillments—not on their symbolic or allegorical status or meaning. Meanings are not superadded but emerge in a historical arena, whether the history of Western literature, Pound's biography, or the composition of the *Cantos*.

While repeats give order to sequentiality, moments of vision "bust" through the order to the "divine" world to offer a glimpse of the "Things themselves," the total design that underwrites historical or sequential patterns. Such a "permanent" basis, which justifies all the repeats, isomorphisms, and metamorphoses of types in the *Cantos*, is a natural, linguistic, animate force. " 'As a wind's breath / that changing its direction changeth its name' " (106:752), this force can be variously called the Ovidian "sea," Confucian "process," or Dante's "thrones." Whether the typology is Christian or Poundian, an ideal dimension of permanent truth ensures equity in all representations and substitutive exchanges.

The figure that accesses this permanent world is an "image," a "direct treatment" ("a more lively and exact Representation") of what surpasses representation—"the 'thing' whether subjective or objective" ("the Things themselves"). The image offers a perception of a " 'complex' instantaneously" and thus liberates us from "time limits and space limits" (*Literary* 3–4). In later reincarnations, an image becomes an ideogram— "a form of superposition . . . one idea set on top of another"—or a "vortex," a "radiant node or cluster" (*Gaudier* 89, 92). These figures of timeless configurations enfold time and history within their scriptural shape. Like the statements of analytic geometry, they are " 'lords' over fact. They are the thrones and dominations that rule over form and recurrence": "Great works of art [are] lords over fact, over race-long recurrent moods, and over to-morrow" (*Gaudier* 91–92). It is in this sense that the "Paradiso" is, for Pound, an "*image*" (*Gaudier* 86).

Canto I, an intertextual ideogram that enfolds temporality, serves as an exemplary Poundian "image." Hugh Kenner calls the canto a "chord" of various beginnings, including Homer, Virgil, "The Seafarer," and Pound himself translating "The Seafarer" in 1911 (*Pound* 349). It superimposes epic journeys of the same type from different times and traditions and fits the modern poet's enterprise into a recurrent pattern. The shape such journeys share—a descent into an underworld to consult the past for prophecy and guidance for the future—is, we might say, the "metaphysical form" of "beginnings." The pattern itself is the "universal" *forma*, "existing in perfection, in freedom from space and time," for the image does not just give a rule that "applies to a lot of facts"; it "grip[s] hold of Heaven" (*Gaudier* 91). Aptly, the specific pattern here is that of figural typology.

Superimposing a translation and new beginnings, Canto 1 could also be called an "image" of Pound's modernism. Beginning by translating the Nekuia, the oldest part of *The Odyssey*, Pound masters his extreme belatedness precisely by acknowledging it. His invocation of Homer's authority at the beginning of the *Cantos* also in effect annuls Homer's beginning, for Pound's translation of a translation—his detour through Andreas Divus's Latin version—reduces the "original" Homer to a mere metaphor for beginnings. An ideogram of "generic" beginnings, the canto metaphorically substitutes for Homer's "genetic" beginning—to borrow Burke's terms—and thus masters Homer's precedence and Pound's belatedness. And this feat is accomplished via the intervention of Latin; already late by Divus's 1538, the use of Latin signifies a distinctly literary continuity and a separate, "sacred" language, where lateness is all.

Canto 1, then, enables Pound to begin by deranging temporal sequence, very much as figural prophecy confuses temporal order, and such a derangement is possible only because history has a total, "providential" order. In this confused sequence of events, either Odysseus or Pound could be the "live man" descending, for both descents would be merely casual without their repeats; the significance of each depends on their reciprocity. We could view Pound as repeating Odysseus's journey, or the other way around—Odysseus as repeating Pound's journey. We can work in either direction, depending on whether we are focusing on Homer or on Pound's translation of Homer—that is, whether we privilege temporal or logical priority. Tiresias's question—"A second time? why? man of ill star"—could be directed at Odysseus, because Pound has already been there, translating and sacrificing "blood" to Homer's ghost to let him speak and prophesy the course of the modern poet's present journey.[6] Or Tiresias could be addressing Pound the epic-quest hero, as distinct from Pound the translator-poet. As hero, Pound is second to Homer's Odysseus; as poet-translator-transmitter, he is prior.

Translation is the crux of Pound's typological literary history. That translation is possible at all attests to the existence of certain "cores" independent of "codes," whether of different languages or period styles. Pound's poet is a medium of a two-way passage, not only between the

originals and their historical translations but also—by virtue of the possibility of such translation—between history and what transcends it and
thereby legitimates translation. "Making it new" day by day also means
making it old, because "it"—here, the process of natural change—does not
change; "it" is the "unwobbling pivot" that authorizes historical changes
and translations. Like typological interpretation, then, translation fulfills prior "types" and perceives timeless patterns, ultimately "busting"
through to a vision of universal principles or "thrones"—"something God
can sit on / without having it sqush" (88:581).

Pound regards the poetic process itself as a form of typological translation, as his early poem "The Tree" (1908) spells out:

> I stood still and was a tree amid the wood
> Knowing the truth of things unseen before,
> Of Daphne and the laurel bow
> And that god-feasting couple olde
> That grew elm-oak amid the wold.
> 'Twas not until the gods had been
> Kindly entreated and been brought within
> Unto the hearth of their heart's home
> That they might do this wonder-thing.
> Nathless I have been a tree amid the wood
> And many new things understood
> That were rank folly to my head before.
> (*Collected* 35)

Here, the psychological adventure of an Ovidian metamorphosis also enables a historical understanding, for the speaker now recognizes the truth
of earlier texts telling such stories of "Daphne and the laurel bow." In repeating the psychological experience that is the source of this myth (cf.
Literary 431), he learns both a truth of nature and the truth of poetry,
which meet in the "laurel bow." He becomes a poet, awakening at once to
the timeless truths of nature and to a historical tradition—specifically, the
tradition of metamorphosis from Ovid's myths through Browning's masks,
whose voice echoes in the poem's final line. The truth of tradition lies in
its truthfulness to the nature it patterns, for the "laurel bow" links the
metamorphoses of natural process, psychic fluidity, figurative language,
and literary tradition.

In "The Tree," then, the poet's psychological experience validates the
tradition, and tradition validates psychological truths. Without this vali-
dating translation across languages and through history, the psychological
experience would be merely aberrant, accidental, or sheer "nonsense" (*Literary* 431) and the tradition "rank folly." The value—of both present experience and past poems—does not reside in either alone but in the reciprocal relationship they enter. The private, historically specific experience

assumes value when it fits into and clarifies an established pattern, and the past's value lies in the light it sheds on the present. This is the same "illuminating reciprocity between type and antitype" (Rowe, "Prophetic" 61) that figural typology provides.

For Pound does not aim for mere novelty; he is careful, for example, to distinguish his program from the Futurists' "curious tic for destroying past glories" (*Gaudier* 90). Neither is he kind to "the laudatores temporis acti": to claim "that the sh-t used to be blacker and richer" (15:64) in the past is antiquarianism, a blockage of the distribution of knowledge, or usury. His translations constitute the kind of prospective archaeology he praises in Leo Frobenius's digging into "past and forgotten life" for the kind of knowledge that will point to "tomorrow's water supply" (*Guide* 57). If Pound's work is a radical break with precedent, it breaks only with "the conventional taste of four or five centuries and one continent," which is *not* his idea of "the tradition" (*Gaudier* 90). He can authorize his derangement of a sequential historical tradition by invoking an older tradition that predates the Reformation, Christianity, and even the classics and runs through many languages. By beginning again, out of the unspeakable prehistoric sources of Book 11 of *The Odyssey*, he renders the entire Western tradition into his currency, and because he is translating not the original Greek but a Latin translation, his repetition of this radical beginning also masters the interim between Homer and Pound—the interim occupied by Latin, Italian, and Anglo-Saxon, by Virgil, Dante, Divus, and "The Seafarer" poet.

Such a progressive recapitulation or translation of earlier texts and translations is, in fact, the hallmark of Pound's modernism, and the operative trope in progressive typology is metalepsis. Richard Lanham describes this trope as the deployment of a remote cause to authorize a present effect in a way that, in effect, nullifies the cause. For example, in the statement "The ship is sinking: damn the wood where the mast grew," the "remote cause, because several causal steps intervene between it and the result, seems less like a cause than a metaphor substituted for a cause" (65–66). Metalepsis disarms the cause and strips the original of its originality in the very act of appealing to it. For Harold Bloom, too, metalepsis masters lateness by figuring it as a new earliness, producing the "illusion of having fathered one's own fathers" (20).

But metalepsis on the scale of Homer and the Bible clearly lies beyond an anxious response and does not proceed through repression. "Influence" would not be the right word for Pound's relation to those he chooses as his predecessors—Homer, Ovid, Dante, the Provençal poets, and so on. We cannot talk about Homer "influencing" Pound in the same way that we can talk about Pound influencing W. C. Williams, say. Rather, the pantheon of classical and medieval poets constitutes a kind of Scripture, and their modern translator fulfills everything that they project by taking them upon himself—by breathing their words now and making them new. Pound's history does not repress anteriority; rather, he begins in translation and completely reaffirms the legitimacy of his predecessors, so that he can legitimize and prove his historical supervention, his actual progress beyond them.[7]

Pound's strategy is the same "perfectionist" strategy that Douglas Robinson finds in Bible translation: "Inspiration by the Holy Spirit makes it possible to reach beyond the words of the original text to God's true meaning, God's Logos, and to translate it so perfectly that the translation supersedes the original" (55). The translation compensates for the historical contingencies and linguistic idiosyncrasies of the original text by attaining to God's true, intended meaning. "In the beginning was the Word," the origin prior to all translations—Aramaic, Hebrew, Greek, Latin, and English, including all historical "translations" like the narratives of the Hebrews and the life of Jesus. Like John's Gospel—"a belated text that claims priority over what came before" by establishing his "Master as originary, the Word that was with God at the beginning" (192)—such metaleptic translation turns belatedness into an origin. The Christian, metaleptic troping of the Old Testament is repeated with each translation of the Bible, which must be "perfectionist"—given the odd fact that the Christians' sacred text is originally a translation. Pound's metaleptic translations similarly enable a typological mastery of belatedness.

In Burke's terms, metalepsis is a species of synecdoche, which presumes a total, closed order to authorize not only substituting "part for the whole, whole for the part" but converting before and after, cause and effect, and temporal and logical sequences into each other endlessly. Synecdochic representation stresses "a relationship of convertibility" between "two sides of an equation, a connectedness that, like a road, extends in either direction" (*Grammar* 507–509). Synecdoche also fosters a confusion or conflation of texts and experience, which is one of its attractions for Pound. It enables a return, at the end of a history of fragmentation, long after "mankind has been commanded" not to write epics (*Selected Letters* 180), to an "image" of totality. For a synecdochic vision is, generically speaking, an epic vision. Georg Lukacs describes the "integrated" world of the epic as one of immanent value: "Being and destiny, adventure and accomplishment, life and essence are then identical concepts" (30). The "totalitarian" world of the epic, where microcosm and macrocosm coincide, has a paradisal clarity, where "each action of the soul" is "complete in meaning—in *sense*—and complete for the senses" (29).

Or, in Pound's own formulation of such a synecdochic vision, "an epic is a poem including history" (*ABC* 46). But who can write such a poem?

The author of an epic would have to be a scribe recording the historical tale of the tribe, as Pound's repeated "ego scriptor" tag acknowledges. And he would have to command a god-like perspective on the whole story—on what must have been, in a sense, already "written" before the first word was spoken. Synecdochically, Pound keeps figuring the "whole tribe" as "from one man's body, / what other way can you think of it?" (99:708); conversely, one man's breath sounds the whole tribe speaking its different tongues: "This is not a work of fiction / nor yet of one man" (99:708). The author of this tale, then, is "no man"—both anonymous and more god than man; as Zeus says of Odysseus, one of whose names is "no man," "A chap with a mind like THAT! the fellow is one of us. One of US" (*Guide* 146).

The design this author perceives is pervasive, for, following Plotinus, he believes "the body is inside the soul." The macrocosmic design may be apprehended anywhere and everywhere—through texts or Scripture, the book of nature or historical events. A superior mind can see the permanent beneath its ever-changing aspects. Pound, for example, can perceive the single pattern—what Kenner would call the "slipknot" (*Pound* 360)—informing myths of the death and rebirth of ancient fertility gods, Odysseus's journey to the underworld, Christ's death and resurrection, Dante's journey through the Inferno on up, the "brother" wasp's natural life cycle, the modern epic poet's search for permanent values through the hell of twentieth-century Europe, and his own biography—his incarceration at Pisa in 1945, his stint in the "bughouse" (105:747), and his repeated rise to "affirm the gold thread in the pattern" (116:797). Seeing these mythic, literary, natural, and historical metamorphoses as isomorphic changes, Pound achieves a vision of the principle of metamorphosis, of divine energy that patterns myths, epics, histories, and individual lives. For such a vision, the betrayals of history are not insurmountable problems; neither are individual "failure" and errors. For "it coheres" (116:797), even though Europe is "a broken ant-hill" (76:458), Pound's "errors and wrecks lie about" him (116:796), and his "notes do not cohere" (116:797): "Heaven's process is quite coherent / and its main points perfectly clear" (85:552).[8]

Accordingly, the *Cantos* themselves "cohere" as a series of typological foreshadowings and fulfillments. This design governs both textual repeats and the traffic between textual patterns and historical events. Odysseus-Pound's progress toward "home," for example, suffers a rude setback with Pound's imprisonment in Pisa; the typological pattern proves its resilience, however, by incorporating even that radical historical break. The first Pisan canto, 74, begins again by representing itself as the historical fulfillment of some of the epic themes prefigured in Canto 1. Now, not only older literary and historical texts but Pound's earlier cantos provide him with types, as the whole poem becomes a self-fulfilling prophecy. For example, Tiresias's prophecy, "Lose all companions" (1:5), gets its historical fulfillment with "these the companions" listed in Canto 74 (432–33). With this canto, the themes of exile, alienation, and homelessness that inform Pound's poetry from the very beginning are rescued from being merely psychological idiosyncrasies or historical accidents and become typological fulfillments of the epic hero's trials and wanderings. Similarly, the refrain "A man on whom the sun has gone down" (430) biographically repeats the earlier literary pattern of the Homeric descent to "the sunless dead and this joyless region" (1:4) and its Dantean repeat, "Io venni in luogo d'ogni luce muto" (14:61).

In proportion as the *Cantos* grow more historically specific, they grow more figurally ambitious: "nox animae magna from the tent under Taishan / amid what was termed the a.h. of the army" (74:437). At the moment the pattern becomes most biographical, it enlarges to incorporate Christ: "magna NUX animae with Barabbas and 2 thieves beside me, / the wards like a slave ship" (436). Within the synecdochic framework of typological interpretation, historical realism and universal patterns are validated in and as one move; neither is sacrificed to the other. Pound's awareness of the clash between his dream and his actual historical situation "amid the slaves learning slavery" (431) leads him only to reiterate the dream — "I surrender neither the empire nor the temples / plural / nor the constitution nor yet the city of Dioce" (434) — and, indeed, to blow it up even bigger. Now Odysseus is also Elijah (426), and Pound also Christ. To put it differently, at the very point that Pound most openly acknowledges the betrayal of history — "the enormous tragedy of the dream" with the "crucifixion" of "Ben and la Clara" (425) — he most emphatically reaffirms the dream: "dell' Italia tradita / now in the mind indestructible" (430).

The subject rhymes with which Pound structures his epic — whether between texts, historical periods, or texts and history — are not, for him, poetic metaphors; they are not mere rhetoric, products of human ingenuity that creates excess meanings "*ex nihil.*" An image or ideogram is "absolute metaphor," "the furthest possible remove from rhetoric" (*Gaudier* 85, 83), for it spells out connections ordained by nature: "The plan is in nature / rooted" (99:709). These connections are not fanciful analogies, imposed by our puny human faculties, but authorized metaphors; the Puritans would call them Types.

Both Pound and the Puritans insist on distinguishing willful rhetoric, trivial metaphoric ornaments, and usurious increases of excess meaning from types that reveal the pervasive design — whether Providential or in "nature / rooted" — which does not need our "polishings" or embellishments. "Does god need a clay model? gilded?" Pound asks. "The celestial wants your small change? / or bears grudge when he does not get it"

(98:688). In fact, something is morally wrong with rhetoric; the Puritans' preference for a "plain" style over smoothness or elegance and for typal figuration over tropes indicates that aesthetic choices imply moral values. This is no less true for Pound, who may have begun as an aesthete but did not end as one; making a telling analogy, he writes: "Aestheticisme comme politique d'église, / hardly religion" (96:651).

Hostility to rhetoric is implicit in the distinction between typological and allegorical interpretation. Typological interpretation, Rowe writes, believes "God's redemptive design becomes visibly manifest in Christ," in the "fabric of history," but "in allegorical exegesis the individual creates his own patterns of symbolic meaning rather than attempts to discover God's already woven pattern" (*Saint* 5–6). While Pound as "interpreter" does not rely on a providential design, he is far from secular; he believes in an immanent "God, *Theos*" (*Selected Prose* 49), and insists that the design of the "universe" is not man-made: "In nature are signatures / needing no verbal tradition," for a "tradition" exists that is "not mere epistemology" (87:573). And the readers of this design are far from mere individuals interpreting according to their lights: "To see the light pour, / that is, toward sinceritas . . . all astute men can see it encircling . . . With splendour, / Catholicity, / Woven in order, / as on cords in the loom" (99:695).

Like the Puritans, Pound condemns any "artful" interference with, or distraction from, God-given Truth. The purpose of art is to reveal the "woven" design, and any blockage of truth, through obfuscation or "excess" meaning, is immoral. "To communicate and then stop, that is the / law of discourse" (80:494), he warns: "Get the meaning across and then quit" (88:581). Geryon, his figure of usury, also represents rhetorical excess, ill-gotten meanings that hide the true pattern under a rich, "marvellous patterned hide" (*Literary* 211). As William Scheick argues, the Puritans also distinguished between denotative language and connotative excess. Denotative language names things by their proper names; "Call things by the names" (52:261), Pound never tires of repeating, "get a dictionary / and learn the meaning of words" (98:689). By contrast, "Satanic" language, with its "subtle sinuous ambiguities," is usurious; like Geryon's twisting serpentine form, it hides truth, rather than revealing it. Such excess or perversion is endemic to human language after the fall: "postlapsarian human language is coiled," deviant, deceitful (Scheick 19). In short, rhetoric is the postlapsarian complication, and we must be ever watchful for its tricks.

Typology appeals to both the Puritans and Pound in their similarly radical-reactionary programs, because typological figuration comes with metaphysical authority and confirms a totalitarian, closed system of meaning that enfolds historical development. The rhetorical strategy Pound shares with the Puritans is, in fact, a repression of rhetoric as figuration, a "willful" misreading of rhetorical or tropological links as absolute connections. Synecdoche, a totalizing trope that naturalizes its rhetoric, underwrites all totalitarian projects. And the politics of the Puritan state and Pound's ideal Confucian state are not that different. John Winthrop figures a "community as members of the same body," "knit together . . . as one man" ("Model" 91), and defines "civil" liberty as "a liberty to that only which is good, just, and honest. . . . This liberty is maintained and exercised in a way of subjection to authority" ("Speech" 92). Ideally, liberty and "subjection" to "just authority" would coincide, and the same holds true for Pound's ideal of Confucian government, where liberty is submission to the Way or Process. "The State is corporate / as with pulse in its body" (99:707), for "There is a must at the root of it / not one man's mere power" (99:709). So that: "The Sage Emperor's heart is our heart, / His government is our government" (99:695). Since both Pound and the Puritans know what is inherently "good, just, and honest," they have as little tolerance for other value systems as they have doubts about their own.

Poetry, however, necessarily disturbs such airtight systems. For example, Puritan poets' allusions to classical texts and verse forms, Lawrence Rosenwald suggests, acknowledge a special language and a special community of poets that does not entirely coincide with the community of the believers to which it belongs (313–15). Here, Latin marks a "special" or poetic language, which has a different connection to the "domain of the sacred." Acknowledging a separate allegiance to a poetic community and to tradition mediates poetry's relation to official doctrine, and American Puritan poets' recognition of the pagan-humanist tradition is a sign of the built-in distance poetry commands not only from dominant social and political practices but from its own conscious, ideological burden. The specialness of poetic language interferes with, modifies, and may even subvert the poet's ostensible ideology. This is one argument for not dismissing Pound's work simply on the basis of its ideology; his very medium, with its moments of "Mediterranean sanity" and "moderation," tempers the distemper of a poet who can plead, with justification, "remember that I have remembered" (80:506).

By comparing Pound and the Puritans, I do not mean to suggest a typological link between them; Puritan ideology and experience are not chapters in Pound's scriptural inheritance. I only propose analogies between Pound's figuration of literary history and the Puritans' figuration of biblical history, and between the ways both deploy scriptural patterns to write more than scriptural history and thereby consecrate their secular experiences. To read their relationship as more than analogous would mean to posit a transcendent basis for the comparison — the *forma* of American beginnings, for instance. Typological readings privilege history, and if we read typological thinking typologically, we could say that it is the rhetorical form by which temporal and historical discontinuity may be mastered. For a nation whose beginning is a violent rupture with the past, typology proves a useful strategy; as Bercovitch argues, "the function of Puritan figuralism in American Culture" has been to ensure the "inseparability" of "the event interpreted and the interpretation become event" ("Ends" 171, 173)—in a word, of history and rhetoric. The Puritans' "poignant and defiant transvaluation of fact into trope" rhetorically compensates for "history's betrayal of the New World" (188), and this strategy is deployed, Bercovitch claims, at every important subsequent crossing in American history—"from the Great Awakening through the Revolution and the Westward Movement to the Civil War, and from that 'Armageddon of the Republic' to the Cold War and the Star Wars of *our* latter days" (186-87).

But analogy, too, requires a shared ground. In this case, I suggest that the common ground is the "form" or generic structure of epics, which conflate temporal and logical sequence. Instead of seeing Pound's enterprise as shaped by the form of the Puritans' historical experience in the New World, then, we could say that the Puritans' vision of their history was shaped by the generic requirements of epic narratives. History and poetry meet in the middle ground of epic, a genre originally inseparable from tribal history. Thus I would privilege a literary form in reading the Puritans' typological rhetoric, rather than a Christian form in reading Pound's enterprise. If "an epic is a poem including history," and if in the totalitarian world of the epic everything is already significant in the mere telling of it, the Puritans' historical experience—no less than Pound's—is represented on the epic model. Once the "touch of rhetoric in the whole" (9:41) is repressed, there is no contradiction between truth and history, truth and poetry, or history and poetry. Spats between "Truth and Calliope / Slanging each other sous les lauriers"—" 'Slut!' 'Bitch!' "—pose a problem only in compositions whose "fragments" are indeed only "shelved (shored)" fragments (8:28). My notes, necessarily sketchy, might be best construed as notes toward a definition of the American epic genre—or, more properly, of epic rhetoric, given the original lateness of both American history and poetry. This special rhetoric, which proceeds by repressing its rhetoric, may govern historical narratives, literary texts, and the commerce between them.

Notes

1. References to the *Cantos* cite the number of the canto, followed by a colon and the page number.
2. Pound also links "semitic" thinking to the Enlightenment: when this "system emerged from low life into high life . . . it produced the Encyclopedists. Things

were so or not so" (*Selected Prose* 151). Thus Protestantism leads to both a coarsening of moral thought and the rise of capitalism and scientific rationalism alike.

3. "I was brought up in American school and sunday school. Took the stuff for granted, and at one time with great seriousness," Pound admits; "I don't in the least wish that I had missed a Xtian education in childhood" (*Guide* 300).

4. If we agree with Kenner that the modern "era" belongs to Pound (*Pound*), we can engage, via Pound, a larger question: how can modernism's commitment to change, to the destruction of outdated conventions, and its commitment to resuscitating the "true" tradition be understood as parts of the same process? Other modernists like James Joyce, T. S. Eliot, and H. D. also correlate texts of pagan antiquity or the Bible with modern episodes and experiences. Schneidau connects the "conception of reality held by Joyce and Pound" to Christian and, before that, primitive ideas that "the whole of nature is, as it were, a hieroglyph of revealed truth" (Gombrich, qtd. in Schneidau 84–85); "some of the most powerful ideas of Western Christianity, including that fateful statement of immanence in the doctrine of Incarnation, percolated through various channels and indirect ways until they reached modernism, as it were, devoid of content but intact in shape" (85). Gelpi, stressing its Puritan roots, classifies Pound's symbolism as typological as opposed to tropological (53). But in both readings—as in the more common arguments for a continuity, via Jonathan Edwards, between the Puritans and later New England writers like Emerson, Thoreau, and Frost—the emphasis falls more on the epistemological claims of typological symbolism than on the ambitions of developmental typology over the shape of secular history.

5. Auerbach's discussion of Dante and Virgil provides the precedent for a literary-historical application of typology. Virgil at once precedes Dante in secular or poetic history and foreshadows his city of the future: "Dante believed in a predetermined concordance between the Christian story of salvation and the Roman secular monarchy; thus it is not surprising that he should apply the figural interpretation to a pagan Roman" ("*Figura*" 67). Here, "the figural structure proves the historical event [Virgil and Rome] while interpreting it as revelation; and must preserve it in order to interpret it" (68): "the historic Virgil was for him a *figura* of the poet-prophet-guide, now fulfilled in the other world" (69). Of course, Dante's mission surpasses that of Virgil, who can guide him only to the threshold of the kingdom of God precisely because he came before Dante, too early for the vision granted *him*. Dante's assimilation of Virgil into a Christian design exemplifies a typological figuration of literary history on the model of scriptural sequentiality.

6. For translation as "blood" sacrifice, see Kenner (*Pound* 149, 360); for translation in Canto 1 and in Pound's work in general, see Alexander 142–44, 66–79.

7. Auerbach notes how, in the two oldest examples, *figura* occurs in combination with "nova," and adds, "Even if accidental, it is significant, for the notion of a new manifestation, the changing aspect, of the permanent runs through the whole history of the word" ("*Figura*" 12). The progressivism of Puritan typology is discussed by many, notably Bercovitch ("Ends").

8. As Bernstein writes, "Coherence in *The Cantos* never really resided in 'the notes' themselves (the actual situations presented in the poem)—it was always posited outside the text, in the realms of history, nature, and myth. . . . Only the entire tribal heritage can unite all of the work's juxtaposed details as part of its larger, all-encompassing tale" (181).

LORIS MIRELLA

T. S. Eliot's Calvinist Modernism

"*Those who regarded Calvin only as a theologian do not know the extent of his genius.*"
—Jean-Jacques Rousseau, *The Social Contract*[1]

T. S. ELIOT's identity as a modernist poet and critic stands in a problematic relationship with his identity as a religious poet and critic. In some cases, the poetry and religion come together in positive ways, as when Eliot is said to explore the spiritual dimensions of experience.[2] In other cases, the poetry and religion are antagonistic, especially when one considers his conversion in 1927 as the decisive act that split his experimental, modernist period from the later period that C. K. Stead characterizes as his "resignation" from the world (209). The former period includes discussions of the special realm of the poet, while the latter offers writings expressive of a clearly Christian ideal.[3] Further clouding the nature of Eliot's religious thinking is the fact that his conversion was to Anglo-Catholicism. Self-consciously European in its orientation, Eliot's Anglo-Catholicism distracts our attention from the American roots of his religious identity, even as it binds our consideration of his poetic career to religious questions (such as whether his turning toward religion was a turning away from poetry). His admiration for poets as religiously varied as Donne, Dante, and Baudelaire tells us little about the actual impact of religion, specifically Calvinism, on his formative years.

A powerful and constant undercurrent in American intellectual life, Calvinism runs as deep in Eliot as it does in the rest of the culture. Eliot's immediate family history was dominated by his grandfather, a Unitarian minister dedicated to service, whose memory was revered by his family as inspirational. The intersection of Eliot's spiritual background and his family history is portrayed in *East Coker* (1941), named after the English town in Somerset from which Eliot's Calvinist ancestor emigrated to America in the seventeenth century. The specific relationship between Eliot's intellectual, moral, and spiritual concerns, involving a Calvinist heritage that is both personal and cultural, is the subject of this essay.

Examining Eliot's career more closely, we can see how Calvinist themes and motifs permeate his poetry and prose, and more importantly, how Calvinism as a system of thought presents an alternative, analogous mode in which to understand his conception of how poetry formalizes consciousness and experience. With the discussion cast in these terms, it is unnecessary to distinguish Eliot's Calvinist roots from the Anglo-Catholicism he ultimately adopted. While much of this analysis focuses on Eliot's pre-conversion work, where the Catholic dimension is irrelevant, the close affinities between Calvinism and Eliot's brand of Catholicism render the conversion itself irrelevant. The hierarchy of artists (and critics) in Eliot's early works becomes a spiritual hierarchy in later work, as a comparison of "The Function of Criticism" (1923) with *After Strange Gods* (1934) makes clear. My purpose is to demonstrate how various dimensions of Calvinism comprise a distinguishable mode of thought in Eliot's work.

We must begin by recasting the terms with which we define modernism and Calvinism. Calvinism is more than a set of religious values; it is also, crucially, a complex or structure of beliefs and attitudes that, operating systematically, functions as an intellectual framework for articulating certain attitudes and emotions. Just as modernism is celebrated as a radical attempt to recast the experience of the contemporary and increasingly urbanized world in new, modern terms, so should Calvinism be considered, in its epoch and in its subsequent development as an "urban movement" with "intense self-consciousness," as the "only form of Christianity adapted to modern life" (Green 41, 26). Both Calvinism and modernism offer modes of "coming to terms" with a new social and cultural reality. They share a capacity to function as intellectual paradigms, providing frameworks for expression and germinating new representational forms. The comprehensive changes in forms of thought inspired by Calvinism intersect in Eliot's work with modernism's rewriting of contemporary experience.

I

One way to recover the Calvinist legacy is to review its historical trajectory. Calvinism is one of the essential spurs toward modernity that propelled European culture out of medievalism. Rousseau's claim that Calvin should be considered as more than a theologian asks us to look beyond a strictly religious frame of reference when evaluating Calvin's impact and relevance. Calvinism's diverse tendencies are frequently reduced to a single perspective. Though it presents a unified body of doctrine, Calvinism contains distinctive currents, most visible when we look at the major differences between American and European Calvinism.

One associates with American Calvinism the origins of the United States, and thus its fulsome preoccupation with revelation, with sinfulness, and with the irredeemability of the fallen world exist as a legacy that leaves people in the position of either strictly venerating or rejecting that tradition. But the Calvin usually cited in European tradition is a political and social radical who stands as an inspiration against the corrupt, vested interests of medieval authority and is thus part of a process of social transformation that allows people to think more critically about the whole tradition. This European version of Calvinism incorporates a notion of political radicalism spurred by moral indignation against injustice; such is the Calvin recognized and praised by his fellow Swiss citizen, Rousseau, himself an icon of political radicalism.[4]

In general, the European version of Calvinism registers the interconnectedness of the social, political, and cultural dimensions, as clearly demonstrated in such studies as Max Weber's. *The Protestant Ethic and the Spirit of Capitalism* (1904) treats the Reformation movement, including Calvinism, not as a haphazard series of discrete and individuated gestures,[5] but as an organic whole or framework that marked an epochal or structural change in the spirit or "ethos" of the Middle Ages (67). In Weber's view, Calvin's reformulation of the individual's identity and responsibility vis-à-vis God and society proved to be one of the fundamental supports for the emerging modern epoch of capitalism and its related social forms, ideas, and institutions. Calvinism's insistence on a remote God unconnected with human action; on a personal, atomized relationship to salvation; and on the irrelevance of "good works" as defined by the medieval system of indulgences and clerical intercession—all contributed to the revolutionary transformation of the communal forms of medieval social life into the individuated forms necessary to modernity.

By contending that Calvinism defines a socially constitutive change, Weber's study asserts the primacy of Calvinism's stress on the structure of social life, a structure of social life in which a personal, atomized salvation was bound over to a communal definition of what behaviors indicated salvation: what counted above all was "not single good works, but a life of good works combined into a unified system" (Weber 117). Thus, while Calvinism is associated primarily with the religious challenge to medieval Catholic authority, it contributed also to an irrevocable social reformation of Europe that encompassed family and individual life as well as cultural and national identity.[6] Calvinism proposed a break with the religious forms ruling the social status quo, sweeping away the accumulation of dogma that had gathered around religious scholarship and discourse and that Calvin saw as having generated corruption as well as deleterious social effects. Calvin rejected the dominant medieval outlook that saw human effort as ultimately redeemable through the intercession of the Church.

The Church, in his view, overstepped its true bounds, usurping power that can belong only to God, by claiming to control access to the eternal, and, in effect, making possible the leap from the worldly to the spiritual. Transcendence was built into the very identity of the Church as mediator (serving as the source of its justification and authority).

For Calvin, the possibility of transcendence is unthinkable given the necessary gap between fallen humankind and God. His ground-clearing return to first principles rested on the belief that it is impossible for humans, who are by definition "fallen," to approach God, the Absolute. For the community to reflect this revised conception of humankind's relationship with God necessitated not only a transformation of values but also a redefinition of the human being.

The effects of Calvinism's rewriting of medieval Catholicism can be charted as a shift in representational strategy. Essential to Calvinist doctrine is the notion that the fallenness of the world defines the human condition. By definition, to be human is to be essentially limited, bound by the world in sin. From this premise, one must logically accept both that God cannot be directly involved with this world and, conversely, that humans cannot have knowledge of God or God's will.

Calvin remapped the spiritual landscape from this perspective, reconsidering all aspects of human activity. Following out the line of thought that humans cannot get beyond their own fallen nature in order to come close to God, we see that any representational model humans may devise to explain and understand God's will or purpose not only must be willed by God but is also, to use a Calvinist technical term, an "accommodation" to the limitations of human categories of representation. In this respect, any attempt to represent God's plan must be regarded as provisional and imperfect; in short, "since the object of knowledge transcends any possible analogy the whole process must be in some sense fictive" (Keefer 146). Here, Calvinism implies that representations of God can be no more than human-devised models of truth. By its nature, representation is necessarily limited, if not inadequate to the object of representation. The notion of accommodation emphasizes that, even though its terms are human, representation issues from beyond the human; it is a process originated and mediated by God. Accommodation defines how "a wholly unintelligible and incomprehensible deity represents himself, in human terms, to mankind" (Keefer 148).

II

If we think of Calvinism in epochal terms as creating new social, political, and cultural forms (as Rousseau and Weber did), then Eliot's modernism, and arguably modernism as an identifiable movement in general, shares at least an analogous relation to Calvinism in that it also reformulates a previous practice in its totality. Calvinism and modernism sweep away previous forms of expression, rewriting the relationship of the individual to the whole. Modernism is more than a series of stylistic revolts against previously entrenched artistic practices; it is a wholesale revision of artistic practices (evident in the explosion of stylistic experimentation), as well as an attempt to transform the world in which those practices take place (as seen in the proliferation of the means of disseminating art, which alters the relation between artist and audience).[7]

Eliot's energetic and imaginative rejection of what he saw as the useless chatter of poetry and criticism that dominated the London literary scene during the post–World War I period comes to define a dominant current of modernism (as later he will reject the corruption and degeneracy of the contemporary world in religious terms). He reacts against what he considers to be the status quo, the "critical Brahminism" in literary activity (*Letters* 314), the presiding hegemony in attitudes, values, and taste. His literary essays set themselves consciously and vehemently against the powers of literary opinion in London, no matter how "obnoxious" he appeared to be in this role "to perhaps the larger part of the literary world of London" (*Letters* 541–42).

The notion of a "framework" ("Blake," "Dante" in *Sacred* 158, 165) is crucial for considering the character of Eliot's modernism, not only because it insists that modernism consists of more than a collection of certain stylistic elements, but also because Eliot himself stresses the importance of what he considers the framing context for poetry, the "organic wholes" ("Function" 31) within which we must consider individual works of art. He uses other terms—"scheme" in "The Function of Criticism" (32; 1923), "temper of the age" in "The Possibility of a Poetic Drama" (*Sacred* 63–64; 1920)—but the implication is the same. The tendency to consider art, religion, politics, and culture as aspects of a unified system marks many of Eliot's writings as he consistently and emphatically associates a specific set of values with a given artistic practice. The framework defines and determines the work of art, affecting the quality and character of the representation.[8] In Eliot's view, for example, "Elizabethan morality" facilitated literary production as well; "it provided a framework for emotions to which all classes could respond, and it hindered no feeling" ("Function" 31–32).

At the same time, even in his early essays concerned primarily with poetry, Eliot expresses literary values in terms that carry the weight of moral distinctions. For example, in "The Perfect Critic" (1920), the title of which alone suggests a purified ideal, bad critics are those whose "feelings are impure" and who offer in their criticism "nothing but an expression of emotion." The "perfect" or "good" critic, on the other hand, is one who is free of such feelings and desires, not tempted to express a "suppressed creative wish," who in the end resembles a religious as much as a literary practitioner: "the end of the enjoyment of poetry is a pure contemplation from which all the accidents of personal emotion are removed; thus we aim to see the object as it really is" (*Sacred* 56–58). The artist must be purified of imperfections and blemishes such as "personality" that are the condition of being human. While primarily literary, Eliot's absolutist separation of poetry from worldly concerns—both objectively (the existing monuments form themselves into an ideal order) and subjectively (the separation between the man who suffers and the mind that creates)—is also moral.

There is in Eliot's poetry a powerful awareness of a necessary accommodation as well. In fact, one could define Eliot's modernism as a search for a proper model that can both equal and accommodate reality or experience. He searches for a single adequate and permanent form or framework to express reality; but he is not concerned with defining "truth, or fact, or reality"; he wants "only to find a scheme into which, whatever they are, they will fit, if they exist" ("Function" 42).

This notion of framework, which appears in a number of the essays that comprise *The Sacred Wood* (1920), promotes the study of poetry qua poetry, but only within an appropriate intellectual and aesthetic context. The framework rather than the poet determines the quality and nature of (any) social or cultural activity. In Eliot's work, and especially in "Tradition and the Individual Talent" (1919), the most familiar version of the framework is tradition, an aesthetic framework within which individual poets find their voice and their place.

Eliot's notion of framework brings coherence to the two halves of his career. In the light of it, we can understand his conversion as another example of a shift in the strategy or mode of representing truth or reality, and his conversion statement appears, not as a simple rejection of his family's Unitarianism, but as an articulation of a unified political and cultural identity. Indeed, his Preface to *For Launcelot Andrewes* (1927), in which he announces his conversion to Anglo-Catholicism, also explicitly includes an aesthetic and political component: he declares himself to be "classicist in literature, royalist in politics, and anglo-catholic in religion" (iv). More than just settling accounts with his American cultural heritage, Eliot here stakes out a comprehensive position that, composited, forms a complete frame of reference for his attitude, perspective, and values. Although he shifts from the language of poetry to the language of religion, the problem throughout his career remains one of representing or formulating adequately experience and consciousness.

Eliot's attraction to the work of the English philosopher F. H. Bradley shares a similar impetus. Eliot is drawn to a model that recognizes a gap between experience or sensations, and the concepts built from the languages that are supposed to explain them. He claims that "the first condition of right thought is right sensation," and goes on to say that "if you have seen and felt truly, then . . . you may be able to think rightly" (*On Poetry* 247). The unalterable "truth" value of sensation is most evident in his high valuation of poets with developed sensibility and taste. Language offers a fragile or tenuous grasp of that reality of experience. Thus, the concepts devised by humans can be, finally, no more than partial or provisional representations of reality, models of an external world they cannot really grasp. The relation between thought and the world Eliot absorbs approvingly from Bradley could be derived from Calvin as well: "Our principles may be true, but they are not reality" (Eliot, *Sel. Essays* 361).

In Calvinist terms, human-based principles and tenets are not to be confused with those devised by God. Calvinism issues from a protest against presumptuous human overreaching that dares to identify itself with the Absolute. Alongside it, in a similar vein, stands Eliot's "classicist" doubt about approaching the artistic absolute. In aesthetic terms, Eliot opposes the classicist and romantic primarily in their respective attitudes toward the nature of art. The romantic attitude is based on the possibility of glimpsing and identifying with the eternal or absolute, whereas the classicist is based on the belief in art's limitations, accepting and respecting the inherited models of representation. Broadly speaking, the classicist view of art springs from some acknowledgment of inadequacy, a necessary, untranscendable gap between representation and reality, between language and truth. But in asking whether classicism as a principle should be applied strictly to literary criticism "or whether it has meaning only in relation to a view of life as a whole" ("Commentary," Sept. 1927, 194), Eliot answers with more than an aesthetic conclusion.

Eliot's understanding of the division between language and the world, between representation and truth, matches his preference for the classic as opposed to the romantic in literature. The twin components of this view, as Eliot sees it, are the humility of the artist and his "allegiance" to "outside" principles rather than to the "inner voice" ("Function" 35). The classicist perspective accepts and applies, humbly and consciously, the restrictions inherent in any human endeavor, whereas the romantic perspective ignores or denies any such limitations: "the romantic is deficient or undeveloped in his ability to distinguish between fact and fancy, whereas the classicist . . . is thoroughly realist—without illusions, without day-dreams, without hope, without bitterness, and with an abundant resignation" ("Function" 39).[9] Eliot emphasizes the maturity and sensible responsibility of the classicist perspective, a clear-eyed, unsentimental acceptance of one's potential to know truth or reality. He cites T. E. Hulme as the emblematic modern practitioner, herald of the "dry classical spirit" (*Use* 142), who tends toward the ascetic in art and in whose spirit one finds "a more severe and serene control of the emotions by reason" ("Idea" 5). Thus portrayed, Hulme resembles Calvin himself, whose reportedly "favorite idea was considering 'things in themselves, not words'" (Green 66).

Eliot's preference for classicism appears most clearly in his rejection of the American transcendentalists. The preeminent American literary tradition that Eliot knew had grappled with, opposed, and sought to overcome the implications of its Calvinist heritage. Basically, the transcendentalists, from Emerson onward, sought to reconcile the distinction between the physical and metaphysical by erasing the line between the natural and the supernatural, thereby neutralizing the Calvinist finality of the Fall and the resultant social and natural divisions. The transcendentalists claimed that the knowledge available through the senses included also that knowledge previously attained solely through nonsensory means (i.e., spiritually). Once the necessity of this distinction between reason and revelation is removed, there is no longer any need for a specialized language to describe or represent religious experience, leaving only "the secularization of language for the description of religious experience" (Shurr 44).

Eliot rejected the transcendentalist tradition because it proposed that a human-centered understanding of truth is adequate and possible. Emerson's vision lies on an essentially romantic continuum, where human potential, the supernatural, and the language needed to describe it are blended and interspersed. Eliot's work seeks to retain the classicist distinction among them: first, because he does not believe that any human rendering of the world can be sufficient; and second, because a human-constructed universe reduces the world to intolerably meager proportions. Without any external authority or standard of values, any human attempt to establish values becomes hopelessly muddled and chaotic, impossible and relative. There must be a reference point beyond the human in order to give the human meaning and value and to anchor the models of representation; thus, the importance for Eliot of classicist historical periods: "surely a moment of stasis, when the creative impulse finds a form which satisfies the best intellect of the time" ("Commentary," 1924, 232).

Hence the significance of Eliot's anti-romantic assertion that "there is no freedom in art" (*Sel. Prose* 32); art is structured and informed by the entire history of artistic practice. He argues for the privileged role of the artist only in relation to his or her art, not indiscriminately licensing freedom as such. Moreover, "freedom is only truly freedom when it appears against the background of an artificial limitation" (*Sel. Prose* 35), a view that places freedom within bounds. Again, while this view describes Eliot's conception of literary tradition, it also traces a moral dimension, resembling the Calvinist doctrine of human freedom (with its tortuous explanation of how free will operates; human actions are free yet simultaneously predetermined). The value of freedom in art makes sense only against some kind of boundary, just as Calvin's Elect have their place of salvation only insofar as the rest must be damned; otherwise salvation is without meaning or value (precisely the terms in which Eliot, in the essay "Baudelaire," elaborates his esteem for a poet usually perceived to be "immoral"). The forms of representation must embody this belief.

III

Calvinism influences not only Eliot's intellectual heritage, his academic study, and his early criticism, but his poetry as well. Eliot's Calvinist inheritance is most visible as a discrete element in the theme of spiritual desolation and the meaninglessness of the world, famously treated in poems such as "The Love Song of J. Alfred Prufrock" and *The Waste Land*.

One can also discern this inheritance in Eliot's concern with an approbation of the metaphysical as a means to devalue and dismiss the physical. In fact, "Whispers of Immortality" makes this distinction dramatically. Opposed to the exotic and foreign Grishkin with her rank "feline smell" are the two native English poets Webster and Donne, who are preoccupied with the decay of the body, with the disintegration of that illusory physical temple rather than with its celebration. Donne is described as the "expert beyond experience," the metaphysical poet either unconcerned with or unattracted to the realm of the physical, while Grishkin is ridiculed as no more than a physically preoccupied body, a "friendly bust" that "Gives promise of pneumatic bliss." The poem leaves the two realms of the physical and metaphysical unreconciled, "And even the Abstract Entities / Circumambulate her charm."[10] Similarly, in "Prufrock," the narrator's meditative quest for significance is constantly deferred or delayed; he is drawn away from the "deeper," pressing philosophical questions of existence (which the women in the poem address in comic fashion, "talking of Michelangelo") by the pungent presence of the female body, associated here with the senses of smell and touch: "Is it perfume from a dress / That makes me so digress?" (65–66). Eliot draws an absolute distinction, clearly valuing the visual as a mode of thought at the expense of the physical.

What is excluded from the female's purview in these poems is the sense of sight, associated with understanding, which in Eliot's poetics constitutes the principle medium of poetry. He celebrates not only these individual metaphysical poets but also that whole era of poets by associating the sense of sight with thought and abstraction, lamenting the later lapses into the "dissociated sensibility" of the eighteenth-century and romantic poets. Holding fast to this principle of visuality later in his career, Eliot articulates his suspicion of the value of Milton and Joyce as influences on younger poets by conjecturing that their blindness had a negative impact on their poetics (it is called "poetic vision," after all), while endorsing Dante's poetics for its powerful visuality. The ability to present hard, clear images, to think in images, as the essential attribute of great poets, underlies Eliot's supreme praise for Dante. Eliot lauds him, above all other poets, for the most comprehensive and complete vision, as the poet who best "succeeded in dealing with his philosophy . . . in terms of something perceived" (*Sacred* 171). Thus, Eliot's work, informed as it is by a strong sense of dichotomies that posits transcendent and metaphysical values against the earthbound and physical, demonstrates and operates on a clear understanding of Calvinist demarcations.

Eliot's attitude toward the Elizabethan era in general, and the metaphysical poets in particular, is a good index both of his modernist values and his Calvinist views. In "Metaphysical Poets" (1921), he proposes to treat the practices of this group of poets as historically unique, using them strategically to attack the subsequent developments in English verse. According to Eliot, the Elizabethan poets and dramatists had a common social and intellectual framework within which to assimilate experience. The epoch of Donne and others was "a period when the intellect was immediately at the tips of the senses." The Elizabethan period was a harmonious one when "sensation became word and word was sensation" (*Sacred* 129). For some reason that Eliot leaves tacit, this harmonized relationship between language and reality was subsequently broken.

The dissociation of sensibility that occurred basically describes the Fall as it takes place in language when language becomes separated from reality. Language became corrupt, decadent, flabby, vague, intricate for its own sake: as "the language became more refined, the feeling became more coarse" (*Sel. Prose* 64). The previously "unfallen," the undissociated or as sociated, sensibility had a purity and clarity, and the language of the chosen practitioners of this sensibility, according to Eliot, was "as a rule simple and pure" (*Sel. Prose* 62). An earlier essay, "Philip Massinger" (1920), anticipates the wider claim about the dissociated sensibility. Eliot shows how Massinger himself inaugurates the next period, the era of decline dominated by Milton, because his work demonstrates the gap between vision and language: "his eye and his vocabulary were not in cooperation" (*Sacred* 128).

Eliot employs a Calvinist distinction to account for the importance of the metaphysical poets: their greatness does not belong to them, but their

shortcomings and failings do. In installing the metaphysical poets collectively in a privileged place within literary tradition, Eliot accounts for their
primacy by featuring a nonindividual characteristic: their greatness comes
from the enabling framework of Elizabethan culture. At the same time,
their failure is their own fault. The failure of individuals—first of Massinger and later, when Eliot changes his opinion, of Donne—results from a
human defect that prevented them from adapting a new framework: "The
defect is precisely a defect of personality" (*Sacred* 143). As Eliot develops
this notion in later essays, he distinguishes Donne from other metaphysi-
cals such as Marvell, and ultimately devalues Donne because he is less
identified with his framework than they are. Unlike Marvell, a "product
of European culture," "Donne would have been an individual at any time
and place" (*Sel. Essays* 252).[11] With increasing clarity, Eliot locates the
source of literary value in an expanding set of objective circumstances, in a
framework that initially consists of literary factors (such as tradition), but
increasingly includes more social elements.

Since he is concerned primarily with the context for his own poetry, the
framework he defines in relation to the Elizabethans has features that he
seeks in his contemporaries. Thus, this framework is not a tool for static
historical analysis. Rather, it is constantly transformed as "the poet must
become more and more comprehensive, more allusive, more indirect, in
order to force, to dislocate if necessary, language into his meaning" (*Sel.
Essays* 248). Eliot argues that the new poets are engaged in the process of
constructing a new framework, evident in their vigorous experimentation
with language to express or embody their experiences of contemporary
life. The most important language "is that which is struggling to digest
and express new objects, new groups of objects, new feelings, new aspects"
(*Sacred* 149–50). Language thus allows for the assimilation and control of
the world as the world changes. A glimpse of how this preoccupation with
the frame operates in Eliot's contemporary context comes in his praise of
Joyce's mythical method in *Ulysses*: where Joyce's "scaffolding" of myth is
"simply a way of controlling, of ordering, of giving a shape and significance
to the immense panorama of futility and anarchy which is contemporary
history" (*Sel. Prose* 177). The function of myth, as a kind of framework,
is to produce an accommodation to and of reality.[12] Thus, the framework
defines the quality and nature of the accommodation; and the poet is responsible for making the accommodation culturally current and relevant,
showing how Eliot's Calvinistic claim that "the chief distinction of man is
to glorify God" applies to the artist ("Literature" 241).

Put in these terms, the nature of Eliot's critical values is suddenly illu-
minated. His summary dismissal of poets such as Milton and Shelley is due
in part to the framework with which each is identified, a schismatic social

context brewing a political and religious radicalness that Eliot abhors. The reasons that make them bad politically or morally are also the reasons that make them bad poetically. The framework encompasses both literary and extraliterary features. In a less strident way, Eliot also criticizes Donne and Blake, whose spectacular achievements give definition to his model for individual genius. In "Blake," he describes the poet as standing "naked," unaided by any outside circumstances and thus handicapped: he had need of "a framework of accepted and traditional ideas which would have prevented him from indulging in a philosophy of his own, and concentrated his attention upon the problems of the poet" (*Sacred* 157–58). Eliot associates this type of creative attitude with eccentricity (later to be renamed heresy); genius is significant only insofar as it is a symptom of a faulty social order, pointing to the inadequacy of a proper framework. Genius is a marker of individualism that can only lead to a preoccupation with personality; it is eccentric because it must compensate for the lack of a proper framework, and it is ultimately heretical because it attributes human greatness to human achievement. As such, Eliot's idea is an elaboration and revision of Calvin's belief that human feebleness and inadequacy require an accommodation—from God (Keefer 154).

Because genius is secondary for Eliot, the determination of individual artistic greatness is made by other criteria: "The difference between Shakespeare and Dante is that Dante had one coherent system of thought behind him" (*Sel. Essays* 116), a "boost" (as Eliot calls it) from the framework of thought provided by St. Thomas Aquinas. In fact, enjoying a kind of aesthetic predestination, the greatest artists are those who managed to belong to the greatest civilizations, namely Virgil as poet of the Roman Empire and Dante as poet of Catholic Europe. That both are products of the highest cultural period of European culture is stressed in "Dante" (1929) and "What is a Classic?" (1944), and is implied in "Kipling" (1940). From the perspective of creating the conditions for great cultural achievements, it is clear why Eliot dedicated himself and the journal he founded to the "European Idea," to the goal of reestablishing a common, unified, European culture.

IV

The two major phases of Eliot's career intersect at *The Waste Land* (1922). While this poem, Eliot's supreme achievement as a modernist poet, can be viewed as the culmination of his poetic experimentation, his own valuation of it as a spectacular failure meshes with our new appreciation of his Calvinism. Its ambiguity, allusive richness, and resonances permitted it to be appropriated by the very culture he sought to oppose. *The Waste Land* became an icon of the very status quo, supporting, reinforcing, and even celebrating the proliferation of meaninglessness throughout the culture. Consequently, Eliot is forced to redirect his creative energies into channels that he feels will be more fruitful both socially and spiritually. In light of *The Waste Land*'s failure, two subsequent developments in Eliot's work are crucial to any evaluation of his Calvinist heritage.

First, from the highly allusive and associative language of *The Waste Land*, Eliot turns to a simple imagery based on allegory. The increasing importance of allegory in his poetry after this time can be explained as an attempt to convey meaning objectively, separated from individual influence or arbitrary reading, as "objectively purposeful" and beyond human intervention as Weber defines Calvinist doctrine's goal. Moreover, allegory downplays the importance of the "surface" meaning, discarding the exterior "flesh" of language for the interior "soul" of meaning;[13] but also allowing one to find one's own level of understanding and thus to enter into an individual relationship with the poetry (in a Calvinist logic, one's ability to read it is the primary proof of the fitness of one's ability).

Second and more importantly, Eliot became absorbed in drama. Whereas poetry tends toward abstraction and allusiveness, drama is concrete, local, and rooted in a commonality of experience among a specific and physically present audience. It thus offered Eliot new possibilities of meaning and altered the framework of that meaning's reception. Drama is "naturally" (inherently) restricted, requiring a common language, a common culture (or at least a collective capacity for "reading" the signs on stage), and a limited number of viewers at any one time, and these features more closely control the play's reception by the community. By this means, Eliot hoped to control the "over-production" of meaning to which *The Waste Land* fell prey. The poem, he felt, meant too many things to too many different people. Given Eliot's view of the structural interconnectedness of social practices, it follows logically that the discipline necessary for art would also have to be manifested in the spiritual as well as the economic realms.

Eliot's turn away from the individual addressed by lyric poetry to the community addressed by drama was thus necessitated by his belief that his cultural epoch needed to control its rising consumerism. "I cannot understand," he said in a 1931 editorial, "the concurrence of over-production with destitution and I cannot help feeling that this has something to do with people wanting . . . the wrong things" ("Commentary" 309). Like Calvin, who turned to the individual in order to discipline him or her not to indulge in the corruption of the Roman Catholic Church, Eliot attacked modern capitalism by also disciplining the individual. The drama *Murder in the Cathedral*, for example, encourages its audience to think of themselves as separate persons requiring extraordinary restraint. The central figure, Thomas à Becket, overcomes the temptations of the flesh, resolving the problem of desire for himself and achieving martyrdom; but in doing so he experiences and reveals what Max Weber describes as the "unprecedented inner loneliness of the single individual" that resulted from Calvinist doctrine (104). In this play, Eliot illustrates that the way to counter the tendency of the contemporary social framework toward overproduction is to articulate an alternative social framework by promoting discipline, regulating corruption, and focusing, as the Calvinists did, on the primary importance of the individual subject.

The image of Becket defeating temptation and achieving sainthood offers the ideal model for the disciplined individual subject. But even more significant from a Calvinist perspective is the nature of Becket's ultimate victory over the Tempters. His success comes in recognizing that "The last temptation is the greatest treason: / To do the right deed for the wrong reason" (*Murder* 44). Acting on a fundamental Calvinist tenet, Becket achieves sainthood once he experiences a revelation: that one cannot try to anticipate nor rationalize the will of God, which was by definition impossible so far as Calvin was concerned (Keefer 155). One description of Calvinism's dynamic applies to Eliot's conversion as well: that it produces "an intellectual as well as practical otherworldliness" (Green 11).

Eliot's preconversion period can be characterized as the almost transparent effort to alter the framework using language (again, a modernist ideal), an effort celebrated in the metaphysical poets and also in Joyce's mythical method. It is the framework, for Eliot, that authorizes a structured freedom, ordering experience and society in the same way. Through the character of Becket, Eliot shows how asceticism and self-discipline are essential both for Becket's individual salvation and for that of his flock. Asceticism did not free one from the world: for Calvinism, and in Eliot's play —contrary to the impression of Catholic resignation—it meant a closer engagement with it (Weber 120–21).

Eliot's conversion—misread by critics as a turning away from the world —consolidates and realigns his disparate spheres of interest and activity within one clearly stated set of values. It represents an alternate mode of engaging with a world that Eliot saw as confined within an unsatisfactory social framework. Thus, the notion of a framework clarifies Eliot's turn toward religion as a significant political action responding to the social and economic crises of his time. His career as a modernist poet reinvests and reapplies in various ways the implications of Calvinist moral precepts to counter his own social framework's drift toward meaninglessness and chaos. Eliot the poet may not stipulate that the world is fallen, filled with imperfection, lacking in grace, and structured by human inability to over-come these limitations, but these Calvinist values are implied by his critical approach to literary matters.

Notes

1. Quoted in Shurr 145.
2. See Lyndall Gordon's two-volume biography, which organizes Eliot's life in terms of a spiritual quest, within which religion came to play the dominant role. In addition to this type of study, in which the poetic career is seen as an expression of religious interests, a number of studies trace diverse patterns of religious themes in his poetry. See, for example, Brooker, Bush, and Calder.
3. Essays typical of Eliot's earlier, modernist period include "Tradition and the Individual Talent" (1919), "Hamlet and His Problems" (1920), and "The Meta-physical Poets" (1921). Some works that typify his later, religious period include "Dante" (1929), "Religion and Literature" (1935), and *The Idea of a Christian Society* (1939).
4. According to Shurr, Calvin and Rousseau represent two poles of America's spiritual experience: that seen from the perspective of religion and that seen from the perspective of nature (145–46).
5. The most significant aspect of Weber's study lies not in its explicit amalga-mation of a religious form with a social attitude and set of values, but in its attempt to demonstrate that the social, economic, and political framework necessary to ac-commodate them was both historically unprecedented and socially constructed.
6. The fracturing of European culture and civilization was of immense con-cern to Eliot; to it he dedicated much intellectual effort, including *Criterion*. The familiar aspect of this quest is Eliot's promotion of individual asceticism and piety, but its collective aspect is the "European Idea," an attempt to reorganize Europe in the aftermath of World War I and the social upheavals of the mid-twenties around a common set of political, cultural, and religious values. See Eliot, "Commentary," Aug. 1927, 98.
7. On the general stylistic revolt initiated by modernism, see Bradbury. Ray-mond Williams divides the modernist period into three distinct but related phases: an initial period of artistic innovation; followed by a period of promoting alterna-tive forums for the production and distribution of these works; leading to a period of advocating a reorganization of "the whole social and cultural order" in support of these new practices (51).
8. Eliot's view of the relationship between art and its enabling framework can be contrasted with that presented in Auerbach's *Mimesis* where the evolution of lit-erary forms as representational models reflects and measures the progress of social evolution.
9. I have not been able to trace why this particular passage appears in *Criterion* but not in *Selected Prose*.
10. The image of women offered here occupies an ambivalent thematic space in Eliot's poetry. As representatives of civilization or culture, as in "Portrait of a Lady," women can be subjected to the Calvinist tenet that models are necessary but inadequate. However, their identity as models for what is human, "fallen," and thus limited and inadequate can often, in Eliot's poetry, be taken also as their identity as

women (is it the attenuating influence of the Lady or of civilization that leads the young man to a state of enfeebled refinement?); thus fusing a constructed image with an essentializing belief. Men are then "victims" not of their general inadequacy as humans but of the particular inadequacy of women. Women — as women — then become the source of evil, as in "Sweeney Among the Nightingales" where the vague but palpable threat of the two women, Rachel and the caped lady ("thought to be in league"), to the narrator is emphatically confirmed by the murder of Agamemnon (leader of the forces of civilization), which takes place "offstage" in the final stanza.

11. Andrewes is superior to the preacher Latimer for roughly the same reason: the latter speaks as "merely a Protestant; but the voice of Andrewes is the voice of a man who has a formed visible Church behind him" (*Sel. Prose* 181).

12. Brooker confirms the centrality of a functioning framework for Eliot: how he was primarily "attracted . . . by a scheme," any scheme, as long it was comprehensive and inclusive, whether intellectual, like Bradley's philosophy, or religious, like Buddhism. And although Eliot retained some awareness of the "emptiness" of these forms, and of these schemes as "inadequate," Brooker points out that his religious conversion was clearly a self-conscious acceptance of (in his words) a "Christian scheme" (12, 25).

13. Herbert Read echoes Eliot's appraisal of Hulme as the exemplary modern classicist: "He despised 'words,' regarding them as mere counters in a game, 'beads on a chain,' mere physical things carrying no reality" (485).

ELSA NETTELS

"Inherited Puritanism"
The Legacy of Calvinism in the Fiction of William Dean Howells

WILLIAM DEAN HOWELLS set nineteen of his thirty-five novels in New England and portrayed characters from New England in almost all the others. None of his characters profess to believe in Calvinistic theology; they do not refer to the doctrines of predestination or the elect or innate depravity; they read Emerson, not Jonathan Edwards. In a number of novels, Howells notes that the old theology is dead, that churches and ministers must rely on social events, personal counseling and eloquent sermons to attract and hold parishioners. However, although Calvinism as doctrine appears defunct, its legacy is powerful in Howells's fictional world. It survives in characters who exhibit traits that Howells explicitly identified as Puritan. It also endures in the need it inspires in characters, especially ministers, to refute its dogmas and find different answers to the eternal questions about the nature of God, the purpose of suffering, the just basis of morality, and one's rightful duty to oneself and to others. In seeking answers to these questions, characters are moved to turn inward, examine their motives, and judge the effects of their actions upon others. Ironically, refutation of Calvinist theology promotes the introspection and preoccupation with one's spiritual condition that Calvinism inspired in Puritans two hundred years before the rise of realism.

Although not a modernist in the strict sense, Howells's critiques of Calvinism involved the use of some modernist motifs and techniques. Indeed, what is most modernist in Howells—his analysis of physical and mental disorders that isolate sufferers, his fondness for open endings and unresolved mysteries, his refusal in later years to impose interpretations on morally ambiguous situations that characters read in different ways—all these elements are part of the heritage of Calvinism that confronted the novelist with unanswerable questions and inspired his mistrust of "inherited Puritanism" expressed in spiritual pride and dogmatic judgment ("Puritanism"

282). Howells's critique of Calvinism, implicit in his narrative practice, also informed his attack on sentimental fiction: both, in his view, encouraged morbid preoccupation with moral purity, duty, and self-sacrifice—false idealism from which enlightened male characters in Howells's fiction seek to rescue susceptible readers. Howells's is a modernism, however, that, in refuting the doctrines of Calvinism, often affirms their vitality by representing in different terms their fundamental ideas and practices.

Any one of a dozen of Howells's novels illustrates the effects of "inherited Puritanism," but its pervasiveness is revealed only in a broader survey of the fiction of the 1880s and 1890s, in novels as diverse as *A Modern Instance, The Son of Royal Langbrith,* and *The Shadow of a Dream.*

I

To define Calvinism as Howells perceived it, one must first distinguish his opinion of Calvinist dogma itself from his view of seventeenth-century Puritanism and its legacy of traits, attitudes, and habits in the nineteenth century. Not surprisingly, during the 1860s and 1870s, when Howells reviewed books on colonial New England in *The Atlantic,* he dwelt on the strengths and virtues of the Puritan forefathers to whose descendants he owed his position of editorial power. Behind the "garb and visage" of the Puritans in Palfrey's *A Compendious History of New England,* Howells the reviewer perceived "the tenderness and strength" of a people who lived "with unostentatious dignity and with an unremitted endeavor of verity and justice." He found aesthetic as well as moral value in "the poetry of the first Puritan invasion of the wilderness" and in the "austere picturesqueness of the first magistrates and ministers" (Rev. 31:745–46). To Howells, even the Salem witchcraft trials showed the Puritans' virtue. The tragedy, he stated, proceeded not from the evil will of tyrants but from "the delusion of just and good men," who afterwards confessed their errors "with grave publicity" and proved able to "learn mercy as well as righteousness" (Rev. 31:746). Apparently, religious intolerance and zealotry were inseparable from the power to withstand disease, privation, and attack—ordeals that "only a people of heroic pith and force could have survived" (Rev. 30:622).

In "Puritanism in American Fiction" (1898), Howells most explicitly affirmed his belief in the survival into the nineteenth century of traits fostered by Calvinism. Although he acknowledged that belief in the doctrine was gone—the power of "puritanic theology" was a thing of the past—he observed the endurance of Calvinist theology in the character of the people: "its penetrating individualism so deeply influenced the New England character that Puritanism survives in the moral and mental make of the people almost in its early strength." In short, "conduct and manner conform to a dead religious ideal" (281).

For Howells, "individualism" is not necessarily negative, but in the Puritanism of nineteenth-century Americans he saw the degeneration of the heroic example of their stalwart ancestors. The dominant traits fostered by Calvinism were on balance negative ones: spiritual pride, self-righteousness, and obdurate will. But Howells acknowledged that virtue survived in the children of the Chosen People, that although "stiffened in the neck" and "hardened in the heart," they "are of an inveterate responsibility to a power higher than themselves, and they are strengthened for any fate" ("Puritanism" 281).

What especially interested Howells in the "inherited Puritanism" he analyzed in scores of essays and novels were the defects of the virtue he most valued in the Puritans—their moral seriousness. At its most beneficent, the Puritan conscience, that part of the Calvinist heritage that acted most powerfully in its inheritors, made them scrupulous in their dealings with others and exacting judges of themselves. But conscience become morbid subjected its victims to crippling doubts and fantastic scruples, to the "ugliness and error and soul-sickness" for which Howells held Puritanism responsible (*Heroines* 180).

Conscience could also be fatal to literature when it required the sacrifice of artistic integrity to the elucidation of moral purpose. Even though he respected, and even revered, Hawthorne, Lowell, and Longfellow, to whom he made his youthful pilgrimage, in later years Howells found their art "marred by the intense ethicism that pervaded the New England mind for two hundred years, and still characterizes it." The writers who welcomed Howells to Cambridge—Lowell, Norton, Longfellow, Holmes— were Unitarians whose art was Puritan, "the Socinian graft of a Calvinist stock." They could not sever themselves from the ancestral trunk: "they still helplessly pointed the moral in all they did . . . they felt their vocation as prophets too much for their good as poets" (*My Literary* 101).

Howells admired the fortitude of the early Puritans; he found Puritanism rich in psychological interest, fascinating to the novelist in the tragic ironies inherent in its complex nature. For the doctrines of Calvinism, however, he expressed unambivalent abhorrence. An optimistic temperament, the Swedenborgian beliefs in free will and a benevolent God that were imbibed in childhood, and a cultivated sense of detachment from the New England character (if not its cultural institutions) combined to place Howells in unrelenting opposition to the doctrines of innate depravity and election. He made his most vehement attack on Calvinist theology in his review of Stedman's and Hutchinson's *Library of American Literature*,

which appeared in his column "Editor's Study" in August 1888. After praising Roger Williams for his religious tolerance, "that highest gift of the
Divine Mercy to mankind," he condemned Calvinist theology as "atrocious
dogma," an "infernal doctrine" that sanctioned intolerance and persecution, "a deadly creed" that in Cotton Mather "rotted into a yet deadlier cre-
dulity." The Puritans, once praised for their "heroic pith and force," were
now self-appointed Saints who "wandered in error more cruel and dismal
than the forests that blackened their New England shores." Belief in the
"pitiless and unjust God" of the Calvinists, he concluded, "defame[s] the
ideals of divine justice and mercy." The literature of the Puritans, however,
still gratified the critic's aesthetic sense. Howells admitted that a poem such
as Michael Wigglesworth's "Day of Doom" possessed "a dark fascination"
that made the early literature of Virginia, in its "delightful freedom" from
spiritual torment, seem shallow and superficial by comparison (477–78).

What is striking is the similarity in tone and language between Howells's
denunciation of Calvinist theology and his attack on the false ideals of
self-sacrifice and dutiolatry purveyed by popular romantic fiction in the
late nineteenth century. He condemns both Calvinism and the destructive
romanticism that the Reverend David Sewell deplores in *The Rise of Silas
Lapham* in the same language: both are "cruel," "perverted," "immoral,"
and antithetical to true Christianity. The similarity is not accidental. In
Howells's view, impulses fostered by Calvinism—the longing for spiritual
perfection, obsession with one's spiritual condition, distrust of sensual
pleasure, spiritual pride coupled with the sense of personal sinfulness—
powerfully reinforced and were reinforced by the romantic novels he attacked in his fiction and criticism. The decay of religious faith invested literature, especially fiction, with the cultural authority and power to create
ideals and define standards of conduct that once belonged to the churches.
Bromfield Corey, Howells's social analyst in *The Rise of Silas Lapham*, declares, "All civilization comes through literature now, especially in our
country. . . . Once we were softened, if not polished, by religion; but I
suspect that the pulpit counts for much less now in civilizing" (118). Observing the "enormous influence which fiction . . . has upon the young"
("Editor's Study" 75:477), Howells believed that the emotions and desires
generated by romantic novels filled a vacuum created by the extinction
of the Calvinist faith. The novels and the feelings they inspired were one
manifestation of "sentimentality, or pseudo-emotionality," an "efflores-
cence from the dust of systems and creeds, carried into natures left vacant
by the ancestral doctrine" ("Puritanism" 282).

Howells does not identify these natures as feminine, but it is his female
characters who are readers of romantic fiction and victims of the self-
deceptions and morbid fantasies they induce. Likewise, the female char-

acters have a virtual monopoly on the power of what Howells called "our intensely personalized American conscience" (*Heroines* 180), that product of "the ancestral doctrine" that enhances susceptibility to false idealism. For instance, the behavior of Rhoda Aldgate and her aunt, Mrs. Meredith, in *An Imperative Duty* causes the protagonist, Dr. Olney, to wonder "how far the Puritan civilization has carried the cult of the personal conscience into mere dutiolatry" (89). Rhoda, soon to learn that her grandmother was a Negro slave, could speak for a number of Howells's young women when she declares, "I can imagine myself sacrificing anything to duty" and finds in the role of "slave of duty" self-gratification and freedom from the painful responsibility of making choices (47). Dr. Olney, who persuades her not to go south to live with "her people" but to marry him instead, diagnoses her mental state as symptomatic of "the Puritanism . . . which so often seems to satisfy its crazy claim upon conscience by enforcing some aimless act of self-sacrifice" (101).

The "pitiless Puritan conscience" (214) by which Lydia Blood in *The Lady of the Aroostook* judges her worldly aunt's activities in Venice drives several of Howells's New England women, notably Marcia Gaylord in *A Modern Instance* and Persis Lapham in *The Rise of Silas Lapham*, who are ignorant of their own deficiencies, to severe moral judgment. More often, however, the "Puritanized woman" in Howells's fiction inflicts the harshest moral judgments upon herself. Grace Breen, the morbidly scrupulous young New England doctor in *Dr. Breen's Practice*, so doubts her own competence that she can feel in control only by blaming herself for what others cause her to suffer. She endures the ordeal of medical school as a penance for being jilted, endangers her life in a boating excursion as payment for a well-intentioned decision that misfires, regards pleasure in wealth or the arts as sinful self-indulgence, and when she marries finds happiness only in sacrificing herself to the welfare of the workers in her husband's mills. After charting her course through "the lonely Calvinist country of the soul" (Eakin 103), the narrator concludes, "At the end of the ends she was a Puritan; belated, misdated, if the reader will, and cast upon good works for the consolation which the Puritans formerly found in a creed. Riches and ease were sinful to her, and somehow to be atoned for; and she had no real love for anything that was not of an immediate humane and spiritual effect" (270).

Grace Breen's asceticism and spiritual rigor are genuine. In Alice Pasmer of *April Hopes*, Howells shows Puritanism manifesting itself in self-deluding romanticism at its most pernicious—a pathological condition seemingly beyond cure. Fancying herself a romance heroine moved by the highest sentiments, Alice is blind to the egotism, disguised as selflessness, that demands the obedience of her suitor Dan Mavering to the impossible ideals of devotion and self-abnegation she imposes on both of them. The language suggests the sublimation of physical desire in masochistic pseudo-religious exaltation. Alice looks at Dan with "an ecstasy of self-sacrifice in her eyes" (161), tells him, "I *like* to be commanded by you," and begs him to require of her "continued self-sacrifice" (256). Dan's adoring belief in her perfection and in his own unworthiness of it heightens the irony of their comically painful relationship.

Howells does not trace the errors and morbid impulses of characters like Alice Pasmer to the teachings of modern churches. In a secular age, he ascribes them not to religious doctrine but to social customs and institutions. Indeed, in *April Hopes*, several characters observe that the Episcopal Church, where Alice is a devout communicant, "makes allowances for human nature," unlike Alice, whose insistence on perfection in her suitor and herself hearkens back to "the old Puritan spirit" (280). Howells explicitly blames her egoistic ideals of duty and self-sacrifice upon "disordered nerves, ill-advised reading, and the erroneous perspective of inexperience" (246). In *April Hopes* and elsewhere, he also portrays women as victims of a society that denies them the opportunity to achieve fulfillment in the masculine world of business and the professions, forces them into a state of idleness favorable to morbid self-scrutiny, and encourages them to exert their influence through the exercise of severe moral judgment and self-aggrandizing sacrifice in the name of duty.

Unlike Grace Breen and Alice Pasmer, whose essential character and attitudes do not change, several of Howells's young New England women, likewise inheritors of the "old Puritan spirit," who are beguiled by the false idealism of romantic fiction, are led by male guides to a sound view of their situation. However, Howells's solutions to these sentimental heroines—the firm guidance of rational male figures—threaten to reinscribe the same kind of patriarchal authority found in Calvinism. For Penelope Lapham (*The Rise of Silas Lapham*), Jessie Carver (*The Minister's Charge*), and Parthenope Brook (*The Vacation of the Kelwyns*), the fictional sacrifice that captures the imagination and inflames the conscience is the same: the heroine's renunciation of the man whom she loves and who loves her, for the sake of a woman whose love he does not return. In each novel, the voice of sanity and reason is male. David Sewell, the minister who tells the Laphams that Penelope's refusal of Tom Corey, who loves her, would be "foolish and cruel and revolting" (*Rise* 242), warns Jessie Carver against "a romantic notion of self-sacrifice" that may "do more harm than good" and later blames the girl's "novel-fed fancies and her crazy conscience" for believing that suffering proves her unselfishness (*Minister's* 324, 340). The presence of Parthenope's enlightened lover Emerance causes her romantic plan of sacrifice to collapse of its own flimsiness. That each novel ends with the prospect of a happy marriage for all concerned validates the authority of the male guide, confirms the rightness of his counsel, and exposes the falsity of the novels he condemns and the dangers to which the Puritanized conscience subjects susceptible readers.

Howells's attack on the romantic fiction that beguiled Puritanized readers always informed his definition and defense of realism. Did he see his exposure of the dangers of false idealism as modernist as well? In some ways, his resolution of the dilemmas that misguided characters force upon themselves and others looks backward, not forward to a new spirit and new literary forms. For example, the happy marriages promised at the end for Lemuel Barker and Jessie Carver, Rhoda Aldgate and Dr. Olney, Penelope Lapham and Tom Corey, Parthenope Brook and Emerance[1] suggest that women will be most completely fulfilled in the traditional roles of wife and mother. In uniting youthful lovers whose misunderstandings threaten to separate them, Howells satisfied readers who desired the conventional happy ending. The sermon-like counsel of guides like Sewell and Olney, as well as the moral reflections of third-person narrators, suggest that the didacticism of the New England writers was not so alien to Howells as his criticism of it might indicate.

But what Howells's characters and narrators preach is not necessarily the accepted conventional morality—that one should always tell the truth, expose falsehood, and live for the happiness of others. In *The Shadow of a Dream*, Howells creates a situation in which the morally enlightened act would have been to lie, not tell the truth.[2] In *An Imperative Duty* and *The Son of Royal Langbrith*, he pragmatically defends the suppression of the truth when the revelation of it will cause suffering and will benefit no one. The narrator of *An Imperative Duty*, who exposes Mrs. Meredith's corrupted sense of duty and asks whether "a wiser and kinder conscience" (88) might not have concealed the truth of Rhoda's birth, speaks for Howells, who rejected absolutist readings of human experience and created narratives to show that what is truth or duty may depend on the circumstances. Howells's rejection of rigid morality, reflective of the "pitiless Puritan conscience," is in keeping with his desire that fiction and drama, so often "the creature, the prisoner, of plot," should be freed from conventions that have their source in tradition and not in human experience. By Howells's definition, writers who freed art from such falsifying conventions were writers "in touch with the most modern spirit" ("Editor's Study" 79:315).

II

With few exceptions, Howells's male characters either preach against the evils of false romanticism or show no interest at all in the romantic fiction that female characters read. Likewise, most are indifferent to Calvinist theology or articulate the anti-Calvinist beliefs that Howells himself expressed. Implicit in David Sewell's denunciation of romantic novels is his rejection of the Calvinist doctrines of the elect and innate depravity. He affirms the power of the will to choose the good when he counsels Jessie Carver: "You know that in everything our help must really come from within our own free consciences" (*Minister's* 322). His sermon on complicity, which declares that "man . . . in his responsibility for his weaker brethren . . . was God-like," is anti-Calvinistic in its affirmation of "the spiritual unity of man" and its definition of God as "the impersonation of loving responsibility, of infinite and never-ceasing care for us all" (341–42). Unlike Grace Breen and Annie Kilburn, who blame themselves for the unfortunate consequences of their well-intentioned deeds, male characters reject as delusion bred by Puritanism the idea that deeds should be judged by their effects, irrespective of motives. When David Sewell blames himself for causing harm he never intended, "his reason protested against his state of mind as a phase of the religious insanity which we have all inherited in some measure from Puritan times" (*Minister's* 88–89). In *April Hopes*, the businessman Elbridge Mavering blames his wife's "inherited Puritanism" for blinding her to the difference between "harm" that results from good intentions and "evil" that proceeds from "ill-will" (310–11).

Sewell denies that the human will is powerless to initiate its own regeneration. But his faith in the "spiritual unity of man" and the existence of a "free conscience" raises questions that may lead characters back to the original premise of Calvinism. If the conscience is free, why are some people capable of seeing and willing the good while others are not? Why are some able to triumph over adverse conditions that destroy others? If people are seen as "mere creature[s] of circumstance," powerless to be other than they are, as the lawyer Putney argues in *The Quality of Mercy* (359), are they not as helpless as those whose salvation depends upon the inscrutable will of God? Howells's sense of unknowable but all-powerful forces recalls the Calvinist's subjection to a masterful deity.

The lawyer Atherton in *A Modern Instance* insists that his friend Ben Halleck is responsible for his acts and feelings: "You've never been out of your own keeping for a moment," he tells Halleck. "You are responsible, and you are to blame if you are suffering now" (368). But he identifies a "free conscience" and moral responsibility with membership in his and Halleck's educated genteel class, a kind of secular equivalent of divine grace. Atherton argues that one cannot hold uncultured people like Marcia and Bartley Hubbard responsible for what they do, for they cannot help themselves. "It's the implanted goodness that saves,—the seed of righteousness treasured from generation to generation, and carefully watched and tended by disciplined fathers and mothers in the hearts where they had dropped it" (417). Atherton ascribes to human parents, not to God, the saving power; but their children, a social elect, are, like the Puritan elect, the recipients of blessings that were predestined at birth.

Howells never repudiated his Emersonian vision of spiritual equality, which Atherton appears to deny. Howells's belief in the power of Americans to eradicate social ills rests on his faith, expressed by the Altrurian traveler, in "the potentialities of goodness implanted in the human heart by the Creator" (*Through* 290). Howells's ideal of complicity, of brotherhood "that centered in the hand of God" (*Minister's* 341), was the fundamental premise of his ideal realist who "feels in every nerve the equality of things and the unity of men" ("Editor's Study" 72:973).

But no less essential in his realism was his portrayal of differences attributable not only to social conditions but to inborn temperament. Words such as *weak, strong, jealous, selfish* denote innate qualities that render some characters better able than others to know and choose the good. Howells's definition of the "higher function" of the novelist—"to teach that men are *somehow* masters of their fate" ("Psychological" 873, emphasis added)— expresses the wish, not the certainty, that they be masters. He praised novels that represented "the prevalence of psychologism over determinism" ("Psychological" 875), but "psychologism" here simply means fiction in which events proceed from the psychology or "temperaments" of the characters, not from arbitrary plots imposed on them. Temperament is a given, beyond the power of characters to change. The very terms in which Howells repudiated the determinism of Calvinism are deterministic: "inherited Puritanism," that "tremendous force which has permeated and moulded" Americans of all regions (*Heroines* 179). Conceptions such as these presume an inexorable transmission of traits that lies beyond the power of the individual will to resist.

In his fiction, Howells responded to the collision of doubt and yearning faith by representing the conflict in the divergent views of characters and narrator, whose positions he simultaneously supports and undercuts, leaving the reader to ponder alternatives, choose one view over another, or rest in the impossibility of conclusion. Howells most fully develops this modernist method of engaging the reader in *The Son of Royal Langbrith*, in which the moral significance of events, not their ontological status, is in question.

The novel, set in a New England town named Saxmills, presents its main characters—the widow of an evil man, her adolescent son, and the middle-aged doctor who wants to marry her—as prisoners of their knowledge or ignorance of the past. Although the widow Amelia Langbrith and Dr. Anther know her husband to have abused her and defrauded his business partner, they have felt themselves unable to reveal the truth to her son. James Langbrith, never having known his father, worships an image of him as noble and selfless, commissions a statue to commemorate him in a public ceremony, and denounces his mother and the doctor when they inform him of their intent to marry.

The question whether the truth about Royal Langbrith will be made known to his son and to the townspeople precipitates the debate in which Howells assigns to different characters the beliefs he struggled to reconcile. The meliorist position is taken by the Episcopal minister Dr. Enderby, who (like Calvin) affirms the inscrutability of God's will but also declares that a "man of good will" can recognize "the will of God" and save himself from error (265). As if to counter the power of the Puritan legacy of righteous men in judgment—immortalized by Hawthorne in *The Scarlet Letter*—Enderby declares that "we have a duty to mercy." Because only God can know the full truth of every act ("every extenuation in motive and temperament"), only He can render justice. "If we press for judgment here," Enderby warns Anther, "we are in danger of becoming executioners" (158).

Like Enderby, Dr. Anther ultimately chooses to remain silent, but not because he believes that only God has the knowledge to judge evil. Striving to banish "old theological cobwebs [that] hang on in the corners of the brain," Anther comes to see Royal Langbrith in purely naturalistic terms. The man he had once called "the Devil" he finally sees as a victim of a "morbid condition with which the psychological side of pathology rather than morals had to do" (86). By this definition, Langbrith is no more responsible for his evil acts than "some treacherous and cruel beast whose propensities imply its prey" (262). By the same reasoning, the timorous passivity of Langbrith's wife exempts her from responsibility. In her failure to sustain her will to defy her son and marry Anther, she reminds him of "those weak forms of animal life," exhausted after the "sudden spurt" of their strength is spent (200). Whether or not Anther's determinist view is his way of resigning himself to what he cannot change, his alternative to the "cruel" and "abominable" doctrines of Calvinism leads to conclusions no less bleak.

The narrator of the novel expresses beliefs that support Enderby's optimism, but in his characterization of the two men he elevates the doctor above the minister. The narrator, like Enderby, affirms the capacities that create moral responsibility: he seeks to bring readers to full consciousness of their power "to make choice of their better selves against their worse"; he warns against the danger of remaining passive in the presence of evil and so becoming its agent, "though as little its masters as before" (251). When Anther allows himself to imagine Langbrith justified by his wife's helplessness, which operates as the "irresistible lure" of his cruel appetites, the narrator calls such thoughts "vagaries" that Anther rightly puts from him (227). But the narrator repeatedly emphasizes Anther's unique virtues: "a character of rare strength," "a nature of exceptional type," who "could accept the logic of his self-knowledge" (228). More than any other character in the novel, Anther has a novelist's recognition of the individuality of persons whom others would take for types. His first name is Justin; he looks at the woman he loves and excuses her weakness with "pitying intelligence [that] was very sweet to her" (229). His are the first words in the novel, and he remains the center of gravity throughout. At times the narrator treats Enderby and his "conscience inherited from Calvinistic forefathers" (131) with mild irony, but none of his irony touches Anther.

On one essential point Anther, Enderby, and the narrator agree: the sins of the father are not visited upon the children. Observing the gaiety and resolution of Hope Hawberk, the daughter of one of Royal Langbrith's victims, Anther reflects that each generation lives in its own concerns, that the "sins or sorrows" of one generation cannot be "livingly transmitted" to the next (110). James Langbrith does not inherit his father's cruel and abusive nature, and he will not be deprived of happiness because his father was evil. The novel ends with Enderby's reminder to his wife of the promise of the Scripture, that "the son who has not done the iniquities of the father shall not pay their penalty" (277). Thus characters, by their words and their actions, refute the Calvinist doctrine of Original Sin.

In concluding his novel with the marriage of Hope and James Langbrith, Howells was not merely giving readers the conventionally happy ending. He was expressing his abiding faith in the power of each generation to free itself from the wrongs and sufferings of past generations and to create new life for itself. In this faith Howells found his strongest defense against the logic of determinism.

III

Contradictions and inconsistencies inherent in the legacy of Calvinism do not seriously threaten the equanimity of characters such as Atherton and Sewell and Enderby, blessed by gentle birth, native intelligence, physical health, a Harvard education, happy marriage, and success in a congenial profession. But when no longer protected by such defenses, Howells's male characters, predisposed to introspection and self-judgment, may, like the female characters, suffer torment akin to spiritual sickness. The difference is that women's Puritanized consciences subject them to needless suffering that reason should dispel. Men of conscience suffer in situations that remain morally ambiguous, leaving open to question what determines the morally right course of action or whether any authority exists to sanction a standard of conduct. The modernist spirit that yearns for certainty and closure but seeks them in vain is most fully dramatized in *A Modern Instance* and *The Shadow of a Dream*, the two novels in which a male character questions his moral right to marry a woman he loved, or feared that he loved, during her marriage to another.

The case of Ben Halleck in *A Modern Instance* is the more simple in that, unlike the central characters of *The Shadow of a Dream*, he knows what he is and what he feels. Indeed, the act of self-definition is the chief source of gratification to the man whose crippled leg symbolizes a crippled spirit. Because "for sectarian reasons" (26) his parents sent him to a college in Maine instead of to Harvard, he feels himself thwarted from the start. Instead of a well-balanced Unitarian he has become "an orthodox ruin, and the undutiful step-son of a Down-East *alma mater*" (212). (The college is not named but one assumes that Howells thought of Bowdoin, Hawthorne's college, which maintained its close ties to the Congregational ministry until the end of the nineteenth century.)

That Halleck should be all but consumed by his suppressed passion for a woman of such unenlightened and jealous spirit as Marcia Hubbard, the wife of a college friend, is not made convincing. The reader may wonder with Atherton "what should have infatuated Halleck with that woman" (452). But accepting the fact, the reader can appreciate the depth of Howells's insight into the nature of a man whose sexual hunger is gratified not by human contact or even by the imagination of consummated love, but by awareness of wallowing in his sense of degradation and by confessing his pleasure to an exacting confidant. "Somewhere in my lost soul—the blackest depth, I dare say!—this shame has been so sweet," Halleck tells Atherton; "it is so sweet,—the one sweetness of life" (368). John Crowley has observed that in Howells's fiction characters are determined by their feelings so long as they are unconscious of them (183), but in *A Modern Instance* characters can be even more powerfully imprisoned by feelings of which they are aware.

The depth of Halleck's pleasure in sinfulness kept secret makes less compelling his expressed desire to marry Marcia after her husband dies. But the morality of such a marriage is the question Atherton and his wife debate at the end of the novel. She rejects his contention that Halleck's loving Marcia while she was married to another is "an indelible stain" (453); he claims that, given Halleck's moral nature, the marriage he contemplates could only be corrupting. Halleck's mistrust of his own conscience and his supplication to Atherton—"I humbly beseech you to let me have your judgment without mercy" (451)—suggest that Atherton may be right in his estimate of Halleck; such a man *would* feel his love to be a stain forbidding marriage. Does Howells believe that Halleck is morally enlightened or morbidly scrupulous? The final pages give no conclusive answer. To Halleck's question, "Am I not . . . bound by the past to per-petual silence?" (452), Atherton would reply in the affirmative, but his final words, "Ah, I don't know! I don't know!" express uncertainty. But the nature of his uncertainty is unclear. Is he merely responding to his wife's demand: "You're *not* going to write that to him?" (453)? Or is he reflect-ing more widely upon the whole situation, doubting his own judgment of it, perhaps even wondering whether judgment is possible?

In *A Modern Instance*, Howells portrays a society in which the authority of churches and creeds has collapsed. Bartley Hubbard, the protagonist, regards church-going as like other activities, a means of making con-tacts and getting ahead. His wife, Marcia, seeks security and social accep-tance in church rituals without understanding the beliefs they represent. Ben Halleck takes refuge in the Congregational ministry of a backwoods church solely to escape his personal torments. The elder Hallecks retain the religious faith of their youth but know themselves anachronisms in late-nineteenth-century Boston. Such is Howells's realism in depicting the modern world that he confronts readers with the doubts and questions of those who inhabit that world, leaving readers, like characters, to determine for themselves the morality of actions and the meaning of words.

In *The Shadow of a Dream*, the meaning of events becomes even more elusive and the desire to reach conclusions more urgent, consuming the energies of all the main characters. The entire action of this short novel, the most ambiguous and resistant to closure of any of Howells's fiction, turns on the way characters interpret one character's obsessive dream, which readers, too, must judge according to their own lights.

The source of the dream is the disordered psyche of a Midwestern lawyer, Douglas Faulkner, destined to an early death from heart disease, perhaps hastened by his recurrent nightmare that his wife, Hermia, and his beloved college friend, an Episcopal minister named James Nevil, are secretly in love and merely waiting for his death so that they may marry. In Faulkner's dream, Hermia and Nevil are married at the funeral service for Faulkner, which Nevil performs in his own church. Once Nevil and Her-mia know the nature of the dream, which they discover only after Faulkner dies and they become engaged to each other, they must try to determine their feelings when Faulkner was alive and decide whether they now have the moral right to marry. That the crisis is precipitated by a dream forces characters and readers to confront the unfathomable terrain of the uncon-scious, to seek meaning in signs that may express not only the repressed desires and fears of the dreamer but the subconscious needs of those who interpret the dream. Nevil and Hermia must ask whether they did in fact desire each other during Faulkner's lifetime and, if so, whether they be-trayed their love in ways that may have caused his death. In short, to assign meaning to Faulkner's dream is to define the nature of their own responsibility.

Neither Hermia nor Nevil seems initially burdened by a Puritanized conscience. At his first appearance, Nevil smokes and drinks claret punch with Faulkner and Basil March, the narrator, and he seems the image of physical and spiritual health—"the very embodiment of strong common-sense and spiritual manliness" (58). But he and Hermia seem as little able as any of Howells's characters to escape their Puritan legacy, as quick to doubt themselves, to agonize over their possible complicity, to read situations in a way that proves them guilty. That Nevil, unlike Halleck, does not absolutely know whether or not he desired another man's wife during his marriage makes his torment more agonizing. In its portrayal of characters beset by irresolvable questions about identity and the force of unconscious motivation, *The Shadow of a Dream* is the most modernist of Howells's novels. Its inconclusiveness is heightened by the uncertainties of the first-person narrator, Basil March, who can only infer from his observation of Hermia and Nevil what feelings they might be suppressing. Did Nevil and Hermia feel desire for each other while Faulkner was alive? Does Nevil remain with Faulkner merely out of compassion for his friend, who is dying of a malady of unknown origin? The novel never conclusively answers these questions.

What the dream reveals of Faulkner is also open to conjecture. As Crowley observes, Faulkner's dream is a text that characters read in different ways (120). To Faulkner, the dream foretells the future. To Hermia and Nevil, it exposes the possibility that they had loved each other without knowing it. To Faulkner's doctor, the dream is the symptom, not the cause, of organic disease. How the implied reader imagined by Howells is meant to read the dream can be inferred from the descriptions of Faulkner's disordered appearance ("restlessly brilliant eyes," nervous hands, trembling yellow-stained fingers); his close attachment to his widowed mother; his looks of hatred directed at his wife; and his dependence on Nevil, expressed as admiration for the minister's moral purity. All these signs confirm the interpretation of recent critics who read in Faulkner's dream an unrecognized homoerotic bond to Nevil, precipitating Faulkner's jealousy—not of Nevil as rival for Hermia's love, but of Hermia as rival for Nevil's.[3] By this reading, Faulkner refuses to question the prophetic power of his dream because it so completely satisfies his psychological needs: to express in disguise his unsanctioned desires and to punish himself for them by suffering that assuages his sense of guilt and shifts the burden of wrongdoing to others.

Significantly, Hermia removes herself from the arena of mental suffering by leaving the final decision to Nevil. Like Hester and Dimmesdale in the forest, briefly united in their vain hope of escaping together, Nevil and

Hermia imagine that their marriage is possible. In a confessional scene in his study, Nevil tells March, "For a moment—for an hour—we were happy in the escape which my defiance won for us, and we built that future without a past, which you think can stand." But like Dimmesdale, tormented by a Puritan conscience, Nevil discovers that escape is impossible. "We had deceived each other, but the deceit could not last" (110). Unlike Dimmesdale, Nevil is not even sure that he has transgressed, but he imagines a fate like Dimmesdale's were he to marry Hermia and "with my lying tongue" continue to preach "submission, renunciation, abnegation, here below," as his church teaches. "Every breath I drew would be hypocrisy" (111). In Howells's novel, no figure such as Chillingworth exists to body forth evil that characters must exorcise. But the absence of such a figure does not release Howells's characters from the desire for closure, from the need to find an explanation for tragedy and a basis for conclusive action. Nevil satisfies this need by convincing himself that he was guilty of desiring Hermia and that the desire now forbids his marriage to her. March seeks closure in rational judgment, attempting to convince Nevil that he wrongs himself and Hermia by condemning himself without any proof but a dream, that his duty as an enlightened man lies in resisting "the powers of darkness that work upon our nerves through the superstitions of the childhood of the world" (112). If Nevil and Hermia were fated, March reasons, they were fated by "their own morbid conscientiousness, their exaggerated sensibility" (113-14). *Morbid* and *exaggerated* indicate March's view of their scruples as unwholesome, unbalanced—in short, the unhealthy effect of the Puritanized conscience. Howells does not let his narrator go so far as to argue that physical passion has its own justification, that whatever Nevil and Hermia had felt for each other during Faulkner's lifetime, they sinned against themselves by denying their love for each other after his death. Howells was not D. H. Lawrence. But in March's concluding words—his wife "does not permit it to be said, or even suggested, that our feelings are not at our bidding, and that there is no sin where there has been no sinning" (115)—he obliquely proposes the way to free Nevil and Hermia from any possible guilt.

Readers unsympathetic to Howells's irony may find his narrator evasive and coy, afraid to commit himself. But the indirection is typical of Howells's refusal to impose a judgment on actions when even the crucial facts of a situation seem beyond everyone's knowledge. March's final statement can also be read as a sly dig at the moral rigidity of his wife, who is proud of her New England ancestry of seven generations. In any case, the reader can infer from earlier statements March's support of the view his wife rejects.

Like the speaker of Robert Frost's poem "Design," who suggests that what most appalls is not the design of darkness but the absence of design, March reflects, "We become so bewildered before the mere meaninglessness of events, at times, that it is a relief to believe in a cruel and unjust providence rather than in none at all" (113). March rejects this kind of providence that Howells equated with the Calvinist God, but he cannot explain why Nevil and Hermia became prisoners of "that perverse and curious apparatus which we call the conscience" (112). If they were not damned by the Calvinist God per se, they were destroyed by Calvinism's legacy in the form of "their own morbid conscientiousness," and they seem as little able to escape that legacy as were their Puritan ancestors to escape the fate decreed by an inscrutable God.

In *Literary Friends and Acquaintance*, Howells declared that the "intense ethicism" of the New England writers allowed them to excel in poetry and the romance but precluded their success in the novel. "New England yet lacks her novelist, because it was her instinct and her conscience in fiction to be true to an ideal of life rather than to life itself" (102). Howells might well have claimed to be the novelist that New England lacked. In novel after novel, he made the legacy of Calvinism itself his subject: he analyzed in the lives of his characters manifestations of "inherited Puritanism"; he showed how romantic fiction filled the vacuum left by the waning power of Calvinist theology; he dramatized the struggle of characters to free themselves and others from the false ideals and morbid scruples fostered by sentimental novels and the Puritanized conscience. He and his fictional spokesmen—ministers, doctors, and lawyers—affirm the freedom of the individual conscience and the existence of a just and merciful God, yet they face the reality of human weakness and evil that rejection of a Calvinist God does not make any easier to explain or eradicate.

To portray the legacy of Calvinism was thus for Howells to affirm in modern terms the moral seriousness and sense of mystery that Calvinism once inspired in its believers. His analysis of the interaction of romanticism and the Puritanized conscience led him to reject moral absolutes, to deny that "truth" and "duty" have but one meaning. He questioned the morality that compels such morbidly scrupulous figures as Grace Breen and Ben Halleck and James Nevil to torture themselves, but he did not unequivocally affirm a different standard of judgment. Aware that the concepts of "inherited Puritanism" and the "free conscience" implied premises difficult if not impossible to reconcile, he transferred the conflict to his fiction, where characters represent divergent views that remain unreconciled. The unresolved debates, the unanswered questions, the multiple readings of events were to Howells essential elements of realism, which he equated with the modern spirit in literature and which constitutes his in-cipient modernism. No less than the "inherited Puritanism" that inspired them, they were a vital part of the legacy of Calvinism.

Notes

1. Other novels by Howells that end with the happy marriage of central char-acters include *A Foregone Conclusion* (1875), *The Lady of the Aroostook* (1879), *The Undiscovered Country* (1880), *Dr. Breen's Practice* (1881), *A Woman's Reason* (1884), *Indian Summer* (1886), *Annie Kilburn* (1889), *The Quality of Mercy* (1892), *The Coast of Bohemia* (1893), *Ragged Lady* (1899), *Letters Home* (1903), and *Miss Bellard's Inspi-ration* (1904).

2. According to the narrator, Basil March, Faulkner's doctor should have spared Hermia the truth about her husband's dream: "he would have done wisely and righ-teously to lie to her about it" (*Shadow* 97).

3. For instance, see Prioleau 110–14 and Spangler 110–19.

JOHN J. MURPHY

The Modernist Conversion of Willa Cather's Professor

Preface

THE PROFESSOR'S HOUSE is a primary example of the eclectic nature of Cather's art, as this attempt to situate Godfrey St. Peter's crisis within the tradition of conversion literature should illustrate. The challenge to the reader involves sorting the universal implications of the protagonist's individual story from those of Cather herself as creator of that story.[1] This challenge demands not only thorough analysis of the text of the final book, "The Professor," but an explanation of the religious as well as psychological dimensions of the 1925 novel.

Cather's early experience of religious revivalism on the Nebraska prairies (she was a member of the Baptist church in her childhood) acquainted her with the phenomenon called "conversion."[2] Because of our Puritan heritage, conversion is for many Americans (and probably was for the young Cather) synonymous with being Christian; it is Calvinism's inner call bringing God's elect to salvation (Steele and Thomas 48–49). It is the process defined in Jonathan Edwards's "A Divine and Supernatural Light" and dramatized in "Personal Narrative," an experience of grace in which the supernatural impinges on the natural person to create a new person. However, before she wrote *The Professor's House* Cather had been confirmed as an Episcopalian and would no longer have either defined Christianity according to primitive forms of conversion or restricted conversion to religious experience. She would have sympathized rather with the admonition of Teresa of Avila to her nuns when describing her own ecstasy; that they "will merit no more glory for having received . . . these favors," for "many saintly people . . . have never known . . . a favor of this kind" (192). This novel, in fact, betrays Cather's interest in the psychological need for and process of conversion as well as its religious dimensions. William James had psychologized conversion for Cather's generation in *The Vari-*

eties of Religious Experience (1902), combining Edwards's and Teresa's traditions (quoting generously from the writings of both mystics) and reflecting an interest in so-called "High Church" Christianity as he investigated the integration of the divided soul.

My strategy here, after a close reading of the Cather text, is, first, to explain Professor St. Peter's dilemma and its inchoate resolution according to Jamesian theories of the sick, divided soul and of incursions or uprushes from the subconscious; second, to show how these are reflected in the modernism of *The Professor's House* through a brief comparison of the novel with the surrealistic art of René Magritte; and, finally, to use "A Divine and Supernatural Light" and Leo Tolstoy's *My Confession* to situate the novel firmly within the conversion tradition.

Edwards's treatise on grace is not only applicable to the self-surrender James equates with Calvinism's inward development of Christianity (205–06) but explains the name of Cather's protagonist while clarifying the rich Catholic Christian imagery surrounding his crisis and emergence as a new person. The autobiographical Tolstoy text analyzed thoroughly by James is a probable source for St. Peter's dilemma — the sense of futility and desire for death that defines the sick soul. Although it is unlikely that Cather knew of Magritte during the genesis period of her novel (his career began in the early twenties), she seriously followed modern trends in art, and his studies of the surreal (a dimension of conversion emphasized in James) clearly portray an experience like the professor's and illustrate Cather's achievement in transforming a traditionally Calvinist "Christian" phenomenon into a modern one through surrealistic structuring — for example, the intrusion of a first-person narrative by the professor's former student, Tom Outland, into the professor's story.

I. Close Reading of "The Professor"

The inconsequent nature of the concluding section, "The Professor," especially its location after "Tom Outland's Story," is underscored with opening references to chance, accident, and fate: the important things in Professor St. Peter's life "had been determined by chance. His education . . . had been an accident." The coming of Tom Outland "had been a stroke of chance," and the elements of Tom's story "all fantastic" (257). In reviewing his own life, "St. Peter thought he had fared well with fate" (258) by being granted a romance of the heart (involving his wife Lillian) and one of his head (involving Tom). The conflict quickens when the professor, separated from his vacationing family and lounging on a Lake Michigan beach to delay annotating Tom's record of mesa explorations, begins to develop a "twilight stage" of reacquaintance with his primitive self, the Kansas boy who had unexpectedly (by chance?) "come back." This boy—"the original, unmodified Godfrey St. Peter" (263)—represents the unsegmented protagonist, what he had been before developing a secondary self, a self "accidental and ordered from the outside" (264), and before the subsequent division between heart and head within the life of this secondary self.

The professor's present crisis involves chronic failure to integrate the original, primitive self and the secondary, social self: "adolescence grafted a new creature into the original one, and . . . the complexion of a man's life was largely determined by how well or ill his original self and his nature as modified by sex rubbed on together" (266–67). St. Peter had intended to share life with this original self but abandoned him for study in France and then forgot him after meeting Lillian. The life that subsequently developed was "the work of [the] secondary social man" and "shaped by all the penalties and responsibilities of being and having been a lover" (265). Tom's arrival and unexpected involvement in the professor's Southwestern research kept the Kansas original forgotten and delayed the return with which the professor now grapples: "Just when the morning brightness of the world [created by the secondary self] was wearing off for him, along came Outland and brought him a kind of second youth" (258). This youth improved the books St. Peter wrote, made them "more simple and inevitable," and provided the opportunity for recapitulation on an intellectual level of the growth and dominance of the secondary self, the creature that adolescence had grafted onto the original one. "A boy with imagination," Outland "had in his pocket the secrets which old trails and stones and water-courses tell only to adolescence" (259). The professor's rejuvenation proved costly, however, complicating the inevitable mid-life adjustment. What Cather examines in the novel's final section involves both multiple divisions of the self and the arbitration among the resulting selves that is necessary to resolve the divisions.

The "romances" St. Peter had with Lillian and with Tom are, to echo the novel's opening sentence, "over and done" (St. Peter feels alienated from his wife, and Tom had died in World War I) when the forgotten self returns with its contributions. That self has qualities of the patriarch Solomon, whose name is given to the valley of the professor's origin: "he [the original self] was terribly wise. He seemed to be at the root of the matter; Desire under all desires, Truth under all truths" (265). He respects the appropriateness of natural life sources and cycles: the curly root, the end of day, the turning leaves of autumn: "He was only interested in earth and woods and water. . . . He was earth, and would return to earth." He is a solitary, had never married and been a father—a condition resulting from St. Peter's failure to integrate him during those years of "conjugating the verb 'to love'" (264).

The professor considers his reunion with this self a "reversion," remembers his grandfather's continuous meditation as a symptom of a similar reunion, and feels that at fifty-two "he might be quite as near the end of his road" as the old man had been in his eighties (266). St. Peter compares this feeling to anticipations of approaching dawn and proximity to the sea, both underscoring the death motif developed in lines he remembers from Longfellow:

> For thee a house was built
> Ere thou wast born;
> For thee a mould was made
> Ere thou of woman camest.
>   (272)

Thus the boy restorer of St. Peter's original self turns out to be the harbinger of death (or at least of the ending of a life), and the professor welcomes him as relief from the worldly griefs experienced in the novel's long opening section, "The Family." That this death essentially involves the secondary lover self is suggested through dramatic changes in St. Peter's thoughts about death. He recollects once being terrified and wanting his wife to share his coffin: "his body would not be so insensible that the nearness of hers would not give it comfort." Presently, however, "he thought of eternal solitude with gratefulness: as a release from every obligation, from every form of effort" (272).

Such resignation and relief qualify the professor's condition when he receives news that Lillian and the Marselluses are returning from France because his daughter Rosamond is pregnant. The professor is decidedly shaken: "He sat down . . . his face damp with perspiration. He sat motionless, breathing unevenly" (274). Apparently he is *not* going to escape the return of dreaded family complications. During this crisis his thoughts become extreme; he feels incapable of living with his family again—especially with Lillian, whom he equates with a die upon which he has been beaten out; his great misfortune, he feels, is falling out of love, falling out of his place in the human family. As he tries to determine the mistake that makes him want to flee others, he contemplates a storm emerging from the lake and duplicating the one in his own psyche. At this nadir, convinced that the storm will discourage the dreaded intrusion of seamstress Augusta, who stores her work in his attic study, the professor takes to his box-couch. The wind increases, blows out the gas heater, and awakens him to contemplate possible asphyxiation before he drifts into unconsciousness.

He awakens at midnight, after being rescued by Augusta and examined by his doctor, to listen to the bell from Augusta's church and her account of his near asphyxiation. His crisis is over, and much has changed: rather than dreading Augusta, he wants her with him; rather than desiring solitude, he feels lonely, "outward bound" to the humankind she represents (281); he resolves to live without the delight he had demanded of life and to face the "bloomless side of life" he has always fled (280). He no longer feels obligated to his immediate family—an obligation that was perhaps that "something very precious" of the secondary self relinquished during unconsciousness (282)—but he will be able to face that family with fortitude and, by implication, to live with them, if not as the same man.

II. Jamesian Division and Conversion

William James's analysis of the melancholia of the divided self and the conversion, or unification, process in *The Varieties of Religious Experience* clarifies Godfrey St. Peter's crisis. According to James, unhappiness characterizes the period of order-making when the divided self struggles toward unification (166–70). The second chapter of "The Professor" details the protagonist's sad awareness of problematic divisions in himself: the secondary social and sexual self, and the original, primitive self. What is felt to be a "reversion" to the original self is merely a component of the conflict between the selves, since the secondary self and its obligations are very much on the professor's mind. Cather's next two chapters explore what James calls the "sick soul," pathological melancholy involving desire for death and "passive joylessness and dreariness, discouragement, dejection, lack of taste and zest and spring" (142). Godfrey St. Peter's loss of zest and spring takes him to the doctor, although he fails to confide his feeling that death is near.

Although St. Peter's process of regeneration is the kind James defines as slow and volitional rather than abrupt self-surrender, it involves, like all conversions, periods of self-surrender (James 208). The professor has been building up a new set of moral and spiritual principles, and at the critical final stage he must surrender his will. Tantamount to these new principles is what St. Peter considers the misfortune of falling out of love: "Falling out, for him, seemed to mean falling out of all domestic and social relations, out of his place in the human family, indeed" (275). James cites as a classic conversion the case of a man falling out of love with a woman who has obsessed him to the point of insanity. "The queer thing was the sudden and unexpected way in which it all stopped," testifies the sufferer. "I was going to my work . . . one morning, thinking as usual . . . of my

misery, when just as if some outside power laid hold of me, I found myself . . . almost running to my room, where I . . . got out all the relics of
her I possessed. . . . [These] I made a fire of . . . [or] crushed beneath my
heel. . . . I felt as if a load of disease had suddenly been removed from me.
That was the end" (177). The professor approaches his final step of surrender when he discovers his family is returning from France, takes to the
coffinlike box-couch, and contemplates asphyxiation. The nature of what
the tormented lover calls "some outside power" (James terms this power
"other forces" [204]) and the positive results of an apparently negative experience in Cather's novel now need to be addressed.

    As a psychologist, James identifies such forces as subconscious allies—
new ideals or self-definitions working toward rearrangement—incubating
within the subject and coming to the fore when the personal will, protective of the old self, is relaxed (204-05). This theory, which he develops from
the work of Edwin Starbuck, James then applies to what he calls "the discovery" in 1886 of the subliminal consciousness, the discovery that "one's
ordinary fields of consciousness are liable to incursions from [the subcon-
sciousness] of which the subject does not guess the source, and which,
therefore, take for him the form of unaccountable impulses to act, or in-
hibitions of action, of obsessive ideas, or even of hallucinations of sight
or hearing" (229). More radical effects, like automatic speech or writing,
James attributes, with the help of Frederic Myers, to " 'uprushes' into the
ordinary consciousness of energies originating in the subliminal mind."
While the effects of St. Peter's surrender are hardly radical, they are dramatically abrupt, and there is evidence of automatic response in his effort
to counter his wish for death. As Augusta tells him, "You were stupefied,
but you must have got up and tried to get to the door before you were
overcome" (279).

    During the recovery from near death, the professor mysteriously quali-
fies falling out of his place in the human family (in particular his immediate
family) with a sense of obligation toward humankind: "There was still . . .
a world full of Augustas, with whom one was outward bound" (281). This
is the positive response to a negative, the alienation from or falling out
of love with the family whose return he now anticipates with fortitude:
"His temporary release from consciousness seemed to have been beneficial. He had let something go—and it was gone: something . . . he could not
consciously have relinquished, possibly" (282). The new man the professor becomes possesses that assurance Martin Luther associated with faith,
"something not intellectual but immediate and intuitive" (James 241): "he
felt the ground under his feet" (Cather, *Professor* 283).

III. Surrealistic Dislocations and Concoctions

Phyllis Rose has compared the "massive dislocation" achieved by Cather in introducing "Tom Outland's Story" into the professor's to the visionary art of René Magritte (127–28). Just as Cather attributes the intrusion of Tom's story to "an exhibition of old and *modern* Dutch paintings" she attended before writing the novel (*On Writing* 31; emphasis added), my introduction here of the Belgian Magritte, which I hope will prove as pertinent as Tom's story is to the novel, is the result of an exhibition of his work I saw in New York while developing this essay.

John Canaday argues that the concoctions of surrealism must, like dreams, have meaning, that the bits and pieces must reveal the subconsciousness involved (467). The inchoate nature of subconsciousness evident, for example, in Magritte's *Youth Illustrated*, with its apparently inconsequential trail of objects—barrel, torso, lion, pool table, bicycle, tuba, etc.—suggests not only the unsettling intrusion of Tom's first-person account of the discovery of Blue Mesa (Mesa Verde) into the stuffy Midwestern story of St. Peter's domestic squabbles but the odd array of items Cather assembles with symbolic intent throughout the entire novel: dressforms, box-couch, mummies, tower, pines, garden, mesa, stove, etc. Similar "irrational" combinations are evident in Magritte's *Eternity*, with its heads of Christ and Dante on either side of a mound of butter, and *The Marches of Summer*, where a flesh-colored torso placed upon a darker pelvis echoes Augusta's "forms," and the architectural frame on the left and bottom echoes the view of Lake Michigan the professor enjoys from his attic study window. The relief of that window, the "long, blue, hazy smear" that becomes "a part of consciousness itself" (29–30), is suggested in Magritte's *The Six Elements* and *On the Threshold of Liberty*, as is the disturbing truth that, as Sarah Whitfield suggests (item 52), the painted sky, like the professor's window view and Tom's story itself, is merely another means of concealment. Magritte develops this idea in *The Human Condition*, which he explains illustrates how we see the world "as being outside ourselves even though it is only a mental representation of it that we experience inside ourselves. In the same way, we sometimes situate in the past a thing which is happening in the present" (qtd. in Whitfield item 62). This externalization not only suggests that Tom's mesa adventures (the desecration and exploitation of the mesa and the collapse of Tom's friendship with Roddy Blake) function subjectively in St. Peter's crisis but reminds the viewer/reader, as Rose observes, of the artificiality of a canvas depicting a canvas and a story "depicting" a story (128).

Pertinent to the professor's problem, if not as illustrative of his sub-

René Magritte, The Marches of Summer, *1938.* © *1997 C.Herscovici, Brussels/Artists Rights Society (ARS), New York. Courtesy Museé National d'Art Moderne Paris.*

René Magritte, The Human Condition, *1933. © 1977 C. Herscovici, Brussels/Artists Rights Society (ARS), New York. Courtesy the National Gallery of Art, Washington. Gift of the Collectors Committee. Photograph © Board of Trustees, National Gallery of Art, Washington.*

René Magritte, Memory of a Journey, *1955.* © *1997 C. Herscovici, Brussels/Artists Rights Society (ARS), New York. Courtesy The Museum of Modern Art, New York. Gift of D. and J. de Menil. Photograph* © *1996 The Museum of Modern Art, New York.*

consciousness, are several Magritte paintings on petrification, a condition reflected in the professor's name, in his fondness for rocks and rocky landscapes, and in his desire "to watch the sunrise break on sculptured peaks and impossible mountain passes" in Outland's country and "to drive up in front of Notre Dame, in Paris, again, and see it standing there like the Rock of Ages" (270). Whitfield notes how in taking over a domestic interior the boulder in *The Invisible World* assumes human attributes (item 113), reversing St. Peter's transformation into stone at his lowest point; it is as if the massive boulder poised on an illumined mountain between a shadowy foreground and background in *The Glass Key* had moved indoors, much as the mesa landscape, equally dehumanized (considering Tom's dismissal of Roddy Blake), had moved indoors—into the professor's story. The result is echoed in *Memory of a Journey*, a portrait of a gentleman beside a table with a candle and a lion, all petrified, and before a petrified painting of a tower in a landscape.

Magritte told his New York dealer that the light emitted by the stone flame of the candle is the only instance in his series on petrification of an object behaving as it would if restored to its natural state (Whitfield item 115), the natural in this case becoming the supernatural. Allow me now to make a surrealistic transition from this mysterious light to the Calvinistic component of my essay, Jonathan Edwards's polemic on the divine origin of those forces intruding upon the exhausted psyche during conversion, forces that James, in a secular age, would associate with subliminal energy.

IV. Edwardsian Sanctifying Light

If Calvinism represents a major phase in the psychological development of Christianity, Edwards's "A Divine and Supernatural Light" is a significant clarification of that phase. Its subtitle—explaining that the "light" is "immediately imparted to the soul by the Spirit of God"—clarifies Edwards's argument, and his introductory example—apostle Peter's statement of faith in Christ's divinity in Matthew 16:17—makes the argument particularly appropriate in a discussion of Cather's novel. At the end of *The Professor's House*, Peter as petrification (the professor who has lost the ability to love) transforms into Peter as rock of faith ("he felt the ground under his feet"), and the prefixed distinction of "Saint" becomes startlingly meaningful, for the light of conversion is bestowed only upon saints.

The abrupt nature of the grace experience is clarified in Edwards's insistence that God infuses light, or faith knowledge, "immediately, not making use of any intermediate natural causes, as [God] does in other knowledge" (*Selected* 67)—a distinction that takes faith knowledge beyond the rational

realm in both its source and quality. Light can best be described as "a sense
. . . in the heart" (72), continues Edwards, which distinguishes it from the
speculative or notional; unlike the rational, it mainly concerns "the will, or
inclination" (73). John Gerstner notes that, for Edwards, "grace produces
new life and will," rather than understanding, and would be opposing itself
in not responding to God (65). Edwards writes that, "in the renewing and
sanctifying work of the Holy Ghost, those things are wrought in the soul
that are above nature. . . . [The Spirit of God] unites himself with the
mind of a saint, takes him for his temple, actuates and influences him as
a new supernatural principle of life and action" (69). Later, Edwards describes the process as a transfiguration, an inward vision of spiritual glory
exceeding the outward manifestation granted Peter and his companions:
"Doubtless . . . the outward glory of [Christ's] transfiguration showed him
to be divine, only as it was a remarkable image or representation of that
spiritual glory" (81).

Edwards concludes with the fourfold effect of divine and supernatural
light: divine wisdom, knowledge of the ineffable, inclination of the will
toward heavenly things, and disposition of the heart toward the universal
will (87–88). If we are not put off by Edwards's rhetoric, this concept can
be applied fruitfully to the professor's case and make meaningful several
textual factors: the religious nature and role of Augusta, the oft-mentioned
seven pines, and the windstorm in the final book.

Augusta, the St. Peters family seamstress, becomes a factor early in the
novel, on the September morning when the professor surveys his study
above the now dead house. Identified as "German Catholic and very devout" (16), Augusta functions as a religious conscience and conversion vehicle for the professor, and her two dressmaker "forms," part of the novel's
surrealistic concoction, reflect his impending crisis (one suggesting the
unsympathetic and the other the restraining qualities of the women in his
life). Prodding her to continue using the old attic study, he tells her, "You'll
never convert me back to the religion of my fathers now, if you're going
to sew in the new house and I'm going to work on here. Who is ever to
remind me when it's All Souls' day, or Ember day, or Maundy Thursday,
or anything?" (24–25). Much later he meets her coming from Christmas
mass and questions her about the Magnificat, the Virgin Mary's canticle
in Luke 1:47–55, which celebrates surrender to the Holy Spirit and the resulting gifts of the Spirit.

The text of the canticle has significant bearing on Cather's, especially
the line about the "rich [being] sent empty away," which is echoed in the
final book when the professor reflects on the text of Brahms's *Requiem*:
"He heapeth up riches and cannot tell who shall scatter them!" (258). An
earlier reference to the ringing of the Angelus, a prayer honoring the An-

nunciation and Incarnation, anticipates the Magnificat discussion. As the bell rings, the professor recalls the faces of his daughters, proud Rosamond and jealous Kathleen—both had loved Tom and are feuding over Rosamond's handling of the fortune realized from the rights to his invention. Looking in the direction of the physics building, St. Peter wonders, "Was it for this the light in Outland's laboratory used to burn so far into the night!" (89–90). Augusta represents a world of escape from all this, but one he has unfortunately relegated to the Middle Ages, when "every man and woman who crowded into the cathedrals on Easter Sunday was a principal in a gorgeous drama with God, glittering angels on one side and the shadows of evil coming and going on the other . . ." (68).

The seven pines, introduced immediately after the professor's lecture on art and science (the source of this insight on the Easter drama), assume importance when the professor is renewing acquaintance with his original self in the novel's final section. Lying on the triangular beach at the lake where they grow, St. Peter watches "for hours . . . the seven motionless pines drink up the sun" (263). Relating them to the wisdom and solitude of his Kansas original, St. Peter knows that "when the seven pine-trees turn red in the declining sun, [the wise boy] felt satisfaction and said to himself merely: 'That is right' " (265). Putting off reading the letters from his family in France, the professor "would lie on the sand, holding [the letters] in his hand, but somehow never taking his eyes off the pine-trees, appliquéd against the blue water, and their ripe yellow cones, dripping with gum and clustering on the pointed tips like a mass of golden bees in swarming-time" (270). Just before he takes to the box-couch, St. Peter notices that the pine trees around the physics laboratory, substitutes for those at the lake, "were blacker than cypresses and looked contracted, as if awaiting something" (275).

These pines—flamelike ("shaggy" [70] as well as red), honey-laden, mystical, and ominous—anticipate the reflexes infused at conversion. The four effects of the divine light in Edwards's Calvinistic tradition become in Augusta's Catholic tradition the seven Gifts of the Holy Spirit, qualities manifest in the Virgin's Magnificat: wisdom (possessed by the Kansas boy), understanding (of revelation), knowledge (of providential purpose), fortitude (enabling the professor to face his returning family), counsel (supernatural intuition), piety (perfection of religion), and fear of the Lord (humility and hope) (Hardon 229–31). The pines suggest the supernatural dimension of the experience they anticipate, St. Peter's conversion during his "absence from the world of men and women" (279).

Wind, a traditional symbol of the Spirit (see Acts 2:1–4), operates in the novel's penultimate chapter. The professor watches a storm blow up "great orange and purple clouds" from the lake, and after a half hour of rain "a heavy blow had set in for the night" (275). At this point he lights the stove and lies on the box-couch: "The fire made a flickering pattern of light on the wall. He lay watching it, vacantly; without meaning to, he fell asleep. For a long while he slept deeply and peacefully. Then the wind, increasing in violence, disturbed him. He began to be aware of noises—things banging and slamming about" (276). The professor takes comfort in the storm as a protection from Augusta, thinking that she would not venture out in it. But she rides the storm: "I came over in the storm," she tells him as she explains that she has dragged him from the gas-filled room. The professor, having experienced no resistance to the gas and seeming to have "let chance take its way as it had done with him so often" (282), can recall only his resignation and then "a crisis, a moment of acute, agonized strangulation"; he has forgotten springing up from the couch, as Augusta is convinced he had. The narrative strategy here—with its byplay of wind, flame, and the banging and slamming of exorcism—is obviously intended to generate mystery, to suggest a process beyond the natural, at least beyond waking reality: "His temporary release from consciousness seemed to have been beneficial. He had let something go . . . something very precious [his former self], that he could not consciously have relinquished, probably" (282). The issues of passive and active will that apparently divide Calvinistic and Catholic versions of conversion (Edwardsian reflex activity [Gerstner 61–62] and Thomistic cooperation [Haight 66–67]) are straddled here in Cather's resolving of the professor's crisis as one beyond consciousness.

V. The Tolstoy Source

While Cather combines several traditions in developing St. Peter's conflict, her immediate source, I believe, is Tolstoy's autobiographical *My Confession*. James analyzes this work as an example of the conversion of the sick soul, but Cather probably discovered it directly, for Tolstoy was one of her early favorites, and then drew on it decades later for *The Professor's House*. In the journalism of her twenties, Cather lamented Tolstoy's sacrifice of fiction to tracts written for the glory of God and the welfare of peasants (*World* [291–92]), but as David Stouck notes, "Tolstoy's belief that art must be imbued with a religious consciousness and that it promotes feelings shared by all humankind can be seen as informing Cather's later works, especially *The Professor's House* and *Death Comes for the Archbishop*" (17). *My Confession* reflects Tolstoy's midlife spiritual crisis about the meaning of his life and work. David Patterson claims that it "marks a turning point in Tolstoy's career as an author, and after 1880 his attention was concentrated quite explicitly and almost exclusively on the religious life that he believed to be idealized in the peasant" (5). In the concluding section of this essay, I deal with aspects of the Tolstoy work pertinent to the professor's story, beginning with Tolstoy's surrealistic postscript, the dream that transforms the work from confessional to conversion literature.

Tolstoy experiences this dream when he reviews his manuscript three years after its completion, and the dream repeats "in a condensed form all that [he] had lived through and described" (72). He sees himself lying on his back on a bed too short or ill made ("something is not right"), and after adjusting his position he discovers that he is on a bed of cords. His legs slip and hang down "without touching the ground" (73); one after another of the cords give way, and he realizes in horror that he is holding himself up by his upper back on "a height beyond all [his] previous powers of conception" over a "bottomless abyss." When he feels about to slip down, "all at once comes into [his] mind the thought that this cannot be true — it is a dream — [he] will awake," but he cannot awaken (74). Both Tolstoy's sleeping figure and Cather's St. Peter on the box-couch are comparable to Magritte's *The Daring Sleeper*, in which the subject is suspended in a coffin-like box at night over a void camouflaged with (instead of a network of cords) a concoction of familiar images on a lead tablet. Whitfield describes this painting as "a traditional surrealist salute to the unconscious and to the dream, but it is also an expression of one of the most recurrent themes in Magritte's work: a terror of the void" (35). She notes a similar relationship between the sleeper and the objects in the writings of the artist's friend Paul Nouge: "The mind is so terrified of the void that it cannot help imagining it everywhere, whereupon it immediately arranges to fill it with the kind of scenes it already sees in its inner eye" (qtd. in Whitfield item 35).

Tolstoy's solution to the problem of the void is to direct his eyes to the gulf above in order to forget the abyss below: "The infinite depth repels and horrifies me; the infinite height attracts and satisfies me." A voice in the dream encourages him to "Look well: it is there!" Then he no longer hangs down but balances on a stay running from a pillar, "the solidity of which is beyond doubt, though there is nothing for it to stand on." He concludes that by looking up and relying on this cord, "there cannot be even a question of [his] falling" (75). As this reliance becomes clear, he expresses ease of mind: "It seemed as if some one said to me, 'See that you remember!'" At this point he awakens. When we meet him after his speculation on asphyxiation, Cather's professor has already awakened and is experiencing the security of Augusta's presence as she sits beside him reading her religious book: "Seasoned and sound and on the solid earth she surely was" (281). The assurance blossoming in the professor characterizes newfound faith: "he felt the ground under his feet. He thought he knew where he was, and that he could face with fortitude the *Berengaria* and the future" (283).

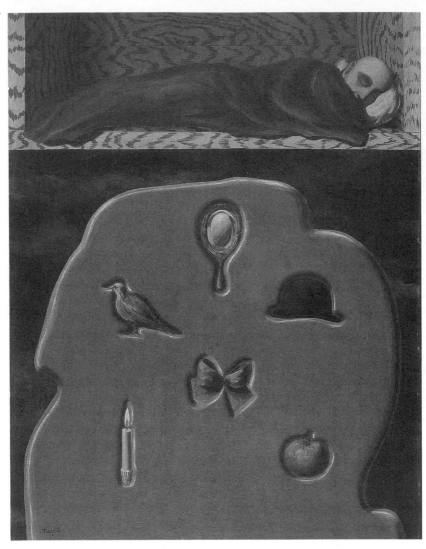

René Magritte, The Daring Sleeper, *1928.* © *1997 C. Herscovici, Brussels/Artists Rights Society (ARS), New York. Courtesy The Tate Gallery, London.*

The professor enjoys the effects without the memory of conversion, and the reader is restricted to his consciousness—thus the essential *experience* remains the thing not named. But the *problem* is named—sufficiently at least to bring it into focus through comparison with Tolstoy's analysis of what he experienced when approaching fifty; a strange state of low spirits and increasingly frequent "moments of perplexity, of a stoppage of life, as if [he] did not know how to live" (12). Confused as to life's purpose, Tolstoy felt "that the ground on which [he] stood was crumbling, that there was nothing for [him] to stand on" (14). Not knowing *how* to live develops into not wanting to live: "The force that drew me away from life . . . was a force like that of my previous attachment to life, only in a contrary direction. . . . [T]he idea of suicide came as naturally to me as formerly that of bettering my life" (14-15). Yet, he admits, he "had a good, loving, and beloved wife, good children, and a large estate, . . . was more than ever respected, . . . praised by strangers, and . . . enjoyed a mental and physical strength . . . seldom found in men of [his] class and pursuits." St. Peter struggles with this dilemma that Tolstoy has understood enough to articulate: "It is possible to live as long as life intoxicates us; as soon as we are sober again we see that it is all a delusion" (Tolstoy 16). The challenge for both lies in facing the bloomless side of life, the heavy and dreary truth that Augusta both confronts and represents in Cather's novel.

Tolstoy's midlife crisis is a recapitulation of youthful questioning after years of preoccupation with family affairs. Raised by aristocrats who were religiously haphazard, by fifteen Tolstoy had lost faith in the Orthodox Christian Church in which he had been instructed, although he admits to neither denying the existence of God nor understanding the essence of Christ's teachings. Placing his faith in progress and the possibility of personal intellectual perfection, he began to write. Yet he yearned for a "something better," concealing his feelings "under the mask of indifference or pleasantry" (6) while recognizing himself and fellow intellectuals as teachers without solutions to life's simplest problems or knowledge of right and wrong: "I had gained . . . an insane self-confidence in teaching men what I myself did not know" (7). This superficial faith in progress was soon shattered by two events: his witnessing a bloody execution in Paris and the death of his brother. The execution contradicted his ideas about the development of civilization, and his brother's failure to understand either life or death confronted Tolstoy with his own insufficiency.

Tolstoy's subsequent search for meaning in establishing schools for peasants and instructing the elite through a scholarly journal was interrupted by domestic involvement: "My life was concentrated at this time in my family, my wife and children, and consequently in the care for increasing the means of life. The effort to effect my own individual perfection, already replaced by the striving after general progress, was again changed into an effort to secure the particular happiness of my family" (11–12). One is reminded here of Godfrey St. Peter's abandonment of the earlier self that later returns to him: "Because there was marriage, there were children. Because there were children, and fevers in the blood and brain, books were born as well as daughters. His histories, he was convinced, had no more to do with his original ego than his daughters had; they were a result of the high pressure of young manhood" (265). Tolstoy's productive years as author were during his domestic period: "I continued all the time to write. I had experienced the seductions of authorship . . . and gave myself up to it as a means of improving my material position" (12). During midlife crisis the work of these years, including *War and Peace* and *Anna Karenina*, seemed to him valueless.

Concerns similar to those of Tolstoy's reversion incubate in Cather's professor. He realizes that his efforts have not saved education from commercialism, that Tom's research has led to jealous bickering, and that family life has become insupportable. What haunts Tolstoy is more direct: "What will come from what I am doing now, and may do tomorrow? What will come from my whole life?" (20). To discover any meaning in life not destroyed by death, Tolstoy explores science and philosophy. If one goes to science for guidance, he says, science will respond, "Study in infinite space and time the infinite combinations and changes of infinite particles, and thou wilt know what thy own life means" (24). Tolstoy's dissatisfaction with this answer is echoed by Cather in the professor's lecture: "I don't myself think much of science as a phase of human development. It has given us a lot of ingenious toys; they take our attention away from the real problems" (67–68). Philosophy fares no better in Tolstoy; it addresses the real problems but fails to solve them: "if it keep firmly to its sphere, it can only answer the question, 'What am I and the whole universe?' by saying, 'All and nothing,' and to the question, 'Why' by adding, 'I do not know' " (25). Pseudo-sciences like history Tolstoy dismisses for proposing "a false conception of [human] development and perfection" (27).

This dim view of progress explains why Cather's mesa dwellers are superior to modern city dwellers in "Tom Outland's Story," why historian St. Peter's philosophy of life is inadequate, and why Tom is unable to deal with Blake after a summer of examining and recording historical artifacts. Tolstoy's escapes from this failure of human knowledge are also echoed in Cather's novel: they are suicide, which the professor considers, and Epicureanism—the latter evident at the end of "The Family," during the professor's special summer with Tom: "When [St. Peter] cooked a fine leg of lamb, *saignant*, well rubbed with garlic before it went into the pan, then he asked Outland to dinner. Over a dish of steaming asparagus, swathed in a napkin to keep it hot, and a bottle of sparkling Asti, they talked and watched night fall in the garden. If the evening happened to be rainy or chilly, they sat inside and read Lucretius" (176).

Something like Edwardsian light prevents Tolstoy from choosing death and defines *My Confession* as conversion literature: "There . . . worked in me a force, which . . . drew me out of my desperate position, and completely changed the currents of my thoughts. This force led me to the idea that I . . . was still ignorant of what human life was" (39). This "force" leads him to seek meaning among the masses, "in their unreasoning knowledge of life which gives meaning to it" (41), although his search merely returns him to the religious faith he "cannot accept while [he] keep[s] his senses." However, the essence of faith, its ability to give meaning even to a life of misery, is now revealed to him: the "irrationality" that, unlike human reason, relates the finite to the infinite and the infinite to the finite. "It was now clear to me," he writes, "that for anyone to live, it was necessary for him either not to see infinity or to accept an explanation of the meaning of life which should equalize the finite and the infinite" (45).

Tolstoy's story is not pious propaganda: he rejects orthodoxy of all kinds, believing that religious institutions merely reflect human flaws. His faith is placed in humankind: "If I wished to understand life and its meaning, I must live, not the life of a parasite, but a real life; and accepting the meaning given to it by the combined lives of those that really form the great human whole, submit it to a close examination" (54). Sustaining such faith while rejecting orthodoxy, he is led to theology, "which [he] had once thrown aside with such contempt as useless" (71), in order to sift doctrinal truth from falsehood. Godfrey St. Peter does not journey this far, having had no faith to return to. However, his direction is similar to Tolstoy's in his recognition of "a world full of Augustas, with whom one was outward bound" (281).

Coda

In contemporary theology, as in *The Professor's House*, psychology and conversion meet comfortably. The late Jesuit theologian Karl Rahner considered all human beings as incomplete, as made to be complemented by the conversion grace offered universally by Deity:

The supernatural and immediate vision of God . . . is [humanity's] end and fulfillment. And conversely: the ontological nature of the doctrine . . . can be grasped in all its radicality . . . as the natural fulfillment of that innermost and really ontological divinization of [humanity] which comes to expression in the doctrine of . . . justifying sanctification . . . through the communication of the Holy Spirit. (118)

For Edwards, conversion, as in his own vision of Christ in "Personal Narrative," involved being emptied of evil and filled with God: "I felt an ar-
dency of soul to be . . . emptied and annihilated; to lie in the dust, and to
be full of Christ alone . . ." (*Selected* 41). For Emerson in the next century
the irresistible grace and evil identified by Calvinist orthodoxy are secularized as afflatus and ego: "all mean egotism vanishes. . . . the currents of the
Universal Being circulate through me" (1:10). Yet another century later,
with Cather's professor, transcendental revivalism is replaced by near-
asphyxiation and a matter-of-fact statement of new life defined against the
values rather than the evils of the former one: "He had let something go —
and it was gone: something very precious, that he could not consciously
have relinquished, probably. He doubted whether his family would ever
realize that he was not the same man they had said good-bye to. . . . At
least, he felt the ground under his feet" (282–83).

Notes

1. I would like to reverse the early and persistent tendency, reflected in both
Edel and Schroeter, to reduce this novel to Cather's personal response to loss
through the marriage of her friend Isabelle McClung.

2. See B. Baker for a discussion of revivalist Fundamentalism in Cather's earlier
fiction.

GEORGE MONTEIRO

Grace, Good Works, and the Hemingway Ethic

The New Englanders were correct in claiming that they were not followers of John Calvin, because they honestly believed that they were reading the Bible with their own eyes. Yet in the historical perspective, their way of interpreting the Bible must be called Calvinist.
—Perry Miller, *Errand into the Wilderness* 49

Christian asceticism . . . strode into the market-place of life, slammed the door of the monastery behind it, and undertook to penetrate just that daily routine of life.
—Max Weber, *The Protestant Ethic and the Spirit of Capitalism*, 154

The valuation of the fulfillment of duty in worldly affairs as the highest form which the moral activity of the individual could assume . . . gave every-day worldly activity a religious significance, and . . . created the conception of a calling. . . .
—Max Weber, *The Protestant Ethic and the Spirit of Capitalism*, 80

WHILE OTHER MODERNS were transforming Christianity through myth, Ernest Hemingway was transforming Christianity—and specifically Calvinism—through ethics. This ethical emphasis belonged as well to the larger culture of advertising and capitalism, as we can see in Bruce Barton's best-seller, *The Man Nobody Knows*. Max Weber has explained in *The Protestant Ethic and the Spirit of Capitalism* how capitalism and Calvinism in the United States are interrelated; Hemingway demonstrates how much he both shares in, and departs from, this culture, particularly in his creation of an aestheticism unanticipated by either Weber or Barton.

In *American Literature and Christian Doctrine*, Randall Stewart takes his definition of "Calvinism" from *Webster's New Collegiate Dictionary*: "The doctrines of the French theologian John Calvin (1509-1564), including election or predestination, limited atonement, total depravity, irresistibility of grace, and the perseverance of the saints. Calvinism especially emphasizes the sovereignty of God in the bestowal of grace. Cf. Arminian" (12). It is not greatly useful to approach Ernest Hemingway's fiction as in any way purely or even directly reflective of Calvinism. If he deals with anything resembling predestination, he does so ironically under the guise of naturalistic determinism, which theologically is quite a different matter. And anyone looking for evidence that his fiction endorses notions of man's natural depravity must account, for example, for his trenchant criticism of such latter-day "puritanical" notions as the uncleanness of adolescent thoughts of sex, in a story such as "God Rest You Merry, Gentlemen," in which a boy mutilates himself because he cannot adhere to Pauline principles of bodily purity.[1] Yet the Christian notion of grace underwent several changes in Hemingway's work and remained present—unnamed or misidentified—throughout his career. Calvinist doctrines of grace, in particular, did interest him, though it was never the strictly Calvinist view that grace was totally within the sovereignty of God that appealed to him but the notion, far more amenable to the Arminians, that grace might be achieved by human good works. As Thomas Shepard pointed out, "the Arminians, though they ascribe somewhat to grace, . . . yet, indeed, they lay the main stress of the work upon a man's own will, and the royalty and sovereignty of that liberty" (Miller, *Errand* 57).[2]

The Arminian heresy that plagued the Puritans in early America as well as orthodox Calvinists everywhere else was no heresy at all in the Oak Park that saw the baptism of Ernest Miller Hemingway in 1899, the year of the installation of the Reverend William E. Barton, Bruce Barton's father, as pastor of the First Church. The theme of grace and good works would in one way or another mark much of Hemingway's fiction. But over the years he handled it differently from text to text, registering changes that can be recognized by an examination of key texts published at different times. Particularly fruitful in this regard are "Today is Friday" (1926), "A Clean, Well-Lighted Place" (1933), "The Snows of Kilimanjaro" (1936), *Across the River and Into the Trees* (1950), and *The Old Man and the Sea* (1952).

An "Oak Park Literary Map" acknowledges Ernest Hemingway as that city's "Most Famous Native Son." Even had they been born in Oak Park, it is doubtful that either of the Bartons—Bruce or William—would have posed a serious challenge for such primacy. Yet in 1925, a year after Reverend Barton had retired from his pastorate in Oak Park and his businessman son published *The Man Nobody Knows* in book form, the fame of both Bartons surely far exceeded that of Ernest Hemingway, who published in the same year a small book of stories, *In Our Time*. Since the Hemingways were communicants of the elder Barton's church (he wrote to young Ernest at the front [C. Baker 52]), Bruce Barton's book could not have escaped Ernest's attention.[3] In New York, on his way to the war in Italy, Hemingway planned to visit the younger Barton.[4] Bruce Barton would later review

Ernest's 1926 book, *The Sun Also Rises*, for the *Atlantic Monthly*. As the author of a book emphasizing the "manly" qualities of Jesus, Barton found his fellow townsman's novel appealing. "A writer named Hemingway has arisen, who writes as if he had never read anybody's writing, as if he had fashioned the art of writing himself," he announced the good news. "It is true that his book deals with people who have no morals. They drink too much. . . . They have no religion, and no ideals in the accepted sense of the word. But they have courage and friendship, and mental honestness. And they are *alive*. Amazingly real and alive" (Hanneman 353; Stephens 46).[5] Courage, friendship, mental honesty—these are qualities that Barton, the advertising man, found in the historical Jesus and extolled in his intentionally buoyant book, the subtitle of which is "A Discovery of the Real Jesus." "There is a success which is greater than wealth or titles," he quotes Jesus as saying, "It comes through making your work an instrument of greater service, and larger living to your fellow men and women. *This* is my Father's business and he needs your help" (189). No more perfect fit for the Christian ascetic calling defined by Max Weber could have been found in the American world shared by Hemingway and the Bartons.

Bruce Barton has not been featured much in Hemingway scholarship. Sometimes critics mention him in relationship to his father—as the author of the review of *The Sun Also Rises* just alluded to—or in a footnote such as this one: "In the twenties, Dr. Barton's son, Bruce, would vulgarize his father's liberalism in an astonishingly successful book, *The Man Nobody Knows*, a portrait of Jesus as supersalesman and rugged he-man" (M. Reynolds 11, Meyers 5, Mellow 334–35, Lynn 21).[6] Barton's epigraph, taken from the Gospels—"Wist ye not that I must be about my Father's *business?*"—points to his understanding of the nature of Jesus's way of being in the world. Indeed, as Barton's book argues throughout, Jesus has chosen this calling. In this way, Barton's Jesus fits right in with Max Weber's description of Calvinism, in which "calling is not a condition in which the individual is born, but a strenuous and exacting enterprise to be chosen by himself, and to be pursued with a sense of religious responsibility" (Tawney 2). Implied in Barton's promotion of Jesus as businessman is his concurrence with Weber's view that "the fulfilment of worldly duties" "alone is the will of God, and hence every legitimate calling has exactly the same worth in the sight of God" (81).

Barton also portrays Jesus as a "he-man" and an "outdoor man," a depiction that obviously held some attraction for the Hemingway who wrote a playlet about the death of Jesus.[7] In "Today is Friday" Hemingway focuses on the immediate aftermath of the crucifixion on that Friday, as T. S. Eliot observed, that we call Good (*Complete* 271–73). The setting is a drinking-place at eleven o'clock that same night. Three Roman soldiers are present, along with a Hebrew wine-seller. The "3rd Soldier" is persuaded to drink down what the wine-seller provides for his "gut-ache." Making a face, he exclaims, "Jesus Christ," to which the "2nd Soldier" responds, "That false alarm!" The "1st Soldier" chimes in: "Oh, I don't know. He was pretty good in there today." The 2nd and 1st soldiers go back and forth. The former is skeptical. "Why didn't he come down off the cross?" he asks assertively. "He didn't want to come down off the cross. That's not his play," answers the latter. The 2nd soldier is not convinced. "Show me a guy that doesn't want to come down off the cross." The 1st soldier appeals to the wine-seller, but he avoids getting involved, saying "I'll tell you, gentlemen, I wasn't out there. It's a thing I haven't taken any interest in." The 1st and 2nd soldiers continue the argument, the former continuing to insist that Jesus "looked pretty good in there today," and the latter insisting that no one would not want to come down off the cross—"When they first start nailing him, there isn't none of them wouldn't stop it if they could." Neither one of them is convinced by the other's argument. The talk moves on to a consideration of what happened to his followers. His "girl" and the other women "stuck by him," says the 1st soldier, but his followers "faded out," he admits. That "gang," says the 2nd soldier disdainfully, "were a pretty yellow crowd. When they seen him go up there they didn't want any of it." The 1st soldier admits that he surreptitiously slipped "the old spear into him," a merciful act that, as the 2nd soldier reminds him, will get him into trouble some day. In the course of things, the 2nd soldier calls the wine-seller a "regular Christer" to his face, and later, out in the street, refers to him as "a kike just like all the rest of them." Since the conversation takes place on Good Friday, there is naturally no talk about the resurrection or the divinity of Jesus.[8]

The Jesus of "Today is Friday" would have been recognized by Bruce Barton, though in *The Man Nobody Knows* he emphasized the work of a strenuous "Outdoor man," an "Executive," the "Sociable Man," who built an organization in which the "blood of the martyrs was the seed of the church," not on the Jesus Agonistes of the crucifixion (123). Yet the "athlete" who "was pretty good in there today" would have recalled Barton's own Jesus, who "would probably have been Captain of the Princeton Football Team," suggests Montgomery, "and just the man that we would 'root' for" (25). Barton and his readers would have been comfortable with either of two titles Hemingway entertained for his story before settling on "Today is Friday," one of which echoes Barton (who was quoting Tertullian), "Today is Friday, or The Seed of the Church," the other being "One More for the Nazarene" (P. Smith 154), which also recalls Barton, who is fond of referring to Jesus as the "Nazareth carpenter" and "the young man from Nazareth" (*Man* 31, 33). Like Hemingway in "Today is Friday," Barton seems not to be interested in the matter of Jesus's resurrection. His narrative stops with the crucifixion. Of that "pretty yellow crowd" (*Complete* 273)—Jesus's disciples—Barton writes that with Jesus's arrest "already they had made their swift escape—the last of the deserters" (*Man* 219). Both Barton and Hemingway turn to the everyday responses of the Roman centurions, the latter transforming the Centurion at Calvary (Matt. 27:54), perhaps, into the 1st soldier (P. Smith 156), the former describing the Centurion at Capernaum (Luke 7:2–10) as "one of the anonymous characters in history that every business man would have liked to meet" (*Man* 26).

The most important similarity between the Jesus of Hemingway's story and the Jesus of Barton's book is that it is the man—the athletic man—not the God (or the Son of God) who is the focus. One need not go along with Barton's notion that Jesus invented modern business or that he was a genius at advertising before the fact (as Hemingway assuredly did not) to respond to his desire to see Jesus as a human being first and foremost. Hemingway would not have disagreed with Emerson—nor would Barton, probably— that the divinity of Jesus was nothing less or more than the divinity that exists, to a greater or lesser degree, in every person. Finding irrelevant to his purposes the argument for Jesus's unique divinity as set forth in *His Last Week*, an exceedingly successful pamphlet published by the senior Barton (with the help of other Oak Park ministers) "to facilitate the reading of the gospel story of the last days of the earthly life of Jesus" (W. Barton 264), Barton efficiently clears space for his own book about Jesus:

Theology has spoiled the thrill of his [Jesus's] life by assuming that he knew everything from the beginning—that his three years of public work were a kind of dress rehearsal, with no real problems or crises. What interest would there be in such a life? What inspiration? You who read these pages have your own creed concerning him; I have mine. Let us forget all creed for the time being, and take the story just as the simple narratives give it—a poor boy, growing up in a peasant family, working in a carpenter shop; gradually feeling his powers expanding, beginning to have an influence over his neighbors, recruiting a few followers, suffering disappointments and reverses, finally death. Yet building so solidly and well that death was only the beginning of his influence! Stripped of all dogma this is the grandest achievement story of all! In the pages of this little book let us treat it as such. If, in so doing, we are criticized for overemphasizing the human side of his character we shall have the satisfaction of knowing that our overemphasis tends a little to offset the very great overemphasis which has been exerted on the other side. Books and books and books have been written about him as the Son of God; surely we have a reverent right to remember that his favorite title for himself was the Son of Man. (*Man* 8–9)

The timing for Barton's book was right. Intended largely as a revelation of a personal and family discovery, it immediately found its place as a Christian apologia for the business and advertising ethics of the 1920s. Christianity and business were not at odds. The Reverend William Barton had celebrated his twenty-five years in Oak Park by resigning his pastorate in 1924. Even the muted boasts of his autobiography, published eight years later, made it clear that the elder Barton was an executive, a booster, a huckster, a fundraiser, and a builder. As he said, triumphantly and smugly, "I believe in a successful God" (W. Barton 303). No wonder, as his son could claim in the introduction to his father's autobiography, that "Hundreds of the leading business men of Chicago sat under his preaching and looked forward to his sermons as the intellectual high point of their week" (xiv). What he provided for them was nothing less than an ideology that not only purported to be Christian but was at the same time functionally secular. "The sneer that rich churches are useless, that heaven is not attained by means of them, that rituals are nonsense, is not new," wrote an anonymous American in 1896. "The day for such misconception of the church is past, however," he continued. "The fact that the spiritual and practical sides of religion are interwoven is beginning to be understood" ("Book Notices" 570). The Reverend Barton understood it clearly and made it his business to promote that very understanding—to the prosperous, to the wealthy. "I respect in the rich man the order of Providence" (Miller, *Errand* 201).[9] The book written by the Reverend Barton's son, fully in keeping with his father's most effective teachings, was an instant success.

Ever watchful of publishers and their books, Hemingway could not have avoided knowing about Bruce Barton's interpretation of the life of Jesus, that secularized "imitation of Christ" for the times. His own orthodox upbringing in the teachings of the elder Barton's church alone, it would seem, would have led him to *The Man Nobody Knows*. It is doubtful that he would have been sympathetic to the book's overall thesis. But there were things about Barton's view of Jesus with which he substantially agreed. Barton's description of Jesus's courage displayed in the last year of his work when "the forces of opposition took on a form and coherency whose significance was perfectly clear":

If he refused to retreat or to compromise, there could be but one end to his career. He knew they would kill him, and he knew *how* they would kill him. More than once in his journeys he had passed the victims of the justice of that day, writhing, tortured beings nailed to crosses and waiting piteously for release. Sometimes they wilted for days before the end. The memory of such sights must have been constantly with him; at every sunset he was conscious that he had walked just one day nearer to his own ordeal. (*Man* 54)

Everywhere in Hemingway there are figures, like Barton's Jesus, who, conscious of the fate that awaits them—the bullfighters of *In Our Time* (1925), Robert Jordan of *For Whom the Bell Tolls* (1940), and Thomas Hudson of *Islands in the Stream* (1970)—do not flinch at the end. Yet it is doubtful that Hemingway would have entirely endorsed Barton's view of the Jesus who, "never falter[ing]," went forth "calmly . . . cheering the spirits of his disciples, and striking those fiery blows against hypocrisy and oppression which were to be echoed by the hammer blows upon his cross. And when the soldiers came to arrest him, they found him ready and still calm" (*Man* 54–55).

Barton's interest in the crucifixion, unlike Hemingway's, shows itself less in the event itself than in his Jesus's anticipation of it. Jesus's fears and his sense of an anticipated great loneliness work away at him, but he will not let them keep him from his public task:

Already one of his disciples had slipped away to betray him. That very night the soldiers would take him, bind him, throw him into prison. The priests and Pharisees whom he had taunted would have their turn to taunt him now. He would be harried through the streets like a hunted thing, the butt of every corner loafer's jest. All this he anticipated, and with the vision of it fresh before his mind, he lifted his head and looked beyond, into the far distant ages. "Be of good cheer," he said to them [at the "final supper"], in tones whose splendor thrills us even now. "I have overcome the world!" (*Man* 215)

Of Jesus's physical suffering and psychological courage during the hours of the crucifixion, Barton says nothing. Jesus is the first martyr to the church for which he was the seed. The Jesus who had refused to be king, not wanting to spend a lifetime "in the defense of his throne and title, a lifetime of bloodshed and intrigue, while his message remained unspoken," would now be recognized by "a crucified felon" at his side (a final convert): " 'Jesus, . . . remember me, . . . *when thou comest into thy kingdom!*' " (*Man* 187, 220)

"Today is Friday" cannot be aligned with *The Man Nobody Knows* as a corroborating text. There is too much about Barton's idea of Jesus as the super-salesman and an organizer of men, not to mention the exuberance with which Barton spells out his discovery, that is alien to Hemingway's own personally nuanced Christianity marked by the commission of disinterested good works and by final stands of stoical bravery. Barton's desire to view Jesus as a man rather than as a supernatural being, however, Hemingway did share.

After "Today is Friday" Hemingway never again wrote directly about Jesus's life or his crucifixion, though the figure of Jesus and his sufferings on the Cross would surface occasionally in his imagery and diction, in his description of the Colonel's wounded hand in *Across the River and Into the Trees* and, of course, throughout *The Old Man and the Sea*. Still in the late 1920s, Hemingway became preoccupied with the "Twenty-Third Psalm," which Barton had called "the greatest poem ever written," consisting of only "one hundred and eighty-eight words" (*Man* 148). He praised the line "the Lord is my shepherd; I shall not want" for its economy and efficiency, as a parallel to Jesus's use of "few qualifying words and no long ones" (*Man* 150). That same line became the basis for Hemingway's "Neothomist Poem," published in the spring of 1927 in the first issue of *The Exile*:

> The Lord is my shepherd, I shall not
> > want him for long.
> > (*88* 83)

The published poem constituted the final, much pared down version of a modernist parody of the "Twenty-Third Psalm" that Hemingway had been trying to write for some time. A study of the extant manuscripts for these unpublished parodies of the "Twenty-Third Psalm" shows that Hemingway was depressed, probably suicidal, during the period of their writing.[10] In particular, Hemingway targets faith in God's providence, the principal theme of the "Twenty-Third Psalm," in each version of the parody.[11]

Echoes of the "Twenty-Third Psalm" and of Hemingway's parodies surfaced, in combination with the dual themes of death and suicide, in one of Hemingway's strongest stories, "A Clean, Well-Lighted Place." In this dark parable the psalm provides a context for the full meaning of the nihilistic parodies of "The Lord's Prayer" and the Catholic prayer to the Virgin recited by the so-called older waiter. Before he utters them, he has conversed with a fellow waiter about a "client's" unsuccessful attempt at suicide—an attempt, from the Church's point of view, to commit the unpardonable sin against the Holy Ghost. "He was in despair," the waiter admits, but it was despair (in what is, after all, a privately grim joke) over "Nothing" (*Complete* 288–91). Three times on the opening pages of this story we are told that the old man, who deliberately echoes the line, "though I walk through the valley of the shadow of death," is sitting in the "shadow" made by the leaves of the tree. The old man, deaf and alone, orders another drink of brandy. The younger waiter pours him one, filling up his glass. But then, making literal one of the most familiar metaphors employed in the "Twenty-Third Psalm"—"my cup runneth over"—the text reads, "The old man motioned with his finger. 'A little more,' he said. The waiter poured on into the glass so that the brandy slopped over and ran down the stem into the top saucer of the pile." This incident distinguishes the "sloppiness" of the waiter from the orderliness of the old man, who always drinks without spilling. At some point good manners turn into good works, but why that should be so remains mysterious in Hemingway's emblematic story.

This waiter, who does not understand the old man, also differs from the older waiter, who does. When the younger man asserts, "I have confidence. I am all confidence," the older one replies, "you have youth, confidence, and a job." As for himself, he is no longer young, and he has never had "confidence"—a key term here. If confidence means self-assurance for the younger waiter, it also means "faith"—the Spanish term *confidencia*. Indeed, if the older waiter has never had such *confidencia*, such "faith," then it is even more certain that his expressions of nihilism are a form of displaying his acedia or spiritual malaise. The consolations to his believers—to men of faith—that are the "Lord's Prayer" and the prayer to the Virgin Mary are not available to those who lack "confidence."

Neither can the "Twenty-Third Psalm"—sometimes described as *"David's confidence in the grace of God"*—serve as repository of sentiments and images that must be taken ironically by the author who not only constructed parodies of the "Twenty-Third Psalm," but also wrote "A Clean, Well-Lighted Place." To the expansive pastoral consolations of the "Twenty-Third Psalm"—its "still waters," "paths of righteousness," the "table" prepared "in the presence of mine enemies," and the promise of anointment—one can only counter with the narrow virtues of a localized cleanliness and man-made light. For the "house of the Lord" in which the psalmist, confident in God's grace, shall "dwell . . . for ever," Hemingway's older waiter offers only the café, "clean, well-lighted," which, though he would "stay late," will perforce close each night while the night is still dark and will remain so long, ostensibly, after the first glimmer of "daylight." "It is probably only insomnia," the waiter says to himself, "many must have it." And indeed they must in Hemingway's world, from the rattled Nick Adams of "Now I Lay Me" (an ironic titular reference to the common child's prayer) to the author who himself, in the late 1920s, compulsively parodied the "Twenty-Third Psalm" (the message of which—an almost naive acceptance of life—Hemingway opposed). Parody also emerges in "A Clean, Well-Lighted Place" when the older waiter prays to *"nada"*:

Our *nada* who art in *nada, nada* be thy name thy kingdom *nada* thy will be *nada* in *nada* as it is in *nada*. Give us this *nada* our daily *nada* and *nada* us our *nada* as we *nada* our *nadas* and *nada* us not into *nada* but deliver us from *nada; pues nada.* (*Complete* 291)

To make clear just what is at stake in this prayerful blasphemy (or blasphemous prayer), we need only recall the prayer itself. The words the older waiter has replaced by his *nadas* are underlined to bring to the fore just what he is denying:

Our *Father* who art in *heaven, hallowed* be Thy name; Thy Kingdom *come*; Thy will be *done* on *earth* as it is in *heaven*. Give us this *day* our daily *bread*; and forgive us our *trespasses* as we *forgive those who trespass* against us; and *lead* us not into *temptation*, but deliver us from *evil. Amen.*

Denied here are words—not their value but their very existence—such as *Father, heaven, hallowed, earth, day, bread, trespasses, forgive[ness], temptation,* and *evil*. Father, heaven, and hell, in this context, might well be considered conceptual abstractions, but surely earth, day, and bread would be considered by most to be as real as anything else in the material world.

If "A Clean, Well-Lighted Place" is as clearly about acedia as anything Hemingway ever wrote, it may also be his strongest statement about the almost deterministic persistence of faith within blasphemous prayer. The fundamental religious point about prayer, writes William James, is that in it "spiritual energy, which otherwise would slumber, does become active, and spiritual work of some kind is effected really" (467).[12] In the world Hemingway creates, a parodied prayer might well do, willy-nilly, the same spiritual work. "The heart lives by the faith the lips deny" reads a line of poetry quoted by William Barton (300).[13] On this the Christians—Calvin, Barton, Hemingway—were agreed.

In 1936, *Esquire* published Hemingway's African story, "The Snows of Kilimanjaro." This extended parable, reinterpreting the Calvinist notion of calling and vocation, takes up the case of a professional writer in extremis. In danger of dying an apostate to his profession, Harry faces the hard fact that he has failed to live up to what he conceives of as his essential self by betraying his trust and his calling. Within Hemingway's third-person omniscient narration there is imbedded a series of flashbacks conveying Harry's final memories and thoughts, including his fantasy or dream of an eleventh-hour rescue. The memories come to Harry as he lies in camp amidst the greenness of Africa, passing through the valley of the shadow of death, within sight of the snow-capped Mount Kilimanjaro. His Villon-esque memories of the "*nieges d'antan*" in Paris, Spain, Greece, serve to prepare him for the grace that will come to him in death. As he "sees" the world about him (and therefore experiences it) when the rescue plane flies him out of the valley of death and toward the western summit of Kilimanjaro, which, the epigraph to the story tells us, the Masai call Ngaje Ngai—the "House of God"—Harry finds himself on a metaphoric journey through life:

[T]hey began to climb and they were going to the East it seemed, and then it darkened and they were in a storm, the rain so thick it seemed like flying through a waterfall, and then they were out and Compie [the pilot] turned his head and grinned and pointed and there, ahead, all he could see, as wide as all the world, great, high, and unbelievably white in the sun, was the square top of Kilimanjaro. And then he knew that there was where he was going. (*Complete* 56)

Indeed, in the words of the psalmist, Harry's experience tells that he is going to "the house of the Lord" where he will "dwell for ever." Harry's "visionary journey" makes sense within the story only if it is seen either as a meaningless, illusionary, psychological experience or as, potentially, a journey of the spirit. The narrative enables both a materialistic, naturalistic reading and a spiritual, Judeo-Christian one. The dream vision gives way to the still life of Harry's corpse. Yet by his eleventh-hour "writing" Harry has achieved grace and has become worthy of the house of heaven that is the summit of Kilimanjaro. It is important to note that it is not enough for Harry's salvation that he be in the right frame of mind for writing, but that he be in the active state of writing—an odd exchange for what Max Weber calls "the Puritan capitalistic valuation of action" (192, n.3). Unless it was meant to be entirely ironic, the earlier title of "Snows"—"The Happy Ending" (Johnston 34-37)—is not inappropriate to this reading.

Hemingway prepares for Harry's reception of the grace he must earn by evoking his religiously couched notions of professionalism. Here he crosses them with the idea of writer as priest, affirming that writing itself is, in the religious sense of the word, vocational. Hemingway focuses on his writer-priest's eleventh-hour recapitulation of a life, that though seemingly begun well enough, soured along the way. Hemingway's writer, Harry, who "never infects," is nevertheless dying of an infection. He counts his time less in days than in hours and minutes. There are only two activities of value left to him: to remember and to write. To remember in order to write. But writing, in any practical sense, is no longer possible. Not even dictation, he reminds Helen, is possible. Yet at a crucial moment in the story he insists, in answer to Helen's question, that he *is* writing. No longer able to write things down, Harry radically redefines writing as an act of pure composition. He now composes in his head.[14] And it is Hemingway's intention that we see that Harry at the very end of his life is writing *well*, that is, to use Hemingway's most honorific term, writing *truly*. Only at the end, for hours or minutes, perhaps, does Harry write, but in so doing he has earned the fantasy of his final journey, that apocalyptic rescue that would lead not to the healing of his infected leg but to his spiritual redemption. In finally recovering his capacity to write, this "spoiled priest" begins to "work the fat off his soul" (44).

Hemingway's notions of vocation and profession enter the fictional debate of "The Snows of Kilimanjaro" in two other ways. First, he pays particular attention to Harry's obsession with the term *trade* (which can be seen as analogous to Weber's term *calling*). And he focuses further on his *talents*. And second, he sees Harry's life as if it were lived within the context of Samson's life, that of another apostate professional with a calling.[15] Like Samson (and like every person, it is argued), Harry has lied to himself, for "somewhere or other every man is a liar: he is false, that is, to the divine idea, which he was meant to embody, and fails to bring it out in all the fulness of its perfection" (Trench 24-25). Harry lies most grievously about his true *trade*—writing—having long ago betrayed it, as he puts it, by *trading* on his talent. He has done so, he admits, by lying and by taking up lesser trades such as loveless love-making. Indeed, he has sold out his talent for the "blood money" that came with that "rich bitch" who destroyed his talent.

> The steps by which she had acquired him and the way in which she had finally fallen in love with him were all part of a regular progression in which she had built herself a new life and he had traded away what remained of his old life.
> He had traded it for security, for comfort too, there was no denying that, and for what else? He did not know. (46)

Whatever his reasons and elaborate rationalizations, it cannot be denied, however, that Harry had married into the world of the rich: Helen's "goddamned Old Westbury, Saratoga, Palm Beach people" (46). The land of the rich, to Harry the priest-writer, is his land of the Philistines. Like John Milton's Puritan Samson, whose betrayal of his priestly vocation and his "Heav'n-gifted strength" began when he married a woman "of another people," Harry dates his apostasy from the date of his marriage to Helen. Just as Delilah is traditionally associated with the hyena—a deceiver and devourer—Helen herself—an emblematic reminder of Harry's spiritual decay (and therefore his chosen scapegoat)—is abetted by the obscene hyena that stands as the omen of Harry's physical death. If imprisoned, blind, ridiculed Samson meditates sorrowfully on the way in which he came to betray his priestly vocation, gangrenous, embattled, cynical Harry rides his reason through his memories to a just assessment of his betrayal of his talent. In a famous sonnet a Samson-like Milton marvels bitterly at his own fate in having been implicitly commanded to employ his innate talent in the service of his God, though afflicted with the blindness that would seem to prevent the fulfillment of that talent. More deeply, his complaint was that blindness impeded, if not prevented, that "rational organization of his life in the world in accordance with the divine will" (Weber 220).[16]

Harry's affliction—his blindness—has not been physical but metaphoric. Afflicted by self-deception, Harry has told himself that he has not traded on his talent: having married money he would some day write *well* about the rich, which is to say, write the truth about them.[17] Like Milton, Hemingway draws on the parable of the talents in Matthew, which charges the lord's steward with failure to increase the fortune entrusted to him. A hard fate it is to be endowed with God-given talent and then to be ordered to exercise that talent to the fullest, regardless of the personal risk or ultimate cost involved. Yet it was part of rationalized Calvinist doctrine that "man owes to God" the cultivation of "the slightest seed of grace that he may receive" (Miller, *Errand* 58). For Milton and Hemingway, writing itself was a great gamble, as it is for Harry, who at the end of his allotted time once again becomes a writer. His triumph over his apostasy allies him with the redeemed Milton and the Samson who tears down the pillars of the temple. Of him might be said, "God blesseth His trade," a familiar "remark about those good men who had successfully followed the divine hints," writes Max Weber (163).

The fate of Hemingway's writer-hero, fulfilled in his fantasy of an apocalyptic translation to the "House of God" at the top of Kilimanjaro, followed by his wife's shrieking recognition that—naturalistically—Harry is dead, is clear. The infection that will kill him, coming from a seemingly minor scratch left too long unattended, has been the providential event that has enabled him to do the good work that will put his spiritual house in order and earn the grace that has eluded him before he undergoes the imminent death he cannot evade.

Early critics blasted *Across the River and Into the Trees*. But they missed the point, Hemingway argued; for this novel about a career army officer whose calling is to what he calls the "*triste métier* of war" (253) offered an artistic complexity exceeding that of any of his previous works, a meaningful performance beyond the grasp of the critics. As in "The Snows of Kilimanjaro," the narrative again takes up the last few days of a life, the business of which is a final reckoning. Over and over Colonel Richard Cantwell insists that he has followed a trade, a "sad" (94) and "strange" (50) trade, a "*sale métier*" or "dirty trade" (114), "*la vie militaire*" (79), an "*oficio*" (93, 97); a trade that has been the "dispensing" of death (220), the "killing armed men" (63) but also the trade of "making things clear" and "breaking spells" (63, 148).[18] But if one disdains the spiritual value of Cantwell's "soldiering as a trade," (27) it might be recalled, as Weber points out, that "every legitimate calling has exactly the same worth in the sight of God" (81), a notion not unrelated to Barton's emphasis on Jesus' view of his and his "Father's *business*" (*Man* iii). But as dedicated as the Colonel is to his trade, he has not been single-minded. Weber points to the radical change in the nature of calling, in which "several callings" may be combined, "if it is useful for the common good or one's own" (162). Besides his military trade, Cantwell has been called to aestheticism—a possibility not allowed for by Weber or envisioned by Barton. The Colonel's actions imply not only an ethic but a system of self-defining morality.[19]

The narrative everywhere reveals the Colonel's attempt to rationalize his quotidian life so that it will be extraordinary for its order, form, and intensity. Out of a wealth of evidence, consider only the account of the Colonel's early morning visit to the marketplace. Observing that "a market is the closest thing to a good museum like the Prado or as the Accademia is now," he studies "the spread and high piled cheeses and the great sausages," moving "through the market inhaling the smell of roasted coffee and looking at the amount of fat on each carcass in the butcher section, as though he were enjoying the Dutch painters, whose names no one remembers, who painted, in perfection of detail, all things you shot, or that were eatable" (190–92). For the Colonel it is natural to move from the "calling" of the Dutch painter who attended to detail, to that of the butcher, to his own as appreciative witness to the arts of painter, hunter, or butcher.

Then the Colonel cuts to the fishmarket, which he calls the highpoint of his morning pilgrimage. There is God's plenty here, a full spectrum of shapes and smells and colors.

In the market, spread on the slippery stone floor, or in their baskets, or their rope-handled boxes, were the heavy, gray-green lobsters with their magenta overtones that presaged their death in boiling water. . . .
There were the small soles, and there were a few albacore and bonito. These last, the Colonel thought, looked like boat-tailed bullets, dignified in death, and with the huge eye of the pelagic fish. . . .
There were many eels, alive and no longer confident in their eeldom. There were fine prawns that could make a *scampi brochetto* spitted and broiled on a rapier-like instrument that could be used as a Brooklyn icepick. There were medium sized shrimp, gray and opalescent, awaiting their turn, too, for the boiling water and their immortality. . . .
Now he looked at the many small crustaceans, the razor-edge clams you only should eat raw if you had your typhoid shots up to date, and all the small delectables. (192–93)

The Colonel asks a seller of clams where his wares have come from. They come from "a good place, without sewerage," he is told, and the Colonel asks for six of them. "He drank the juice and cut the clam out, cutting close against the shell with the curved knife the man handed him" (193). In this exchange in the marketplace, the buyer no less than the seller is engaged in the good offices of trade in a world whose wealth is endless to the innocent eye. Hemingway's Colonel walks in grace through the Venetian marketplace.

The critics who were unkind to Hemingway's novel of grace and graceful death may have influenced Hemingway's theme in his next work. Although *The Old Man and the Sea* is not without its moments of aestheticism, this novella about an unlucky fisherman returns to Hemingway's earlier notions of how Christian grace is achieved through suffering and good works. Its ethic replicates that of "The Snows of Kilimanjaro" and "Today is Friday."

The Old Man and the Sea allows Santiago his graceful triumph. But the grace he achieves is humanistic. Weber writes of the great change when the Christian ascetic "had strode into the market-place of life, slammed the door of the monastery behind it, and undertook to penetrate just that daily routine of life with its methodicalness, to fashion it into a life in the world, but neither of nor for this world" (154). Santiago's ethic both anticipates this historical change and is a product of it. The great difference, of course, is that his triumph (destruction, if necessary, but not defeat) has its existence in and for this world, not for the next. Testing his limits and going beyond them, he does what no one else (except the boy) expects him to do. Enhanced by self-knowledge, this triumph of spirit recalls that of Jesus, as recognized by the knowing Roman soldier who in "Today is Friday" remarks that Jesus "was pretty good in there today." It is the abandoned Jesus's behavior on the cross that earns the Roman soldier's professional respect. It is not far-fetched to see *The Old Man and the Sea* as an extension of the story of "Today is Friday," one in which the whole of Jesus's ordeal—a week of passion, crucifixion, burial, and resurrection—is replayed in the old man's three-day ordeal.

Santiago's humanism is defined, as readers have always seen, by other "Christ features" (Brumm 206)—indicated by imagery, language, and situation. Santiago's is a saint's name, he makes "a noise such as a man might make, involuntarily, feeling the nail go through his hands and into the wood" (*Old* 107); he climbs a hill to his shack, shouldering a cross-like mast, and he talks of prayer. But as is made clear, victory for Santiago does not lie in his elation at first landing his fish or his battle with the sharks, or even his making his way safely back to port. His victory lies in the way he has managed his ordeal. The good has come in the way he has worked. He has met Colonel Cantwell's standards for high regard, by being "hit solidly, as every man will be if he stays"—a "tough boy," "a man who backs his play" (*Across* 71, 49). At the end he sleeps in a state of grace, feigning the graceful death of Robert Cantwell, perhaps the death of Harry in the "Snows," and probably the death of the Jesus who "was pretty good in there today."[20] In Hemingway's world, grace is earned through good and hard work, not bestowed by a sovereign power. From the outset Santiago has good reason to feel good about his work. "His hope and his confidence had never gone. But now they were freshening as when the breeze rises" (13).

That Hemingway often tended to see such unexpected triumphs by professionals—"outdoor men"—in their enactment of the rituals of sport should not be taken to mean that he saw such experiences as merely convenient metaphors for more profound human experiences. Like war and writing, certain sports potentiate the earning of grace, as Hemingway saw it. Consequently, he could see his man of grace embodied not only in the old

Cuban fisherman but, as Santiago does, in a professional baseball player beset by injury and age. Santiago's regard for the "great" DiMaggio coincides with Hemingway's own view of Santiago—of his professionalism, courage, and achievement of grace.[21]

One final observation about Hemingway's engagement with the Christianity of his fathers. Weber points out that the Christian ascetic, in the process of working out his relationship with the world, abandoned at an early stage the sacrament of private confession, a sacrament of which Calvin had been suspicious. "The means to a periodical discharge of the emotional sense of sin," he affirmed, "was done away with" (106). Hemingway's quiet revolution—resembling those of modernists like Eliot and the Southern Agrarians—was to reinstate private confession in its unmediated form. "The Snows of Kilimanjaro" makes the reader privy to Harry's litany of sins that were not until then expiated by his writing. *Across the River and Into the Trees* walks us through the soldier's replaying of a life of regrets and failures. *The Old Man and the Sea* offers three days of Santiago's drama of courageous competence and self-chastising regrets, along with his said and unsaid prayers of expiation and hope. Even "A Clean, Well-Lighted Place" has its place in this paradigm, though sin becomes acedia, confession deteriorates into the ruminations of angst, and prayers of supplication and expiation give way to parody. For the most part, Hemingway resorts to ways that are not entirely alien to "the way in which the conscientious Puritan continually supervised his own state of grace" (Weber 124). Surely, in this, Hemingway's older waiter differs little from T. S. Eliot's supplicants, including the old man in "Gerontion" whose thoughts are those "of a dry brain in a dry season" (*Complete* 23).

After 1921 Hemingway moved at great distances from Oak Park, transcending at an early age the significantly secularized religion of the Bartons, father and son, to embody in his life the fundamental element of spirit of "all modern culture: rational conduct on the basis of the idea of the calling," as Weber said, "[born] from the spirit of Christian asceticism" (180). Unlike most of his fellow modernists, who saw in Christianity only a myth, a human construction that promised (often ironically) some sense of order, Hemingway found in it the source of an ethic. Oddly enough, in this, if in nothing else, he was rather like his fellow Oak Parker, the author of *The Man Nobody Knows*. His callings, though, were not those of the businessman or man of advertising, but of the soldier, the writer, and the fisherman, as he tried to the last to work out his own spiritual way to a writer's good and graceful place. Not always graceful himself, he was truly our modern poet of humanistic grace.[22]

Notes

1. See Monteiro, "Hemingway's Christmas."

2. Compare with the Arminian's position on works and grace, John Winthrop's, as spelled out by Perry Miller: "though there would be hard work for everybody [in the Massachusetts Bay Colony], prosperity would be bestowed not as a consequence of labor but as a sign of approval upon the mission itself. For once in the history of humanity (with all its sins), there would be a society so dedicated to a holy cause that success would prove innocent and triumph not raise up sinful pride or arrogant dissension" (*Errand* 6).

3. Ernest's father knew Bruce Barton; and William E. Barton refers to Anson T. Hemingway, Ernest's grandfather, as his "deacon emeritus" (265).

4. Ernest Hemingway to Clarence Hemingway, May 19, 1918 (Griffin 59).

5. Six months after his review of *The Sun Also Rises*, Barton's name surfaced in Dorothy Parker's explanation of why critics had dismissed *In Our Time*: "Well, you see, Ernest Hemingway was a young American living on the left bank of the Seine in Paris, France; he had been seen at the Dôme and the Rotonde and the Select and the Closerie des Lilas. He knew Pound, Joyce and Gertrude Stein. There is something a little—well, a little you-know—in all of those things. You wouldn't catch Bruce Barton or Mary Roberts Rinehart doing them" (92).

6. Grimes mentions Bruce Barton merely as the author of *The Man Nobody Knows* (1), while Isabelle does not mention him at all.

7. Curiously, Barton's he-man Jesus is anticipated in the Jesus of Ezra Pound's *pre*-modernist poem "Ballad of the Goodly Fere," one whose strong-man exploits— driving the money changers from the Temple and eating the honeycomb—are celebrated in the narrative voice of Simon Zelotes. Barton also uses the story of the money-changers to support his view of Jesus the "Outdoor Man" (*Man* 32–56). Brought up on a Jesus meek and mild, the adult Ernest might have welcomed Barton's Jesus. The seeds were there. "When I get to be a big boy, I don't want to be an Onward Christian Soldier," the child is reported as having said; "I want to go with Dad and shoot lions and wolves" (Griffin 8).

8. An entry in "Fragments from Ernest von Hemingstein's JOURNAL" reads: "Friday.—Attended the Crucifixion of our Lord. Tintoretto was there. He took copious notes and appeared to be very moved. Dined with Boys. He asserted the entire spectacle was a fraud. He was his usual irascible self but sound company. He says Joyce drinks too much and confirmed several new anecdotes of Gide. The unfortunate Gide it seemed was refused admission to the Crucifixion as they had decided (officially) to call it. Goya offered me La Alba for the evening. Really charming of him. A well spent evening" (*Letters* 768).

9. Miller quotes the words of Mary Moody Emerson, Ralph Waldo Emerson's aunt, within this context: "Speaking as a Calvinist, she anticipated Max Weber's discovery that the Protestant ethic fathered the spirit of capitalism, in the pungent observation, 'I respect in a rich man the order of Provident'" (*Errand* 201).

10. Three such manuscripts appear in facsimile in Hemingway's *88 Poems* (82).

11. Hemingway's parodies of the "Twenty-Third Psalm" led not only to the short poem he published in Ezra Pound's magazine but to the opening paragraph and the overall mood of *A Farewell to Arms* (Monteiro, "Ernest" 83–95).

12. Reverend Barton extends James's notion to the prayer of the agnostic. "I

think that the man who is alleged to have prayed, 'Oh, God, if there be a God, save my soul if I have a soul,' prayed a very good prayer" (303).

13. Reverend Barton affirms that "the heart lives by the faith the lips deny," and quotes a poem in support:
There is no unbelief.
Whoever plants a seed beneath the sod,
And waits to see it push away the clod,
Trusts he in God.

There is no unbelief.
And day and night and night and day unceasingly,
The heart lives by the faith the lips deny—
God knoweth why.
(300)
The older waiter's truncated parody-prayer to the Virgin anticipates the scene in *For Whom the Bell Tolls* where the official communist adoration for the icon of the Revolution, La Passionaria, turns at the moment of his imminent death into a young partisan fighter's prayer to the Virgin Mary.

14. Consider Marti-Ibanez, who invokes Hemingway: "The best place for writing is inside the writer's head, as Hemingway has said" (51).

15. Bruce Barton accounts for Samson's failure differently: "Samson had almost all the attributes of leadership. He was physically powerful and handsome; he had the great courage to which men always respond. No man was ever given a finer opportunity to free his countrymen from the oppressors and build up a great place of power for himself. Yet Samson failed miserably. He could do wonders singlehanded, but he could not organize" (*Man* 29). In *Across the River* Cantwell recalls that the French marshal Foch was one of those who "both fought and organized" (27).

16. Weber goes on to say that this "rational organization" of life in accordance "with the divine will" forms "the permanent inheritance of later times from Calvinism" (220).

17. Oak Park would not have disapproved of Helen's money. After all, its famous minister was "a business man's minister, who saw nothing ironic about his crusade for 'clean money,'" writes M. Reynolds. "Filthy money," Barton said, "was not only a menace to health but had its influence on the character of those who used it, while clean money, like clean clothes and cleanliness of person, tended to tone up one's morals and self-respect. He could get something of an index of the character of the young man he had married not by the size of the fee but by the quality of the money in which it was paid, its newness and cleanliness" (10-11).

18. Cantwell's definition of a "jerk" as "a man who has never worked at his trade (*oficio*) truly" (*Across* 97) recalls Weber's warning against individuals guilty of "unfaithfulness" in their "callings" (162).

19. The *locus classicus* for the modernist's dramatization of the conflict between aestheticism and the ancient religions is Wallace Stevens's poem "Sunday Morning" (1915).

20. Interestingly, F. Scott Fitzgerald thought otherwise. One notebook entry reads: "Showing off. Well, then, so was Christ showing off" (15).

21. Santiago's empathy with DiMaggio, along with Hemingway's portion in the literary transaction, is discussed in Monteiro ("Santiago").

22. This essay draws on materials published in *Journal of Modern Literature*, *Fitzgerald/ Hemingway Annual*, and *Hemingway Review*.

JEREDITH MERRIN

Sites of Struggle
Marianne Moore and American Calvinism

MARIANNE MOORE AND the Calvinist tradition: for champions of Moore, the topic incites certain resistances. During the past decade or more, in the all-out effort at critical reclamation of Moore as a major modernist, her supporters have been willing (for the most part) to give the nod to the poet's inarguably ethical sense of purpose. Yet they have as a rule avoided the word "Puritan," which carries common, and commonly unfortunate, alliterative associations: piety, prudery, pedantry—together, perhaps, with the idea of a fatally dated, rather rigid politeness. After all, isn't the *true* modernist marked (among other things) by skepticism; by a bold, frequently competitively bluff or *mano à mano* approach to sexual subject matter; by a disinclination for moral didacticism; and by a cleansing or salutary anti-Victorian anti-gentility? This question of the credentials for, and what we might call the conscience of, modernism is one to which I will return.

Opening the door of Moore criticism to the Calvinist inheritance—a rich and lasting *imaginative* inheritance, as Sacvan Bercovitch and others have pointed out[1] (*American Puritan*)—need not make way for her modernist demotion. Rather, Moore's brand of modernism and her traditional Presbyterian religiosity manage in an unusual way to brace and interanimate one another. Moore's commitment or calling—or, as the Puritans would say, her "errand"—is at once spiritual and aesthetic. And this twofold purpose is specifically *American* in nature for the poet who sees, like a true pilgrim, opportunity in resistance and salvation in struggle. She imbibed, after all, this dual sense of mission and these American Protestant ideals with her mother's milk.

In *Marianne Moore: Vision into Verse*, Patricia C. Willis's 1987 catalogue to a Rosenbach Museum & Library exhibition, I find a powerful visual emblem of Moore's combined Calvinist, modernist, and familial "errand." The Moore family owned an unsigned nineteenth-century American oil painting, *View of the Ohio River from above McKees Rocks* (37). At the lower

View of the Ohio River from above McKees Rocks, *circa 1880, artist unknown. (Courtesy Rosenbach Museum & Library)*

right it portrays, on a wooded hill in western Pennsylvania overlooking the broad Ohio River, a mother and two children saying grace before their picnic lunch. This competent, pleasant work with its typical Hudson River–school perspective may be seen, like Moore's much more remarkable poetic *oeuvre*, as wonderfully linking private and public mythos, the Moore family condition and that family's perception of the manifest destiny of the nation.

A bit of biography is in order. On November 15, 1887, Marianne Craig Moore, the second child of Mary Warner Moore, was born into a fatherless household. Mary Warner, separated from John Milton Moore after his mental breakdown in the months before Marianne was born, had moved with her then year-old son, John Warner, into the Kirkwood, Missouri, parsonage of her Presbyterian minister father, John Riddle Warner. Mrs. Moore's insistence on the patronym "Warner" in both her own name and that of her son (whom she habitually addressed as Warner rather than John), as well as her bequeathment of her deceased mother's surname "Craig" to Marianne, suggests how fiercely she cleaved to the values and sense of self acquired in her childhood home. Mary Warner's devotion shows, too, in her posthumous publication, at some cost to herself, of the Reverend Warner's collected sermons — including the rather famous address he had delivered at Gettysburg, which at that time and place evidently rivaled Lincoln's for the attention it received (Molesworth 2).

When Reverend Warner died in 1893, Mrs. Moore took her two small children to live near Pittsburgh with her uncle Henry. When Henry in turn died in 1895, she then resettled in Carlisle, Pennsylvania. Fate had insistently and repeatedly erased from the picture, as we might say, any father figure for Marianne and her brother. It is clear why, then, the painting previously described must have had special resonance within Mary Warner's household: an isolated group of three with no adult male in view, huddled closely, dwarfed by and praying in the lush garden/wilderness of Pennsylvania.[2]

I have just imported into my discussion, as the reader may have noticed, traditional Calvinist terms for America: "garden" (the New World as Eden, or as the *hortus conclusus* of the redeemed soul) and "wilderness" (the Puritan settlers' experience as akin to the Exodus or other biblical ordeals or tests of spirit). Since the group in the painting is portrayed on a hill, that image may bring to mind as well the Puritans' typological figuring of America as the "City on a Hill" or New Jerusalem. In Moore's poetry and in the mythos of her family, such traditional terms do not seem artificially or anachronistically imposed, so deeply ingrained into both poetry and family psychodynamics is unswerving American Protestant purpose.

Just listen, for only two of many possible examples, to Mrs. Moore ardently reinstilling, in passages from two 1905 letters addressed to both of her now college-aged children, a sense of mission in peculiarly Puritan terms (Marianne then at Bryn Mawr, and Warner—nicknamed "Toady"—then at Yale):

Don't forget that we three are "a Peculiar people;" that is, acc. to the Scriptures, a people *set apart*. We have a mission in the world; as the old prophets used to call their message, "*a burden*," and it behooves us to carry it directly. As Jesus said about his mission to earth, "how am I straitened—until it be accomplished?" Never, dear Toady, forget that; more than to get teaching, more than to do well in athletics, more than to make pleasant friends, you have the burden of delivering to every soul with whom you come in contact, *the impress of the Lord Jesus*.

You are both out at sea now, and those who are in the harbor are full of anxiety—as to the gales you are called upon to weather. Were you in a company of "your own people" I should know things with you to be wholly different. But you are as if young Cromwell and young Milton were taken up bodily and put down in the French Court, there to grow up. I pray the stamina may be in you to do as they would have done in such a case; for I think Milton would have come forth at last, the unsullied soul he pictured "the Lady" in Comus, to be, and Cromwell alike have come out unscathed; the valiant, the fighter of evil. (*Letters* 19 Oct., 23 Oct., 1905)

Of course, in the way high seriousness always invites deflating levity, these maternal sermons-in-miniature may carry somewhat comical moments for us, Mary Warner's latter-day and unintended audience: the inconsonant address to Warner by his babyish nickname from *The Wind In The Willows*, for example;[3] the straight-faced summoning of "unsullied" Milton—in his own day dubbed by his peers at Cambridge "the lady of Christ's [College]" for his excessive nicety; or the xenophobic ruffling of feathers at those always decadent devils, the Catholic French!

Still, the Moore family correspondence is strangely poignant in what we can gather from it about the anaclitic intensity of this little circle's bonding in the face of felt vulnerability. In one letter, Mrs. Moore actually tells her children that although she herself has taken to writing extra notes to them, they need not feel obliged to contribute to more than the usual *two* round-robin letters each week. And the letters are striking, as we've just seen, in their reliance on Puritan tropes and types: Mrs. Moore's typological identification of her family with the Old Testament Israelites ("a Peculiar people"); her likening of their family mission to that of the "old prophets" crying in the wilderness: her deployment of the twin role models, Milton and Cromwell; and, finally, her figuration of spiritual life as a battle and of her children's college experience—echoing the Pilgrims' Atlantic ordeal—as a hazardous sea voyage. John Warner's and Marianne's letters as well as their mother's explicitly and implicitly subscribe to this mythos—as when Marianne, in a move meant to reassure her mother, refers to her own "stiff

Puritan nature," or when she bucks freshman homesickness in battle terms: "No one has died of mere unhappiness and I will get over it sooner or later so why not now. But my philosophy seems almost vanquished sometimes" (*Letters* 14 Oct., 15 Oct., 1905).

The voluminous and lifelong correspondence of brother, sister, and mother attests to their shared Calvinist convictions that the path of the Elect must be hacked through the forest of adversity and that the Enemy, or Satan, lurks not only outside—in the hostile or indifferent or immoral world—but also inside, most balefully in the shape of that most dire sin: despair. The weapon they all wielded against disbelief and despondency was the written and spoken word. As Presbyterian minister and sometime navy chaplain, John Warner Moore, like his grandfather, wrote and delivered sermons. Mrs. Moore, preserver of her father's sermons, in Marianne's youth taught English at a girls' high school, and then later consistently commented on or even "corrected" her adult daughter's poetic drafts. Marianne composed verse and stories from childhood, contributed wide-ranging and influential editorial "Comments" during her years at *The Dial* magazine (1921–1929), and authored, throughout her long life, some of the most idiosyncratic and shrewd literary letters ever penned.[4] Most importantly, she created that unlikely—even apparently oxymoronic—article: an audaciously *modernist* religious poetry.[5]

What drives Moore's indubitably modern poetry of spirit and permeates its subjects, tropes, and forms is a literary-*cum*-spiritual ethos of struggle —a complex drama of external and internal resistances that originates in orthodox Protestantism and, as we have seen, has been fervently privatized within the Moore family matrix. Struggle or resistance, variously contextualized, is the subject of virtually every Moore poem. "The Fish," from her ground-breaking 1924 book, *Observations*, provides a particularly compact and memorable example. Here, Moore finds in an ocean-battered cliff an emblem of spiritual endurance:

> All
> external
> > marks of abuse are present on this
> > defiant edifice—
> > > all the physical features of
>
> ac-
> cident—lack
> > of cornice, dynamite grooves, burns, and
> > hatchet strokes, these things stand
> > > out on it; the chasm-side is
>
> dead.
> Repeated

> evidence has proved that it can live
> on what can not revive
>   its youth. The sea grows old in it.
>   (*Complete Poems*, 26–40)

The poem, with its insistence on the values of fortitude and faith, is, as Andrew J. Kappel points out, one of Moore's "inspirational statements of a religious belief" (46). It is also, like so many of Moore's early works, a statement of her determination and artistic defiance. With its chiseled five-line verse units, "The Fish" has what John Hollander reminds us so many of Moore's poems possess: the look of seventeenth-century lyric stanzas (88). And, in another Renaissance association, the word "hatchet," together with the punning linebreak on "ac-," may even recall those Protestant courtiers who defied "mere" physical execution on the scaffold: "What matter," said Walter Raleigh, consummate self-fashioner of his own legend, "how the head lie, so the heart be right" (qtd. in Greenblatt 29).[6]

Yet Moore's "The Fish," with its apparently arbitrary syllabic measure that leaves syllables or articles ("ac-," "an," "the") oddly stranded on individual lines, is not a Renaissance religious poem, after all; its doughtiness has a distinctly modern cast. For William Carlos Williams, Moore was a paragon of modern "scientific" writing with a sort of genius for surgery: "Miss Moore gets great pleasure from wiping soiled words or cutting them clean out, removing the aureoles that have been pasted about them or taking them bodily from greasy contexts" (87). We are so used to thinking of modernist strategies in tandem with profound or postured religious skepticism that we may be baffled by this technically advanced poet who was so absolutely a believer and whose writing is, as her younger friend Elizabeth Bishop once wrote in "Invitation to Miss Marianne Moore," "all awash with morals" (82–83).

But what if we learn to see—as Moore's poetry so often asks us to see—with new eyes? What if, as I have been suggesting in these pages, we view Moore's Presbyterian morality and her formal modernity not so much as conflicting, but rather as complementary? Her famous and famously collage-like deployment of quotations we could then allow owes something also to sermonic citation and to the writings of Protestant biblical commentators (Kappel 49). Her predilection for containing her material in neat, syllabically symmetrical stanzas might come to seem not only, as Hugh Kenner finds it, a sign of contemporary keyboard culture,[7] but also evidence of participation in psalm-book culture. We might even see in Moore's fastidious poetic patterning what Albert Gelpi locates in the strict stanzas and container-images of the Puritan poet Edward Taylor: a means of evoking the fixed limits within which all created beings labor, and a reminder that the lot of humankind is both to contain and be contained by

God (38). And finally, that surgical slicing of syntax, so admired in Moore by Doctor Williams: might that appear to us not only in the guise of cool experimentalism, but also as a Protestant passion—like the Puritans' rapt absorption in anagrams and acrostics—for uncovering or discovering in words hidden associations or latent truths? Here we might pause to look again at the final stanza of "The Fish." Notice the way Moore has positioned "it can live" at the end of one line and "can not revive" at the end of the next: she has unearthed or dis-covered in riven syntax the Christian paradox of eternal life in death.

I would like to linger for a moment on that last point about Puritan anagrams and acrostics, both because such wordplay is inherently interesting and because the topic leads us to consider a fundamental Calvinist dilemma underlying Moore's choice of subject matter as well as her formal decisions. According to Roy Harvey Pearce, anagrams and acrostics, based on persons' names and generally in the form of elegies, were popular among the Puritans because they uniquely satisfied a Ramist poetics: "a poetics of discovery, of examining and stating, of coming upon, of laying open to view" (*Continuity* 34). In other words, the following early American anagram is based on the presumption that, jumbled somehow within the letters of a name, God had planted evidence of a man's nature or fate:

Thomas Dudley
ah! old, must dye

The Puritan elegist who sent this verse in 1605 to old Thomas was probably not expressing, in proleptically Freudian fashion, a wish that Dudley die; nor was the poet claiming the status, sinful within the Calvinist worldview, of clever creator. Instead, the author was pointing to something he or she had detected within that vast system of correspondences and linked analogies—all of them waiting to be sighted and then cited—which was God's creation. A 1693 dissection of Samuel Arnold's name, for example, revealed that it was time for him to "Leave old Arms." Lydia Minot's name yielded three deciphered truths for her 1667 elegist: "I di to Al myn," I di, not my Al," and "Dai in my Lot." And, for a final seventeenth-century example, in Elizabeth Tompson's name a relative descried her departed spirit's joyful exclamation: "O I am blest on top" (Pearce, *Continuity* 29). (Because the game has proved irresistible, here is an anagram on my name: "Jeer in red mirth." And, taking just one last turn, I will now—none too soon— conclude this digression, "Ere J. M. Di Therr-in.")

The previous paragraph may itself be seen as illustrating, albeit in a somewhat trifling way, the Calvinist dilemma to which it refers. The action of looking, or of attempting to look, *outside* oneself to find God-given *objective* or literal truths can revert so easily—as in my own anagrams—to plainly *subjective* activity: the self just playing around or showing off, the self projecting its own inescapable preoccupations or anxieties. This inevitable human tendency to manipulate, to project, to find only what we are looking for works against that other, self-effacing search for objective knowledge; for, as the Puritans saw it, God's own Truth, hidden variously in His Word and world but available to be discerned. Summarizing the problem succinctly, Bercovitch writes: "The Puritan's dilemma was that the way from the self necessarily led through the self" (*Puritan* 165).

Having sternly repudiated not only Catholic but also Anglican hierarchical systems of authority, the Puritan relied on the authority of the Bible alone, the doctrine of *sola scriptura*. This left every Puritan his or her own exegete, poring over Scripture to gain understanding. The discovery of truths in anagrams is an obvious analogue to this scriptural process. To rephrase the problem, if you were looking for truth outside yourself *with your own eyes and mind*, how could you be certain you had not misconstrued or contaminated the text in the process? The dilemma was felt most strongly by the Puritans, at the epicenter of radical Protestant reformation, but tremors were widely registered. Both this Protestant faith in Scripture and this indissociable suspicion of self-as-interpreter are captured, for example, in the seventeenth-century Anglican George Herbert's couplet from "The Flower": "Thy word is all / *if* we could spell" (156–57, italics mine).

Marianne Moore's poetry is made out of the very stuff of the Puritan dilemma. Hers is a poetics of profound self-suspicion. It is also, *par excellence*, a poetics of the *text*. Moore was, after all, a bookish poet, gathering exotic information and images from the library rather than (in the manner of her younger friend Elizabeth Bishop) from actual travel experiences. She kept tiny, fastidiously cross-indexed notebooks of useful phrases: scraps from the Bible, from her mother's conversation, from sermons she had heard and books and articles she had read. And as is well known, most of Moore's poetic subjects (her cat named "Peter," for example; her paper nautilus; or her armored anteater, the pangolin) are drawn from the Book of Nature, God's other book, whose importance was acknowledged by the Renaissance humanists and the Puritans alike.[8]

When he was not staring into the abyss of damnation, even the fierce Puritan divine Jonathan Edwards, as Susan Howe points out, was wont to open this second book and read in peaceful contemplation: "God's excellency, his wisdom, his purity and love, seem to appear in every thing; in the sun, moon, and stars; in the clouds, and blue sky; in the grass, flowers, trees; in the water, and all nature. . . ." (46). Edwards's choice of words is echoed in this psalm-like outburst from one of Moore's best and longest poems, "The Pangolin":

Sun and moon and day and night and man and beast
each with a splendor
which man in all his vileness cannot
set aside; each with an excellence!
(31-35)

What I am suggesting is that Moore's habitual, we might even say scriptural, study of words and of the created world rises directly out of her Calvinist inheritance and faith. Tirelessly, her poems scrutinize both nature and language, describing and deciphering "God's excellency, his wisdom."

It is a small step, within this scheme of things, from pointing out how words contain or resemble other words to pointing out, as Marianne Moore will also do, how creatures or things resemble other created things: how a swan possesses "maple- / leaflike feet" ("Critics and Connoisseurs") or an elephant "fog-colored skin" ("The Monkeys"); or how a cat can suddenly jump with "froglike accuracy" ("Peter"). The emphasis here, as in Puritan anagrammatics, is on self-effacing scrutiny and on the revelatory juxtaposition of found things. And Moore's Puritan-like avoidance of subjectivity propitiously dovetails with modernist collage techniques and with the modern poet's objectivist credo. Moore's much-anthologized poem "Peter," about a pet cat, particularly revels in this depersonalized descriptive strategy. Peter has whiskers "like porcupine quills," a "prune-shaped head" and "alligator-eyes": strikingly odd images all, but all unimpeachably objective.

Yet even this latter poem, which takes what we might now call Moore's Calvinist objectivism to an extreme, is always on the brink of reverting to the subjectivity that it resists. After all, Moore's cat—who, we are informed, has a perfect right to "the disposition invariably to affront"— clearly does also stand for the defiant young poet herself. And even if the poem did not toy with personification as it does (by giving Peter a "disposition," for example, or by conjuring up a cat who "does not regard the published fact as a surrender"), even then it would bear the unmistakable imprint of its author's uniquely impersonal personality. In the end, Marianne Moore's "Peter" might best be described as a poetic paradox: an expression of self-assertion that robustly resists self-assertion.

Moore, then, is not merely retooling selected Calvinist writing tropes and strategies for modern times. In all her best poetry she vividly encapsulates that same warfare between the forces of self-effacement and self-assertion with which the Puritans were obsessed. The bald, abstract expression of Moore's more usually implicit and concretely embodied theme of psychic struggle may be found in a line from her much-contested World War II poem, "In Distrust of Merits": "There never was a war that was not inward."[9] For a seventeenth-century Puritan parallel, popular in its own time, here are the opening lines of George Goodwin's "Auto-Machia":

> I sing my SELF; my *Civil Warrs* within;
> The *Victories* I howrely lose and win;
> The dayly *Duel*, the continuall Strife,
> The *Warr* that ends not, till I end my life.
>   (Bercovitch, *Puritan* 19)

The very title of Goodwin's poem, from the Greek, means Self-Fight. And the poet's rhymed couplets work hard to contain the opposed forces of self-love and self-loathing, confidence and dejection, while managing at the same time to convey something of the constantly remustered energy and accompanying exhaustion that must have marked Puritan spiritual life.

We might pause for a moment to notice in "Auto-Machia" certain wide-ranging intertextual connections. Goodwin's lines glance backward at the martial imagery of John Donne's holy sonnets (and "dayly *Duel*" specifically recalls the alliterative title of Donne's most famous sermon, "Death's Duel"). More important for the purposes of this discussion, Goodwin's poem also uncannily presages American poetry to come: most obviously, Walt Whitman's *Song of Myself* (beginning, "I celebrate myself, and sing myself"); and more subtly, the centripetal verse of the mid-twentieth-century confessionals, since Goodwin claims as subject matter "my *Civil Warrs* within."

The American poetic future foreshadowed in a popular Puritan verse: this tells us something about the endurance in our poetry of inherited Calvinist concerns, however shape-shifting those concerns have proved to be. It also suggests, I think, something important about the American literary centrality of Marianne Moore, a writer who has too often been scoffed at—or what is perhaps worse, condescendingly smiled at—for writing non-mainstream poetry.[10]

Of course it is a long way from Goodwin's early American couplets to Moore's characteristic modernist syllabics; a long way from the Puritan poet's contained verse to the sprawl of Walt Whitman, or from "Auto-Machia" to the confessionalism of, say, "Skunk Hour." Yet the American obsession with "SELF" in the form of either self-celebration or self-excoriation continues to leave clear tracks. Not all of us, to be sure, come from Calvinist stock or share Marianne Moore's Presbyterian beliefs, as I myself do not. But American life and literature nevertheless remain inescapably shaped by the conflicts, still with us, out of which not so long ago the nation was born.

American Puritans were not only seekers of religious freedom who became, with history's usual bitter irony, themselves implicated in religious oppression: The Puritan enterprise was, in addition, every bit as material as it was spiritual. These people settled on and claimed as their God-given right physical terrain. Some would insist the were visionaries and brave settlers of a new world; others that they were that world's self-justifying plunderers, even rapists. The land was a site of brutal conflict for native Americans and Puritans alike. The former were slaughtered, pushed from their homes, robbed of their food-sources, exposed to cruel new diseases. The latter—threatened by starvation, by harsh weather and aggressive beasts, by gruesome Indian attack and captivity—felt themselves surrounded by a wilderness that was, as they variously described it, "howling, hideous, boundless, unknown, Satanic, wild, forlorn" (Bercovitch, *Puritan* 102). Conceived in linguistic terms, the Calvinist New World must include not only the words *spirit, wonder,* and *hope,* but also *matter, fear,* and *guilt.* As Susan Howe has remarked of Puritan New England, "Contradiction is the book of this place" (*My* 45).

In the terms of this discussion, the fraught and beleaguered beginnings of American nationhood might be seen as the individual Puritan's "Self-Civil-War" writ large. On the one hand, the Puritan "errand" was to search for spiritual purity in a new world, attending always with an open-hearted and open-minded alertness to God's secret signs. On the other hand, the group mission amounted to settling a punishing and inhabited terrain, putting one's stamp upon it, enforcing one's will. At the troubled heart, then, of the Puritan settlers' endeavor were both prayer and plunder. In the beginning, there was the open heart, there was the closed fist.

This "Auto-Machia" or "Self-Fight" at the *fons et origo* of the national enterprise is the focus of one especially energized poem that Moore wrote after she moved with her mother to New York City in 1918. "New York," first published in the *The Dial* in 1921, begins by referring to that city as "the savage's romance," with those three words conjuring up at once precolonial America and the savagery of contemporary commerce. At its conclusion— with Moore's characteristic penchant for the precisions of negation—it arrives at an affirmative definition of New York (and, as is implied, of the New World) through a complex list of rejected alternative definitions:

> It is not the dime-novel exterior,
> Niagara Falls, the calico horses and the war-canoe;
> it is not that "if the fur is not finer than such as one sees others wear.
> one would rather be without it"—
> that estimated in raw meat and berries, we could feed the universe;
> it is not the atmosphere of ingenuity,
> the otter, the beaver, the puma skins

> without shooting-irons or dogs;
> it is not the plunder,
> but "accessibility to experience."
> (16–25)

In her notes to this poem, Moore scrupulously attributes that last quotation, "accessibility to experience," to Henry James, a personal hero. That Moore would look to James as an exemplar of what it means to be American is telling in a number of ways, some importantly related to her Calvinist perspective. "Accessibility to experience" may have been a phrase pieced together from a jacket blurb for a 1910 English edition of James's *The Finer Grain*, or it may (which seems more likely) later have been extracted whole from Dixon Scott's 1917 *Man of Letters*, which Marianne and her mother brought along with them on a trip to California in 1920—and from which Mrs. Moore copied down the following phrases:

> The elder Henry James had a sunny loathing for the literal, caring for our spiritual decency supremely. . . . All he cared to produce was that condition of character which his son calls "accessibility to experience." You were interested only when you were interested—your very conscience ought to work unconsciously—and so our Henry James was equipped for life without plundering it. (M. W. Moore 13)

Moore's poetic use of material first copied by her mother reconfirms our sense of the extraordinary, familial nature of this literary/spiritual venture; and it is in this shared quotation that we find "accessiblity" opposed outright to the notion of "plunder."

Obviously, for Moore, to be an American artist meant to be spiritually receptive rather than materialistically acquisitive. But more than that, it had something to do with an individual's "condition of character" and with respect for personal idiosyncracies and tastes ("You were interested only when you were interested"). A Calvinist suspicion of subjectivity is counterpoised by an equal advocacy of individualism. This balance is part of what Moore sees embodied in James and what makes her claim, as the title of her 1934 essay, "Henry James as a Characteristic American," attests. At the end of this essay, Moore (who makes it a point in her critical writings to allow her subjects their individual voices) jigsaws together sundry quotations from James himself to complete her portrait of him:

> Love is the thing more written about than anything else, and in the mistaken sense of greed. Henry James seems to have been haunted by awareness that rapacity destroys what it is successful in acquiring. He feels a need "to see the other side as well as his own, to feel what his adversary feels"; to be an American is not for him "just to glow belligerently with one's country." Some complain of his transferred citizenship as a loss; but when we consider the trend of his fiction and his uncomplacent denouements, we have no scruple about insisting that he was American: not if the American is, as he thought "intrinsically and actively ample . . . reaching

westward, southward, anywhere, everywhere," with a mind "incapable of the shut door in any direction." (*Complete Prose* 321–22)

Aside from suggesting Moore's personal motive for avoiding matrimony, which she referred to (in her poem "Marriage") as "This institution" (an institution, too often, alas, manifesting itself as "Love . . . in the mistaken sense of greed"), the quoted passage delineates Moore's American aesthetics: broadly speaking, an imaginative open-door policy that avoids "rapacity." That openness means respect for the individuality of others, effort expended "to feel what [one's] adversary feels," as well as room for personal idiosyncrasy, the freedom to follow one's own nose. As Moore asserts in her 1958 essay on "Idiosyncracy and Technique," once again calling on her American exemplar, "In saying there is no substitute for content, one is partly saying there is no substitute for individuality— that which is peculiar to the person (the Greek *idioma*). One also recalls the remark by Henry James: 'a thing's being one's own will double the use of it' " (*Complete Prose* 514).

To interfere with or suppress individuality is to lose something of intrinsic value and potential usefulness, regardless of the necessary "Self-Fight." For this reason, Moore all her life protected her own singularity (or *idioma*) and generously applauded that of others: "Blessed is the man," she quotes from the first Psalm of David, "who does not sit in the seat of the scoffer" (*Complete Prose* 512). For the same reason she celebrated in her poetry the individual forms of animal life. And for this reason, also, Marianne Moore (together with her mother) ardently supported women's suffrage. As evidence of her thinking on that last subject, here is a sentence she jotted down with evident approval from a speech by Professor Zeublin in 1915: "Suffrage is not a question of superiority or the lack of it; it is a question of personality, and that of the woman is as sacred as that of the man" (qtd. in Molesworth 56). In the end, then, although the Calvinism of others may have lent itself to sexism and to the suppression of individuality, Marianne Moore's Calvinism recognizes any given personality as "sacred"—as much the proper focus of human admiration and study as any other manifestation of what Jonathan Edwards called "God's excellency, his wisdom."

I have called special attention to Moore's active feminism in this context because it is perhaps easy for us to presuppose any form of Calvinism as inimical to feminism. It may be tempting for contemporary feminist critics to view the Puritan fathers as an all-male police force, with hapless American women poets—Bradstreet and Dickinson, in particular—fleeing from their aggregated menace like earlier versions of those plucky cinematic outlaws Thelma and Louise. But strong poets have always owned astonishing survival tactics. And there are, as Wendy Martin in her book on Bradstreet, Dickinson, and Rich has pointed out, ways in which the Puritan inheritance actually lends itself to the feminist cause: "Although there is a dramatic contrast between the content of the feminist vision and the Puritan vision, it is instructive to understand that there are striking parallels in form and that these shared patterns are an important part of American culture. . . . The pattern of protest and reform and this belief in regeneration and renewal—of the possibility of beginning again—is a prominent characteristic of much American psychological and social life" (*American* 7). What Moore does not lose sight of is that American "possibility of beginning again" of which Martin speaks—the same possibility that of course propelled the Puritan endeavor. The still-youthful New World for her remains more pliant than the Old. Like the mind. America may in this sense be seen as "an enchanted thing"; like the mind, it is "not a Herod's oath that cannot change" ("The Mind Is an Enchanting Thing").

Living in New York in the teens and twenties of this century, Marianne Moore was in the theater when the curtain rang up on American Modernism, and became herself a leading actor in the play. Lending to that movement her own personality, her own unique and Calvinist-based aesthetic, she came up with a poetics whose particular "difficulty" (to use Eliot's acid test for modernism) was also unique. It does not plunge us into the cold waters of nihilism, for one thing. Neither does it possess the difficulty—not infrequently come across in the work of Moore's masculine compeers—of a self-promoting and reader-abusive abstruseness. Moore is, after all, the poet who let us know, in her poem "England," that she *wished* to write "in plain American which cats and dogs can read!" Moore's reader is not faced with the embarrassment of encountering the author's amplified erotic angst or self-flagellation. Nor, finally—although citation is a specialty of Moore's—is her reader forced by ostentatious allusiveness to become an unpaid researcher or source-hunter: quotations in Moore's poems are generally meant to be taken as they are found, gaining little for her text by being restored to their original contexts.

Moore's poems are, rather, difficult in that they ask us to become, together with their author, "actively ample"; to increase our "accessibility to experience"; to be capable of wonder without "rapacity." In Moore's "An Octopus," for example, her frequently baffling yet breathtaking catalogue-poem about the Nisqually Glacier atop Mt. Rainier, a waterfall observed on the goat-inhabited heights seems freed not only from Newtonian Law, but also from the force of the poet's own moral "gravity":[11]

> And farther up, in stag-at-bay position
> as a scintillating fragment of these terrible stalagmites,
> stands the goat,

its eye fixed on the waterfall which never seems to fall—
an endless skein swayed by the wind,
immune to the force of gravity in the perspective of the peaks.
(54-59)

Returning to the Moore family's nineteenth-century painting with which this essay began, allow me fancifully to propose that when reading Moore's modernist poetry we are in imagination located with her on that gentler promontory, the hill overlooking the Ohio River—at the time of the painting, as Patricia C. Willis reminds us, "the gateway to the west." Not all of us share Moore's conception of the sites (or sights) of struggle, in which spiritual warfare or the "dayly *Duel*" holds out the hope of Christian salvation. Even so, we can comprehend such struggle as she proposes, and certainly without needing to categorize her effort as minor or unmodern for vocalizing an important set of American beliefs. It should be remembered that "modernism" now is as "modernism" is taught in English department classrooms, in which too often too little is understood of American cultural history, the history of ideas and of religion. To know Moore well is to become familiar with these disciplines, and to become avid in general for expanded understanding. As Moore said when she received the M. Carey Thomas Award of her alma mater, Bryn Mawr College, in June of 1953: "the test of culture is the ability to pay voluntary attention" (qtd. in Molesworth 360).

Notes

1. As Bercovitch explains: "the Puritan legacy to subsequent American culture lies not in theology or logic or social institutions, but in the realm of the imagination" (*American Puritan* 7).
2. Marianne Moore's paternal grandfather, Captain William Moore, piloted and owned, with his brother, the steamer *Hope*, which plied the Ohio and Mississippi Rivers before the Civil War: thus an ancestral male figure is suggested by, although absent from, the painting. (Marianne Craig Moore, letter to the author, July 8, 1993). Ms. Moore also informed me that she and her sister recall seeing the painting in question in the living room of their grandmother's and aunt's apartment at 260 Cumberland Street in Brooklyn.
3. Following this *Wind In The Willows* nicknaming, Mrs. Moore was Mole, and Marianne Rat. The close-knit family was addicted to pet names, and there were others: "Nunky" for Marianne, "Weaz" for John Warner, "Bunny" or "Bunny Long Ears" for Mrs. Moore, and so forth.
4. A volume of *The Selected Letters of Marianne Moore* is in progress: general editor, Bonnie Costello; associate editors, Cristanne Miller and Celeste Goodridge.
5. For a discussion of Moore's Presbyterianism as it relates to her modernism, see Kappel.
6. Raleigh's remark was in response to a member of the crowd who suggested

that he ought to face the east, with its traditional association of resurrection (Greenblatt 29).

7. Kenner writes, "the words on these pages [of Moore's poems] are little regular blocks, set apart by spaces, and referable less to the voice than to the click of the keys and the ratcheting of the carriage" (*Homemade* 98).

8. I discuss Moore's deployment of the Book of Nature in relation to Renaissance prose writers, and particularly the prose of Sir Thomas Browne, in the first chapter of *An Enabling Humility*.

9. For a discussion of the contention surrounding this poem, and particularly the critique of Randall Jarrell, see Susan Schweik, chapter 1.

10. Roy Harvey Pearce is particularly virulent in his support of the *masculine* mainstream: "It might well be that there will be no American poetry in the next half-century, that it will be a new international poetry, deriving from a sense of the do-or-die community of men. Whatever else, it must surely be a poetry of *men*: men conceived as in their history representing the infinite range of possibilities of being and acting open to them when they realize that as man they are nothing if not men" (*Continuity* 433).

11. Moore visited Mt. Rainier in Washington with her mother and brother in July of 1922, sightseeing and clambering on the mountain whose topmost meadow was called "Paradise." For the family of three, who had not been reunited since John Warner had gone to sea as a navy chaplain in 1917 and who had long held to a special sense of shared religious mission, this western vacation was highly charged, nearly allegorical.

ELISA NEW

Awe, Wonder, and Wit
Elizabeth Bishop and the Modernization
of Calvinist Mood

SURPRISE IS AT the root of religious feeling, and at the root of much modern poetry too. But even people who are not religious and not poets will also sometimes recall a moment when the world became surprising, when suddenly the particular arrangement of things, their involuted, tensely meaningful and textured complexity provoked the question: why? Such moments reveal just how contingent and loosely mortised ordinariness is, just how "rotten [a] covering"—as Jonathan Edwards would have it—is the sheath of phenomena we walk upon guided by habit and insensibility (*Selected* 101).

I once had such a reorienting experience with the word "green," the recollection of which is one source of this essay. While driving on an interstate with my parents, "green" suddenly assumed a firm shape—pinched and then lengthening nasally like a whistle. Its look in my mind had nothing to do with grass or trees, but rather with the way its sound, transcribed, imposed itself cylindrically with all the insistence that it had ever exerted semantically. "Green" became, as Elizabeth Bishop puts it in "In the Waiting Room," so decidedly "unlikely"—so contrived and yet at the same time so impossible to disconnect from the circumstances of its appearance—a summer drive down a highway lined with trees—that I knew I had experienced something unforgettable. Now I know from Saussure that the relationship of signifier to signified is arbitrary, and I have learned that the cognitive retraction from phenomena I underwent has various names, alienation among them. But neither intelligence has wilted the surprise "green" held for me that day or has slaked my interest in the sudden onset of dread, or awe, or quizzicality that can fill moments when—as a Calvinist would put it—the sharp difference between human works and the Creation reveals itself.

If the onset of such moods is a defining Calvinist experience—conversion depends, remember, on a rush of clarifying feeling—it does not take

Calvinist faith to have such experience. Indeed, it is a critical common-place that modern literature shows a nearly morphological solicitousness to states of mood. Nausea, elation, futility, depletion, suspense, surprise are all moods subject to overdetermination in the modern text, made to in-dicate not only something beyond themselves but something omnisignifi-cant: the vertiginous condition of man, the ephemerality of inspiration, the dessication of expression, the world's incompleteness. This hypostatization of mood notwithstanding, modernism is, of course, not Calvinism. The Calvinist's sense of dread is nourished by faith rather than skepticism, and the Calvinist's sense of the self by a more rueful sense of human chosenness than modernists tend to countenance (Adam's fall can never be appeased by song, his transgression of the complete Word never redeemed by inveter-ately dualistic language). For the Calvinist, humanity is lost to the world's meanings, while, for the modernist, the world's meanings are lost to man.

If, however, this difference is intellectually crucial, it is not, perhaps, lyrically so, since the lyric habitation of lostness has nothing to gain, lyri-cally speaking, from securing intellectual *bona fides* (a means of orientation) and everything to gain by concentrating itself in, occupying itself with, this lostness—the intense experience of which undergirds its lyric authenticity. As Kierkegaard himself knew when he called *Fear and Trembling* a "dia-lectical lyric," in a world fallen into dualism, expressive form must school feeling, and good faith, belief. It is not that poetry converts the modern to faith, or even that it simulates the conditions of faith. It is rather that the discipline the lyric exacts, the strenuousness of affective commitment it entails, conditions the discovery of the poem (the modernist quest) on the discovery of its gratuity. The romantic temperament might deem a "work" so laboriously hacked out of obscurity proof of truth's rare pre-ciousness and, accordingly, of the valorous will of its discoverer. But the modern poet, like the Calvinist, views her work rather more curiously. How, she asks, could the product of such restrictive assiduity and affective insularity as a poem possibly express anything but its own stranded sin-gularity? Poetic labor, and the "work" this labor yields, reveals a distance from Being—sustained by human will—that the poem does not bridge but simply verifies.

Elizabeth Bishop is a poet whose Calvinist patrimony gives special acuteness to her modernity. By Bishop's own account, she was "three-quarters New Englander" and thus bore all her life "a peculiar Boston sense of guilt" that bound her temperamentally with great-uncles who went to sea as Baptist missionaries (qtd. in Millier 2). Bishop's very geographical remoteness from New England for most of that life confirms rather than contradicts her Calvinist heritage. Her strain of modernism—a modern-ism of dazzled and stricken surmising—exemplifies that mainstream strain of Protestant inquiry that finds in modern lyricism a means of feeling its lostness, and finds in the exercise of poetic labor an inlet to the currents of the larger processes of Creation. The supple coordination of a modernist gravity (the gravity of the poet self-appointed "to lay up shards against ruin" [Eliot], or to attain the "Incognizable Word" [Crane]) with older strains of Calvinist accountability gives the poetry of Bishop an uncanny power deriving in seemingly equal measure from her awe, or perhaps better, from a faithful habit of incredulity that takes a modern temper to sustain. Her Protestantism is best described as marrying the subject's sense of the ego's smallness with a broad receptivity to and indeed, active solicitation of, an engulfing complexity. Thus, when Bishop recounts that "as a child I used to look at my grandfather's Bible under a powerful reading glass. . . . The letters assembled beneath the lens were suddenly as big as life as as alive, and rainbow edged" (Kalstone 130), her recollection is testimony to experience of a kind her poems enact and reenact. Through a man-made lens the poet glimpses a world our seeing abuts, or snags, or holds, but always queerly, a world mere seeing does not ever compass. Thus, the flat letters "assembled" have mysteriously irridescent "rainbow" edges: from beneath the glass of our limited scrutiny, these letters look back at the looker with that encompassing wisdom Bishop will later attribute to her "fish"—whose eye looks away and past the eye of the fisherwoman vaunting her inevitable "fish story."

The openness of American writers, and particularly American poets, to the affective exigencies of such revelation is a feature of the national literature at least equal in significance to the national proclivity for projective romancing, and a feature whose flourishing into the modern period bespeaks the hardihood of the Calvinist ethos. From Samuel Sewall's attentiveness to Plum Island's patterned yet artless beauty through Annie Dillard's resolution that since "beauty and grace are performed whether or not we will or sense them . . . the least we can do is try to be there" (Dillard 8), the earliest of Calvinists share with and sometimes bequeath to their modern heirs a disinclination to indulge in the more adventitious forms of making, along with an inclination to revere what is already made. Thus, the characteristically implicated posture of the modern writer—on whom the burden of meaning rests despite her apparent insufficiency, despite indeed the collapsed foundations of belief on which meanings once were reared—echoes the implicated posture of the believer who depends on grace alone yet is obliged withal to works.

The template for this strain of American attentiveness, and thus for a certain kind of poetic observation, was struck in the seventeenth century with the Calvinist inquiries into human control that eventually culminated in Jonathan Edwards's study on the freedom of the will. For Edwards, the will properly adjusted to the rhythms of creation had executive rather than originary power, and so his whole philosophical and theological corpus may be seen as a continuation of the question that occurred to him when, as a boy of eleven or twelve, he watched spiders spin laddered webs down to the sea. The intricate beauty of their spinning simultaneously declared to Edwards the ultimate futility of busyness on the part of the created and, at the same time, the avenue for expression God had left his creatures as a sign of his grace. A century later, Melville renews this Edwardsian awe— and the delight in the gratuitous that goes with it—in a book that makes its own gratuity a harbinger of the modern. Melville's *Moby-Dick* magnifies the paradox Edwards first expressed by setting the phantasmagoric, hypertrophied romance of Ahab and the whale (an Edwardsian exemplum on the barrenness of egotistic desire) against a jubilee of human works (a Reformed compendium of "callings"). Most of *Moby-Dick* is taken up in demonstrations of what Warner Berthoff has eloquently called "mankind's laborious tenure of the physical earth" (82). With death impending, Ishmael and Queequeg make the choice of cod or clam; amid breakers and sharks, Stubb perfects pitchpoling. The assertion of action and decision in the face of their certain undoing, that begins with Edwards and runs through Thoreau, Melville, Dickinson, Moore, and Frost, may be said to culminate in Bishop, whose poetic work is more entirely given over to this question of works and their meaning than that of any other poet of the modern era.

From the "uncontrolled, traditional" crowing of her roosters, to the "obsession" of the sandpiper and the reaction formation of the Unbeliever, who yet fills his agnostic life with the superstition that "I must not fall," Bishop frets the relationship of purposive action, and especially human intentionality, to the larger Creation. Bishop's concern is with the relationship of Providence to contingency, and by extension, of Providence to the freedom of the will: her purview is Edwards's own. From this set of theological and philosophical interests come powerful poems that evoke radically "unlikely" or contingent realizations of the Divine intention. It is the tension between the substratum of Divine continuity and the fitful, arbitrary, and decidedly strange varieties of human making that gives Bishop's poetry its strange power. In such poems as "In the Waiting Room," "The Fish," and "Filling Station," Bishop will suggest, on the one hand, the factitiousness of human culture and, on the other, the sturdiness and coherence wrought in the space Providence clears for human exercise. Her poems pivot on the question of whether our labors are a cosmic joke—utterly insignificant—or whether (however outré or insignificant they seem) such wafer-thin things as magazines and names and dates and feathers and wicker furniture and wallpaper somehow enhance, or glorify, the Creation that comprehends them. As I will describe, it is the dramatic oscillation between these two poles that gives Bishop's work its character-istic and striking affective power. A mercuriality and unsteadiness of voice is the poet's means of internalizing and so submitting to personal spiritual examination the question of what larger design our idiomatic quirks could possibly anchor. Addressing the classic questions vexing Protestant theo-logians from Edwards through the Niebuhrs, Bishop's poems disclose, as they are nourished by, the three states of soul occupying cardinal points on the Calvinist register: dread, wonder, and wit.

dread: *"In the Waiting Room"*

Understanding of Bishop's vision perforce begins with inquiry into her concept of dread, which functions in her work in classic Reformed fash-ion: dread opens contemplation's ducts. "Dread," wrote Kierkegaard, is "sympathetic antipathy and antipathetic sympathy" (38). For the Protes-tant, the psyche's sense faculty and its spiritual compass, dread, is not to be squelched but nurtured. As Edwards knew when he began his most fa-mous call to redemption with the verse from Deuteronomy 32, "Their foot shall slide in due time" (*Selected* 96), the consciousness of disjunction that dread registers is redemption's anteroom, its waiting room.

Now I do not mean to suggest by this juxtaposition that Bishop's "In the Waiting Room" should be labeled an orthodox poem or that the Bishop who wrote it was the kind of orthodox Protestant of whom Edwards would have approved. The speaker's juvenile realization of the extreme tenuous-ness of all human organization is so impartial, and her exactly simulta-neous, even superimposed apprehension of New England outerwear and the female equipment of African breasts so homogeneous, that it is clear that whatever the religious quality of her experience, it has nothing of sec-tarianism or tribalism about it. The attraction-repulsion established be-tween the speaker and the actual tribeswomen—a figurative rendering of her alienation from her own Aunt Consuelo—confirms that. At the same time, though, the refusal of orthodoxy confirms the poem's essential piety. Bishop's poem estranges all phenomena equally from the somatic experi-ence of the self stripped and islanded in its moment of knowing; in much the same way, the very sermon taken to typify American Protestantism, Edwards's "Sinners in the Hands of an Angry God," will sacrifice narrow appeals to orthodoxy for the sake of dramatizing, and indeed simulating, the condition of sin—thus streamlining doctrine and creed in order to make vivid, as Perry Miller has shown, the *sensation* of the Fall (*Jonathan* 147). By the time we join Bishop's speaker undergoing her trial by dread, she is well beyond any of the more refined solaces that association, or credal clubbishness, can offer. Her sense of self is, at this pass, so retracted and so acute that all the ligatures of contact, including those of human association, like the absurd contingency of a "dentist's appointment," have snapped, and she grasps for ballast more fundamental: a knowledge of knowledge itself as it might define her humanness, as it might anchor her status. What, in effect, Adam knew in the instant just after the fall—Time, his body, and the estrangement of being from knowing by words—these are what she knows. Her experience is religious in the most essential sense.

> I said to myself: three days
> and you'll be seven years old.
> I was saying it to stop
> the sensation of falling off
> the round, turning world
> into cold, blue-black space.
> But I felt: you are an *I*,
> you are an *Elizabeth*,
> you are one of *them*.
> *Why* should you be one, too?
> I scarcely dared to look
> to see what it was I was.
> I gave a sidelong glance
> —I couldn't look any higher—
> at shadowy gray knees,
> trousers and skirts and boots
> and different pairs of hands
> lying under the lamps.
> I knew that nothing stranger
> had ever happened, that nothing
> stranger could ever happen.
> Why should I be my aunt,
> or me, or anyone?
> What similarities—
> boots, hands, the family voice
> I felt in my throat, or even
> the *National Geographic*
> and those awful hanging breasts—
> held us all together
> or made us all just one?
> How—I didn't know any
> word for it—how "unlikely" . . .
> How had I come to be here,
> like them, and overhear
> a cry of pain that could have
> got loud and worse but hadn't?
>
> The waiting room was bright
> and too hot. It was sliding

> beneath a big black wave,
> another, and another.

Like Adam waiting in the garden, all this speaker knows is that she is there, that she has been, and that *her* occupation of time, as distinct from that of others, is delimited by this arrangement of sounds rising sharply to the thin "is" before dropping to the sibilant rustle: "abeth." The uncanniness of this defamiliarized name—its denotative relevancy all of a sudden become unpromising as the faculty of clasping that those "hands under lamps" now also seem never to have possessed—is enhanced by the poem's lineation. The poem's narrow silhouette stands consciousness up in a vacuum: it is as if the vacancy of page around the vertebral column of self-discovery runs cold hands over the frailty of this human subject, over this soul reduced, in Luther's words, to a "lonely church of one" (Pelikan 174). Utterly alone amid hats and coats and cultural artifacts, Bishop discovers what Edwards knew for original sin in a "sidelong glance" at herself falling off the world in all the busyness of Worcester, Massachusetts, a "slippery covering." And yet, rather like the "Man-Moth" in another Bishop poem of that title, the child surprised by sin in the waiting room does not, in fact, slip and does not fall through the floor of the dentist's office into totality. She clings: "eyes glued to the cover / of the *National Geographic*."

Notwithstanding the sublime and terrible consciousness of the "wave" approaching to swamp her, this obdurate clinging distinguishes Bishop from the more apocalyptic American poets (not only Lowell, Crane, and Robinson, but Emerson too, who, as I have elsewhere described, makes the hortatory mode action's replacement rather than its impetus) whose aversion to timeserving left them also impatient of *occupations*. In her regard for the ontological significance of occupations, Bishop is more revealingly associated with such pragmatists as Emerson's Hosmer, and with Frost, Moore, and Williams. Like these, she would hold the immensity of divine Design in mind while pacing, surveying, and tending her smaller patch (New 25–55). All the world may be, as Edwards held, a waiting room, but this intuition is not sufficient warrant for boredom, eschatological hoarding, or a nihilistic withdrawal from temporality. Any of these withdrawals from worldly commerce Bishop will deem, with Kierkegaard, mere inversions of the transcendental ecstasy—that detemporalizing ecstasy whose lust for self-expenditure is as inauthentic as anomie. All court the Kierkegaardian "shut-upness" that presages sickness-unto-death.

Fighting such shut-upness by means of dread, then, Bishop addresses herself to the element in which we live, that element which, however unpredictable, local, and knobby with arbitrariness, still has its significance, still issues its call. It is such a call that draws the "Man-Moth," whose struggle parallels that of the child in the waiting room. An absurd creature of clueless inquisitiveness and compassless momentum, the Man-Moth, we remember, "must investigate," and "must / be carried through artificial tunnels and dream recurrent dreams." His arduous efforts allow traversal without breakthrough, speed without penetration or arrival. As the Man-Moth is a creature moved by faith alone, the country of faith he travels is a Reformed principality. Realizing and revealing the Creative energy in all its contingency, the Man-Moth's world yet solicits engagement rather than withdrawal, movement rather than immobilized contemplation, action as the affirmation and acknowledgment of awe. This creature who "must" fill his days with odd, habituated motions of his body is, in this sense, the phylogenic ancestor to the child who reads straight through the *National Geographic*, noting names, dates, and ephemera close at hand as well as far away. As the Man-Moth's homemade compass virtualizes his profession of faith, the *National Geographic* functions in "In the Waiting Room" as a kind of primer of works: it functions to chart and inventory the endless varieties of human enterprise (it is a *Pequod* in the sense of vessel of trades) and also to model certain kinds of intellectual errand (it is a *Pequod* in the sense of a vessel of quest). Its centrality in the poem is a sign that the "blue-black" *answer* of action's ultimate inutility in no way nullifies those "questions of travel" that the *National Geographic* prosaically, and fragmentarily, meets: inadequacy is no exemption from the imperative to go on the errand.

Pursuing this Calvinist aspect further, I propose that Bishop's understanding of Creation's repleteness not only permits, but exacts, "works." Her "blue-black" eternity sustains and supports historical time, and not because works or history can direct the design, but rather because they, somehow, bless it by consenting to it—by allowing free exercise to the prolific creativity that is Being's most salient feature. The syllables in the name "Elizabeth," the wire-wound necks of African women in the *National Geographic* looking "like the necks of lightbulbs," the fact that Aunt Consuelo's foolishness would permit a worse cry than she utters but this time (for some reason, *this* time) doesn't—all these freeform but self-confirming circumstances are embedded like fossils in other circumstances. These, like continents, are in turn embedded in other multifarious, enwhorled, and interconnected circumstances until the vast yawning distance between Nothing and a small girl reading in a dentist's office is closed by whole cities and continents of "geographics," contingent but somehow manifesting Being's consent to itself in various kinds of patterned concord. This consent is what forms the habitable world, the world which, though it floats on nothing but blue-black space, sustains significance.

Reading, naming, cartography, and poetry are all means of transfiguring dread into a mode of pregnant and fertile waiting, a state whereunto the gap between us and the All can be abided not simply as an absence: but as a room. In this room one can feel the illogical but immutable felicity that differentiation—the curse but also the boon of the Fall—nevertheless yields. To feel the grade and slope of one's own difference from the rest of matter (as Adam did, as *Elizabeth* does) is doubtless unnerving: but it is also galvanizing. The recognition of difference, after all, engenders occupation, and occupation the associated pleasures of place and texture, congruity and fit. These are the pleasures Bishop thinks of in "The Map" when she lets the printer who engraves it "experienc[e] the same excitement / as when emotion too far exceeds its cause." The printer's intangible joy at the printing, like his child-reader's quenchless thirst for the reading, is a version of that literally frictive attraction that Stevens called "inarticulate pang." Bishop locates its global expression in peninsulas that take "the water between thumb and finger" and in the more local: "women feeling for the smoothness of yard-goods." The fact that differentiation permits the articulation of relationship, Elizabeth Bishop (echoing Edwards) deems the wellspring of beauty. That Being's governing law is the elastic, responsive tendency of things to draw to other things (as in "land [leaning] down to lift the sea from under, / drawing it unperturbed around itself")—this is a fact capable of subduing dread. To address oneself to such facts is to seine and salvage wonder from the grave of human expectation.

wonder*: "The Fish"*

"The Fish" is, of course, Bishop's best known instance of such salvaging, and, not incidentally, her most religious poem. A work of passion—albeit with a small "p"—"The Fish" is not strictly christological, but it is richly imbued with the sentiment of pity Passions teach. Built on another poem—Marianne Moore's of the same name—Bishop's "The Fish" answers with consolatory psalmody Moore's pitiless, Job-influenced vision of the terror of contact. Bishop's poem follows the piercing of flesh beyond the collapse of external surfaces to reharvest the mystery of Flesh—and its wisdom. "In the Waiting Room" is a poem that asks why culture is as it is. "The Fish" asks a more fundamental question still: why bodies are, and what their complex organization might say about the Law that made them.

Remember that Moore's "The Fish" had investigated the erosive force of nature in all its impartiality. It gave brief tenure to individuated acts of resistance, and scarcely more to the principle of differentiation itself. The final wisdom of Job, that nothing but annihilation "escapes" to bring the tidings of annihilation's wave, infuses a poem whose final contemplation of the sea that "can live / on what can not revive / its youth" confirms the extreme fragility of what Helen Vendler calls "interfaces." As Vendler notes of Moore's poem, "the fish poem reproduces the sliding motions of the sea creatures, the brutal pressure of the water, and the stolid endurance of the cliff, all intermixed in what one might feel to be a transcription of conflicting motions of the nervous system transliterated into earthly symbols" (86). Vendler shows how Moore's poetry uses the interface to mark the dissolution of interfaces. Matter conceived as abraded surface, and time's law as an irresistible erosion—the undeniability of the insight lends an uncanny fatalism to Moore's poem that is no more alleviated by observation of its beauties than Edwards's sermon on the Fall is alleviated by experience of ground underfoot. Beauty and footing are, in Moore's and Edwards's parallel works, the veneer on Doom, its epidermis. Experience, flimsy, is punctured by Providence, which eventually engulfs it and dissolves all interfaces in the solution of change. Time is a grave.

Bishop's poem, on the other hand, stands itself up, to paraphrase Hart Crane, in Doom's "despite." Her poem "The Fish" allows Experience the stoutness to defer, not by mastering, but by abiding with, Providence. In this poem, glorious knowledge may dwell within ordinary appearance, being within becoming. *Doxa*, or true glory, may imbue the visible semblance of that glory. Such *doxa* somehow floats itself in an element in which mere mentation sinks. Recall once more the "Man-Moth," who stood in "battered moonlight" on his hat, which "lies at his feet like a circle for a doll to stand on, / and he makes an inverted pin, the point magnetized to the moon." Fashioning an instrument out of insubstantial material, the Man-Moth uses insubstantiality to guide himself and so makes his life, all absurdity of circumstance aside, not only a space but an engrossing "city" richly traveled. He gives silence the efficacy of a word.

Indeed the Man-Moth imitates Christ himself inasmuch as he performs the office of what he is not: he drives mere flesh to an Infinite task. Similarly, by setting "The Fish" in a "rented boat"—a makeshift and pathetic vehicle of paradoxical bouyancy—Bishop reels in the same "unlikeliness" that was a byproduct of dread in "In the Waiting Room"—but with effects more closely approaching those represented in "The Man-Moth." In "The Fish," as in "The Man-Moth," an unsustainable environment becomes a borough sanctified by *savoir faire*, and its protagonist, a *verbum infans*, mysteriously incarnates that Totality of Being that Flesh itself cannot sustain.

Bishop's marine veteran has this *savoir faire*, the worldly name for *doxa*, in abundance, and it is his *savoir faire* that the poem named in his honor salutes. To say that it is the fish's "experience" that saves him from harm is almost too obvious to mention, except insofar as the fish reanimates for us just what experience is. In its deepest aspect, experience is not avoidance of fate but execution of fate: the fish is exemplum of Providence given embodiment. Thus the fish's physical hardihood, proof of his marvelous making, is not in the least secondary to his salvific function.

In "The Fish," the material products of Creation—contrived either by nature or man—attain to value insofar as they reflect on, and consent to, the principle of Creativity that sponsors them. While in "In the Waiting Room" such bizarre cultural formations as dentist drills and wire-wrapped necks had an excrescent, gratuitous relation to the truth of the "blue-black space" they filled, here such phenomena attain to talismanic, ritual status. The materials of which the fish is made, painstakingly evoked, have, indeed, the same status that they have in Scripture, where the grain, hue, or patina of a thing is significant for that aspect of divine Creativity it burnishes. The slow cataloguing of stuffs and methods that God appends to his instructions to Noah to build the ark; the repetition of the same that fills the chapters devoted to the building of the tabernacle, and then the board-by-board, wall-by-wall specifications that fill the chapters on the building of the Temple in Kings, and on the City of God in Revelations—all these testify to a sense that *technique* has its divine aspect, that the inwrought wondrousness of the Creation issues its call, bids us hew to its Image. The God who is exacting about materials, who prefers cedar to other woods, who loves David the harpist and Bezalel the silver worker, is a God who blesses skill of all kinds. Practitioners of such skill are, accordingly, in Jerome Rothenberg's phrase, "technicians of the sacred": they seek grace of their and all things' Maker.

Moore's fisherwoman speaker—who has an experience of Creation's motion—rises to such status by attaining mastery in the guise of technical wisdom rather than in the guise of dominion. Her hook, a kind of sword made ploughshare, harvests from the sea the differentiation, both physical and affective, that Moore's earlier poem flooded. To put this another way, Bishop's "The Fish" makes a pragmatic incision in the irresistible tide of determination against which Moore's distinct creatures could not secure their distinctness. Bishop's "The Fish" does not credit miracles any more than Moore's, yet her poem allows life itself, which "Repeated / evidence has proved" ephemeral, the distinctness that experiential usage can give to matter. Make no mistake. Interfaces will eventually collapse in Bishop's sea as they do in Moore's, but Bishop affords them the durability of a pragmatic rather than a determinist vantage point. The sturdiness of experience from within its centripetal wheel is enhanced by a certain participatory suspension of disbelief, what William James called the "will to believe" and Moore in other moods knew for "gusto." The lapidary phenomena of Moore's "pink / rice-grains, ink- / bespattered jellyfish" can be rescued, then, not by sentiment (a mere evasion of determinist force) but by technique, which is practiced engagement feelingly informed. As

Bishop's reprise of Moore's poem reveals, this discovery of technique's affective register—and conversely of affect as a mode of action—is what distinguishes her poetry most decisively from that of her teacher.

The poem begins more pugnaciously, though, with what Moore might call an "externalist's" boast. Its human tone is unbecoming in a familiar way:

> I caught a tremendous fish
> and held him beside the boat
> half out of water, with my hook
> fast in a corner of his mouth.
> He didn't fight.
> He hadn't fought at all.
> He hung a grunting weight,
> battered and venerable
> and homely.

The metrical thrust of the first line, with its ascending, exaggerated distention of "tremendous," does just about all language can do to convey the bellicosity and heedlessness of human domination. Held "beside" the boat, "half out of water" and with the hook in the "corner" of his mouth, the fish is a badge of victory on a dualist interface. Not killed, but "hooked," his very weight and age lend gravity to the woman who caught him, since the world in which she operates is a strategic one where values are differential, a world in which one expects the fish to fight as one fights oneself. Later in the poem, Bishop's martial metaphors will be transformed, and the pugnacity of the poem's opening will be reversed in the final representation of fish as victor: whiskered, beribboned, and sage. But this transformation cannot occur too fast—lest we miss the different set of values by which the fish the speaker catches is honored. It cannot occur until the fish's armor is exposed for precisely what it is—hardly armor at all, but sheet after sheet of the most permeable stuff. It cannot occur until the fish's victory in extremity and ordeal is distinguished from the punier, shallower repulses of extremity passing for triumph on the dualist frontier. These latter kind of victories—of bodily passion averted—Bishop's poem reduces to mere "fish stories," while the former ones—of passion victoriously undergone—earn the status of revelations. Her slow dissection of the fish will reveal the sanctity and eloquence of mortal permeability. Her fish will illumine the Mystery of that force that incarnates the Logos in perishable flesh, exfoliating unitary truth in the rough or delicate, membranous or gossamer, solid or fluid stuffs of living tissue.

The lines that follow, though vivid, are of necessity enigmatic, since the deliberate dissection of the fish's anatomy they perform make glisteningly transparent nothing but the fish's insuperable corporeality. The wonder of the fish, in other words, is twofold. On the simplest level, the poem evokes amazement that the fish could be constructed so artfully, so cunningly, his body with its "dramatic" patterns and antique trim eliciting the "admiration" (rather than, say, awe) that one tenders a couture gown or a well-preserved tunic or hanging of museum quality. And yet the ornamental look of the fish is deceptive, since it is not of the surface. The fish's "brown skin [hanging] in strips / like ancient wallpaper," his body "speckled with barnacles, / fine rosettes of lime," presents a visible surface whose exterior qualities are not the sheathing but the actual product of wisdom by ordeal. The fish's coat is, in other words, not hieroglyphic of some other, far different stratum of meaning, above or beyond physical realization, but is itself the realization of that "skilful workmanship" God approves in himself and in men like Bezalel (R. Scott xvii) and that Jesus eventually brings forward in his own person.

Note carefully that as the poet's description penetrates the visible membrane of the still living fish, the affective register of her language deepens: the oxygen is "terrible"; gills are "frightening," they "can cut so badly." The emotive tension tautens along the literal line of the speaker's contact with the fish on her hook; his mortality conducts into her speech. But more subtly, the Christian paradox of material stuffs harboring the most profound of meanings is underscored in the odd pairings of "oxygen" with "terrible," "gills" with "frightening," and, more generally, in the way the decorative language of flowers and textiles, wholly aesthetic, is given surreal inflammation by affective predication:

> the coarse white flesh
> packed in like feathers,
> the big bones and the little bones,
> the dramatic reds and blacks
> of his shiny entrails,
> and the pink swim-bladder
> like a big peony.

Bishop's interest in density refracted into insubtantiality—nonsubstance transposed as substance—is ineluctably religious. It reveals, chiefly, her interest in the capacity of Being to incarnate itself in a form *different* from itself that is *still* itself; the fish is a meditation on diversity out of unity, the complexity Edwards finds everywhere in beauty. Thus when Bishop describes the eyes of the fish—

> far larger than mine
> but shallower, and yellowed,
> the irises backed and packed
> with tarnished tinfoil

seen through the lenses
of old scratched isinglass.

—her rendering of a transparency "backed" by so much stuff—by tinfoil
and especially by isinglass, rendered from fish bladders (i.e. difference from
the same)—becomes a meditation on the most basic, but most mysterious
operations of Creation, those producing particularity out of All. The rainbow that heralds God's mercy toward human survival in Genesis 11 (and
that is a leitmotif in Bishop's work) is also a figure of this paradox—a coherent knitting together of something out of nothing, its weightless truss-
ing of variegated color epitomizing the ineffable and altogether "unlikely"
consolidation and preservation of firm matter in the midst of the Flood.

Further, we might note that in the Flood narrative to which the poem
refers, a marvel of human handiwork—the ark—will preserve both diversification of matter and the continuity of such diversification in reproductive pairings. Bishop's little *Pequod*, her "rented boat," is such a saving
vessel. The capacity of human craft to preserve God's Creation and the
contribution of skill or expertise to the "victory" of this preservation are
signaled in the epiphany of her last lines. There the "rusted engine," the
"bailer rusted orange," the "sun-cracked thwarts," and the "oarlocks on
their strings" merit that homage earlier tendered the fish. From the clev-
erly rendered parts of the little craft a film of emitted oil spreads like a
nimbus, the iridescence of the suspension imaging the brilliance and variation of substance that nonsubstance supports. The primary allusion to the
miracle of Noah's survival of the Flood is itself subtly iridescent with allusions to other miraculous suspensions of death by water—Moses's, Jesus's,
and the species still floating its small craft on the Flood of "blue-black
space." The wonder that is the signal mood of "The Fish" is emitted by
dread. It is emitted by Bishop's apprehension in "In the Waiting Room"
that beneath the film of calendrical marks and outside the borders of ven-
tures merely geographic is a wider, deeper realm whose wavelike motion is
the movement of nothingness folding into itself. That this wave should sustain something, and so many things, is not only unlikely: it is miraculous.
The more unlikely the more miraculous, the more miraculous the more
absurd, the more absurd the more victorious. The absurdity is of great moment. As I will now describe, Bishop's particularly Calvinist wit—the wit
that renders the fish not only an emblem of Christ but a tough, corpulent,
grunting, decorated old salt—is a constituent feature of her vision. It is a
feature that undergirds awe and wonder both.

wit: *"Filling Station"*

As Carol Bensick has recently noted in an essay on Edward Taylor's *God's Determinations*, we no longer need persuading that Calvinism can be fun, or that even such an ostensibly grave doctrine as the doctrine of predestination could yield amusement, and even sometimes an absurdist kind of mirth (133). Absurdity, as both Edwards and later Kierkegaard knew, is one of grace's anterooms, an expedient route into edification. It is the absurd that dramatizes just how slight our claims to sustenance must be such that Being so extends itself to preserve what so little earns preservation. The disproportion of the humorous instructs the proportionings of Law.

Following up on Bensick's suggestion, let me go so far as to notice that the very fearsomeness of Edwards's warning in "Sinners in the Hands of an Angry God" is, after all, a bit funny as well. Edwards plies a special kind of physical comedy, a solemn banana-peel kind of irony out of human complacency when he writes: "your healthy constitution, and your own care and prudence, and best contrivance, and all your righteousness, would have no more influence to uphold you and keep you out of hell, than a spider's web would have to stop a falling rock. Were it not that so is the sovereign pleasure of God, the earth would not bear you one moment" (*Selected* 104). Edwards's rhetorical effect depends not only on his auditors' cognitive acquaintance with the downward pull of gravity, and with the incongruity of rock's buoyancy in an atmospheric element manifestly thin; it also depends on their own experiences and observations of the stumbling and skidding of the foot when it slips. Edwards's technique, in other words, is to allow the inescapable logic of human susceptibility to gravity's force to expose the unlikeliness—and so the ludicrousness—of our confidence in stability. His use of ridiculous disproportion in this endeavor instances the classic Calvinist humor, a humor hardly optimistic, to be sure, but not misanthropic either. Edwards allows ludicrous images of physical disproportion to elbow the faculty of dread. The ridiculous provokes a kind of surprise that is cousin to the surprise of dread. Both spasms occupy one affective spectrum.

Bishop's technique in "Filling Station" has essential affinities to that of Edwards inasmuch as she writes of human survival in an element that logic dictates should preclude this survival, upstanding in an element that should compel slipping. The very setting of the poem, from which its title is drawn, names this element: the poem is set in a "filling station," where a conflagration waiting to happen is deferred only by the grace of that "somebody 'who' loves us all." The last line of the first stanza, sliding after an initial agitated bump into an attenuated skid—"Be careful with that match" — suggests a physical and an emotional inflammability at extreme odds with the stable "living" the filling station provides and is.

At the same time, however, a "living" is what "Filling Station" precisely is about — a living full *and* unfulfilled, or perhaps better, simply full of unfulfillment. The filling station feeds and fills automobiles as well as it feeds and fills the lives of the family who own the station, saturating this family with fuel just as their private lives are permeated by station life. At the same time that this "filling" suggests a certain stability of intake if not fulfillment, its gerund form also implies a temporariness, and tenuousness, reinforced by the "high-strung automobiles," the urgent coded alarm of the cans that "softly say: / ESSO — SO — SO — SO" (read: SOS!), as well as the skittish darting voice of the speaker. The cars, after all, are only the vehicles of the "high-strung" types who drive them, and the filling station itself vehicle of those vehicles, serving the served: it has no role but to serve. It is a *service* station.

We do not need to know more about the "quick and saucy / and greasy sons" who "live in the station" to know how their full lives could be running on empty. (What could life be like, the poem invites us to imagine, in a place so provisional as a "station"?) And we do not need to know much more about the father in an "oil-soaked monkey suit / that cuts him under the arms" to imagine his unfulfillment despite the seams he overfills. Busyness and saturation of life, even to the impregnation of the "wickerwork" with the oil that also stains his monkey suit, is no guarantee of durability or significance. The viscosity of the oil permeating and coating everything with a "disturbing, over-all / black translucency" epitomizes the instability of substantive works — however "refined" — to fill the world up. The station represents the Christian pilgrim's ephemeral connection with the stopping places of this world, even as it marks and plots the necessary movement of this pilgrim to a better one. In sum, Edwards's metaphor for insecurity, the slippery covering of the material world, is thus updated in Bishop's poem of anxiety coated over with refined petroleum. In this world of slippery footing, unsatisfaction puts off crisis, letting it slide.

There is yet more, though, to be said about oil and especially about "Father" in his "oil-soaked" monkey suit. "Father," his name the Ur-cognomen of the male progenitor of the species, leads the poem back into the deep time that is one of Bishop's chief interests as a poet. His function is to name the ridiculous, atavistic drive that propels his line. But again, as in "The Fish," and as in "In the Waiting Room," the truth of things — the truth of their ultimate inutility — does not imply that such inutility cannot be worked with. Rather, inutility becomes the measure of wonder, and insignificance the index of grace. The absurdity of the things we misguidedly deem necessary once revealed, the mind can open to all the excess and paraphernalia the world contains, and thus to its bounty. To this end, Bishop's filling station patriarch, covered with oil and outgrowing his clothes, is drawn in contrast to the family pet who snoozes while "Father" labors. On the "cement porch / behind the pumps" is a set of "crushed and grease- / impregnated wickerwork" and "on the wicker sofa / a dirty dog, quite comfy." Perfectly gratuitous, this pet (as unnecessary to the family's survival as the hairy begonias and crocheted chair ornaments they also keep) is introduced to shed light on the most gratuitous things of all: satisfaction and desire, pleasure and sense of privation: the feelings. Through this dog Bishop brings into view the whole complement of moods—no more fated, after all, than hairy begonias—that the world sustains, contains, and allows play and expression.

In this way, Bishop's idiomatic use of "comfy" and her sly, slangy "dirty dog" provide the poem's richest vein of wit, but also its interpretive fulcrum, since it is through the knowingness of the language applied to this dog that the poem's overall message of the world's surplus can find resolution. The dog's complacent self-possession makes him anything but a "dirty dog"—the clever or urbane hustler the idiom suggests—while "comfy" is so anthropocentrically unsuitable, so obviously displaced from somewhere else, as to bring into sudden view what has been lurking around the edges of the poem all along: an eagerness of advance, the odor of ambition thick enough to cut, the human imperative—connoted in the urgent cars, the saucy sons, and the very atavistic arrangement of a family business—to "get ahead."

Indeed, the contrast between Father in his monkey suit (a sly allusion to the evolutionary beginning) and the dirty dog on his "comfy" wicker perch (a bemused allusion to the dingy dream of retirement) conveys some of the paradoxical devolution of the human by acquisitive desire that Thoreau had noted in *Walden* in his portrait of John Field, bog-trotter. But not only. The contrast is also rich with a certain kind of delight at the variety of sublimations human desire will compel, at the dexterous and cunning complexities simple *wanting* will produce, the morse code of culture founded on a primal reservoir of energizing desire. As in Bishop's mesmerizing "Sleeping Standing Up," where the drive for survival conjures the pebbles and breadcrumbs of narrative, of Hansel and Gretel; or, again, as in "The Man-Moth," where the tracks disappearing under the feet of the creature trace a delicate filigree around his world—in "Filling Station," the assiduities of Father and his kin are so peculiar, so cryptic and obscure, that even as their complications weaken rather than strengthen the case for their necessity or preservation, still, by their very gratuitousness, they glorify the Force permitting them. If, in short, the tendency to take complexity of civilization as assurance of its continuance or renewal has no foundation, as these primevalisms of Bishop reveal, it is also the case that this complexity is a source of wonder, beauty, and delight.

The absurd works that Bishop surveys with incredulity sharpened by anxiety escape the sterility a nihilist's reading of the gratuitous might arrive at. They answer to something. Gas in a combustion engine siphons energy and speed out of annihilating explosions; the energy created thereby provides Bishop with an instance of primary force parallel to Edwards's downward pull of gravity that may drag us down to death but allows us to travel through deep zones of sensation on the way. It is oil, the enriched product of the death and decay of life itself and a substance moreover threatening to life, that upholds the family of man, just as nature, inimical to human survival and foiling human persistence, still somehow supports human buoyancy in blue-black space.

The adjustment in Bishop's poetry of perceptual power to natural force, and the alignment of her percipient eye with the turning world in "blue-black space," measure the vitality of the Edwardsian consent in American thought. Edwards's notion that Beauty is "that consent, propensity and union of heart to Being in general" resists the human tendency to project its own desires, requiring instead that the eye school itself in an adhesiveness that modes of romance necessarily refuse (*Works* 8:540). The vitality of such adhesiveness in the American poem tells of the still signal influence of such thought as Edwards's on American representation. More importantly, it bespeaks the continued capacity of the poem to channel, conduct, compose, and reanimate that surprising experience which, despite the world's determinations, broadly unfolds as we open to it.

IVY SCHWEITZER

Puritan Legacies of Masculinity
John Berryman's *Homage to Mistress Bradstreet*

The discourse of man is in the metaphor of woman—Gayatri Spivak, "Displacement," 169

Woman then stands in patriarchal culture as a signifier for the male other, bound by a symbolic order in which man can live out his fantasies and obsessions through linguistic command by imposing them on the silent image of woman still tied to her place as bearer, not maker, of meaning.
—Laura Mulvey, *Visual and Other Pleasures*, 15

The woman who is truly Spirit-filled will want to be totally submissive to her husband. . . . This is a truly liberated woman. Submission is God's design for women.
—Beverly LaHaye, *The Spirit-Controlled Woman*, 71

IN 1953 JOHN BERRYMAN published a long poem in *Partisan Review* about—of all things—the little-known colonial New England poet Anne Bradstreet. In an interview, Berryman claimed that he did not like Bradstreet's poetry but that he "fell in love with her; and wrote about her, putting myself in it" ("Interview" 7). Despite the work's confessional quality, Berryman insisted that *Homage to Mistress Bradstreet* was a historical poem and liked to quote Robert Lowell's pronouncement that it was "the most resourceful historical poem in our literature" ("Changes" 101). I will argue here that Berryman's poem is "resourceful" in its appropriation of the feminine for decidedly masculine and hegemonic purposes, and "historical" not in the way he and Lowell meant (and many readers have taken it), in its evocation of the "reality" of a figure in our country's colonial past, but as a document of the continuity of certain cultural constructions of masculinity, most particularly, Puritan legacies of masculinity.

In what ways, however, can we speak about "inheriting" cultural constructions of gender roles and expectations? David Rosen, in a recent study of the "changing fictions of masculinity" in English literature, argues for "a sense of the necessary instabilities of the idea of masculinity . . . and the need men have felt to stabilize the idea of masculinity from age to age" (215). Although I stress here that strategies and elements persist, I believe, in strong contradistinction to the mythopoetic views sparked by Robert Bly's work of the early 1990s, that masculinity, like femininity, is not trans-historical but is shaped by historical contexts and constructed by social and cultural forces; that there are multiple definitions of masculinity that are associated with particular cultural sites and manifested in specific social institutions, such as religious and political movements; and that the dynamic definitions of masculinity reflect as well as shape material conditions and especially relations of power. I agree with Rosen that "masculinity functions as a cultural and subcultural marker, working even within groups to define privileged loci of power" (221).

If gender roles are culture- and site-specific, can they be inherited? I would argue that our modern-day inheritance of Puritan legacies of masculinity is part of a particularly tenacious bequest of a specifically "American" set of ideologies—what the Protestant ethic has left to our modern era—that are also strongly linked to gender ideologies pervasive in the Western intellectual tradition.[1] In seeing John Berryman as one of many "inheritors" of Puritan legacies of masculinity, I do not mean to imply that he held their beliefs; Berryman struggled all his life with religious issues, and late in his life finally converted to Roman Catholicism. Nor do I mean that he was "Puritanical" in the conventional sense of that term. Given what we know of his personal life, he certainly was not. However, in his choice of Anne Bradstreet as subject, Berryman declares himself an "American" poet rooted in a tradition that has been deeply scored by Calvinist influences. When, for example, in an essay written in 1965, Berryman tried to answer the often-asked question of why, in his own words, "I chose to write about this boring high-minded Puritan woman who may have been our first American poet but is not a good one" ("Changes" 100), he sketches out a complicated, one might even say, Bloomian, relationship to Bradstreet as the personification of that American tradition. In doing so, he reenacts certain dynamics of the Puritan ideology of masculinity.

Berryman claims, first, that, in fact, he "did not choose her—somehow she chose me," thereby casting himself in the traditionally "feminine" position as the one chosen. We will look more closely at the gender politics at work in this remark. Next, he admits that "one point of connection, at any rate, [is] the almost insuperable difficulty of writing high verse at all in a land that cared and cares so little for it." Here, at least, he acknowledges Bradstreet's status as a poet attempting to write "high verse." Their shared rejection as poets is another ambivalent tie to the American "land." Despite this grudging and oblique acknowledgment of Bradstreet as poet, Berryman confesses he "was concerned with her, though, almost from the beginning, as a woman, not much as a poetess" ("Changes" 100). Aside from the condescending connotations of that last word, what can this mean?

I argue that the threat posed by the woman-as-poet, a magnification of the "ordinary" threat posed by "woman" in patriarchal culture, is revealed when Berryman, with seemingly nothing to fear from the long-dead and "boring poetess," grants her a power over his imagination but at the same time has to put her back into her "rightful" place, which is, as Laura Mulvey says above, "as bearer, not maker, of meaning." Ambivalently, he makes her both an object that he appropriates and his persona, with which he identifies. She is the means by which he, as Mulvey says, "can live out his fantasies and obsessions through linguistic command" of a silenced woman. In doing so, Berryman exhibits what poststructuralist feminist theorists identify in critical as well as textual practice as a masculine recuperation of "woman." Furthermore, these gestures and attitudes that Berryman expresses poetically about sexual difference and masculine entitlement also echo the attitudes of seventeenth-century Puritan New Englanders about the place of "woman," as well as their discursive use of the feminine.[2] While we can draw some conclusions pertinent to the work of John Berryman from the comparison, I also believe we can venture some more general speculations about the on-going practices of contemporary ideologies of masculinity as well as masculine critical practice.

In an earlier study of self-representation in lyric poetry, I explored how the Puritan doctrines of conversion and salvation, understood and idiosyncratically applied in colonial New England in conjunction with the Massachusetts Bay's theocratic social and political arrangements, constituted a profoundly troubled and troubling set of paradigms for masculinity. Gender roles in Puritan New England were clearly demarcated and believed to be divinely imposed and biblically justified. Not just about individuals or individual behavior, they enmeshed people in an interlocking network of social and cultural structures. Men were the linchpins of the colonial New England social structure, which was organized as a patriarchal theocracy (Rotundo 11-12). Although Puritan doctrine taught men the necessity of learning to accept submission to superiors and to God, in a very broad way masculinity was identified with patriarchal order and public social power.

However, the discourse of Puritan piety as it developed in the New England colonies unsettled this easy identification. Puritan men and women were exhorted by their ministers, who promulgated a metaphorical understanding of the Song of Songs, to become the spiritual Brides of Christ, wooed by and betrothed to the divine and loving Bridegroom. This was the pervasive image for the saved soul. Would-be saints of both sexes had to quell the "masculine" aspects of their fallen selves—willfulness, independence, activity—and strove to achieve a redeemed state of "femininity" as passive vessels cleansed and receptive for the pouring in of divine grace. While females only had to go along with "nature" in accepting a submissive and obedient role in religious worship, males, understood by the Puritans as "naturally" willful, active, and assertive, spent their spiritual lives attempting to subjugate the very qualities their society told them they could not help but embody and were expected to manifest in daily life.[3]

Philip Greven, a historian of the period, bluntly summed up the dilemma that Puritanism posed: "for men to be saved they had to cease being masculine" (129). Furthermore, he suggests that the anxiety many Puritan males experienced as a result of the demand for spiritual feminization produced misogyny and a virulent rejection of effeminacy. Walter Hughes explores the implications of the "figurative homosexuality" that the religious discourse of salvation posed for Puritan males, as expressed in Puritan poetry (103). He finds that poets such as the eccentric Michael Wigglesworth and the more representative Edward Taylor are caught up in a vicious cycle. They struggle to discipline, humble, and feminize their willful selves and turn their errant desires toward an aggressive God. But once achieved, this spiritual triumph results in homosexual panic, self-loathing, and fear of annihilation. Wigglesworth, whose journal records in a secret code his sexual feelings for his male students, resolves his panic by allowing himself only masochistic pleasure in the transgressive loving of a male God. Taylor, in order to stave off his fears of being annihilated by submission to his divine Bridegroom, wildly multiplies the images of mutual objectification that he applies to himself and Christ, and so diffuses both desire and fulfillment into "a kaleidoscopic polysexual ecstasy" (120). Hughes is absolutely correct in pointing out how both poets, as many Puritan men of the time, suffered under the impossible psychic demands of rigorous Puritan doctrine. Yet, we must not forget that they also maintained important, visible public offices, were the pillars of their communities, headed households, and dominated religious and civic life. In other words, spiritual feminization or "figurative homosexuality," while causing private panic and suffering, are a productive part of the schizoid constellations of masculinity maintained by the Puritan patriarchal theocracy.

In fact, the constitution of male spiritual subjectivity by the occupation and/or appropriation of "feminine" positions not only empowered men but consolidated male power by effacing women and further marginalizing socially feminized others like Native Americans and enslaved people. In order to understand this, we need to look at colonial Puritan treatment of women and "woman." Although an essentialized notion of "woman" served as a figure for the regenerate Puritan soul, and womanly functions such as marrying, giving birth, and mothering were used to describe spiritual processes, real women and their biological and social functions were not elevated and ennobled by this use. Puritan women who fit the Pauline model were extolled, but the effect of approving women for being self-effacing would, presumably, be more and better self-effacement. In fact, only a certain scripturally defined and culturally approved notion of "woman" served as the typology of regenerate subjectivity. Carol Karlsen points out that "women who failed to serve men failed to serve God. To be numbered among God's elect, women had to acknowledge this service as their calling and *believe* they were created for this purpose" (166; her emphasis).

Karlsen is talking about the seventeenth century, but she outlines a lesson strategically embraced by Beverly LaHaye, an influential apologist of the 1980s for the New Right's "pro-family" agenda whose doublespeak about woman's place I quote as an epigraph.[4] In the seventeenth century, women like Anne Hutchinson, who swerved noticeably from the Pauline model of passivity, humility, and obedience (and today would be called "feminists"), were considered not just heretical but downright demonic. Governor John Winthrop summed up the prevailing attitude in his frequently cited comment on the tragedy of Anne Yale Hopkins, wife of the governor of Hartford, who allegedly wrote herself into insanity. "For," Winthrop concludes, "if she had attended her household affairs, and such things as belong to women, and not gone out of her way and calling to meddle in such things as are proper for men, whose minds are stronger, etc., she had kept her wits, and might have improved them usefully and honorably in the place God had set her" (*Winthrop's* 225). God set woman in her *place*, a position subordinate to man, and as far as Winthrop was concerned, displacement spelled tragedy for women, chaos for society.

In the hands of Puritan theologians, the spiritualization of feminine imagery had the effect of erasing the earthly and fleshly femaleness from it. The male Puritan saint appropriated female imagery but only as a necessary phase on the way to the remasculinization offered by the Puritan conversion narrative, in which, ultimately, God adopts the saint as his son and heir, while woman/women disappear. According to the logic of conversion, all saints pass through a feminizing process. Brides become sons and heirs and are thus remasculinized, but they remain on the feminine side of the gender/power divide.[5] Edward Taylor makes as much clear in a rapturous contemplation of his many (subordinate) relationships to Christ, who, in assuming the masculine role, finally subsumes "Ev'ry thing":

> In us Relations all that mutuall are.
> I am thy Patient, Pupill, Servant, and
>   Thy Sister, Mother, Doove, Spouse, Son, and Heire.
> Thou art my Priest, Physician, Prophet, King,
> Lord, Brother, Bridegroom, Father, Ev'ry thing.
>   (Med. 1.29.20–24)

Does the absence of "daughters" in this vision of heaven indicate that women also become "sons"? Finally, the paternal and patriarchal appropriation of the mother's role seems to be the point here. John Calvin, quoting John, emphasizes the logocentric—or more precisely, the phallogocentric—nature of faith in Christ, which grants "the privilege 'to become the Sons of God, even to them that believe in his name, which were born not of blood, nor of the will of the flesh, nor of the will of man, but of God' (John 1:12)" (465).[6]

It may be helpful to think about Puritan culture's discursive deployment of "woman" as a form of "gynesis," a concept articulated by feminist theorist Alice Jardine. Textually, gynesis designates "discourse *by, through, as* woman" (36); more generally, it is the effect produced when "woman" is employed as a figure in discourse, used as the vehicle of man's contemplation, as the Other who makes possible his apprehension of interiority and subjectivity. This process, according to Jardine and Gayatri Spivak, who analyzes the effects of gynesis in the thinking of Derrida, is at work in much of Western philosophical thought and recurs frequently in texts of a religious and literary nature (Jardine 63); for example, in the passage quoted above, Edward Taylor conspicuously figures himself as the feminized, and therefore, passive, receptive, and inferior partner in his spiritual marriage with Christ. Most recently, gynesis has been deployed in postmodernism's dismantling of the master narratives of patriarchal culture, including Puritanism. Thus, for example, because deconstruction rejects the notion of a fully conscious, transcendent subject, Derrida cannot speak as "man"; in order to deconstruct his centrality as illusory, he must speak deliberately as "woman," from a position of *dis*placement (Spivak 173, 179). By understanding this conscious rhetorical move, deconstructive feminist theory enables us to see the phallogocentrism of Puritan thought and doctrine. In the light of Paul's metaphysics of gender and colonial New England's theo-patriarchal culture, Taylor's self-feminization can be understood as a form of spiritual empowerment that derives from his speaking from a seemingly disempowered feminine place.

In both cases, spiritually and critically, the male speaker gains power by appropriating a feminized position. How does this gynesis affect women? From the perspective of Puritan doctrine, as I argue above, women are ungendered by the logic of conversion and disappear. Culturally, female functions are appropriated and women as a class become the markers of cultural value, not the makers of culture. Critically, despite the crucial role Derridean thought has played for feminist and oppositional critical practice, a similar effect occurs. Postmodernism's privileging of the feminine does not imply a privileging of or even an equality for women, or a revaluation of our position socially or politically. In fact, as Barbara Johnson argues, in speaking from and thus occupying the place of "woman," male authors continue in reality to silence the sex to whom in theory they give voice (131). In her analysis of postmodern U.S. culture, Tania Modleski finds gynesis "deeply embedded in the American cultural tradition" (7) and traces a similar reinscription of female disempowerment in the thinking of several prominent postfeminist male critics. In their analyses, now de rigeur, of male power, these critics attempt "to reposition the struggle between feminism and the patriarchal tradition as a struggle inhering *in* that tradition" and thus confuse feminism and feminization (8). This "confusion" has been strategically deployed by some male critics to argue for the alleged "feminization" of the discipline and profession and is an example of how gynesis, despite its radical potential, is coopted to serve the interests of male-dominated culture.[7] In the following reading of *Homage*, I argue that Berryman harks back to Puritan attitudes in a gynetic identification with Bradstreet as "woman," which ultimately becomes a reactionary appropriation and erasure of women that reinscribes a patriarchal ideology of masculinity and, in some ways, prefigures the troubled privileging of the feminine of Berryman's postmodern literary and critical brethren.

In 1648, Anne Bradstreet's brother-in-law, John Woodbridge, took a manuscript of her poems to London and had them published without her knowledge or consent. Though this was the first volume of poetry by a single author to come out of the New World, Woodbridge could not bring himself to name Bradstreet a poet. The title of the volume styles the unknown author as *The Tenth Muse, lately Sprung up in America*. But Bradstreet, whose own relationship with the nine sisters of antiquity was uneasy at best, knew that Muses are not poets. The Muse-poet relationship has always been a particularly vexed site of power relations.[8] Up until recently, and certainly in the seventeenth century, it was a rigorously heterosexual relation: muses were female, poets were male. Thus, in naming Bradstreet the "tenth muse," Woodbridge deliberately attempted to manage the threat of a woman quietly defying her culture's double messages about women's capabilities and roles by putting her back into a feminine place. He does this by attributing to her a status higher than that of mere poet, a mythic, even goddess-like, and controlling status. But every woman who has been put on a pedestal knows that this kind of deification is disarming, for it has the effect of denying her the status of subject, speaker, agent, or author.

Berryman employs a similar strategy in his "homage." His allegation that Bradstreet "chose" him suggests, in the spiritual/erotic language in which male poets traditionally addressed their earthly muses, that the power to choose was all on her side. But this courtly discourse is an ancient mode of equivocation. By calling his poem an "homage," he implies that he puts himself under obligation to a figure whom he reveres and also wants to flatter. But Berryman publicly denies his interest in Bradstreet's poetry and asserts instead his interest in her "as a woman"—an "interest" that becomes palpably sexual and manipulative in the middle section of the poem when the male poet's voice enters into dialogue with Bradstreet's voice. Abruptly, the male poet announces, "I have earned the right to be alone with you," to which the Bradstreet voice responds, "What right can that be? / Convulsing, if you love, enough, like a sweet lie" (27.6–8). It seems clear from her response, that "Bradstreet"—and thus her creator, Berryman—recognizes the "sweet lie" in her wooer's rhetoric. The tropes of courtly praise and the equivocal self-abnegation of an homage have always been a polite mask for sometimes illicit sexual desire and a pretext to sexual domination. Ironically, the response and resistance Berryman fashions for his "Bradstreet" indicate a self-consciousness about masculine strategies of domination. His desire to make them public does not, however, result in critique, but in reaffirmation of their effectiveness and his "rights" to them.

Like Bradstreet's brother-in-law's elevating her to the status of Muse, Berryman's equivocal "homage" recognizes and de-authorizes at the same time. The modern appropriation seems more insidious, however, because Berryman dismisses Bradstreet's poetic productions and then is free to raid and deploy them at will. Furthermore, his success in recreating Bradstreet can be measured by the number of critics who use his poem as a guide to Bradstreet's work. Hyatt Waggoner, for example, recommends reading Berryman's poem as an introduction to Bradstreet's poetry and to themes and images particularly "American" (8). Elizabeth Wade White, Bradstreet's most recent biographer, endorses Waggoner's recommendation because, she argues, the strangely wrenched syntax, psychological method, and historical setting of the poem seem to bring the woman and her environment eloquently to life. Neither seems disturbed by the ventriloquistic nature of her voice, the appropriation of her life, or the unsavory central action of the poem. They do not question the male poet's assumption that he can claim the right to be alone with "Bradstreet" because, like all the other Beatrices and Lauras of the male tradition, she is his creation, a figure who has sprung from his imagination and his desire, over whom—in the poetic sphere—he has total control. Berryman exercised this control by distorting the historical facts of Bradstreet's life to suit his own purposes.[9]

The sexual politics implied in the title are supported by the biographical context of Berryman's life and the poem's composition. Several critics argue that Berryman's *Homage* was motivated by the guilt he felt over his own compulsive adulterous affairs. Luke Spenser traces Berryman's ambivalent feelings about his strong-willed mother and her marital in-

fidelities (354–55). Sarah Provost points out that the technical and creative breakthrough represented by *Homage* was preceded by another major
work, *Sonnets to Chris*, which depict the poet at the mercy of a flamboy-
ant woman called "Lise" with whom he had an obsessive and humiliating
affair in 1947. Finally released from his compulsion to compose poetry to
and about "Lise," he cast around for a subject that would allow him to
fathom the tumultuous experience — in publishable form. In the middle of
1948 he wrote the first eleven lines of *Homage* but could go no further. For
the next five years, he read and researched, finishing the poem in an anguished burst of creativity. Comparing the two works, Provost argues that
the figure of Bradstreet is a tempered and pliant version of "Lise" (71).
Thus, in his poetic rendition of the "real" affair, Berryman construed himself as the victim and fool, while in the later, "idealized" affair with his
compliant creation he maintains rigorous control of events as well as his
writing. Berryman's Bradstreet is, by contrast to "Lise" and the women
poets crowding the postwar literary scene, the sign of an earlier version
of masculine power, one that does not call into question traditional gender roles: intensely womanly, patient to a fault, and faithful. Not only is
she the colonial foremother of "American" poetry, but she is also a woman
deeply committed to motherhood, a fact that Berryman will appropriate
as a metaphor for male poetic creativity. For it is precisely the *difference*
of gender that entices and challenges Berryman, a difference he wants to
maintain, exploit, and transcend all at the same time.

But despite the importance of difference for Berryman's project, there
exist complicating identifications between the modern male poet and the
colonial female one. Several critics discuss this identification in terms of
Yeatsian masks (Holden, Haffenden) and suggest that "Bradstreet is herself an antithetical self for the poet" (Mazzaro 125). Provost is surprised
to discover that Bradstreet is both Berryman's idealized, quintessentially
feminine mistress and the persona through which he projects his own
struggles with guilt, creativity, and God. The notion of Yeatsian antithesis, however, does not adequately address the gender politics of Berryman's
gynesis. Several aspects of the poem illustrate this gynesis and its connection to Puritan gynesis, especially Berryman's handling of the different
voices and the means of their dialoguing. For example, at the very beginning, Berryman projects himself upon the deck of the *Arbella* as it landed in
Boston harbor on a windy day in 1630. The poet's voice modulates into the
Bradstreet voice through a repetition of first-person pronouns: "I come to
check, / I come to stay with you, / and the Governor, & Father, & Simon,
& the huddled men" (4.6–8). In the first line, the male poet imposes upon
"Bradstreet" as yet another dominating, restraining male presence in her
life in a hierarchy that is enumerated in the third line — governor, father,

husband, males. This is only his first link with the Puritan patriarchy. In the middle line, the subject and object, "I" and "you," are ambiguous and in direct relation; this is the fleeting moment of identity that is dispelled by the lines surrounding it. Berryman then quotes Bradstreet's well-known words from a letter to her children that record her resistance and resignation to the Puritan and masculine direction of her fate: "my heart   rose, but I did submit" (7.8). But again he acts in concert with Puritan governor, father, husband, males by having her embrace the conventional Puritan notion that women must suffer restraint as protection from the temptations of the devil, of heresy, as well as from the lure of their own impulses: "I must be disciplined, / in arms, against that one, and our dissidents, and myself" (11.7–8).

"Bradstreet's" patience and pliability are exaggerated; Berryman imagines her waiting dutifully in heaven for her husband, who outlived her by thirty years, and likewise waiting several centuries for him to "summon" her from the past (1.3–4; 3.2). Such exaggeration leads to a masochistic submission to male authority that the poem highly eroticizes in what amounts to a perverse celebration of female embodiment and a painful, futile awareness of the oppression that results. In recounting the arrangement of her marriage, she says "That year for my sorry face / so-much-older Simon burned, / so Father smiled, with love. Their will be done" (14.3–5). This Christ-like obedience has a barely sublimated erotic energy, epitomized in her declaration of faith: "I kissed his Mystery" (14.8). Later in the poem, after "Bradstreet" has consented to the "affair" with the modern poet and is consumed with guilt and shame, she imagines her damnation and recalls the devil's promise to spare woman if she agrees to be his tool. But with a painful insight she realizes the uniformly oppressive nature of male power, and cries: "Father of lies, / a male great pestle smashes / small women swarming towards the mortar's rim in vain" (37.6–8). Here Berryman allows his character to recognize and condemn her oppressors while at the same time acknowledging her vulnerability; God, father, and devil coalesce into a looming phallic pestle that grinds helpless, ant-like women into a powder.[10] Her God is not paternally benevolent but sadistic, continually sending her physical chastisements to amend her errant soul. As she ages, and is beset with poor health, the death of children, the burning of her house, she says, "I look. I bear to look. Strokes once more his rod" (50.8), as God satisfies himself in a barely concealed display of phallic power. Yet she begs, "torture me, Father, lest not I be thine!" (39.1).

Berryman's gynesis of identity and difference is further illustrated by the manner in which the male poet enters "Bradstreet's" world. To do so he fantasizes that he must, like the Puritan fathers (including Bradstreet's own father), displace a very powerful, masculine, and thus threatening, female friend: Anne Hutchinson. Hutchinson was the woman most feared by the early Puritan leadership, and her defeat gave them the opportunity to further restrict female visibility and speech. In a tactical move, Berryman portrays Hutchinson as Bradstreet's closest friend, though their sisterhood is based not on strength or resistance, but on the experience of victimization. Though there is little historical basis for this friendship, the connection allows Berryman to replay the repressive authoritarianism of the Puritan fathers. As "Bradstreet" mourns Hutchinson's isolation and exile, crying, "Bitter sister, victim, I miss you," the voice of the male poet interrupts her and the first dialogue of the seduction ensues, their voices alternating, beginning with the male poet's:

> —I miss you, Anne,
> day or night weak as a child,
> tender & empty, doomed, quick to no tryst.
> —I hear you. Be kind, you who leaguer
> my image in the mist.
> —Be kind you, to one unchained eager far & wild
>
> and if, O my love, my heart is breaking, please
> neglect my cries and I will spare you. Deep
> in Time's grave, Love's, you lie still.
> Lie still.
>
> (25.3–26.4)

Echoing her words of empathy, implying a previous acquaintance, and playing upon her "motherly" instincts by comparing himself in his weakness to a child, he imposes his own projected need between the two women. Berryman's note to this passage is illuminating. Speaking of the male poetic voice, he says, "He is enabled to speak, at last, in the fortune of an echo of her—and when she is loneliest (her former spiritual adviser having deserted Anne Hutchinson, and this her closest friend banished), as if she had summoned him; and only thus, perhaps, is she enabled to hear him." The fantasy at work here—a familiar one—is the heterosexist displacement of strong female associations and female desire for abusive male attention. Notice that the male voice comes into speech as an "echo" of the female voice's need, "as if *she* had summoned *him*" (my emphasis), and as if the continuation of his attentions is dependent on her desires. A *fantasy* of female power (voice, desire) underlies this effacing gynetic appropriation and display of linguistic male power.[11]

Despite his ostensible "need," Berryman barely conceals his aggression toward women in the poem. The above passage contains a pattern of words the male poet uses repeatedly, as does his Puritan antecedent John Winthrop, to put woman back in her place. Describing his vision of Bradstreet at rest in "Time's grave," he notes her peacefulness—"you lie still"—and

advises her (against his own urgings) to dismiss his suit and "Lie still"—
that is, remain peacefully at rest in the past. The word "still" also occurs
three times in stanza one and twice in the final stanza. It suggests remaining in a place, motionless, like a still pool or fixed like a "still" photograph,
silent, subdued, or hushed, quiet and tranquil. As an adverb "still" describes an on-going condition. The conflation of adjectival and adverbial
meanings calls up Keats's strangely applicable and subliminally sinister invocation of his Grecian urn, "Thou still unravish'd bride of quietness." At
the same time as the male poet imagines "Bradstreet" peaceful and silent
in the past and wants her to remain that way as a source of constancy for
him, he is maneuvering to drag her into the tumult of adulterous passion,
unquiet speech, and breach of faith. When "still" is applied to the verb
"lie," the gentle imperative "Lie still" takes on threatening implications
of enforced silence or immobility and continuing deception; recall "Bradstreet" 's earlier recognition of the "sweet lie" of "convulsing" love.

The threat surfaces more openly when "Bradstreet" fulfills the poet's
ambivalent desires and asks to be touched, kissed, talked to. Then, in what
Berryman describes as "an only half-subdued aria-stanza" ("Changes" 101),
his love song takes on explicitly aggressive forms:

> —It is Spring's New England. Pussy willows wedge
> up in the wet. Milky crestings, fringed
> yellow, in heaven, eyed
> by the melting hand-in-hand or mere
> desirers single, heavy-footed, rapt,
> make surge poor human hearts. Venus is trapt—
> the hefty pike shifts, sheer—
> in Orion blazing. Warblings, odours, nudge to an edge—
> (31.1–8)

The erotically charged, wet, and burgeoning world of New England spring
fills the poet's heart at the moment he achieves his conquest. But this fades
rapidly into a threatening nightsky world with intimations of conflict between Venus, the goddess of love, formerly a menacing carnivorous plant,
and Orion, a mythic giant and hunter who terrorized the sisters known as
the Pleiades and was eventually slain by Artemis. Venus, who once slyly
trapped men in her "engines" (see Bradstreet's "An Elegy upon . . . Philip
Sidney," l. 27), is now herself trapped by Orion's sharp pikes, and the stars
have become weapons. By the end of this stanza, love is a prisoner and
the sounds and smells of nature that "rapt" Bradstreet and brought her a
glimpse of heaven (see her "Contemplations" ll. 8–15), bring the lovers to
a dangerous precipice.

In the course of their bizarre intimacy, the male poet confesses to mur-
derous feelings and an unrestrained "western lust" that fills his mind with

images of Nazi atrocities: "I trundle the bodies, on the iron bars, / over that fire backward & forth; they burn; / bits fall. I wonder if / *I* killed them. Women serve my turn" (33.2; 34.1-4).[12] "Dreams!" responds his generous mistress; "You are good," she tells him despite all evidence to the contrary, and prays to her God for "mercy for him and me" (34.5; 39.3). Still, he is torn by unbelief. While she can affirm that "God awaits us," he is despondent. "I cannot feel myself God waits" (34.8-35.1), he admits, expressing the dark heart of his fears, which leads to an unexpected enactment of a ritual mutilation of the woman's body:

> Man is entirely alone
> may be. I am a man of griefs & fits
> trying to be my friend. And the brown smock splits,
> down the pale flesh a gash
> broadens and Time holds up your heart against my eyes.
> (35.4-8)

While the speaker doesn't quite believe that the world is devoid of God ("may be"), he implies that he is far from any source of meaning. The next image, a kind of caesarian birth performed on "Bradstreet" 's brown-smocked body by "Time," images forth the effects of his wrenching doubt. Perhaps her faith is unbelievable; perhaps she, his creation, is unbelievable, and he requires visual evidence, her heart—seat of her emotions and faith—delivered up to him. There is also a sense in which time measures her heart (faith) against his eyes (skepticism) and finds him wanting. The excision of her heart, a violation of her body and metaphorical theft of her soul, can be read as an emblem of how in his doubt he has forced her open in an "unnatural" birth where her sex becomes a Christ-like gash, a wound, yet still the only way to her heart, her faith, to that which he does not and cannot possess except through violence. To be loved and known, woman must be sacrificed.

By contrast, Berryman has "Bradstreet" narrate her bodily decline and impending death in sexual terms that contradict the forced, adulterous opening: "Light notes leap, a beckon, swaying / the tilted, sickening ear within. I'll—I'll— / I am closed & coming. Somewhere! I defile / wide as a cloud, in a cloud, / unfit, desirous, glad—" (53.4-8). In an ecstasy of eschatological desire, her body seems to evaporate into the air. But the male poet retains his relentless preoccupation with her body, and reserves for himself the details of her burial, sending her off with imagery alternately tender and grotesque:

> —You are not ready? You áre ready. Pass,
> as shadow gathers shadow in the welling night.
> Fireflies of childhood torch

> you down. We commit our sister down.
> One candle mourn by, which a lover gave,
> the use's edge and order of her grave.
> Quiet? Moisture shoots.
> Hungry throngs collect. They sword into the carcass.
>   (54.1–8)

The movement here is resolutely downward, and the emphasis falls on
"Bradstreet"'s deceased body, not on transcendence or her released soul.
The contradictory image of fireflies "torching" her to her final rest captures his need to return her to a childlike status, diminutive and fanciful —
a small body that glows intermittently. Distancing himself, his voice takes
on the detached tones of a preacher addressing mourners. Then, with a
kind of Marvellian glee, he watches as the "hungry throngs" of worms
pierce her body. Marvell's mistress was more "coy," but her body was just
as indispensable to satisfy the poet's lust for power, immortality, song.

However, just as "Bradstreet"'s imaginary body is the locus for the male
poet's aggression, it provides her with an identity and power he covets. According to Berryman's own account, "the moment of the poem's supreme
triumph" is the birth of "Bradstreet"'s first child ("Changes" 101), a passage that must be set against the forced birth cited above. The tension,
rhythm, and emotions accelerate in an extended, hallucinatory description
of labor:

>   everything down
>   hardens I press with horrible joy down
>   my back cracks like a wrist
>   . . . .
>   I work thrust I must free
>   now I all muscles & bones concentrate
>   what is living from dying?

Then, just as she can no longer endure,

>   it passes the wretched trap whelming and I am me
>   drencht & powerful, I did it with my body!
>   One proud tug greens Heaven. Marvellous,
>   unforbidding Majesty.
>   Swell, imperious bells. I fly.
>   Mountainous, woman not breaks and will bend:
>   sways God nearby: anguish comes to an end.
>   Blossomed Sarah, and I
>   blossom . . . .
>   (19.5–7; 20.1–3; 20.8–21.1–8)

In this irreducibly female and quintessentially feminine experience, "Bradstreet" finds herself competent, powerful, and blessed by God. Through
motherhood, "Bradstreet" eludes the trap of sinful love. Her refuge from

the harsh and oppressive world is her "Beloved household" (22.1) where her delight in her children reenforces her sense of identity: "When by me in the dusk my child sits down / I am myself," she declares peacefully, echoing the declaration of selfhood through birth: "I am me . . . I did it with my body!" (42.1-2). By comparison, "The proportioned, spiritless poems accumulate. / And they publish them / away in brutish London, for a hollow crown" (42.6-8). Literary notoriety for woman is barbarous, worldly. Here, Berryman reimposes on "Bradstreet" the same split that male-dominated Puritan culture imposed on creative women, and that Bradstreet's poetic productions belie: the split between procreativity and artistic creativity. For, in the end, "Evil dissolves, & love, like foam; / that love. Prattle of children powers me home" (39.6-7). "That love" is the adulterous, evil love with which she is tempted; her mother-love allows her to resist her "demon-lover's" blandishments and return to domestic fidelity and religious hope.[13]

In the poem's coda, "Bradstreet"'s resistance to temptation and her achievement of identity are contrasted to the poet's damning declaration of selfhood, in which he ruefully admits to being corrupt and dark:

> I am a closet of secrets dying,
> races murder, foxholes hold men,
> reactor piles wage slow upon the wet brain rime.
> (55.6-8)

Resonating suggestively with the gender politics at work in the poem, this passage associates the male poet's own moral corruption and spiritual emptiness with the decline of modern, postwar society, the rabidity of racist nationalism, and the abuse of nuclear power. This declaration of male subjectivity is rife with the corruptive effects of what is repressed and undisclosed. The masculine psyche is a "closet" whose secret contents are ultimately destructive on a personal as well as a broader political level. In Bradstreet's times, a "closet" was a small private room to which one retreated for private religious meditation; however, we cannot ignore the contemporary connotation of the term, which suggests that Berryman understood that the effects of gynesis were not merely personal but more broadly cultural: to make real women invisible and unthreatening, thereby reenforcing male dominance and facilitating homosocial male bonding.

The triumph of body, will, and faith here is woman's. Despite the male poet's relentless imposition of control, he can only experience these triumphs by appropriating them. In fact, Bradstreet had the children *and* the poems; after much suffering and doubt, she achieved a hard-won faith. Furthermore, "Lise" left Berryman to return to her husband and child (Provost 77). Berryman recreates Bradstreet not simply as an object of love or lust but also as a wishful recreation of himself, empowered by the physical exertion of birth, which he can only experience vicariously, as the "couvade" of poetic creation.[14] By inhabiting her body, he can imagine the "proud tug" that "greens Heaven," and the unqualified love that overcomes devious lust. By speaking through her voice he can try on the beliefs he cannot sustain in his own world, quieting his own doubts with a faith that would elude him for many years. In a note he typed up for the ending of *Homage*, he explained, "Upon her turn away from evil, with her help, *he* finally turns" (qtd. in Haffenden 28; Berryman's emphasis). And by projecting his shameful desires onto her, and watching her agony and redemption, the male poet can exorcise his guilt publicly and be expiated. Despite homages and honorifics, and the trappings of Puritanism, modernism, or postmodernism, female visibility, independence, and agency are once again sacrificed for the spiritual, critical, and rhetorical advancement of the male.

Notes

I would like to thank the editors for their helpful comments, and Dana Nelson for her astute reading and suggestions.

1. See Bordo for a discussion of Descartes's determining "flight to objectivity," "a compensatory turning toward the *paternal* for legitimation through external regulation, transcendent values, and the authority of law," and away from "the *maternal*—the immanent realms of earth, nature, the authority of the body" (58).

2. Spenser, whose analysis of the poem appeared in 1994 (well after my initial reading in *Work* but remarkably close to mine), makes a similar argument. Though he finds "many moments of dramatic power, even empathy" with the Puritan woman's experience, "there is also a current of feeling that seeks to colonize Anne Bradstreet as a 'mistress,' with as much rhetorical insistence as Bradstreet's fellow (male) colonists established their authority over Massachusetts" (356).

3. For a more complete discussion, see Schweitzer, *Work*, especially chapter 1.

4. Compare Winthrop's remarks to the General Court of Massachusetts: "a true wife accounts her subjection her honor and freedom, and would not think her condition safe and free, but in her subjection to her husband's authority" (*Winthrop's* 239).

5. See Romans 8:15-17. "Sonship," Samuel Willard said, proceeds from "our Marriage to Christ; so that by becoming his Spouse . . . we are made the Children of God" (qtd. in Morgan, *Puritan* 165).

6. This point is echoed in Rotundo's conclusion. For more on the suppression or negation of woman in Puritanism, see Ong and, from the perspective of French postmodernism, Jean-Joseph Goux, who argues that "*the* founding fantasy" of Western culture is "the active negation of the Mother" (qtd. in Jardine 32).

7. Jardine differentiates between contemporary instances of gynesis and concludes that the Anglo-American version is reactionary, concerned primarily with reenforcing the status quo (231-36). This supports my argument about Berryman's gynesis; however, Jardine anchors her speculation in the different symbolic econo-

mies constructed by Protestant democracies and a Catholic monarchy. Berryman's later conversion to Catholicism complicates any simple or reductive attribution of ideological content.

8. DeShazer surveys the literary history of the Muse of male as well as female poets. See pp. 1–44.

9. See Holden, who catalogues the discrepancies between the poem's historical claims and Berryman's major source for Bradstreet's life and circumstances, the already semifictional biography by Helen Campbell, *Anne Bradstreet and her Time* (1891). For other critical views that do not condemn Berryman's effacing procedures, see C. Johnson; Provost, who (eerily echoing Winthrop's attitudes about women) says the finale of *Homage* "restores the woman to her proper place . . . serv[ing] to further, rather than hinder, the poet's work" (73); and Rich's reversal of her 1967 claim that *Homage* is a great poem. For feminist interpretations, see Watts, who calls the poem "macho" (34 n.4); Ostriker, who concludes "that Berryman created, out of his own yearning, a lover-anima-muse figure who would never be seen as a colleague, collaborator, or equal" (26–27); and Gilbert and Gubar, who also find that despite Berryman's ostensible reverence for Bradstreet he, like fellow poets Roethke and Lowell who celebrate female contemporaries, has "made a critical gesture that suggests some measure of hostility toward literary women" (158).

10. No one has pointed out that this startling image without the gender specificity occurs in Bradstreet's poetry and prose, for example, in her letter to her children: "when I have been in sickness and pain, I have thought if the Lord would but lift up the light of His countenance upon me, although He ground me to powder, it would be but light to me" (*Works* 243), and in Meditation 19: "Corn, till it have past through the mill and been ground to powder, is not fit for bread. God so deals with his servants: he grinds them with grief and pain til they turn to dust, and then are they fit manchet for his mansion" (*Works* 275).

11. In an interview, Berryman comments: "I decided to tempt her. I could only do this in a fantasy; the problem was to make the fantasy believable" (Stitt 196).

12. Between *Sonnets* and *Homage*, Berryman worked on a series of poems concerning victims of the Holocaust entitled *The Black Book*, which he abandoned because the topic was too painful. During this period he also had recurring dreams in which he killed women (Provost, 70, 78; Haffenden 19).

13. Berryman describes the voices' dialogue as "a sort of extended witch-seductress and demon-lover bit" ("Changes" 101).

14. Berryman's wife at the time, Eileen Simpson, records in her memoir that when Berryman finished the passage on Bradstreet's delivery, he threw himself down and said, "Well, I'm exhausted. I've been going through the couvade. The little monster nearly killed *me*" (226). Provost points out that accounts of Berryman's creative process repeatedly compare it to birth-throes. She argues that the "children" he wanted were his poems, birthed as women birth children, but at their expense (76). Mancini analyzes Berryman's "couvade consciousness" from an "archetypal" perspective and thus ignores the gender politics. I agree with Friedman, who argues that "Men's use of the metaphor [of childbirth] begins in distance from and attraction to the Other" and appears to be a "tribute to woman's special generative powers" but is ultimately "an appropriation of women's (pro)creativity [because it] subtly helps to perpetuate the confinement of women to procreation" (84).

PART TWO

"The Disturbed Eyes Rise / Furtive, Foiled, Dissatisfied"

The Rebellion Against Calvinism

ALIKI BARNSTONE

Mastering the Master
Emily Dickinson's Appropriation of Crisis Conversion

Let Emily sing for you because she cannot pray. —Emily Dickinson (L 278) [1]

Emily Dickinson's religion was Poetry. —Susan Howe, *My Emily Dickinson*, 48

The old words are numb —*and there* a'nt *any* new *ones* —*Brooks* —*are useless* —*in* Freshet-time
—Emily Dickinson (L 252)

ON THE OUTSKIRTS of the city of Madison, Wisconsin, where I once lived, a sign in front of a farm reads, "All the world guilty before God." The Puritan tradition of guilt and original sin, familiar to Emily Dickinson, has sustained its power for a long time.

In Calvinism the world is vanity and the human soul lowly and despicable, but at least the individual has direct access to the Lord—without papal intermediary. Dickinson found the hierarchical relationship with the divinity, wherein the abject soul is unequal, suspect and even intolerable. While she maintained an agonizing discourse with the Master, whom she believed had excluded her from the circle of the elect, she never granted him mastery by accepting a humble and condemned state. Indeed, to the Wisconsin farmer who proclaims, "All the world guilty before God," she might dare ask if God himself is the guilty party: "Whether Deity's guiltless / My business is, to find!" (P 178). So Emily Dickinson talked with the Master but rejected the orthodox premise for the conversation. This intense dialogue, on her terms and with her guiltless lexicon, became her poetry. Because Dickinson invents a language beyond orthodoxy and tradition, one that relies on heterodoxy, ambiguity, and fragmentation, her work, even more than that of her contemporary Walt Whitman, marks the beginning of American modernism.

Dickinson is a religious poet and an appropriator of religious language, who paradoxically excludes the vocabulary of sin from her work. Like Emerson, Dickinson rejects the tenet of original sin, as shown by the virtual absence in her poetry of the words "evil," "sin," and "guilt." When she uses them, she does so satirically. In the poem beginning "The Bible in an antique Volume— / Written by faded men," she mockingly writes that sin is "a distinguished Precipice / Others must resist" (P 1545).

By excluding sin from her vocabulary, however, Dickinson excludes herself from the faith of her family and community. Though each of her family members converted, entering the First Congregational Church through professions of faith, Emily never did. To have joined the faith would have meant having a crisis conversion wherein the self sees its own absolute sinfulness. In this crisis the self is annihilated and submits to divine will. But Dickinson maintained her worldliness, as when she writes, "The mysteries of human nature surpass the 'mysteries of redemption.'" She was an outsider, resisting the religious revivals of her time and her education at the evangelical Mount Holyoke Seminary:

How lonely this world is growing, something so desolate creeps over the spirit and we don't know it's [sic] name, and it won't go away, either Heaven is seeming greater, or Earth a great deal more small, or God is more "Our Father," and we feel our need increased. Christ is calling everyone here, all my companions have answered. . . . I cant [sic] tell you *what* they have found, but *they* think it is something precious. I wonder if it *is*? How strange is this sanctification, that works such a marvelous change, that sows in such corruption, and rises in golden glory, that brings Christ down, and shews him, and lets him select his friends! (L 35)

The letter asserts that she has chosen not to join the flock. She is skeptical about what her companions have found, and that skepticism leads to satire. Dickinson makes fun of the notions of status and size, casting perception into doubt. Heaven *seems* greater and earth smaller. God is a greater father while humanity feels its need increased in the face of its own lowliness. The people around her think they have found "something precious," but Dickinson questions the value of their truth, pointing out that the hierarchy is perceived by some but not by others; she casts her uncertainty in the telling understatement: "I wonder if it *is*." Yet her friends' perception of Christ's ascendancy gives him his power and "lets him select his friends" (while presumably excluding the unelect). The letter also reveals Dickinson's loneliness. That her friends and family converted gave her a double sorrow, for she was shut out of love in two ways: Christ did not come down and "select" her for a friend, and her earthly friends who stood with Christ abandoned her, for they, with the other elect, would be together on the other side. Conversion became something "desolate that creeps over the spirit." It is through satire that Dickinson contends with this desolation, with election's pain-inflicting companions: loss and exclusion.

The tone of the above 1850 letter — also the year her first poem is dated — combines satirical whimsy with lament. And in the poems written in this first stage of her career, she similarly satirizes election from the vantage of her own exclusion. Fighting off her cultural inheritance, an outsider, she sets her language apart from the voices she mocks, frequently framing the mocked voices in quotation marks, as in the humorous lines:

> What is "Paradise" —
> Who live there —
> Are they "Farmers" —
> Do they "hoe" —
> (P 215)

In this poem, as in many early poems, she asks "What is what we call 'Paradise'"? She questions those who imagine the mystery of an afterlife in the terms of familiar social categories.

In another early poem, she transforms prayer into a jesting nursery rhyme:

> Papa above!
> Regard a mouse
> O'erpowered by the Cat!
> Reserve within thy kingdom
> A "Mansion" for the Rat!
> (P 61)

The tone of the line "A 'Mansion' for the Rat!" mixes outrage with the ominous and even the grotesque. This stanza lowers the reverent diction of "Our father who art in heaven" to the familiar and rather taunting "Papa above!" For the lowly mouse, who asks the overpowering cat for notice and a place in the kingdom of mansions, election is not only exclusionary and hierarchical, but predatory. Barton Levi St. Armand writes that "Dickinson constructed a closed imagistic world in which she assumed the role of victim, toyed with by an aloof cat-god who possessed the power of imparting or withholding sanctifying grace" (166). Since she is the victim and he the cat-god persecutor, he remains outside herself; she can wittily dismiss him and repay him for his exclusion with exclusion. As she says in another poem beginning "Going to Heaven" (P 79), "I'm glad I don't believe it." As these poems show, Dickinson is able in her early poems to set her language apart from the voices she satirizes; she is engaged in an externalized battle with her cultural inheritance.

These early satirical poems culminate in 1862, when she internalizes the battle and begins the second period of her career. She has what one might call a grand intertextual experience; when she writes, "The Brain is wider than the Sky / . . . / The one the other will contain / With ease —

and You—beside—" (P 632), she observes that the text of the world forms the text of her mind. Dickinson, always critical of hierarchy, recognized that the masculine dominates both the religious and the literary tradition. Accordingly, her "Master," whether man or God (there is much critical speculation), also becomes an internal problem. Now, rather than regarding Calvinism as a foe she can control with satire, she acknowledges the potentials of her faith and that she must subdue the internal imperative to convert. By transforming the critical religious experience of crisis conversion into poetic practice, she achieves mastery over the Calvinist forces in herself. She emerges from this ecstatic visionary encounter not with prayer but with poems. In a letter she affirms her conversion to poetry: "Let Emily sing for you because she cannot pray" (L 278). Susan Howe observes, succinctly, "Emily Dickinson's religion was Poetry" (48).

As a consequence of her internal combat with her religious and cultural inheritance, in 1862 numbness emerges as one of Dickinson's primary poetic modes. So much internalization inevitably leads to self-division. The pain is so great that the self dislocates from itself, or it stands as two or more selves, or it dies inside itself. In the poems I call the "numb" poems, she appropriates the self-exiling theology of crisis conversion. In conversion the self must be numb to its own sensations and to its attraction to the vanity of the world. This numbness is a kind of dissolution because the self must separate from its sensory parts. Thus, Dickinson observes that the saved man "hath endured / The dissolution—in Himself" (539). Internal forces rage, paining her, overwhelming, dividing, and ultimately numbing her. This numbing is frequently an inner death. Or the self is dislocated or multiple. She depicts her self-division relentlessly, as the first lines of these famous poems show:

I felt a Funeral, in my Brain (P 280).
I got so I could take his name / Without Tremendous gain / That Stop-sensation—on my Soul (P 293).
After great pain, a formal feeling comes (P 341).
I felt my life with both my hands / To see if it was there (P 351).
There's a Languor in the life / More imminent than Pain (P 396).
The Soul has Bandaged moments— (P 512).
Pain—has an Element of Blank— (P 650).

In these numb poems, as in conversion, the self is numb to itself. Because Dickinson contains the self-exiling theology of crisis conversion in the poems, they are a form of mastery—a mastery of containment through language.

The numb poems follow the pattern of Calvinist crisis conversion, in which the self is annihilated to be reborn in God, but they do so with a twist: they achieve self-conversion. Dickinson's mastery means annihilating the self to transform it into art. By mastering the text of orthodoxy, she outwits the Word who is God, and she is reborn into Poetry. Because Dickinson internalizes the visionary religious experience of crisis conversion but does not enter the faith, she converts the language of orthodoxy and the language of the genre. The failure for her of religious orthodoxy also leads to the failure of conventional form and to her triumph in poetic innovation. Her language exceeds conventional boundaries because, as she writes in a letter to Thomas Wentworth Higginson, she is not the subject of a ruler; she has annihilated the governing language of sin and abjectness: "I had no Monarch in my life, and cannot rule myself, and when I try to organize—my little Force explodes—and leaves me bare and charred—" (L 271). Sixty years before Eliot's *The Waste Land*, Emily Dickinson, in a numb desolation in which no monarch prevails, creates an intensely personal idiolect and radical poetics, all of which bloom in her own protomodernism.

In the second stage of her career, Dickinson believes that the boundaries of the self are fluid. Her famous statement, "My business is circumference," refers to the necessity and difficulty of delineating the self. The cultural inheritance that she so caustically fought, she now perceives is contained inside herself. The battle continues internally. Accordingly, in this David and Goliath allegory, she regards her earlier assaults as self-destructive:

> I took my Power in my Hand—
> And went against the World—
>
> . . . .
> I aimed my Pebble—but Myself
> Was all the one that fell—
> (P 450)

To hold in so many internal forces causes pain, overwhelms, and ultimately numbs her. In the poems, this numbing is frequently an inner death. The business of circumference (with its attendant pain and numbness) has, in this second period in her poetry, become her crucial and most agonizing concern. The poems that recount pain—with this wavering circumference and the deadening of that pain—frequently have a male figure as the source of the soul's dilemma. For example, in "I got so I could take his name" (which plays on "taking the Lord's name in vain"), it is a "He" who causes "That Stop-sensation—on my Soul." In some numb poems, there are two internal male figures—one godly, one demonic—vying to conquer the soul. In "The Soul has Bandaged Moments—" a personified thought, "a Goblin," accosts another personified thought, the "Lover," who is "a Theme so fair." In " 'Twas like a Maelstrom, with a notch," the masculine figures are more specifically godly and demonic:

And not a Sinew—stirred—could help,
And sense was setting numb—
When God—remembered—and the Fiend—
Let go, then, overcome—
(P 414)

This vast and embattled self has particular significance for Calvinist election. First, even though Dickinson may have chosen not to heed Christ's call, she reveals that the internal imperative to do so remains. Second, this self with its compromised boundaries corresponds to what the soul must endure in the conversion process. The Calvinist self, like the self in Dickinson's numb poems, will be divided, self-annihilated, and overwhelmed. Crisis conversion, as Mitchell Breitwieser writes in his discussion of Cotton Mather, begins with a "severe trauma" in which the self that

flourished in its daily life learned that it persisted only by the arbitrary kindness of God. . . . Mather repeatedly calls it a kind of dying. . . . [I]nstead of persisting in old thoughts, the fledgling was to ponder them. A part of thought would step out of self and look upon it. It would see two things: sin, that is the baseness and vanity of self; and its inability to correct error. (28–29)

Once the self is annihilated and thereby utterly submissive to divine will, "the law can be seen clearly" and "the mind can rise to survey the whole pattern in which it has accepted its part" (30).

Cotton Mather, Breitwieser's representative Puritan, strives to give himself to God by abasing consciousness. Thus, in his diary he writes, "There is nothing of more Consequence to my Safety and Welfare, than a constant strain, of the most self abasing Humility. Wherefore I would constantly chase all vain Thoughts, and Vainglorious Ones out of my Mind, with the greatest Abhorrence of them" (qtd. in Breitwieser 32). This hunt in which the self is prey is itself a form of consciousness in that it drives out what Dickinson might call "Fiendish" thoughts. By implication, it must maintain the thoughts focused on God, so that, in Dickinson's terms, God will "remember" and the "Fiend—/ Let go, then, overcome."

The Puritan must be always vigilant, for even those who achieve a crisis conversion are not assured of salvation. A perfect assurance, in fact, is considered a sign of the unelect. As Perry Miller writes,

Calvin had wisely advised caution in promising positive assurance, since predestination takes place in the inmost recesses of divine wisdom, where the careless intruder may obtain no satisfaction, "but will enter a labyrinth from which he shall find no way to depart." To him it seemed unreasonable that men should scrutinize what the Lord had hidden in Himself. . . . (*New England* 1939, 370)

Edmund S. Morgan, in a further complication of the labyrinth, writes, "This was the constant message of Puritan preachers: in order to be sure one must be unsure" (*Visible* 70).

Dickinson's doubt goes beyond orthodox uncertainty. She internalizes the conflict—and its attendant doubt—that before was externalized. The numb poems fight dual internal battles: one the Calvinist battle against the self and the other against a cultural inheritance urging just such conversion. For example, the enigmatic poem "Me from Myself—to banish—" (P 642) is a model for Dickinson's transformation of crisis conversion into poetry; it can be read both as a prayer for the self-banishment of conversion and as a description of her poetics. The poem, as in the Bible, proceeds by logical parallelism and speaks in riddles. In the Gospel of Mark, when the Twelve ask Jesus why he speaks in parables he answers that it is to keep the unelect outside, "That seeing they may see, and not perceive; and hearing they may hear, and not understand; lest at any time they should be converted, and *their* sins should be forgiven them" (4:12). In this poem, as in so many others, Dickinson the outsider adopts the strategy of Jesus's parables, in which, as Frank Kermode puts it, "The riddle remains dark, so does the gospel" (*Genesis* 47). Thus, "Me from Myself—to Banish—" poses a riddle that with each line is complicated and questioned, recomplicated and re-questioned; with each articulation, the darkness is intensified, but, as in one of Mark Rothko's dark canvases, there is much to see in the blackness:

> Me from Myself—to banish—
> Had I Art—
> Impregnable my Fortress
> Unto all Heart—
>
> But since Myself—assault Me—
> How have I peace
> Except by subjugating
> Consciousness?
>
> And since We're mutual Monarch
> How this be
> Except Abdication—
> Me—of Me?
> (P 642)

On the one hand, this poem employs the language of Calvinism and expresses Dickinson's desire to convert. On the other hand, the poem turns Calvinist language against itself. Thus, if the questions asked in Dickinson's poem are answered affirmatively, then the poem rehearses the anguish of conversion and advocates banishment, subjugation, and abdication of the self, just as would the Puritan seeking to give herself to God. The assaulted self in Dickinson's poem wants "peace / . . . by subjugating / Consciousness" or, in Mather's terms, must "constantly chase all vain Thoughts" out of mind. Likewise, the self must abdicate its position as ruler in order to be subject to God.

Since one can never be assured of salvation, it is fitting that a Calvinist

reading of "Me from Myself—to banish—" is equivocal. The poem resists theology with its doubting structure in the way each line questions
the previous line. David Porter's observation that Dickinson's poems move
"from belief to questioning and disjunction" (91) is true of the structure
of "Me from Myself," which moves from an assertion in the first stanza to
two questions in the second and third stanzas. The disjunction is in self
from self and, as Dickinson writes in another poem, in "internal difference / Where the Meanings, are" (P 258). That is to say, the first stanza
states that the exaction of conversion is self-banishment and that the desired result is to be invincible to the temptations of the heart. To shut out
the self that cherishes corrupt worldly love would make the speaker free
to accept Christ's love. However, although the poem implies God by the
language of conversion theology, it does not mention God (and as Marianne Moore observes, "Omissions are not accidents"). By omitting God,
Dickinson circles back to the "Fortress" that is "Myself." In this alternative
reading, the double meaning of the pivotal line, "Had I Art," moves away
from the more humble "had I means" and toward the more self-reflexive
"had I Poetry." The self wishes to shut out the love of God, to construct a
fortress of the self that would be impregnable to God's invasive Word. In
the fortress that she constructs with her own human word, God's intrusive
divine Word will not penetrate. In the same moment that the poem seems
to assert faith, it likewise asserts the disjunction in the self-annihilating
requirements of Calvinist conversion. That disjunction turns the poem
toward self-conversion, that is, her conversion to art.

The poem's disjunctive structure is typical of Dickinson's poetic
strategy. Karl Keller writes that Dickinson's

is one of the most remarkable bodies of protest literature we have *against* New
England religion. To the resurgence of Puritanism in her time, her poetry is a formidable veto. . . . Yet she could not escape it. She indeed had what she called "An
Ancient fashioned Heart."
    But this alternating defense and offense creates a tense ambiguity in our under-
standing of her Puritan origins. She stamps her foot at what she stands on. She
yells at the voice she yells with. Like the Brahma, it is with Puritan wings that she
has the power to flee the Puritan past. (67–68)

Seen in this way, the assaulted self in the second stanza is the one that is
attacked by its cultural inheritance; she achieves peace by "subjugating"
the consciousness that contains that inheritance. The poem, then, may be
seeking to banish not the self that resists conversion but the self that is infused with conversion's self-banishing theology.

Once that inheritance has become "subject," however, which self has
achieved ascendancy? The "Me" in the last stanza is a "mutual Monarch,"
who contains all the selves it wishes to "subjugate." The phrase "mutual
Monarch" contains a double dichotomy of four monarchs. The first two are

the ones the poem explicitly names, "Me" and "Me." The second two are
the two immortal masculine forces to which the "Me" might yield: Lucifer,
Prince of Darkness and, as Milton names Him, the "Omnipotent, / Immutable, Immortal, Infinite, / Eternal King . . . Author of all being" (*Paradise
Lost* III: 372–74). "Mutual Monarch" works to hold each of the monarchs
in a horizontal line. Since each monarch is contained in the phrase, no
one of them can rise or abdicate. The rhetorical question at the end of the
poem throws mastery and hierarchical categories into question.

Since the poem ends with a question, it emphasizes the impossibility
of resolution. "Abdication— / Me—of Me" is a formula that mocks the
logic of Calvinist self-annihilation, for to subtract me from me equals
zero. How, after all, can a zero either be saved by the Lord or submit to
him? Thus, the poem addresses the problem of the split self by suggesting that each self is so integrally related to the other that abdication is
impossible. If one returns to the first stanza, one can see that the poem's
impossible formula of self-banishment hinges on the subjunctive "Had I
Art." Art compromises the formula in which self-banishment equals zero
and zero equals numbness. Since the poem is art, it suggests that art is the
path through self-banishment. And since art, not Calvinism, is the result
of this numbness, numbness is the path to art. The poem is the banished
self, an "Impregnable . . . Fortress," that by "subjugating / Consciousness"
has made consciousness its subject. The "Mutual Monarchs," "Me" and
"Me," are the author and the Calvinist text, each subject to the other, and
each author of the other's being.

The poem, then, takes the reader through the steps of a conversion
experience that sincerely searches for the Deity, but ends in union with
poetry rather than with Christ. The self annihilates itself—or attempts
to—but Christ fails to call on the prepared self. Of God, who does not
respond to her fervent supplication, Dickinson bitterly writes in another
poem:

> Of course—I prayed—
> And did God Care?
> He cared as much as on the Air
> A Bird—had stamped her foot—
> And cried "Give Me"—
> (P 376)

Numb poems, such as "Me from Myself—to banish," describe a religious
and artistic practice. Again and again they record a self-banishment that
ends not in conversion but in poetry. These poems, like the experience
of crisis conversion, can be regarded as ecstatic, for *ekstasis* in its Greek
etymology is to be "put out of place," that is to say, to stand outside oneself. The self is moved to some other state. In Dickinson's case, when the
self stands outside, its boundaries can be filled (or expanded) by God or

art. Thus, in Dickinson's lines of numbness ("Pain—has an element of Blank—" [P 650] and "After great pain, a formal feeling comes—" [P 341], for example) the ecstatic religious experience of conversion is an analogy for ecstatic artistic experience. It is Dickinson's art—and not God—that elects her to immortality. I call this practice "self-conversion."

"Me from Myself—to banish" questions the hierarchy of orthodox conversion in which the self must be utterly abased before God's higher Power. The poem also regards love, a crucial component of conversion, as hierarchical; it is a conquest. Thus, the speaker in the poem wishes to be "Impregnable . . . / To all Heart." Like romantic love, the kind of love experienced in conversion could mean an absolute union. But that union is not reciprocal; the self must be so overwhelmed with love that it desires subjugation, even if it means self-extinction. "Conversion," as Susan Howe writes, "is a sort of Death, a falling into Love's powerful attraction" (79). As Cynthia Griffin Wolff points out, conversion was popularly regarded as just such "a falling into Love's powerful attraction": "For the women especially, this Christ Who came to call for them so importunately—offering himself as the 'Bridegroom' of salvation and beseeching them to become 'Brides of Christ' by accepting faith—could be a compelling Suitor" (*Emily* 103). Dickinson makes these connections between conversion and both kinds of love, profane and holy. Since she is always turning toward self-conversion, she, too, is evangelical in the sense that she wants the reader to convert to her. In the following poem, she proclaims that "The Saints" will remember her:

My Holiday, shall be
That They—remember me—
My Paradise—the fame
That They—pronounce my name—
(P 431)

These lines turn the tables on conversion. As in "Me from Myself—to banish," the words simultaneously refer both to salvation and to poetry. The poem, in one reading, is humble; it seeks no other fame than to be able to join the Saints in heaven. In an alternative reading, the poem seems to substitute literary recognition for divine salvation. She may ask for the union of divinity and her subjugate self, but she will settle for the union of the reader and her poem. She will be elected to immortality not by God but by the readers who pronounce her name and who make her poems live.

For all her criticism, Dickinson is not cynical about conversion or love. If conversion were reciprocal, it would indeed be a divine love, a mutual reading in which both selves ecstatically stood aside for the other. We can see this hope in one of Dickinson's most despairing pieces of writing, the second "Master Letter" (which, like most of the numb poems, was written in 1862). Wolff writes that, in this letter, "the microcosm of the lovers assumes the same tragic configuration as the macrocosm that is ruled by God: it is a world desolated by wounding and by the loss of face-to-face communication" (*Emily* 408). Yet, in spite of failed communication, we hear Dickinson implore the Master to *believe*—or, to put it a bit differently —to love her, to convert to her, to *read* her. (The manuscript was written in ink, corrected in pencil; words Dickinson crossed out are in brackets.)

MASTER.
If you saw a bullet hit a Bird—and he told you he was'nt shot—you might weep at his courtesy, but you would certainly doubt his word.
One drop more from the gash that stains your Daisy's bosom—then would you *believe*? Thomas' faith in Anatomy, was stronger than his faith in faith. God made me—[Sir] Master—I did'nt be—myself. I dont know how it was done. He built the heart in me—Bye and bye it outgrew me—and like the little mother—with the big child—I got tired holding him. I heard of a thing called "Redemption"— which rested on men and women. You remember I asked you for it—you gave me something else. I forgot the Redemption [in the Redeemed—and I did'nt tell you for a long time, but I knew you had altered me—I] was tired—no more—[so dear did this stranger become that were it, or my breath—the Alternative—I had tossed the fellow away with a smile.] . . . If it had been God's will that I might breathe where you breathed—and find the place—myself—at night— . . . [T]he prank of the Heart at play on the heart—in holy Holiday—is forbidden me—
I dont know what you can do for it—thank you—Master—but if I had the Beard on my cheek—like you—and you—had Daisy's petals—and you cared so for me— what would become of you? . . . Say I may wait for you—say I need go with no stranger to the to me—untried [country] fold— . . . (L 233)

Critics have been trying for years to identify the Master. I, for one, am glad we know neither who the Master was nor the circumstances under which Dickinson wrote the Master letters. The uncertain identity of the Master allows us to slip with the constant slippage of identity in this letter. We can treat the Master as a figure, as Dickinson does. "The prank of the Heart at play on the Heart" may be "forbidden," but she plays anyway. Each self stands outside itself; each self is linguistically fused with the other, only to be cast aside again.

Although this letter is, as Wolff says, "a world desolated . . . by the loss of . . . communication," it contains instructions to the Master-reader, who, even as he acts on the letter in order to read it, must stand outside himself to make way for the text. Dickinson teaches belief and doubt: "If you saw a bullet hit a Bird—and he told you he was'nt shot—you might weep at his courtesy, but you would certainly doubt his word." This injunction, which might be summarized as "believe not words, but what you see," is followed by a fervent request that the Master believe "not what you see, but words." He is to believe a metaphor: that the words on the page are a drop of blood from the wound on "Daisy's bosom." Wolff explains, "The letter clearly implies that although the beloved ought to have been able to infer her pain (even though she disavowed it when they were together), the written words of this letter must play a role in making the invisible wound apparent" (*Emily* 408).

The structure of the letter constantly questions and affirms what the reader can infer either from words or from the phenomenological world. That is to say, the letter vacillates between doubt and faith, words and phenomena. Thus, after asking the Master to have faith in her metaphorical wound, in the depth and pain of her love, she undercuts the notion of belief: "Thomas' faith in Anatomy, was stronger than his faith in faith." But to what kind of anatomy is she referring? The sentences preceding and succeeding the adage about Thomas refer to the anatomy of the soul, to Daisy's wounded bosom with its self made by God and its heart built by God, the heart that outgrows its boundaries and " — like the little mother — with the big child — " becomes tiring and stands outside as a "him."

This anatomy of the soul is also the anatomy of the "thing called 'Redemption' which rested on men and women." In exchange for standing aside for God, Dickinson would receive absolute union and rest, that is, entrance into the Kingdom of heaven. But redemption won't rest on her. She asks the Master for "it" and he gives "something else." She is "tired — no more" when she forgets "the Redemption." But that Redemption is replaced by another kind of redemption that alters her and is so precious that she would choose "it" over her own "breath"; she seemingly would face self-extinction "with a smile." This redemption, like the other, does not rest but multiplies "Alternatives" so quickly that it is hard to tell what is "it" and what is "something else": "so dear did this stranger become that were it, or my breath — the Alternative — I had tossed the fellow away with a smile." Which "fellow" is it who would be tossed away "with a smile"? Breath, Redemption, the stranger, the heart "built by God," the him, the her, or the *it*?

The letter reenacts the conversion experience by making identity slip away from itself in the same moment that words slip from their meanings. Dickinson speaks both in the first person and in the third person as Daisy; to say "God made me . . . I did'nt be — myself" is to say "I didn't become myself by my own volition," "I didn't have being," and "I didn't have being by my own volition." This kind of "prank of the Heart" points to no absolute redemption by words and meaning.

Dickinson is committed to redemption, but she is aware that her pursuit is through language, through the *Word* of God or the word of poetry. She suspects language can invent what she desires. No sooner is redemption part of her vocabulary than it slips away into doubt, not only religious doubt but also epistemological and linguistic doubt. She is left in the place where "We must meet apart," with her art, wit, the blankness of doubt, and "that White Sustenance / Despair" (P 640).

Yet even as the letter shows the impossibility of redemption through love, it asserts the possibility by asking the Master for empathy. If the Master would *believe*, he would convert. He would become a woman: "but if I had the Beard on my cheek—like you—and you—had Daisy's petals—and you cared so for me—what would become of you?" Of course, this moment of faith, too, will be undercut by doubt, but the words carry with them the hope that this uncertain territory can be mastered. Dickinson wants "to wait," rather than to go alone with the self that is a "stranger." Such an alternative can hardly be articulated; the pain is so utter that it nearly results in syntactical breakdown: "Say I may wait for you—say I need go with no stranger to the to me—untried [country] fold." If the words are to make "the invisible wound apparent," it will be between the lines, in "the gash" (or gap) between Master and Daisy, in "internal difference / Where the Meanings, are."

By the end of this letter, Dickinson has nullified the category of self by constantly positing "Alternatives." She reinvents redemption; it is no longer doctrinal salvation but the transforming redemption of "something else" redeemed by something else. This alternative redemption tends to level the hierarchy between the masculine master and his feminine subject. Margaret Homans writes that, in manipulating "language to reverse its ordinary meanings," Dickinson uses "linguistic power first to reverse the ordinary direction of power between the feminine self and a masculine other, and then . . . uses it to discard the idea of dominance altogether" (201). Dickinson undoes "the idea of dominance" by transforming the contending identities: Daisy has "the Beard" on her "cheek" and Master has "Daisy's petals." Like "Me from Myself—to banish—," the letter follows Porter's pattern of "belief . . . questioning and disjunction" to the extreme place where Dickinson establishes linguistic categories only to undo them.

Dickinson's linguistic transformations have particular implications for reading, conversion, and authority. Reading, as Norman Pettit points out, was crucial to the process of conversion. "Grace came not from God as a removed creator but through a personal experience of the direct operation of His Spirit" (10) as one read the Bible or wrote about the conversion experience. Even the Puritans questioned whether their understanding of the Word was God's absolute meaning or a product of Fancy. Dickinson goes farther than doubting whether her perception is true. She takes pleasure in multiplicity and even in one poem declares, "the Object Absolute is Nought." Although she appropriates religious discourse, she equivocates. Her poems, as Mutlu Konuk Blasing writes, "[rule] out any authoritative reading" (178). The poem "There's a certain Slant of light" invites this sort of equivocating slant on God:

> There's a certain Slant of light
> Winter Afternoons —
> That oppresses, like the Heft
> Of Cathedral Tunes —
>
> Heavenly Hurt, it gives us —
> We can find no scar,
> But internal difference
> Where the Meanings, are —
>
> None may teach it — Any —
> 'Tis the Seal Despair —
> An imperial affliction
> Sent us of the Air —
>
> When it comes, the Landscape listens —
> Shadows hold their breath —
> When it goes, 'tis like the Distance
> On the look of Death —
> (P 258)

An obvious reading of the poem is that an afflicting light oppresses the soul with the knowledge of its unworthiness in the sight of the Lord. Such a realization in an orthodox interpretation would be a prelude to conversion. The phrase "the Seal Despair," a play on the seals of the Revelation, reveals not the crisis leading to rebirth but "the Distance / On the look of Death." The sinner foresees not the heavenly afterlife but the death of the soul. The poem as a cautionary tale is undermined because the poem overtly invites multiple readings. She *should* read the Scripture and find the one absolute meaning in the Word. But she turns to poetry and finds "internal difference" in such terms as "Cathedral Tunes," "Affliction," "Heavenly Hurt," and "the Seal Despair"; she subverts their Calvinist meanings and transforms them into her own multivalent poem.

As in "Me from Myself — to banish," "There's a certain Slant of light" does not mention God, but nevertheless undercuts His Supreme Authority. In "Slant," which deals with oppression, despair, hurt, and affliction, Dickinson undoes the orthodox notion that God inflicts pain for didactic purposes. Dickinson's Puritan predecessors, Mary Rowlandson and Anne Bradstreet, upheld the tenet of affliction as a good lesson. Rowlandson makes her captivity narrative public "for the Benefit of the Afflicted" (317). As she points out, the Scriptures teach that "*For whom the Lord loveth he chastenth*" (Hebrews 12:6). He will help the loved and afflicted "and make them see, and say they have been gainers thereby. And I hope I can say . . . as David did, *It is good that I have been afflicted.* The Lord hath shown me the vanity of these outward things" (365–66). It is through affliction that the Calvinist sees the vanity of the world. Seeing that vanity helps prepare her for turning toward God by turning her away from the self that clings to such worldliness. Similarly, Anne Bradstreet, like Rowlandson a seventeenth-century Puritan, writes in her "Verses upon the Burning of Our House, July 10, 1666": "Farewell, my pelf; farewell, my store; / The world no longer let me love. / My hope and treasure lie above." For all the ambivalence in their work, both women ultimately bless the Lord for His difficult lesson.

Dickinson, unlike Rowlandson and Bradstreet, is not reassured that affliction is the sign of God's Paternal Omnipresence. Rather, affliction is the sign of His absence and His inscrutability. As Wolff explains, whatever sign the Lord may send only further obscures knowledge of Him, thereby intensifying the affliction:

If God's absence is compensated by words and signs, these are forms that . . . [insinuate] falsehood into our beliefs—revising our "sight" so we can accept his mutilations without complaint. God urges us to seek Him, but when "enlightenment" comes, it is knifelike and cold—"*a certain Slant of light,* / *Winter Afternoons*—" . . . . God still refuses to loosen the Seal of Revelation; instead he inflicts the "Seal Despair." . . . And this, too, invades the coherence of the self. . . . God's prevarications and false promises call . . . we turn away . . . and still the mind has been violated and sullied—even if only with the desire for hope. (*Emily* 155)

In "There's a certain Slant of light," Dickinson appropriates God's signs and fills them with empty despair. The poem compares the "Slant of light, / . . . That oppresses" to "Cathedral Tunes" and alludes to the worship of the God with the irreverence of "Tunes" rather than with the reverence of hymns. The grandeur of a cathedral, a monument to the Lord, is juxtaposed not with hymnal songs of praise but ironically with tunes, which are the melodies without the words. "Imperial affliction," too, has been emptied of its ordinary meaning. While the poem links affliction with teaching ("None may teach it—any—"), this religious justification is mocking, since it is "Sent us of the Air." Whether "the Air" is the air we breathe or is an "air," meaning one of those "Cathedral Tunes," the satirical tone suggests a blankness: tunes without words, light without revelation, affliction without reason, not "compensation by words and signs."

This blankness throws affliction's "imperial" modification into question. Affliction seems to come out of nowhere, out of "the air"; it has no sign—"We can find no scar"—and no significance—"But internal difference / Where the meanings, are." Even light, God's emissary, is merely the

object of a preposition, not worthy of being a subject nor of being capitalized. It is the light's "Slant" that is subject and capitalized. And that slant
seems to hit each word at a different angle. The first pronoun "it" seems
clearly to refer to the "Slant." Thereafter, with each reiteration, "its" refer-
ents multiply. By the end of the poem, "it" could be the Slant, Heavenly
Hurt, internal difference, the Seal Despair, an imperial affliction, and/or
the listening Landscape. The slant is also Dickinson's oblique self receiving
orthodox messages.

     Even the speaker is multiple since the poem is written in the first person
plural. She includes the reader among those who are afflicted, but at the
end neither speaker nor reader is present. Distant, we (who are both the
readers and the implied speakers) no longer hurt because we no longer perceive: "When it comes, the Landscape listens." For all the pain the "Slant
of light" inflicts, the landscape is animated by it: "the landscape listens—
/ Shadows hold their breath." "When it goes," the landscape looks distant
and dead. The poem's end is filled with loss: the loss of the light and the
loss of the speaker and the reader as they exit the poem. Like the landscape,
we have lost our animation. We are like the excluded unelect in the Gospel
of Mark: "That seeing they may see, and not perceive; and hearing they
may hear, and not understand; lest at any time they should be converted,
and *their* sins should be forgiven them" (4:12). The light which was the
sign "affliction" now has the detached "look of Death." It has not taught
the vanity of the world and the hope of another. We have been neither converted nor forgiven.

     If the poem refutes the lesson of afflicting light, it paradoxically "lis-
tens" to it and reverses the meanings again. The "Slant of light," in all its
variety, refracts infinitely in each facet of the "it" that it illuminates. The
light, God's sign, is multiple, not absolute. Thus, the "internal difference /
Where the meanings, are" undoes religious doctrine and posits a proto-
modern religious pluralism and a relativity of meaning. Dickinson releases
the signs from their ordinary meanings and points her reader to an alternative, "slanted" signification. Paradoxically, by refuting religious doctrine,
she restores God's unknowability and thereby asserts a fundamental tenet
of Puritanism. In her doubt, she is a most pure Puritan. But she accepts
faith not through Calvinist crisis conversion but through self-conversion.
She annihilates both the self that has internalized a conventional god and
the theology associated with him.

     In that blankness is Emily Dickinson's poetry, a poetry devoted to the
unknowable. In her ambiguity of meaning, her fragmented form, her doubt
and parody of tradition and God, in her finding her home in the wasteland
of self-division, and in her transference of meaning from God to poetry,
Dickinson anticipated the concerns and techniques of the modernists. Her

doubt and radical theology of self-conversion provide her with the language of negation, the tongue of blankness, and the slanted faith of her protomodernist poetry. Brilliant, innovative, *it* is her Faith.

Note

1. References to Dickinson's letters appear in the text in parenthesis with the abbreviation "L" followed by the number of the cited letter. References to poems by Dickinson appear in the text in parenthesis with the abbreviation "P" followed by the number of the cited poem.

CAROL J. SINGLEY

Calvinist Tortures in Edith Wharton's
Ethan Frome

READERS SELDOM ASSOCIATE Edith Wharton either with Calvinism or modernism, but both figure prominently in her 1911 novel *Ethan Frome*. Wharton was attracted to Calvinist theology and its legacies at an early age. As a child, she compared a life-altering, personal moral crisis and its "depressing results" with those produced by "the sternest Presbyterian training" ("Life" 1074); and as an adolescent she immersed herself in reading sermons of every kind, including evangelical ones (R. Lewis, *Edith* 25). As an adult, Wharton continued to be fascinated not only with Calvinist doctrine but with Puritan culture and geography. She made frequent trips to New England, built a home for herself in the Massachusetts countryside, and chose the region as a setting for short stories and for her novel *Summer* (1917), as well as for *Ethan Frome*. Wharton's interest in Calvinism was part of her lifelong religious and spiritual search that included Episcopalianism, the genteel faith in which she was raised; transcendentalism, a philosophy of personal freedom that offered an antidote to Calvinist precepts; and Catholicism, a creed that satisfied her tastes for beauty, order, history, and ritual.[1]

Calvinism, as practiced by seventeenth-century Puritans, was far more balanced than Wharton's selective depictions in *Ethan Frome* suggest. Her equation of Puritanism with harshness or austerity distorts the Puritans' complex beliefs and practices; nevertheless, Wharton did associate early American culture with sensual and aesthetic deprivation. In this respect, she articulates a perspective that is both unique to her and representative of her time. By the end of the nineteenth century, as Warren Susman points out, Puritanism was enlisted to connote stern morality and hostility toward self-expression (42–47). Calvinist dogma, at odds with the genteel manners of Wharton's upper-class society, softened, in Jackson Lears' phrase, to a "platitudinous humanism" (32). Yet the dilution of this earlier robust faith left previously confident believers in a state of spiritual uncertainty that extended to doubt about personal identity itself. Although they eschewed the rigors of past creeds, especially evangelical ones, restless Victorians searched for some kind of assurance that moral value was not entirely relative. Edith Wharton, a Victorian who wrote much of her best fiction in the modernist period, looked to the older Calvinist faith for such certitude, but she also viewed Calvinism with the skepticism and irony characteristic of her time. Wharton's personal history deepened her attraction to Calvinist concepts and forms. In particular, an adulterous midlife affair reignited the Calvinist moral tortures that had wracked her as a child. She wrote *Ethan Frome* amid the turmoil of this romance. A bleak novel that reproduces the despair she felt at this time, *Ethan Frome* demonstrates the sense of guilt, futility, and remoteness of redemption that Wharton experienced in her personal life and found in this exacting Protestant faith.

When composing *Ethan Frome*, Wharton extracted qualities from Puritan culture that corresponded to her own spiritual circumstances and aesthetic practices. She was drawn, in particular, to the extremes of the New England landscape—its brief, delicate summers; its relentless, frigid winters. She was also intrigued by the oppositions she found in Calvinist doctrine: the abject sinfulness of human beings in the face of God's grandeur, power, and love; the horror of hell and damnation in contrast with the glory of salvation; and the states of hope and despair that believers experienced as they alternately viewed themselves as damned or saved. Wharton had extreme and often ambivalent feelings about New England—and about America as a whole, as her expatriation to France suggests. On the one hand, she was drawn to Calvinism's moral absolutism; on the other hand, she decried what she saw as its rigidity, especially when applied to matters of sexuality and art. Like her predecessor, Nathaniel Hawthorne, who was also inspired by Calvinism, Wharton emphasized the Manichaean, or dualistic, aspects of this faith. Such emphasis is evident in her use of light and dark imagery in *Ethan Frome*. Moreover, she stresses Calvinism's negative rather than positive aspects, reflecting her spiritual skepticism: Wharton could not be sure that the fierce God of Calvinism was also a forgiving, loving God. *Ethan Frome* makes selective use of Calvinist materials and presents them disjunctively, in a context of spiritual alienation rather than belief. The novel is modernist in this sense as well as others: in it Wharton explores the psychological as well as theological implications of Calvinism, experiments with narrative perspective and subjectivity, and uses the spare language of the twentieth-century technological age. Ultimately, then, what Wharton gained from Calvinism was of aesthetic as well as theological value.

Wharton was by no means the first American writer to find the Calvinist soil fertile ground for the imagination. Indeed, her novel, like Hawthorne's

The Scarlet Letter, revisits Calvinism in order to denounce it, both as moral force and literary aesthetic. But whereas Hawthorne incorporates a romantic sensibility, Wharton demonstrates a modernist one. She uses the Calvinist past as other modernist writers do—as folk history or mythic frame—but she does so ironically, to convey post-Darwinian doubt. *Ethan Frome* suggests that Christian salvation is no longer tenable in early twentieth-century culture. In her descriptions of sterile domesticity, muteness, and miscommunication, Wharton further criticizes nineteenth-century codes of sentimentality, which deliberately softened the stern, patriarchal Calvinist God and elevated the roles of wife, mother, and Madonna. She rejects hallmarks of sentimental culture such as the home-as-haven, the rewards of self-sacrifice, and the certainty of forgiveness.

In addition to revising history in a modernist fashion, Wharton employs modernist techniques. A narrative frame allows her to render her tale with detached distance. This seemingly objective method makes the narrative a subjective account that leads the reader as well as the narrator to speculate about the causes and effects of Ethan Frome's torment. Before early twentieth-century writers refined the spare language and dislocated narrative structures that are characteristic of modernism, Wharton experimented with such innovations, making her New England portraits— *"granite outcroppings,"* as she calls them in her preface (v, emphasis in original)—forerunners of a new literary movement.

Ethan Frome, then, is a transparent account of Wharton's personal tribulations as well as a complex work of fiction. The novel's devastatingly bleak domestic scenes reflect her unhappy experiences in childhood and marriage, as well as her cultural critique of Calvinist legacies. Through the composition of *Ethan Frome*, Wharton exorcised the Calvinist demons that had tortured her. Her application of Calvinist principles thus resulted in an artistic as well as personal triumph.

I

Edith Wharton's elite background places her in the tradition of genteel Protestantism. Yet a closer look reveals a sensibility that can only be characterized as evangelical—the spirituality commonly associated with Calvinism.[2] Wharton's relationship to Calvinism is complicated and even paradoxical, not only because Calvinism contrasted sharply with her upbringing, but because she resisted, on intellectual and aesthetic grounds, the austere doctrines to which she felt spiritually drawn. Wharton's connection to Calvinism began at an early age. First, it was found close to home, in the Episcopal service book that she read each week in church. At the end of the *Book of Common Prayer* are Calvin's "Thirty-Nine Articles of Religion," a reminder that this genteel faith finds its origins in a harsher one. Whether Wharton familiarized herself with these principles while she sat in the family pew is impossible to say, although in her autobiography, *A Backward Glance*, she describes reading the *Book of Common Prayer* as a child (10). Given her passion for reading, one can reasonably assume that she did study Calvin's articles.

Second, Wharton developed a religious enthusiasm that far surpassed her family's. When she was thirteen, she struck up a friendship with Emelyn Washburn, daughter of her parish rector. She visited Emelyn often at the rectory, where they trimmed hats, typed out archaic languages on Dr. Washburn's typewriter, and read books in the library. About this time, Wharton also "began to read widely and indiscriminately in religious literature, particularly sermons of every kind of doctrinal persuasion" (R. Lewis, *Edith* 25).[3] Third, Wharton's autobiographical writings reveal that she had begun to develop a strict conscience, obsession with truth-telling, and doubts about forgiveness that are associated with Calvinism. In "Life and I," a fragment she never published—and that might be termed her spiritual autobiography—she recounts a childhood trauma that produced "excruciating moral tortures" (1072) and left her in spiritual agony and confusion.

This moral crisis originated in a dancing class when she was six or seven years old. She mischievously called her dancing teacher's mother "an old goat" behind her back. Immediately overcome with guilt, she confessed her transgression and was devastated when her public confession elicited not forgiveness but "a furious scolding for my impertinence." She felt further betrayed when her mother also reproached her—not for a lapse in moral conduct but for social impropriety. Despite her relation to a society that taught that "ill-breeding . . . was the only form of wrong-doing" and parents who were "profoundly indifferent to the subtler problems of the conscience," Wharton herself adhered to a strict code of truth-telling, "the least imperceptible deviation from which would inevitably be punished by the dark Power I know as 'God'." She writes that during this spiritual crisis, she "suffered alone, as imaginative children generally do, without daring to tell any one of my trouble, because I vaguely felt that I *ought* to know what was right, & that it was probably 'naughty' not to" (1072–74). Wharton's experience of guilt and isolation, similar to that felt by Calvinist soul-searchers, lasted seven or eight years. As she explains, "I had been naturally a fearless child; now I lived in a state of chronic fear" (1079). Wharton's emotional trauma and withdrawal recalls that of Hawthorne's clergyman in "The Minister's Black Veil," whose estrangement from others inevitably follows from harsh Calvinist tenets.

Wharton's moral tortures were no less poignant than those that gripped Puritan poet Anne Bradstreet as she wrestled to reconcile her love of life's pleasures with her devotion to God. In Bradstreet poems such as "The Flesh and the Spirit" and "Before the Birth of One of Her Children," for example, the speaker seeks to affirm Christian selflessness over more immediate desires for sensual gratification. In Wharton's case, the joy of sounding clever to her peers competed with her inner sense that such displays of wit were boastful and hurtful of others. Puritan John Norton, in his biography of John Cotton, expressed this same dilemma as a choice "between the word of wisdom [which is God's] and the wisdom of words," which is mere rhetoric (213).

Neither were Wharton's moral tortures any less painful than those of Puritan preacher and poet Edward Taylor as he struggled with his unworthiness before God. As Taylor writes in "The Souls Groan to Christ for Succour": "For in my soul, my soul finds many faults. / And though I justify myselfe to's face: / I do Condemn myselfe before thy Grace" (ll. 4–6). For Taylor, moral tortures were as spiritually empowering as they were exhausting. Self-examination prepared him for his ultimate goal: union with Christ, first in the form of communion and later in eternal life in heaven. For Wharton, however, there was no consoling response such as the one that soothes the speaker in Taylor's poem "Christs Reply": "Peace, Peace, Peace, my Hony, do not Cry, / . . . / Is anything too good, my Love / To get or give for thee?" (ll. 1, 5–6). Instead of the mild-mannered Christ, Wharton faced a formidable mother whom she equated with an inscrutable, unsympathetic, vengeful God.

Two aspects of the dancing-class ordeal are relevant to *Ethan Frome*. First, Wharton associated her mother with the fierce God who tortured her; both were dictatorial and impossible to appease. As she explains:

for years afterward I was never free from the oppressive sense that I had two absolutely inscrutable beings to please—God & my mother—who, while ostensibly upholding the same principles of behaviour, differed totally as to their application. And my mother was the most inscrutable of the two. ("Life" 1074)

Second, Wharton focused on aspects of faith that brought guilt and despair rather than solace. In particular, she was unable to accept the doctrine of Atonement. Instead of Christ's resurrection, she emphasized only his submission, suffering, and alienation. She even questioned the purpose of sacrifice altogether. In "Life and I," still casting her mother as God, Wharton explains her bewilderment:

But passionately as I was interested in Christianity, I was always horrified by the sanguinary conception of the Atonement. I remember saying to myself again & again, in moments of deep perplexity: "But if the servants did anything to annoy Mamma, it would be no satisfaction to her to kill Harry or me." (1091)

For Wharton, punishment was unjustly related to the offense; and God was not a benevolent caretaker, but a "dreadful Being" — "one of the dark fatalities . . . [who] seemed to weigh on the lives of mortals" (1091). The weight of God's ire upon the powerless individual is vividly described in Thomas Hooker's sermon "The Soul's Preparation for Christ": "when God lays the flashes of hellfire upon thy soul, thou canst not endure it. . . . [I]f the drops be so heavy, what will the whole sea of God's vengeance be?" (24). Michael Wigglesworth, in his poem "God's Controversy with New England," also describes an angry Puritan deity who brings his "wrath upon Revolters" (l. 252) and promises destruction unless the believer repents. For all of his awesome power, however, Wigglesworth's God is still a loving deity who prefers obedience to disobedience and offers salvation to penitent sinners. Wharton denies her characters in *Ethan Frome* this opportunity for redemption. Ethan suffers alone and in silence, unable to reconcile passion for Mattie with duty toward his wife Zeena; and increasingly Zeena, who resembles the "dark power" that Wharton associated with her mother and God, exacts high prices for Ethan's bid for freedom.

As Wharton grew older, she expressed her feelings about Calvinism in her response to the New England landscape and way of life and in her reaction to a love affair with Morton Fullerton. Even though she objected to Calvinism's sternness, she was attracted to the New England countryside where it had flourished. In 1904, she built a mansion — which she called her "first real home" (*Backward* 125) — in Lenox, Massachusetts.[4] Although she visited the Mount only during the warm seasons of spring or summer, she never forgot the region's harshness, as her letters to friends show. For example, in a 1911 letter to Sara Norton, she commented on the cold weather's effect on her garden, mentioning a vine that may have inspired the one on the Fromes' porch: "no lovely flowering shrubs or creepers 'do' here. Even the clematis paniculata I had established so carefully is dead" (Letters, 3 July). She also criticized New England manners, which she believed interfered with enjoyment. Urging Sara to join her on a trip to Rome, she wrote, "now, don't raise all sorts of conscientious New England objections, but try to be a pagan, & see how nice this would be" (*Letters* 73).[5] Wharton's prodding of Sara to enjoy life's pleasures shows her disapproval of what she considered Calvinism's restriction of female desire.[6] Although Calvinist doctrine considered women the spiritual equals of men, it upheld a strict social hierarchy in which man ruled over woman, as God ruled over man. This creed also associated female sexuality with human fallibility and temptation. Not surprisingly, then, Wharton's own slumbering Calvinist sensibilities — especially her early ruminations about a fierce diety and the futility of atonement — were awakened in 1908 when, at the age of forty-six, she began an illicit affair with *London Times* journalist Morton Fullerton.

Wharton's affair — and the lies it necessitated — reactivated the "moral tortures" that had obsessed her as a child in the dancing class. Wharton herself discounted this association, perhaps because it was so potent and personal. She claims instead that "a distant glimpse of Bear Mountain brought Ethan back to my memory, and the following winter in Paris [1910–1911] I wrote the tale as it now stands" (*Backward* 295–96). However, Wharton was not in New England in 1909 or 1910 (R. Lewis, *Edith* 300); therefore, a recent visit could not account for her renewed fascination with the area and its culture. More likely, her statement that "Ethan's history stirred again in my memory" refers to the Calvinist "moral tortures" of her childhood. Ethan's drama reenacts Wharton's battle with Calvinist principles. In romantic despair, and judging herself guilty of the same sins as Ethan and Mattie, she created a fictional world in which adulterous love leads to dependence and disfigurement.

Ethan Frome explores the crippling effects of conflict between passion and duty that Wharton saw as part of the Calvinist legacy. As such, it evokes an earlier American novel—*The Scarlet Letter*.[7] Like Nathaniel Hawthorne, Wharton was drawn to New England's extremes; she keenly felt the lack of sympathy and connection that results from polarizing private feeling and social duty. Both writers saw in the New England landscape a fundamental and irreconcilable duality, a Manichaean opposition between good and evil, spirit and flesh, that is indigenous to American Calvinism.[8] *Ethan Frome* and *The Scarlet Letter* both explore illicit passion and the consequences of breaking moral and social law. Wharton's narrative, like Hawthorne's, "runs directly counter to the 'American Dream,' being neither romantic nor libertarian, but distinctly authoritarian and conservative" (Baym, "Passion" 214). The novels are also similar in technique, theme, and tone. Like *The Scarlet Letter*, *Ethan Frome* subordinates action to the effects of action; includes narrators who reconstruct a tale of adultery (in *Ethan Frome*, intended adultery) and failed escape from evocative details (a letter sewn on a scrap of cloth, a stride broken by a limp); and demonstrates how sexual transgression—which William Shurr terms the "one real evil" in the American psyche (123)—incurs repression.[9]

If *The Scarlet Letter* argues against the conflation of female sexuality and spiritual inadequacy inherent in Puritan texts, as Margaret Thickstun notes (132–34), then *Ethan Frome* extends Hawthorne's critique by denying passion altogether. Whereas at the end of *The Scarlet Letter*, Hester's sexual vitality is converted into an abiding, selfless maternity, and Dimmesdale and Chillingworth are released from earthly torment to face whatever afterlife each deserves, Wharton creates a bleaker, more modernist ending, allowing her characters to suffer in "the most enduring triangle that fiction has recorded" (Ransom 273). Mattie and Ethan are physically and spiritually crippled for their passion and attempted suicide; and Zeena, the loveless but legally empowered spouse, triumphs, a relentless reminder of their failures. Finally, whereas the meaning of Hester's "A" gradually encompasses "able" and even "angel," Ethan's "red gash" (3)—his badge of ignominy—remains an ugly scar, a perpetual mark of transgression and punishment. Wharton is thus more Manichaean—and more modernist—than Hawthorne because she allows no tragic heroism or mediating circumstances; she binds her characters, body and soul, to a dark world.[10]

II

Wharton's sense of Calvinist extremes is evident in her descriptions of nature and community, which she also presents in a modernist way. The Calvinist view of nature is immediately apparent in Wharton's setting and, in particular, in the name of Ethan Frome's town. Starkfield is a "stark field," a postlapsarian Eden where "starved apple-trees writh[e] over a hillside" and Ethan struggles for survival. While life in Starkfield is difficult for all its inhabitants, Ethan is especially afflicted. His barren fields and "lonely" New England farmhouse, with a funereal "black wraith of deciduous creeper flapp[ing] from the porch," only "make the landscape lonelier" (11). Material prosperity, a sign to early New Englanders that they were members of the Elect, eludes Ethan. He constantly toils but has no heart for and takes no profit from his work. With his "saw-mill and the arid acres of his farm yield[ing] scarcely enough to keep his household," and more than his share of "sickness and trouble" (8), Ethan has missed his "calling." The Puritans placed high value on the concept of "calling," which minister John Norton describes as God's work upon "the spirit inwardly" in spite of the individual's intentions to pursue other vocations. The human will produces "false hopes and grounds" (212-13); only God can guide the believer to his true calling. Ethan, an unsuccessful engineer and farmer, experiences only the struggle of work and fails to earn God's grace for his efforts.

Seasonal imagery also conveys Ethan's isolation. Winter was commonly used in sermons of Puritan preachers to signify periods of doubt, divine trials, and perseverance. The clergy spoke of lapses in faith arising not from a deficit of grace but from the believer's human inadequacies: "so is it with the graces of God in mans soule, they have their spring and summer seasons, they have also their winter, wherein they seeme cleane blasted and decayed, as if there were no seeds of grace in their hearts" (qtd. in Miller, *New England* 1939, 54). The faithful, recognizing that winter is temporary, work to relieve themselves of doubt. In one minister's words, "it is not the office of faith to cherish and maintaine such feares and doubts, but to resist them, to fight against them, and so much as is possible to expell them, and dri[v]e them out" (54). In Ethan Frome's case, however, winter is a victor: the narrator notes "the vitality of the climate and the deadness of the community" (5). The "storms of February" and "wild cavalry of March winds" (6) vanquish human effort and deny—as does T. S. Eliot's cruel month of April—any promise of spring and rebirth. Ethan succumbs to this winter of the soul so totally that he seems virtually "a part of the mute melancholy landscape, an incarnation of its frozen woe" (8).

Wharton further expresses human alienation from nature in her novel's ending. In the actual 1904 mishap that inspired the climactic suicide attempt, a group of Lenox sledders collided with a lamppost: one girl was killed, one made lame for life, and one badly scarred. In Wharton's revision, Ethan and Mattie clash with a symbol of nature—an elm tree—rather than one of society—a lamppost. Their collision with nature represents the human spirit in battle with itself. Wharton's version is also modernist in its suggestion of psychological conflict and its denial of will. Although the lovers choose death rather than separation, they end up together and maimed, unable to control their destinies.

In addition to representing fallen nature, Wharton enlists Calvinist notions of election to underscore Ethan's social and spiritual alienation. Ethan's house, a "forlorn" "image of his own shrunken body," lacks the structural "L" connecting it to the barn (11-12). This architectural separateness represents Ethan's isolation from community, a concept valued by the Puritans. Hoping eventually to join God's saints in heaven, Puritans sought to replicate community in human relations. John Winthrop articulates the importance of the social body to his parishioners in "A Model of Christian Charity": "true Christians are of one body in Christ. . . . All parts of this body . . . must needs partake of each other's strengths and infirmity; joy and sorrow; weal and woe" (86–87). As cultural critics Perry Miller and Thomas Johnson note, "it was not possible to segregate a man's spiritual life from his communal life" (181). The more confidence an individual had about his own salvation, the more positively he embraced the society in which he lived. Ethan Frome enjoys none of this community. Indeed, only he, Mattie, and Zeena seem singled out for their cruel fate. Other characters find some measure of happiness; in Calvinist terms, they experience relief because they believe they are Elect. For example, Ruth Varnum, a healer like Zeena, is not blighted by moral tragedy; she is healthy—"hale"—as her married name implies. Ruth and Ned Hale marry and have children, unlike Mattie and Ethan. Their house—"at one end of the main street . . . looking down . . . to the slim white steeple of the Congregational Church" (6)—forms a social and spiritual center for the town. Mrs. Hale's knowledge of the Frome tragedy, an event that in Puritan times might be said to precipitate a crisis conversion, accounts for the "insurmountable reticence" and "depths of sad initiation" in her voice when she speaks of the crash (6–7). Intuitively, neighbors keep their distance from Ethan: "his taciturnity was respected and it was only on rare occasions that one of the older men of the place detained him for a word" (4). Ethan's estrangement from community—like Young Goodman Brown's in Hawthorne's story—signifies his spiritual alienation.

Wharton's modernist message in *Ethan Frome* is that paradise lost cannot be regained—in this life or the next. The Puritan sought to balance worldly pleasure with anticipation of eternal joy in the hereafter, as Bradstreet's poem lamenting the loss of her possessions by fire vividly demonstrates. The speaker in "Upon the Burning of Our House" affirms that "all's vanity" and chides herself not to value "wealth on earth" when "there's wealth enough" in heaven (ll. 36–38, 51). However, Wharton, a modern skeptic, is less sure that the God in whom Bradstreet trusts will offer salvation. Wharton also takes to a bitter, logical conclusion the Calvinist belief that human will can effect only evil—not good. It is not that Ethan "lack[s] the force or the courage either to impose himself or to get away" (Wilson 26–27), but that human efforts are already doomed. The self not only fails to assert itself in such a world but is reduced, as Mattie Silver's pained, mouse-like "*cheep*" suggests, to the lower order of animals (*Ethan* 84, emphasis in original). No less etherized than Eliot's Prufrock, Ethan elicits pity because he cannot act; his will is as frozen as the landscape he inhabits. Early Puritan preachers exhorted their congregations to relinquish their wills and humble themselves before God: "There must be contrition and humiliation," writes Thomas Hooker, "the house must be . . . swept by brokenness and emptiness of spirit before the Lord will come to set up his abode in it" ("Application" 177). The Puritan believer effaced himself in hope of God's grace, but Ethan's powerlessness accomplishes nothing but more suffering. Wharton's version of the New England "errand into the wilderness," to use Miller's phrase, is an errand gone awry.

When Wharton wrote *Ethan Frome*, turn-of-the-century liberal theology and positivistic science had blurred the hard edges of old-fashioned religion to the point that *Scribner's* could mourn "The Passing of the Devil" in 1899, and a writer for the *Atlantic Monthly* could complain that "conscience has lost its strong and on-pressing energy" (qtd. in Lears 46). When Wharton resurrects the God force in *Ethan Frome*, then, she reinstates an element missing from secularized bourgeois Victorian culture: punishment for sin and the reality of hell. She rejects sunny interpretations of Darwin and turns instead to Calvinism as a more appropriate representation of modernist uncertainty and alienation. Calvinism and modernism share the same sense of human limitation, understood as original sin in the former case and as natural or social restriction in the latter. Although modern secularism substituted "reason" or "nature" for God, it still found life inscrutable and human suffering inevitable. With the disappearance of religious certainties, a sense of life's ambiguities heightened, as did the irony with which they were depicted. The devil, not God, might be turning the wheel of fortune; faith in reform became a pipe dream; and the individual felt powerless to halt the increasing mechanization of life (Schneider 7–9). *Ethan Frome*—a modernist allegory about this loss of faith in God, community, and self—suggests that despite secular progress, life is still inscrutable and often insufferable.[11]

III

Edith Wharton's modernism is evident in her use of history as well as religion. Modernist writers broke with the immediate past and turned to pastoral or classical ideals, mixing earlier chapters of history in richly allusive, jarring ways. "Instead of narrative method, we may now use the mythical method," writes T. S. Eliot (*Selected Prose* 178). Like other modernists, Wharton draws on classical and folk forms, but she criticizes rather than reinstates them. The chapter of history that Wharton most strongly evokes and rejects in *Ethan Frome* is Calvinist, as we have seen, but she also alludes to classical tragedy and European fairy tales. For example, the description of Ethan's "lean brown head, with its shock of light hair" that once sat "gallantly" "on his strong shoulders before they were bent out of shape" (4), recalls the image of a Greek hero—but a defeated one. And, as in Greek tragedy, we learn the story of Ethan Frome—a "ruin of a man" (3)— from the choral laments of Harmon Gow and Mrs. Hale. Wharton also transforms the traditional form of the fairy tale, which, as Jackson Lears explains, allowed Victorian readers to escape reality and lose themselves in a primitive or mythic past. The fairy-tale movement substituted for lost religious certainty and thereby represented an antimodern impulse (168– 73). However, in *Ethan Frome*, Wharton employs this motif ironically— that is, modernistically—to convey religious skepticism. The wicked witch Zeena is not destroyed, and young innocents Ethan and Mattie do not live happily ever after. By distorting the fairy tale, Wharton subverts Victorian optimism and makes her tale "new" in the sense that Ezra Pound exhorted writers to invent new forms.

Wharton also reveals her modernism by voicing disapproval of the nineteenth-century sentimental religious tradition, which elevated motherhood and espoused domestic felicity as alternatives to an increasingly commercialized and industrialized society. In contrast to much nineteenth-century domestic fiction, Wharton's novel describes a distorted ménage in which home is a living hell rather than heaven on earth. *Ethan Frome* is a modernist nightmare of maternal abandonment and marital neglect. Wharton draws heavily on her own disappointing family life — first as the child of a cold, disapproving mother and later as the wife of an unsympathetic husband — for these portrayals of emotional starvation and misunderstanding. Indeed, Wharton's own life is discernible in all three of her main characters.

We can appreciate Wharton's critique of sentimental dogma by analyzing the characters' relationships to one another and to Wharton herself. She aligns herself with her protagonist through the similarity of their names: Edith Jones and Ethan Frome. Ethan suffers loss when his mother becomes ill and strangely silent. After she dies, he marries her nurse, Zeena, in order to escape his terrible loneliness, but Zeena, too, turns sickly and querulous. Likewise, Edith Jones also suffered from her mother's silence. Lucretia Jones disapproved so vehemently of her daughter's writing that she never spoke to her about it, and she neglected to tell her daughter even the basic facts of life.[12] Hopelessly ignorant about sexuality, Wharton married a man of whom her mother approved — just as Ethan marries the woman closest to his mother. After years of incompatibility, Wharton experienced, like Ethan, the thrill of an illicit passion; and she struggled, like him, with conflict between romantic desire and marital commitment.

If Ethan suggests Wharton's thwarted passion, then Mattie represents the expression of that passion. Mattie is both Morton Fullerton, a charming, carefree lover, and Wharton herself, as she encountered — in middle age and for the first time — the kind of romance usually reserved for youth. Mattie's feelings for Ethan are as unmindful of consequences as Wharton's for Fullerton initially must have been. By the same token, however, Mattie's devastating immobilization at the end of the novel emblematizes Wharton's fear that loving Fullerton might end in her own emotional crippling.

Wharton reserves her most complicated portrayal for Zeena. Zeena is like Teddy Wharton, a wronged spouse, who becomes vengeful rather than forgiving. She is also like Lucretia Jones, a deficient nurturer with all the fearsome, Godlike powers that Wharton associated with her mother during the dancing-class incident. Wharton suggests Zeena's parental role in a number of ways. Although only seven years his senior, she seems old enough to be Ethan's mother; she "was already an old woman" (32). After Ethan's mother dies, he clings to her out of gratitude and need, as a child does to a parent: he had a "magnified . . . sense of what he owed her" and a "dread of being left alone" (35). But Zeena is no nurturer. She takes the dead mother's place by emulating her "silent," self-absorbed, and sickly behavior (36). And just as Lucretia Jones restricted her daughter's knowledge of the facts of life, Zeena guards the gates of passion. She keeps her red pickle dish—a wedding present with sexual overtones—high on a shelf, just as Wharton's mother kept sexual knowledge out of her daughter's reach. When Zeena leaves overnight, Ethan fantasizes about an evening alone with Mattie, but he is denied even this simple pleasure. When they dare to use the red pickle dish—that is, to express their desire—the cat, Zeena's occult emissary, jumps onto the chair, shatters the dish, and ends the romantic interlude.

By investing Zeena with such enigmatic and absolute powers, Wharton extends her role from spouse to parent to deity—just as in the dancing-class episode she identified her mother with the "inscrutable" Calvinist God ("Life" 1074). Although any authority figure might be aligned with a Calvinist patriarch, Wharton specifically compares her mother's ostensibly nurturing role with that of a Calvinist God bent on condemnation and retribution. In *Ethan Frome*, she reproduces this ironic inversion. Faced with an unforgiving scorekeeper whose "fault-finding was of the silent kind, but not the less penetrating," Ethan finds himself filled with "vague dread." Although he tries to "imagine that peace reigned in his house," he can only "postpone certainty" that it does not (30–31). "Nobody can tell with Zeena," Mattie says about her inscrutable methods (47). Zeena's powers are those of the Calvinist God who predetermines human fate. Having vowed vengeance, Zeena "never changed her mind" (60).

Wharton creates this punishing God-force to convey a sense of early-twentieth-century spiritual despair. At the end of the novel, the narrator describes Ethan's futile cry: "And what good had come of it? She was a hundred times bitterer and more discontented than when he had married her; the one pleasure left her was to inflict pain on him" (64). His spirit rises up against such waste, but he can take no action. Ethan's and Mattie's failed suicide also underlines their lack of control over their fate. With "stricken faces," clinging to one another like children, they imagine they "can fetch it" (83) and start down the hill toward the tree. Zeena— "no longer the listless creature who had lived at [Ethan's] side in a state of sullen self-absorption, but a mysterious alien presence" (58)—intervenes. As he points the sled toward the elm, Ethan suddenly sees her face, "with twisted monstrous lineaments, thrust itself between him and his goal" (83). Zeena's image, like that of a wrathful God, causes the sled to veer from its course, and the lovers' hopes—and bodies—are dashed. In Hawthorne's novel of thwarted passion, Chillingworth's power over Dimmesdale and Hester dissolves with Dimmesdale's confession and death, but in *Ethan Frome*, even Ethan's and Mattie's attempted suicide remains under Zeena's Godlike control. They find themselves, to paraphrase Jonathan Edwards, sinners in the hands of an angry Zeena.[13]

Ethan Frome conveys Wharton's personal experience of Calvinism's bleakness and her cultural critique of its influence. However, the novel's narrative structure suggests that she also envisioned escape from such restriction. *Ethan Frome* is the only one of Wharton's novels that makes use of a narrative frame. As Wharton notes in her preface, the unnamed narrator acts "as the sympathizing intermediary between his rudimentary characters and the more complicated minds to whom he is trying to present them" (vi). He also provides distance between the story and its telling. He is an outsider with limited perceptions, whose account is necessarily selective and speculative. Through him, Wharton permits a subjective rather than objective interpretation of Ethan's story.

This unreliable narration—a modernist technique—invites both the narrator's and the reader's participation. The narrator constructs the tale from his observations and neighbors' accounts, deciding on the meaning of what he has learned. The reader, provided with the same information as the narrator, similarly engages in acts of meaning-making. Wharton makes use of ellipses at crucial and vexed moments: for example, before and after the narrator's reconstruction of Ethan's story; when Ethan and Mattie imagine a life together, race downhill toward the tree, and awaken after the crash; and when Ethan introduces the narrator to Zeena and Mattie. The ellipses ask the reader to fill in "the gaps" in Ethan's story (5).[14] As early as 1915, Elizabeth Shepley Sergeant perceived the novel's subjectivity: "it was just Mrs. Wharton's *own sense* of the blankness and emptiness . . . in Starkfield lives, that made her construct that tremendous fourth act for her lovers and condemn them to its gruesome, long-drawn epilogue" (20, my emphasis). A realistic novel might end with the lovers' resigned parting; Wharton's choice—to leave all three characters suspended in pain without resolution—conveys her modernist sense of uncertainty and indeterminacy.

Focusing on the narrator's perception of the story also allows Wharton to present two sides of a conflict that warred within her: the Calvinist despair felt by believers who think themselves damned, represented by Ethan, and the rejection of that fate, represented by a modern scientist and skeptic. The narrator, a sophisticated urban engineer, comes to the remote town of Starkfield to oversee the expansion of an electric power plant. There he encounters his dark double, Ethan Frome, who has forfeited dreams of technical achievement and romance, whose only future is to join his ancestors in the family graveyard. The engineer is associated with technology, education, choice, and worldly accomplishment; Ethan, with unyielding nature, lapsed potential, restriction, and suffering. Wharton herself held these two worldviews in tension, not only during the period that she wrote *Ethan Frome*, but during much of her life.

The narrator expects to mold events to his own plan, but he encounters the same obstacles that hinder Ethan. For example, he must rely on an earlier mode of transport, horse and buggy, to travel to the plant site because the railroad does not fully serve the remote region. Nature has its way when Denis Eady's horses fall ill, and the narrator turns to Ethan for transportation. Snow then blankets the town, requiring a detour to Ethan's farmhouse and the figurative journey back to a time when natural and moral necessity seem to predate and defeat reason. The narrator, an accomplished technologist, represents the post-Darwinian conviction that, as chemist John William Draper says, "there was no limit to understanding the world in natural rather than supernatural terms" (qtd. in Turner 200). Ethan Frome, however, a failed engineer, evokes an earlier chapter in American moral history that focused on human limitation rather than potential. The narrator intuitively understands the effect of this Calvinist past when he takes Ethan for "an old man," even though he is "not more than fifty-two" (3).

The narrator tries to discover the cause of Ethan Frome's misfortune, but he can only speculate that it was "something in his past history, or in his present way of living" (10). He finds the answer in a look on Ethan's face "which . . . neither poverty nor physical suffering could have put there" (7). The narrator senses rather than deduces a "depth of moral isolation too remote for casual access" (8). Thus Wharton suggests that despite reason, science, and technology, the world is still unknowable and beyond human control. In the end, the narrator can only muse over the ruin of a man whose interest in science and books has not saved him. The search for meaning is as frustrated for us as it is for the narrator: we find within the text no rational explanation for Ethan's fate or means of altering it.

If the meaning of Ethan's story is indeterminate for both narrator and reader, it was not so for Edith Wharton. The very act of composing the novel released her from her Calvinist "moral tortures." Wharton clearly aligns herself with both Ethan and the narrator. Like Ethan, she is a sensitive yet discouraged aspirer who has "been in Starkfield too many winters" and cannot "get away" (5, 6); like the narrator, she is a designer with creative capabilities who does get away. Ultimately, however, one sensibility prevails: Wharton, writer and creator, identifies with the narrator rather than the mute and powerless Ethan Frome. Whereas Ethan laments, "Oh, what good'll writing do?" (78), Wharton seized the pen and imparted her story to others.[15]

The narrator gains power over the narrative in yet another way. Initially curious about and sympathetic toward Ethan's plight, he becomes more detached by the end of the story. His narrative ends when he meets Mattie and Zeena; we learn nothing of his reaction to their suffering. We can only imagine his relief at being able to escape the conditions that keep Starkfield under "siege like a starved garrison capitulating without quarter" (6).

Furthermore, the narrator's position is not entirely neutral. If the characters' wracked, ailing bodies bear the marks of punishment by an avenging God who belongs to an outmoded faith, then the narrator's gaze serves to reinforce that punishment. In Foucauldian terms, his surveillance—a play of asymmetrical glances that the objectified individuals internalize—asserts his power over the scene. The novel opens, after all, with the narrator's gaze fixed on Ethan Frome as he pulls his horses to a stop and limps awkwardly to the post office. It ends with his invasive scrutiny of the Frome household—a visit that no Starkfield resident has ever made. Can Ethan feel anything but humiliation and defeat when—already "a prisoner for life," with reality "closed in on him like prison-warders handcuffing a convict" (66)—he is further punished by the narrator's penetrating gaze?

Through the narrative frame in *Ethan Frome*, then, Edith Wharton allowed herself to survey and emerge victorious over the crippling effects of Calvinism. In writing the novel, as Debra Goodman notes, she created a scapegoat to bear her guilt and thereby "exorcized her own demons" (qtd. in Murad 103 n52). Her affair with Fullerton had reactivated her Calvinist morality—what she once called a "cursed" "split between body & soul" (*Letters* 159)—but *Ethan Frome* healed the split.

IV

Despite the critical acclaim it received, Wharton never considered *Ethan Frome* her literary masterpiece. Some twenty years later, she wrote that "far from thinking 'Ethan Frome' my best novel," she was "bored and even exasperated when I am told that it is" (*Backward* 209). Her godson, William Royall Tyler, corroborates: "She was always impatient about *Ethan Frome*. She wished that people wouldn't always talk to her about it. She didn't think of *Ethan Frome* as being her highest achievement or anything like it" (Tyler). Yet Wharton understood that the novel was a technical tour de force that enabled her to experience "the artisan's full control of his implements" (*Backward* 209). She also knew that it helped her lift a heavy personal burden. As she writes in the preface, the subject of Ethan Frome was the first "I had ever approached with full confidence in its value, *for my own purpose*" (vi, my emphasis). Even if the novel's significance was private, it was still a source of power. As Wharton remarked about readers' responses to the novel: "They don't know *why* it's good, but they are right: it *is*" (*Letters* 261, emphasis in original).

Calvinism provided Wharton with a usable past that she could transform into modernist art. Like other female American writers such as Anne Bradstreet, Emily Dickinson, and Harriet Beecher Stowe, she found the patriarchal Calvinist God oppressive, and in *Ethan Frome* she turns an austere theology into an austere aesthetic. She gives her narrator modern values and plain, economical speech. His efficient expression—a language *démeuble*, as Willa Cather puts it—heightens the novel's emotional impact: we feel the characters' suffering all the more because so much of their inner lives is left to be imagined. As Cecilia Tichi notes, a decade before Ernest Hemingway published his first major work, Wharton had mastered "the power of the machine-age plain style"—an "engineering aesthetic" (219, 217). Modernist writers often achieved a hard-edged quality with images of metals, especially steel; in *Ethan Frome*, Wharton accomplishes the same goal with New England granite. Commenting on her artistic method, she explains that in the "construction" of her novel, she resisted the "added ornament, or a trick of drapery or lighting" (vii) that is associated with Victorian realism. It is true that Wharton remained aloof from the Left Bank modernists just blocks away in Paris,[16] and she rejected some twentieth-century literary developments—for example, she called Joyce's *Ulysses* "a welter of pornography . . . unformed and unimportant drivel" and complained that Eliot's *The Waste Land* lacked the warmth of Whitman's poetry (R. Lewis, *Edith* 442). Nevertheless, *Ethan Frome*, although an American story, was drafted in France, amidst the ferment of a new international literary movement. Wharton is a modernist innovator whose *Ethan Frome* helped shape a movement and whose minimalist style influenced Sherwood Anderson, Gertrude Stein, and Ernest Hemingway.

Wharton continued to write about New England, but she never wrote another novel as bleak as *Ethan Frome*. No other fiction is so desolate in setting, theme, and tone because at no other time did Wharton wrestle so intensely with Calvinist issues such as salvation and damnation, free will versus fate and predestination, and the proper balance between pleasure and sacrifice. In this novel, Wharton revived the Calvinist doctrines that her genteel society had so complacently dismissed. And in so doing, she reconciled the American past as well as her own and reinterpreted Calvinism for a modern world.

Notes

1. For detailed discussions of Wharton's spiritual search and the religious and philosophical dimensions of her fiction, see my study *Edith Wharton*.

2. Here I borrow Greven's terms—"genteel," "moderate," and "evangelical"—to describe the range of American religious temperaments (12-14). His classifications refer to the colonial period, but they also help to explain nineteenth-century American religious life.

3. Wharton describes her driving need for spiritual answers: "I read, à tort et à travers [at random], every 'religious' work I could lay hands on" ("Life" 1090).

4. On Wharton's relationship to New England, see Hamblen, Leach, and A. Rose.

5. When Sara Norton declined the offer to play hostess to visitors she did not like, Wharton commented sarcastically to another friend, Gaillard Lapsley: "What fun it must be to be a Bostonian! It's the only surviving habitat of the Moral Imperative" (*Letters* 496). In *A Backward Glance*, she characterizes Bostonians as "a community of wealthy and sedentary people seemingly too lacking in intellectual curiosity to have any desire to see the world" (61–62).

6. Wharton's criticism of the Calvinist view of women is apparent in *French Ways and Their Meaning* (1919), in which she complains, "the long hypocrisy which Puritan England handed on to Americans concerning the danger of frank and free social relations between men and women has done more than anything else to retard real civilisation in America" (112–13). She also criticizes Calvinism in the story "The Pretext" (1908), in which the protagonist must battle "the specter of her rigid New England ancestry" (*Collected* 633).

7. Missing its more compelling similarities to *The Scarlet Letter*, most critics cite *The Blithedale Romance* or "Ethan Brand" as touchstones for *Ethan Frome*.

8. On the Manichaean vision in realism and modernism, see D. Schneider; on Hawthorne and Manichaeanism, see Chase (74–79) and Winters (3–22). Coale's view is particularly relevant to *Ethan Frome*: "Hawthorne looked out upon a dark, imprisoning world. He also looked to a soul imprisoned and isolated. The world oppressed the self, which in turn oppressed the soul, the inner spirit. The ultimate horror, however, was the perception of the inner soul and an outer world both of which were dark and impenetrable. . . . What remains is the sense that the dark soul and the dark world can obliterate each other" (4–5). Wharton may have learned about Manichaeanism from Augustine, whose *Confessions* she quotes in her novel *The Gods Arrive*.

9. The characters in the two novels play similar roles. Ethan, like Hester, commits an act of transgressive passion, silently suffers its consequences, and gradually wins his town's sympathy. Zeena parallels Chillingworth, a wronged, vengeful spouse obsessed with illness. And Mattie, like Dimmesdale, is an impulsive lover who ultimately fails to take responsibility for her plight.

10. Wharton never acknowledged her debt to Hawthorne, but she may have intended her own New England tale of woe to rival his. In a 1908 letter to publisher William Brownell about his article on Hawthorne, she commented that she "especially enjoyed your bringing out his lack of poetry and his lukewarmness. . . . My only two quarrels with you are for calling the Scarlet L. 'our one prose masterpiece'—I'd so much rather we had more than that one" (qtd. in R. Lewis, *Edith* 237). As Lewis notes, Wharton's "grudging reading of Hawthorne, whose impact on *Ethan Frome* a few years later would be unmistakable," conveys a younger writer's need to denigrate a predecessor in order to promote herself (237).

11. See Eggenschwiler, who also describes *Ethan Frome* as a complex allegory. For him, however, Ethan's tragedy is "strictly classical" (245) rather than Christian.

12. Wharton writes that in order to acquire writing paper, she "was driven to begging for the wrappings of the parcels delivered at the house" (*Backward* 73). She also explains that when she asked about the new feelings she had when she "raced & danced & tumbled with 'the boys',", she was always told, "You're too little to understand," or else, "It's not nice to ask about such things" ("Life" 1087).

13. Hays also reads the accident in terms of Calvinism, but he emphasizes Ethan's sense of duty to others. Ethan, "close-mouthed, stalwart, and puritanical," has so thoroughly internalized New England codes that he insists on sitting first

in the sled, an arrangement he believes will allow him to die but will spare Mattie (n.p.).

14. Critics have noted that Wharton's narrative technique invites reader participation. On her use of ellipses, see Blackall (145) and Ammons (62). On the effect of absence in Wharton's fiction, see A. Smith and my essay with Sweeney.

15. Wharton implicitly identifies herself with the narrator in her preface: "only the narrator of the tale has scope enough to see it all, to resolve it back into simplicity, and to put it in its rightful place among his larger categories" (vii). As Brennan notes, the narrator "is actually a writer in disguise with the technical skill of a professional novelist and the sensibility of a poet" (348). Both are sophisticated observers capable of seeing and shaping experience. Wolff also discusses this doubling, reading the novel as a dream vision in which the narrator, as Ethan's double, plunges into the repressed parts of his psyche. The narrator emerges from his "private nightmare" stronger and more whole; the doubling of author and narrator thus serves to validate the young writer (*Feast* 183–84).

16. See Benstock's treatment of Wharton as both a modernist forerunner and an outsider in Paris (61–65).

CYNTHIA GRIFFIN WOLFF

Un-Utterable Longing

The Discourse of Feminine Sexuality in Kate Chopin's *The Awakening*

BECAUSE NOVELISTS ARE particular about beginnings, we should notice that *The Awakening* opens with two things: sumptuous sensory images and an outpouring of babble—words that resemble ordinary speech but that really have meaning for no one, not even the speaker:

A green and yellow parrot, which hung in a cage outside the door, kept repeating over and over:
"*Allez vous-en! Allez vous-en! Sapristi!* That's all right!"
He could speak a little Spanish, and also a language which nobody understood. (19)

Although an onlooker is able to enjoy this vivid scene, the parrot cannot; moreover, there is a sense of enigma (or fraud) about this bird who seems able to communicate but is not. Indeed, the absolute discontinuity between the bird's "discourse," its exotic plumage, and its feelings (whatever they may be) is even more significant to the larger themes of the novel than the fact that he is caged. Or perhaps this very disconnectedness (and the bird's consequent isolation) defines the cage.

Critics admire the "modernism" of Chopin's work, the strong spareness of the prose and the "minimalism" of a narrative whose absences are at least as important as its action and whose narrator maintains strict emotional and moral neutrality. What we may not fully appreciate is the relationship between these elements and Edna Pontellier's personal tragedy, a relationship whose terms are announced by the apparent disarray of the novel's brilliant beginning. This is a tale about *not* speaking, about disjunction— about denials, oversights, prohibitions, exclusions, and absences. It is not merely about things that are never named, but most significantly about stories that cannot be told and things that can be neither thought nor spoken because they *do not have a name*.

After about 1850, the notion of a "woman's sexual awakening" became, by definition, an impossibility—a contradiction in terms—because the medical establishment in America began to promulgate the view that normal females possessed no erotic inclinations whatsoever (and one cannot awaken something that does not exist). William Acton, the acknowledged expert on the nature of women's sexuality and author of "one of the most widely quoted books on sexual problems and diseases in the English-speaking world," wrote: "The majority of women (happily for society) are not very much troubled with sexual feeling of any kind. What men are habitually women are only exceptionally. It is too true, I admit, as the divorce courts show, that there are some few women who have sexual desires so strong that they surpass those of men, and shock public feeling by their consequences."[1] Acton's work elaborated a comprehensive system of women's "inequality" to men; and it was so universally respected that his sentiments can be taken to represent opinions that were held throughout much of America during the second half of the nineteenth century. Certainly they defined the stern attitudes of the society in which Edna Pontellier had been reared, Calvinistic Presbyterianism, a latter-day bastion of Puritan thought.[2]

American Puritanism had always preached that although the woman was to be "regarded as equal to man in her title to grace," she was nonetheless "the weaker vessel" and thus was obliged to pursue all endeavors as a "subordinate to the husband" (Haller 121). From the beginning, this definition of the feminine role had created tensions and conflict: it had often produced instances of strong, passionately outspoken women; however, the assessment of these women's behavior had varied greatly. Nonetheless, until the nineteenth century, English and American Puritanical beliefs about woman's nature were relatively consistent: women were wanting in neither emotional energy (in general) or sexual energy (in particular); indeed, the second was thought to be a concomitant of "innate depravity," which was often associated with other forms of aggressive behavior that were inappropriate for women. In America, Puritanical communities gave considerable attention to the various means that could be employed to *control* a woman's sexual behavior, and early novels that were popular on both continents—*Pamela*, *Clarissa*, *Charlotte Temple*, and *The Coquette*—focused explicitly on the dilemmas that attended feminine sexual drive.[3]

When Anne Hutchinson "stepped out of the role the community defined for her," a special sort of "woman-problem" was defined in America—in part sexual, but more generally political—for "if a woman could instruct men, then all legitimate authority was in jeopardy" (Lang 42–43). The prototypical response had been formulated in Hutchinson's day: require women to assume their divinely ordained, subordinate position. Her failure to do so would result (so the argument ran) not merely in civil misrule but in grotesque sexual misconduct. Thus in the Hutchinson case, the phantoms of both social turmoil and sexual license haunted the trial: "everywhere in the court examination, one finds the insinuation that Hutchinson is, like Jezebel, guilty of fornication" (43).[4]

Although Puritanism in America had begun to lose its vitality as a unifying cultural force by the end of the eighteenth century, and the clearly defined vision of human nature that had characterized its earliest days was gradually eroded, the fear of a woman's transgressing the boundaries that circumscribed her role lingered and seemed to justify a potentially lethal form of repression. Even at the time of Hawthorne's great work—and certainly by the beginning of the Civil War—Americans had displaced the reality and complexity of Puritanism with a trope; and the *trope*, "Puritanical," was used generally (and rather carelessly) to denote *conservatism* and *repression*, especially sexual repression. Paradoxically, although in loose usage repressive "Puritanism" had generally come to have negative connotations where women were concerned, repressive modes of defining women's "appropriate" role persisted and were generally applauded. Such a response may well have been the conservative reaction to the first Woman's Movement—with its outspoken leaders and its demands for female empowerment. Thus it is not surprising that during the flowering of late-nineteenth-century American Victorianism, major changes further constricted these widely disseminated notions of a woman's innate nature.

The superficial attitudes and norms seemed the same: it was deemed inappropriate for a woman to enact aggressive behavior, and it was deemed scandalous for a woman to indulge in passionately sexual conduct. Yet whereas seventeenth-century Puritans had presumed that women (like men) were innately passionate, late-nineteenth-century Americans presumed that women (*unlike men*) had a certain innate "passivity" and "purity": "appropriate" female behavior—silence and a revulsion from sexual activity—was therefore also considered to be "*natural*" female behavior. The deep, persistent Puritan heritage in American culture imparted a virulent force to such attitudes, and a number of Protestant sects actively promoted them.[5]

In the 1870s and continuing through the end of the century, the Presbyterian Church in America suffered a crisis over the role of women that might well be defined by the question, "Shall Women *Speak?*"[6] The embroglio began when a Newark clergyman invited two women into his pulpit to speak in favor of the Temperance Movement. Seeing an opportunity to reaffirm the precedent of women's "naturally" subordinate role, the Presbytery of Newark brought formal charges against the minister. In the minds of the accusers, the issue was far from narrow: "the subject in-

volves the honor of my God. . . . My argument is subordination of sex. . . .
There exists a created subordination; a divinely arranged and appointed
subordination of woman as woman to man as man. Woman was made for
man. . . . The proper condition of the adult female is marriage; the general rule for ladies is marriage. . . . Man's place is on the platform. It is
positively base for a woman to speak in the pulpit. . . . The whole question
is one of subordination" (qtd. in Boyd 287). For both the Puritan Fathers
and their late-nineteenth-century Calvinist descendants, the specter of a
woman speaking out was portentous: at best, it was unsettling to the male
hierarchy; at worst, it augured chaos. Suffragists could also discern the
importance of this case, and the dispute among Newark Presbyterians became a notorious part of "the record of their struggle" and was widely
publicized" (Boyd 291).

Confronted with what they feared might become a similar provocation,
the Presbyterian clergymen of Edna Pontellier's youth demanded that
women keep to their "natural sphere" of home, hearth, and motherhood.
As for women's sexuality, William Acton was their more than sufficient
spokesman.

All of Acton's formulations are sweepingly comprehensive and inescapably normative, and in this respect he resembled the Puritans. He does not
admit of gradations among women; nor does he entertain the possibility
that additional data—testimony from women themselves, perhaps—might
contradict or even emend his pronouncements. Instead, he presents his
ideas as nothing less than a description of both a divinely ordained condition and a condition for middle-class respectability. He clearly considers
the absence of passion in "normal women" to be a good thing (for its presence in a decent female would "shock public feeling"); and he refers dis-
missively to "prostitutes" and "loose, or, at least, low and vulgar women"
whose strong libidinous drives "give a very false idea of the condition of
female sexual feelings in general." In short, the innate frigidity of women
signified a form of refinement and could be used as a touchstone for respectability.

The official "scientific" and "medical" view can be stated quite simply:
an average woman (a "decent" woman) possesses no sexual feelings whatsoever. Thus it is not enough to say that *The Awakening* is a novel about
repression (that is, about a situation in which a woman possesses sexual
feelings, but is prohibited from acting upon them). It is, instead, a novel
about a woman whose shaping culture has, in general, refused her the right
to speak out freely; this is, moreover, a culture that construes a woman's
self-expression as a violation of sexual "purity" and a culture that has denied the existence of women's libidinous potential altogether—has eliminated the very *concept* of sexual passion for "normal" women.

The consequences are emotionally mutilating (in the extreme case, some form of mental breakdown would result).[7] In such a culture, if a "respectable" woman supposes herself to feel "something," some powerful ardor in her relationship with a man, she can draw only two possible inferences. Either her feelings are not sexual (and should not be enacted in a genital relationship), or she is in some (disgraceful) way "abnormal." Moreover, because there is presumed to be no such entity as sexual feelings in the typical woman, a typical (i.e. "normal") woman will literally have no words for her (nonexistent) feelings, will have access to no discourse within which these (nonexistent) passions can be examined or discussed, will be able to make no coherent connection between the (unintelligible) inner world of her affective life and the external, social world in which she must live.[8] Finally, if she feels confusion and emotional pain, her culture's general prohibition against speaking out will make it difficult, perhaps impossible, to discuss or even reveal her discomfort.

Of course there was an escape hatch (infinitesimal, and insufficient). After all, men and women did marry, did have sexual intercourse, doubtless did (sometimes) enjoy their love-making, and did (occasionally) find ways to discuss the intimate elements of their relationship.[9] The range and resourcefulness of their individual solutions must remain a mystery. However, the publicly approved forms of discourse for female desire are a matter of record. Medical and psychological experts concluded that although women had no sexual drives per se, they often possessed a passionate desire to bear children: such ardor was both "normal" and (inevitably) sexual. On these terms, then, sexual activity—even moderate sexual "desire"—was appropriate in "normal" women. However, a profound displacement or confusion was introduced by this accommodation: the language of feminine sexuality became inextricably intertwined with discourse that had to do with childbearing and motherhood.

According to Acton (and to others who followed his lead), nature itself had made the longing to have children the essential, causative force of a woman's sexual "appetite." Thus men and women were essentially different: men have sexual impulses and needs (and these are quite independent of any wish to sire offspring); women crave children (and consequently they might be said—very indirectly—to "want" sexual activity). "Virility" and "maternity" were defined as parallel instincts that were nonetheless fundamentally dissimilar; and a woman's possessing sexual ardor *independent of her yearning for babies* became a defining symptom of abnormality or immorality or both:

If the married female conceives every second year, we usually notice that during the nine months following conception she experiences no great sexual excitement. . . .

Love of home, of children, and of domestic duties are the only passions [women] feel.

As a general rule, a modest woman seldom desires any sexual gratification for herself. She submits to her husband's embraces, but principally to gratify him; and *were it not for the desire of maternity*, would far rather be relieved from his attentions. (Acton 138, 164; my emphasis) [10]

Scholars have accepted almost as cliché the fact that in late-Victorian America "motherhood" was exalted as an all-but-divine state. However, if we do not also understand the oblique (and contradictory) sexual implications of this cultural ideal, we may be unaware of the confusion and conflict it engendered.

This definition of feminine sexuality radically displaced a woman's passionate desires: unlike males, who were permitted to "possess" their sexuality and were consequently allowed to experience passion directly and *as a part of the "self,"* females were allowed access to sexuality only indirectly— as a subsidiary component of their desire for children. It was literally unimaginable that any "decent" woman would experience sexual appetite as an immediate and urgent drive, distinct from all other desires and duties. Men "owned" their libido; women's libido was "owned" by their prospective children.[11]

Any woman would find this concatenation of denials and demands unbalancing; however, in *The Awakening*, Chopin renders these cultural regulations of women's role in ways that are designed to demonstrate their potentially lethal consequences, for in Edna's case, the already vexed situation is brought to crisis by a superadded disjunction: a conflict of "religions" and "cultures." The summer at Grand Isle marks the moment when catastrophe begins.

Reared as a Presbyterian in Kentucky, Edna has been married to a Creole for many years. Nonetheless, she has never become "thoroughly at home in the society of Creoles; [and] never before had she been thrown so intimately among them" (27–28). It is not that Creoles do not have a rigorous sexual code: their customs follow the boundary conditions that Acton and his fellow theorists have postulated. However, far from being Bible-bound, sober and staid, so long as they remain within the rules of this code, they permit themselves an extraordinary freedom of sensual expression. Thus a lusty carnal appetite in *men* is taken for granted. (Robert has his affair with the Mexican girl, everyone knows about it, and no one thinks to disapprove.) However, the case of Creole *women* is different, for their sexuality may exist only as a component of "motherhood." Nevertheless, so long as they accept this model, women, too, may engage in a sumptuous sexual life. Mme Ratignolle, the "sensuous Madonna," embodies the essence of ardor and voluptuous appetite thus construed.

Such a system imposes penalties (Adèle's accouchement is one specific marker for the price to be paid); however, within these limiting conditions,

the Creole world is more densely erotic than any community Edna has encountered. It revels frankly and happily in the pleasures of the flesh—not
merely enjoying these delights with undisguised zest but discussing them
in public with no shame at all. Edna can recognize the inherent "chastity"
of such people, but their habits nonetheless embarrass her profoundly:

Madame Ratignolle had been married seven years. About every two years she had
a baby. At that time she had three babies, and was beginning to think of a fourth
one. She was always talking about her "condition." Her "condition" was in no way
apparent, and no one would have known a thing about it but for her persistence in
making it the subject of conversation. (27)

A late-twentieth-century reader may innocently suppose that Adèle's preoccupation is purely maternal. The full truth is quite otherwise: in the
discourse of the day, Adèle has elected to flaunt her sexuality—to celebrate both her ardor and her physical enjoyment. Robert enters the festive,
flirtatious moment by recalling the "lady who had subsisted upon nougat
during the entire—," and is checked only by Edna's blushing discomfort.

All such instances of candor unsettle Mrs. Pontellier, for example, when
she responds with shock to Mme Ratignolle's "harrowing story of one
of her *accouchements*" (28). This strange world, with its languorous climate and frankly sensuous habits, is a world where "normal," "respectable"
women openly vaunt pleasures that are unfamiliar to her. She is fascinated and eventually profoundly aroused. And although she is bewildered
by these new sensations, once having been touched by them, she becomes
unwilling to pull away. Much of the novel, then, is concerned with Edna's
quest for a viable and acceptable mode of owning and expressing her sexuality: first by locating the defining boundaries for these feelings and thus
being able to define and name what she feels inside herself; second by finding some acceptable social construct which will permit her to enact them
in the outside world and to make an appropriate, vital, and affirming connection between the "me" and the "not-me" (Laing, *Self* 17-53).

Edna's easiest option is "collusion," to become a "mother-woman";
however, she rejects this role violently because of the displacements and
forfeitures that it would impose. If, like Adèle, she were willing to disguise
her erotic drives in the mantle of "motherhood," she might indulge the
many delights of the body as Adele patently does. However, such a capitu-
lation would not allow her really to possess her own feelings—nor even to
talk about them directly or explicitly. It would maim the "self," not unify
and affirm it: like Adèle, Edna would be obliged to displace all of her sexual
discourse into prattle about "the children" or her [pregnant] "condition,"
fettering her carnal desires to the production of babies; and part of what
was really *inside* (that is, her sexual drive) would be displaced on to some-

thing *outside* (society's construction of female appetite as essentially "maternal"). In the process, the authority and integrity of her identity would be compromised, and instead of making contact with the outside world, she would be merged into it and controlled by it. Edna loves her children and is happy to be a mother; however, she refuses to define her sexuality in terms of them.[12]

Thus Edna's rejection of this emotional mutilation lies behind the many tortured examinations of her relationship to the children and informs such assertions as: "I would give up the unessential; I would give my money, I would give my life for my children; but I wouldn't give myself" (67). Renouncing what she can clearly recognize as an unacceptable violation of her emotional integrity is Edna's most confident step toward freedom.[13]

She shrugs away from marriage for many of the same reasons, declaring that she will "never again belong to another than herself" (100). The problem is neither immediate nor personal: it is not Léonce, per se, that Edna repudiates, but the warped forms of intimacy that he represents. Like Adèle, Léonce is acquainted with no discourse of feminine sexuality other than some variant on the language of "motherhood." This conflation is revealed in the couple's first intimate scene. Léonce has returned from an evening of card-playing, jolly at having won a little money — "in excellent humor . . . high spirits, and very talkative" (23). To be sure, he does not "court" his wife; yet he is scarcely brutal or coarse, and his gossipy, somewhat preoccupied manner as he empties his pockets might be that of any long-married man. Indeed, it is *Edna's* unapproachable manner that disrupts the potential harmony of the moment. There is nothing peculiar about the "action" of this scenario, nor is it difficult to read the subtext: Léonce would like to conclude his pleasant evening with a sexual encounter; his wife is not interested.

The real oddity has to do with language. Although the couple falls into a kind of argument over their differing inclinations, sex itself is never mentioned. Instead, when Léonce chooses to rebuke his wife (presumably for her passional indifference to him), he employs a vernacular of "motherhood" to do so. "He reproached his wife with her inattention, her habitual neglect of the children. If it was not a mother's place to look after children, whose on earth was it?" (24). With this alienated discourse, neither party can talk about the real source of unhappiness; however, Léonce at least has "acceptable" alternatives (for example, we should probably not suppose that he is celibate during his long absences from home). Edna has none — not even the satisfaction of being able to define the exact nature of her despondency.[14]

She generally shuns the effort to assert herself, and to a remarkable degree she has detached herself from language altogether. As Urgo has observed, "For the first six chapters of the novel, she says all of four sentences" (23). Moreover, although she has lived among the Creoles for many years, "she understood French imperfectly unless directly addressed" (56). On this occasion, then, it is not surprising that she "said nothing and refused to answer her husband when he questioned her" (24). This is her customary reaction. Although Chopin's narrator refrains from moralizing about Edna's predicament, she does give the reader information from which it is possible to extrapolate Mrs. Pontellier's reasons for avoiding speech.

After her minor disagreement with Léonce, Edna begins to weep: "She could not have *told* why she was crying. . . . An *indescribable* oppression, which seemed to generate in some *unfamiliar* part of her consciousness, filled her whole being with a *vague* anguish" (24-25; my emphasis). At the most literal level, Edna is absolutely unable to "tell" why she is crying: her deepest passions have no "true" name. Society has given them only false names, like "maternity"; and such a discourse of feminine sexuality both distorts a woman's feelings and compromises her authority over them.

Thus Edna's recoil from language — her refusal to comply with this misrepresentation — is a primitive effort to retain control over her "self":

She had all her life long been accustomed to harbor thought and emotions which *never voiced themselves*. They had never taken the form of struggles. They belonged to her and were *her own*, and she entertained the conviction that she had a right to them and that they concerned no one but herself. (66-67; my emphasis)

Nor is it surprising that Edna has always been deeply susceptible to fantasies — to her inward "dreams" of the cavalry officer, of the engaged young man from a neighboring plantation, of the "great tragedian." A person can and does entirely possess the products of his or her own imagination because (like the passions that infuse them) they are a part of the self. Thus, falling into fantasy becomes another way by which Edna seeks to maintain the integrity of self.

In some primitive way, silence also is Edna's only appropriate reaction to society's way of defining female sexuality: for if women were imagined to have no sexual feelings, *not to speak* would (ironically) be the way to "communicate" this absence. Yet not to speak has an annihilating consequence: it is, in the end, not to *be* — not to have social reality. One can never *affirm* "self" merely through silence and fantasy — can never forge that vital connection between the "me" and the "not-me" that validates identity. A "self" can mature only if one strives to articulate emotions; learning to name one's feelings is an integral component of learning the extent and nature of one's feelings, and what is undescribed may remain always "indescribable" — even to oneself — "vague" and even "unfamiliar." Moreover, without some authentic, responsive reaction from another, no one can escape the kind of solitude that increasingly oppresses Edna during the summer of her twenty-ninth year.[15]

Indeed, the dispassionate tone of Chopin's novel may be related to the complexity of Edna's quest, for Edna cannot "solve" her problem without an extraordinary feat of creativity. She must discover not merely a new vernacular with which to name her feelings—not merely a new form of plot that is capable of containing them—but also an "audience" that both comprehends and esteems the story she might ultimately tell. Thus the true subject of *The Awakening* may be less the particular dilemma of Mrs. Pontellier than the larger problems of female narrative that it reflects; and if Edna's poignant fate is in part a reflection of her own habits, it is also, in equal part, a measure of society's failure to allow its women a language of their own.

Most immediately personal is Edna's enchantment with forms of "communication" that do not require words. She is entranced by the ocean because its "language" neither compromises nor distorts her most intimate passions. Yet it cannot allow her to assert and confirm "self"; for ironically, like society, the sea requires an immersion of "self" (and this is, perhaps, the reason Edna has feared the water for so long):

> Seductive; never ceasing, whispering, clamoring, murmuring, inviting the soul to wander for a spell in abysses of solitude; to lose itself in mazes of inward contemplation.
> The voice of the sea speaks to the soul. The touch of the sea is sensuous, enfolding the body in its soft, close embrace. (32)

Music also seems to have "spoken" to Edna, most often conjuring primly conventional emotional "pictures" in her mind. However, as soon as she stirs from her sensual torpor and discards the prim and the conventional, music begins to conjure something more violently demanding: "no pictures of solitude, of hope, of longing, or of despair. But the very passions themselves were aroused with her soul, swaying it, lashing it, as the waves daily beat upon her splendid body" (45). Without the customary "pictures" to contain them, these emotions clamor for expression with an intensity that is all but unbearable.

It is troubling that the narrative conventions to which Edna is habitually drawn are so formulaic, that they decline to attempt some model of feminine initiative or some assertion of explicitly feminine passion. She configures her outing with Robert as "Sleeping Beauty" ("'How many years have I slept?' she inquired" [57]). Her dinner-table story is passive—the romance of a woman who was carried off "by her lover one night in a pirogue and never came back" (90). And if, as Sandra Gilbert has argued, Edna presides over a "Swinburnian Last Supper" just before her death

(44), this moment when the "old ennui" and "hopelessness" overtake her once again must be read not as a new birth of Venus but as a poignant prefiguration of her return to that sea whence she came (Chopin 109).[16]

Yet troubling as Edna's habits of mind may be, Chopin also makes it clear that it would have taken more than daring ingenuity to alter her situation. The demand for women's rights alarmed sexual theorists, who construed all changes in the accepted paradigm as portents of anarchy. Their response was to reaffirm the conventional life story by insisting that women's dissatisfactions could be readily dismissed as nothing but an evidence of their innate inferiority: "In medical colleges, in medical books, in medical practice, woman is recognized as having a peculiar organization, requiring the most careful and gentle treatment. . . . Her bodily powers are not able to endure like those of the other sex" (qtd. in Barker-Benfield 200). When Léonce begins to discern the differences in Edna's manner and takes his concerns to Dr. Mandelet, their conversation recapitulates these nineteenth-century discussions of woman's nature:

"She's odd, she's not like herself. I can't make her out. . . . She's got some sort of notion in her head concerning the eternal rights of women." . . .

"Woman, my dear friend," [the Doctor responded,] "is a very peculiar and delicate organism—a sensitive and highly organized woman, such as I know Mrs. Pontellier to be, is especially peculiar. . . . Most women are moody and whimsical. (85–86)

It would take invention and resolution indeed to counter such a confident weight of received opinion—more than most women (most people) possess.

If the power of Edna's narrative ability is insufficient to retaliate against such fettering force, her primary choice of "audience" merely recapitulates her other problems. Instead of discerning Robert's true nature, she fancies him to be the lover of her dreams. She does not heed the conventions within which their flirtation begins; instead (as Adèle observes), she makes "the unfortunate blunder of taking [him] seriously" (35). Nor does she very much attend to Robert's conversation; for although he has spoken enthusiastically of going to Mexico, his untimely departure catches her entirely by surprise. Thus the exact nature of their intimacy is always best for Edna when it must be inferred (because it has not been put into words):

[Robert] seated himself again and rolled a cigarette, which he smoked in silence. Neither did Mrs. Pontellier speak. No multitude of words could have been more significant than those moments of silence, or more pregnant with the first-felt throbbings of desire. (49)

Neither the reader nor Edna herself can know whose "desire" has been felt nor precisely what the object of this "desire" might be. However, the (almost overtly ironic) use of "pregnant" suggests that it is Edna, and not Robert, who has suffused this moment with unique intensity—and, most important, that she has not yet escaped all of those conventional constructions of female sexuality that bind it to maternity.[17]

Mademoiselle Reisz and Alcée Arobin (characters in and audiences for Edna's nascent narratives) both hold out the possibility that Edna might resolve her dilemma by usurping the prerogatives of men. Yet each offers a "solution" that would constrain Edna to relinquish some significant and valued portion of herself.

Ivy Schweitzer has observed that Mademoiselle Reisz, "a musician and composer, represents one extreme possibility; she exemplifies the artist with . . . 'the soul that dares and defies' conventionality, transgresses boundaries, and transcends gender" ("Maternal" 172). Mademoiselle Reisz also holds out the independence that men can achieve in a career. Yet Edna chooses not to follow this avenue; and Mademoiselle Reisz's admonition that the artist "must possess the courageous soul" (Chopin 83) may have been less of a deterrent than the example of that lady's own life. Fulfillment through aesthetic creativity appears to offer authentic expression to only one portion of the self. Mademoiselle Reisz "had quarreled with almost everyone, owing to a temper which was self-assertive and a disposition to trample upon the rights of others"; having no sensuous charm or aesthetic allure ("a homely woman with a small weazened face and body and eyes that glowed" [44]), she presents a sad and sorry prospect of some future Edna-as-successful-artist. What woman seeking sexual fulfillment would willingly follow the pathway to such a forfeiture of feminine sensuous pleasure as this?

Arobin offers the opposite. Something simpler but equally wounding. Lust. Sex divorced from all other feelings. The expression of that raw libido that was presumed to be part of men's nature (as "virility") but was categorically denied as a component of the normal female. Yet Edna finds that limiting sexuality to this form of expression imposes a distortion fully as destructive as society's construction of "maternity."

Arobin pursues Edna by pretending that casual sexuality is some fuller, more "sincere" emotion (he is careful never to mention love). And although his practiced style invites "easy confidence," it is also filled with "effrontery" (96)—with the desire to treat her as no more than a "beautiful, sleek animal waking up in the sun" (90). His manner could seem "so genuine that it often deceived even himself"; yet "in a cooler, quieter moment," Edna recognizes that it would be "absurd" to take him seriously (98). This form of eroticism explicitly excludes the integral complexity of Edna's unique "self": she might be anyone, any "sleek animal waking up in the sun," any woman whose "latent sensuality [would unfold] under his delicate sense of her nature's requirements like a torpid, torrid sensitive blossom"

(126). Thus the aftermath of their consummation is not an affirmation of identity for Edna but another form of maiming—a cascade of simple sentences in largely parallel form to configure alienation and disintegration—the novel's shortest, most mutilated chapter, less than half a page. These lay bare the harsh realities of existence, "beauty and brutality," and conclude with nothing but a "dull pang of regret because it was not the kiss of love which had inflamed her" (104).

By the time Robert returns, Edna has all but exhausted the limited possibilities of her world; and if her first preference is once again to construe him dreamlike—"for he had seemed nearer to her off there in Mexico" (124)—she has gained the courage to speak forbidden discourse in the hope of inventing a new kind of narrative. "I suppose this is what you would call unwomanly," she begins, "but I have got into a habit of expressing myself. It doesn't matter to me, and you may think me unwomanly if you like" (127). They return to her little house, and when Robert seems to doze in a chair, she rewrites the sleeping beauty story by reversing their roles and awakening *him* with a kiss, "a soft, cool, delicate kiss, whose voluptuous sting penetrated his whole being. . . . She put her hand up to his face and pressed his cheek against her own. The action was full of love and tenderness" (128–29).

Reality is the realm into which Edna would lead Robert: a complex kingdom of sensuous freedom commingled with "love and tenderness," a place where man and woman awaken each other to share the "beauty and brutality" of life together in mutual affirmation. Each owning sexual appetite; both sharing the stern burdens of brute passion.

Edna is shocked, then, to discover Robert speaking a language of "dreams": "I lost my senses. I forgot everything but a wild dream of your some way becoming my wife." Even worse, Robert's "dream" retains the confining accouterments of the narrative Edna has journeyed so far to escape. She wants a new paradigm; he merely wants to rearrange the actors of the old one, and Edna firmly rejects his falsifying, custom-bound notions. "You have been a very, very foolish boy, wasting your time dreaming of impossible things. . . . I give myself where I choose" (129). When Robert responds with perplexity to this new assertion of autonomy, Edna is offered the opportunity to show him what fortitude might mean.

Female sexuality had been falsified by the construct of "maternity"; however, there was one barbarous component of femininity, one consequence of feminine sexuality, that even the mother-woman could never evade. As Carroll Smith-Rosenberg explains:

In the nineteenth century, with its still-primitive obstetrical practices and its high child-mortality rates, she was expected to face severe bodily pain, disease, and death—and still serve as the emotional support and strength of her family. As the eminent Philadelphia neurologist S. Weir Mitchell wrote in the 1880s, "We may be sure that our daughters will be more likely to have to face at some time the grim question of pain than the lads who grow up beside them. . . . To most women . . . there comes a time when pain is a grim presence in their lives." (*Disorderly* 199)

Having confronted the harsh "masculine" fact of unmitigated sexual desire, Edna entreats Robert to comprehend the inescapable pain and danger of the "feminine" by acknowledging the reality of childbirth. Having risked the scorn of being judged "unwomanly" by speaking her feelings and by awakening Robert with an act of love and passion conjoined, she asks him to demonstrate comparable courage. He, too, must leave dreams and half-truths behind, must comprehend the full complexity of *her* experience — both the brutality and the beauty — if he is to share in the creation of this new narrative of ardent devotion. "Wait," she implores, as she leaves to attend Adèle; "I shall come back" (130).

After the delivery, Edna's still-fragile, emergent self is shaken. In response to Dr. Mandelet's queries, she shrugs away from language: "I don't feel moved to speak of things that trouble me." Her desires continue to trail a fairy-tale hope of absolute happiness: "I don't want anything but my own way" (132). Still her anticipated reunion with Robert fortifies her. She foresees the opportunity to resume their love-making; and she believes there will be a "time to think of everything" (133) on the morning to follow, a chance to fashion the story of their life together. However, she has refused to consider his weakness and his fondness for illusions. Thus she is unprepared for the letter she finds: "I love you. Good-by — because I love you" (134). In the end, Edna has discovered no partner/audience with whom to construct her new narrative, and she cannot concoct one in solitude.

Nonetheless, she concludes with a narrative gesture of sorts — a concatenation of the parlance of "maternity." Perhaps it is a tale of the son, Icarus, defeated by overweening ambition: "A bird with a broken wing was beating the air above, reeling, fluttering, circling disabled down, down to the water." Perhaps a tale of babies: "Naked in the open air. . . . She felt like some new-born creature, opening its eyes in a familiar world that it had never known." Most likely, it is a tragic inversion of the birth of Venus: "The touch of the sea is sensuous, enfolding the body in its soft, close embrace" (136).

So Edna has failed. Or rather, being a woman with some weaknesses and no extraordinary strengths, Edna has chosen the only alternative she could imagine to the ravaging social arrangements of her day. (Only seven years earlier, "The Yellow Wallpaper" had attracted wide attention to the same stifling, potentially annihilating constructions of "femininity.") However, we cannot forget that, if her heroine faltered, Kate Chopin fashioned a splendid success. *The Awakening* is the new narrative that Mrs. Pontellier was unable to create: not (it is true) a story of female affirmation, but rather an excruciatingly exact dissection of the ways in which society distorts a woman's true nature. The ruthless contemporary reviews leave no doubt that Kate Chopin had invented a powerful (and thus threatening) discourse for feminine sexuality. And although the novel was forced to languish (like yet another "sleeping beauty") largely unread for three quarters of a century, the current respect it enjoys is a belated affirmation of Kate Chopin's success.

Notes

1. We might be tempted to suppose that this attitude was in some essential way "Puritanical." However, Degler makes it clear that these explicit notions of women as totally devoid of passion entered American culture rather late (251–52). Quoted material within the text is from Degler 250 and Acton 162–63.

2. Chopin makes it clear (though unobtrusive) that Edna's background was repressive in many ways and that Edna was profoundly shaped by it. She writes of Sunday with its "Presbyterian service, read in a spirit of gloom by [Edna's] father" (35). It is significant that the age Edna mentions is both the age at which girls enter adolescence (and might under other circumstances begin to contemplate a sexual awakening) and the age at which Gilligan has found that many women "lose their voice" (12).

3. As early as 1563, the Englishman John Foxe recorded accounts of exemplary strong women in his *Book of Martyrs*; yet in America not many decades later, Anne Hutchinson's "strength" was heartily condemned. The intense mid-nineteenth-century climate of Amherst Puritanism produced probably the most "uppity" feminist voice of all — Emily Dickinson. For an extended examination of this phenomenon see my studies *Samuel Richardson*, "Literary Reflections," and *Emily Dickinson*.

4. One interesting difference between the seventeenth-century Puritans and their nineteenth-century inheritors is in their estimation of women's capacity for sexual passion. In Anne Hutchinson's day, few doubted that the average woman was possessed of sexual appetite (such an appetite was part and parcel of the shared human inheritance: "innate depravity"); the emphasis, then, was upon control of that appetite. However, by the later nineteenth century, the forcible disempowerment of women had advanced to the point where (in Acton's formulation, for instance) the "natural capacity" for sexual passion was missing in women. All serious Christians — perhaps especially the Puritans — would have discerned that the supposed compliment in this construction of the feminine was in reality a grotesque mutilation: she is rendered somewhat *less* than fully human.

5. Acton was an Englishman whose work found wide acceptance in America. Clearly, therefore, the attitudes about a woman's "normally" asexual nature were a feature of high Victorianism in England. The fact that my discussion is limited to America does not mean to imply that our English cousins were more sexually "liberated" with regard to a woman's nature.

6. Penfield suggests that "only the Lutherans, Southern Presbyterians, United Presbyterians . . . and Episcopalians among Protestants are more conservative on issues relating to women in the mainstream of church life" (119). The Congrega-

tionalists had been thrown into disarray almost a half-century earlier by a similar issue concerning women (the Grimke sisters) who had been permitted to speak in churches against slavery. As Boyd and Brackenridge suggest, even "during the last two decades of the nineteenth century, the inherent conservatism of the Presbyterian church caused social customs and traditions to be modified only slowly and not without tension and turmoil" (108).

7. Laing discusses difficulties that result from a failure to relate the "inside-me-here-now-good-real-pleasant" to some "outside" and "recognized" (or acknowledged) self. "The attempt to find a satisfactory stable combination between good-bad, empty-full, inside-outside, me-not-me, may take up a great deal of energy—so [an individual] may feel exhausted, empty, inside *and* outside (*Politics* 91, 93–94). This analysis allows us to understand Edna's profound ennui throughout the novel—her sense of lassitude—for little in her lifetime (either before or after her marriage) has very much facilitated the development of an authentic and socially confirmed sense of self.

8. For a description of the treatment of "hysteria" in women see Smith-Rosenberg, *Disorderly* 206–207, 211.

9. See Rothman, throughout, for some insight into these solutions.

10. For a critique of perspectives like Acton's, see Chodorow, who argues that women's unhappiness stems in part from being forced to "live through their children" (44).

11. Laing's discussion of false naming sheds light on Edna's predicament (*Self*, chaps. 8, 9). See also Yaeger, who ties the linguistic problems of the novel to notions of property and ownership.

12. Almost twenty years ago, I wrote an essay on this novel, "Thanatos and Eros: Kate Chopin's *The Awakening*," reprinted in complete form (Chopin) and in abridged form (Culley). What I am attempting here is not a fundamentally different reading of this novel (which still seems to me to present the tragic plight of a woman whose "identity" is never forged into a coherent, viable "self"), but a reading that traces the *social or cultural origins* of Edna's problem. See also Edna's reading of Emerson and her and Kouidis's discussion of her determination to achieve a "unified self."

13. Since Edna's children make very few actual demands upon her time or energy (she has all the "childcare" one might wish for and a mother-in-law who is apparently quite happy to bestow attention and affection upon her grandchildren), the emphatic quality of her renunciation—the almost obsessive way she returns to the problem—may seem odd unless a reader understands the tortured connection between female sexuality and "motherhood" decreed by American society in the late nineteenth century. Urgo insightfully examines Edna's habit of silence at the beginning of the novel. However, I cannot agree with his conclusion that Edna's story "about the woman who paddled away with her lover one night" represents the "discovery of a narrative voice" (28). This fairy-tale ending does not constitute much of a narrative advance over Edna's adolescent fantasies.

14. Chopin focuses on Edna, but she allows the reader to see that Léonce is injured by this system, too. One supposes that he understands at least *some* of what he wants (more enthusiastic sexual receptivity from his wife); however, he can't *say* such a thing bluntly—because no "decent" or "sensitive" husband would make such a demand of his wife (who presumably only tolerated his advances because she had an interest in bearing children!). Hence he, too, cannot define the sources of his unhappiness:

It would have been a difficult matter for Mr. Pontellier to define to his own satisfaction or any one else's wherein his wife failed *in her duty toward their children.* It was something which he felt rather than perceived, and he never voiced the feeling without subsequent regret and ample atonement. (26; my emphasis)
The problem really has nothing at all to do *with the children,* of course. Yet the discourse of "mothering" is all Léonce has been allowed if he wants to voice his disappointment.

15. See Bauer and Lakritz's excellent discussion of the social and cultural dialogues that inform this novel. They note but do not trace the origins of the quasi-medical terminology that lies at the root of Edna's problem. See also George.

16. Showalter has observed that "the New Women writers of the 1890s no longer grieved for the female bonds and sanctuaries of the past . . . [but] demanded freedom and innovation" (175). Clearly, Edna does not have the creative power to fashion these new narratives.

17. Chopin gives us many clues concerning Edna's inability to see Robert as anything other than an extension of her own desires. Thus, when he cannot be with her, "She wondered why Robert had gone away and left her. It did not occur to her to think he might have grown tired of being with her the livelong day. She was not tired, and she felt that he was not" (59).

SUSAN GOODMAN

The Fatherlode
Ellen Glasgow's Religious Inheritance

Two things, and two things only, were requisite to my identity both as a human being and as a writer—an intense immediate experience, and the opportunity to translate that experience into forms of creative imagination. —Ellen Glasgow (1873–1945), *A Certain Measure*

I

ELLEN GLASGOW'S STRUGGLE with Calvinism was predestined. In her autobiography, *The Woman Within* (1954), she recalls that her father, Francis Glasgow, "regarded every earthly affliction, from an invading army to the curdling of a pan of milk, as divinely appointed by a God" (16). A Scots-Presbyterian, he seemed to need neither comfort nor pleasure: "a God of terror, savoring the strong smoke of blood sacrifice, was the only deity awful enough to command his respect" (85). Although he wept copiously—to his amazed family's scorn—over sentimental fiction recounting a prodigal daughter's return, his own daughter felt that he was patriarchal rather than paternal (86–87). "He gave his wife and children everything," Glasgow writes, but love, "the one thing they needed most." What virtues he did have—"complete integrity, and an abiding sense of responsibility"—she thought alien to his dispassionate character and more "Roman" in their austere practice than Calvinistic (15). Because Glasgow was never able to dissociate her vision of her father's religion from her vision of him, she saw Calvinism as a punitive, authoritarian, and irrationally sentimental system.

Ellen Glasgow believed that her father's unbending Presbyterianism made him one of the last men on earth her mother, Anne Gholson Glasgow, should have married. A creature of light and a figure of tragedy (*Woman* 13), Anne Glasgow provided the model for Virginia Pendleton (*Virginia* [1913]), "the perfect [and doomed] flower of Southern culture" (*Certain* 90). In her daughter's mind, she had survived the occupancy of Richmond, the financial reversals of Reconstruction, and the birth of ten children only to surrender to depression after learning of her husband's one secret pleasure, his affairs with mulatto women (Wagner-Martin 7–8; Godbold 27).

Blaming her father for her mother's unhappiness and disliking him for his cruelty to dogs, Glasgow claimed: "Everything in me, mental or physical, I owe to my mother" (*Woman* 16). Yet she also associated his Scotch-Irish ancestry with fortitude, the "vein of iron" (later the title of her 1935 novel) she thought stoical and necessary for survival. The metaphor reflects not only the iron will Francis Glasgow passed on to his daughter but also the source of his family's income, gained from his management of the Tredegar Iron Works, once the largest supplier of Confederate weapons.[1]

The Glasgow household, just blocks from the Tredegar Works, flourished on two traditions, the myth of True Womanhood and the myth of the Old South. Glasgow's mother, eulogized by friends and family for her unselfish devotion to others, embodied the first; her father, remembered for keeping the Iron Works operating with pig iron produced by slave labor, the second.[2] Glasgow saw these myths as cultural manifestations of a religion she found both sexist and racist. Satirizing True Womanhood in comedies of manners like *They Stooped to Folly* (1929) and offering a revisionary history of the South from the Civil through the First World Wars in novels from *The Battle-Ground* (1902) to *In This Our Life* (1941), she bequeathed future writers another tradition: a brand of modernism that redefines her father's stern and oppressive Calvinism to include the maternal and the aesthetic. In Glasgow's own analysis, her vision of Calvinism belonged more to Massachusetts than Virginia, where religion "had softened in a milder climate to a healthful moral exercise and a comfortable sense of divine favor" ("Novel" 71).

This essay focuses on two crucial texts for understanding Glasgow's vision of both Calvinism and modernism, her autobiography, *The Woman Within*, and its fictional equivalent, *Barren Ground* (1925). Of herself and her heroine, Dorinda Oakley, Glasgow confirms: "We were connected, or so it seemed, by a living nerve" (*Certain* 163). Although the novel predates the autobiography, it grows from the emotional and intellectual context the autobiography reveals. It fixes one stage in its author's development and partly determines another.

Together *The Woman Within* and *Barren Ground* illustrate Glasgow's fluid process of making and unmaking meaning. From this process, both autobiographical and fictional in practice, emerged Glasgow's empowering, modernist version of Calvinism. Glasgow's forays into Darwinism and Freudianism—that is, ostensibly away from religion and into science and psychology—had only highlighted the impossibility of any single discipline explaining human behavior. In a sense, what began as a rebellion against her Calvinist heritage ironically ended as a return to the fold. Religion, science, and psychology proved less oppositional than complementary. If science honored the artist's dispassionate eye, and psychology the labyrinth of the mind, religion recognized an incorporeal realm that Glasgow increasingly valued. *The Woman Within* depicts the Calvinist world of her childhood transformed to house herself, a woman and an artist. *Barren Ground* portrays a parallel world politicized, one that fuses Calvinism and feminism.

More than any other of her novels, *Barren Ground* represented a turning point for Glasgow. "I wrote *Barren Ground*," she recalls, "and immediately I knew I had found myself. . . . I was at last free" (*Woman* 243–44). Most importantly, the novel allowed her to approach the unapproachable—her father's wartime use of slave labor, for example. This "conversion" to a new, liberating creed of fiction (*Certain* 213) that privileged the world within over the one without gave Glasgow "a code of living . . . sufficient for life or for death" (*Woman* 271). What she called "freedom" was an ambivalent reconciliation with the past, for after *Barren Ground* her social history encompasses a more complex and sympathetic attitude toward characters who have survived on the meager diet of faith. This shift—toward a "modernism" defined not by subjects Glasgow thought shockingly unromantic, such as illegitimacy or free love, but by a psychological realism patterned on her response to Calvinism[3]—signaled a new phase of her career and, with the exception of *Virginia*, the beginning of her finest work.[4]

Part *künstlerroman*, part spiritual autobiography, *The Woman Within* articulates the personal myth that informed Glasgow's fiction and gave birth to *Barren Ground*. Both books show how she came to terms with the emotional legacy of her father's religion. Glasgow believed that an autobiography's "truth" depended on its duplication of a state of mind;[5] she also believed that a novel should have a planned, implicit philosophy. *Barren Ground*, the story of a betrayed woman who becomes the victor instead of the victim, illustrates how Glasgow altered the feelings explored in her autobiography into an argument for feminist self-determinism. In this interplay between fact and fiction, there is—to twist a phrase from the preface of Hemingway's *A Moveable Feast*—a chance of what has been written as fact throwing some light on what has been written as fiction.

II

Glasgow worked on the manuscript of *The Woman Within* (kept in a locked black leather briefcase and labeled "Original Rough Draft") for eight years, from 1935 to 1943. During this time, she also wrote the essays for *A Certain*

Measure (1943), which contemporary reviewers later compared favorably with James's prefaces to the New York edition. Because the autobiographical and critical acts coincided, the books sometimes echo one another, suggesting—as *Barren Ground* and the autobiography illustrate—that the private and public sectors of existence cannot be easily divided (Gusdorf 36–37).

The *Woman Within* integrates the worlds of father and daughter. Its content is fundamentally Calvinist; its circular, fragmented, and sometimes repetitive form, modernist. "I have tried to leave the inward and the outward streams of experience free to flow in their own channels, and free, too, to construct their own special designs," she explains. "Analysis, if it comes at all, must come later" (*Woman* 227). To borrow Glasgow's metaphor from *Barren Ground*, the words of the covenant may have altered, but "the ancient mettle" still infuses the author's spirit (*Barren* 460). Like a good Presbyterian, Glasgow struggles against the powers of evil and suffers for a purpose. Like a true modern, she finds "the universal" in the personal. The autobiographical act confirms her being, agency, and talent.

The autobiography's first section recounts Glasgow's awakening to self; the second to art; and the third to "God" (*Woman* 289). Successively focusing on the Calvinist beliefs of particular election, redemption, and irresistible grace, *The Woman Within* reflects her lifelong interest in the mutation and variation of self. It honors those whom her father scorned, including artists, skeptics, and scientists. Glasgow was drawn to the teachings of Charles Darwin and Herbert Spencer for professional as well as personal reasons. Knowing that her father hated anything to do with Darwinism, she read *The Origin of Species* when nearly twenty and assimilated an extended discussion of inherited characteristics and environmental influences into her first novel, *The Descendant* (1897). The "minor religious persecution" (*Woman* 91) that Ellen Glasgow suffered at home for reading Darwin was more than offset by the temporary sense of identity and authority his theories afforded. He became a kind of intellectual father, whose views on heredity vaguely echoed those of her own father on predestination. In a sense, Darwin's beliefs were to the body what Francis Glasgow's were to the soul. If *The Descendant* sides neither with "nature" nor "nurture," later works like *Barren Ground* and *The Woman Within* present "heredity" and "predestination" as almost interchangeable concepts.

Near the end of her life, Glasgow felt that science had failed to cure her body in the same way that religion had failed to cure her soul (*Woman* 138). She spurned the categories of science when writing *The Woman Within* because they seemed to simplify or exclude what she had come to see as unclassifiable: her own "dubious identity" (130). "I am concerned, now," she writes, "only with the raw substance and the spontaneous movement

of life, not with the explicit categories of science" (227). Glasgow assumed
that intellect and sensation were so closely intertwined that "where one
began in pure feeling, and the other ended in pure speculation" (56) remained unfathomable. Such views would have shocked her father as heresy.

Following a pattern more commonly associated with British and American male autobiographers (Mason xiii), Glasgow presents her "self" on a
grandly dramatic, or even epic, scale worthy of Milton. Her soul becomes
a battleground where opposing and "hostile" forces—the "stalwart, unbending, rock-ribbed" (*Woman* 16) Calvinism of her father and the radiant
sympathy of her high-church Episcopalian mother—contend. Feeling like
"the last unwilling scapegoat of Predestination" (275), she is torn between
mother and father, nature and civilization. She belongs everywhere and
nowhere.

Although Glasgow claimed that she was never a disciple and disliked
"the current patter of Freudian theory" (*Woman* 267, 227), *The Woman
Within* favors a universe in which a densely knit cluster of emotions, memories, and perceptions dominate, even predetermine, the historical course
of life (Olney 244). Glasgow identifies this amorphous state—described in
terms that suggest she never fully repudiated scientific categories nor dis-
owned Darwin—with her mother and nature.

The first moment of consciousness thrusts Glasgow from womblike
comfort into a terrifying void. "Moving forward and backward, as con-
tented and as mindless as an amoeba, submerged in that vast fog of existence," she recalls:

I open my eyes. Beyond the top windowpanes, in the midst of a red glow, I see a
face without a body staring in at me, a vacant face, round, pallid, grotesque, malevolent. Terror—or was it merely sensation?—stabbed me into consciousness. . . .
One minute, I was not; the next minute, I was. I felt. I was separate. I could be
hurt. I had discovered myself. And I had discovered, too, the universe apart from
myself. (*Woman* 3–4)

In the child's vision, the masculine sun eclipses the female sphere "of love
and ritual" (Smith-Rosenberg, "Female") where Mother and her nurse,
Mammy Lizzie (Lizzie Jones), benignly reign. The world, now inexpli-
cable, menacing, and revelatory, houses gods less indifferent than pernicious. The face at the window may as well anticipate Jacques Lacan, for
the passage recreates the subjugation of the amoebalike self to an emerging and increasingly insistent "I." The appearance of "a face without a
body" marks the child's fall into a symbolically ordered world of the father,
who "had little compassion for the inarticulate, and as his Calvinistic faith
taught him, the soulless" (*Woman* 4, 14).[6] The law of the father, whether
Calvinist or Lacanian, atomizes the child's existence. As a writer, Glasgow
internalized her father's Calvinist equation of speech and being; however,

she never forgot the child who could not put her fear into words. Her empathy for all the abused, helpless, and mute victims of life grows from her experience of being voiceless when first faced with what her Calvinist ancestors might also have called "the cold implacable inhumanity of the universe" (*Woman* 168).

Glasgow's apparition, which owes its shape to "the late revenge of that [paternal] Calvinist conscience" (*Certain* 111), curiously resembles the Satan of James Hogg's early nineteenth-century text, *The Private Memoirs and Confessions of a Justified Sinner* (1824):

delineated in the cloud [was] the shoulders, arms, and features of a human being of the most dreadful aspect. The face was the face of his [the protagonist's] brother, but dilated to twenty times the natural size. Its dark eyes gleamed on him through the mist, while every furrow of its hideous brow frowned deep as the ravines on the brow of the hill. (39)

In both Glasgow's memoir and Hogg's novel, the apparitions function like mirrors to reveal "the bloated mask of evil" as one's own. Neither author sees an end to the eternal, and therefore predetermined, "conflict between human beings and human nature" (*Woman* 4, 285).

Framing her life story, Glasgow did not shun the religious myths that she termed a form of "evasive idealism"—defined as a "whimsical, sentimental and maudlinly optimistic philosophy" ("Evasive" 123). The "strange transference of identity" (*Woman* 8) that heralds her waking to consciousness also distinguishes her as an artist. Feeling herself chosen for a life of suffering made bearable only by her sense of anointment, she testifies: "I, alone, saw the apparition. . . . I saw it hanging there once, and forever" (*Woman* 5). This sign, which reinforces Glasgow's inherited sense of estrangement and recalls the crucifixion, also establishes, like Hester Prynne's scarlet letter, her moral superiority: "a sensitive mind," she concludes, "would always remain an exile on earth" (*Woman* 271). What Puritan typology would have revealed as part of a universal history of providential significance (Brumm 33), Glasgow individualizes. For her, there is no heavenly reward for earthly torment.

Instead of asking, "How can I best prepare myself for what is to come," Glasgow asks: "How can an oversensitive nature defend itself against the malice of life?" (*Woman* 168). The answer lies in art. The muse is her angel of annunciation. Writing becomes a way "to break through" or "push back into nothingness" the old wall of silence Glasgow first associated with the face at the window: "I was driven, consciously or unconsciously, by my old antagonist, a past from which I was running away" (*Woman* 195). Trying to lessen the gap between the writer and the word, Glasgow approximates reality with a prose style "so pure and flexible that it could bend without breaking" (*Woman* 123). Art, which in some way allows her to relive or

revise the past, further permits her to transcend that past. That self, introduced initially in the present tense and created in language, is modern in
its continual becoming.

The style of the memoir reflects what Glasgow defines as the "modernity" of its structure. "For the modern process," she explains in her interpretation of prose fiction, *A Certain Measure*, "means a breaking up on the
surface of facts, and a fearless exploration into the secret labyrinths of the
mind and heart" (113-14). The enigmatic repetitions and interrupted chro-
nology of *The Woman Within* replicate the "tunnelling process" (Woolf
60) of Virginia Woolf (1882-1941), a writer whom Glasgow admired. They
also serve to obscure meaning. She mentions her brother Frank's death
three times, for example, before the reader can confidently guess suicide
as its cause. Reverting perhaps to the genteel tradition in which she was
raised, she rationalizes the waste: "In a last effort to spare us as far as it was
possible, he went, alone, from the house, and, alone, into a future where
we could not follow him" (*Woman* 67). The false starts and hesitations
underscore the ways in which Glasgow makes meaning, while her recurrent memory of Frank and particularly of the setting sun highlights how
she alters essence.

The image of the setting sun accrues meaning each time it occurs.
Glasgow first associates her unchildlike, brooding sense of exile with the
"half-forgotten presence of the evil face without a body" (*Woman* 25).
Later, she agonizes over God's indifferent gaze and Judas's despairing face.
These "hallucinations" are far less frightening than their prototype (the
evil face), for imagination can "convert" Christ's grimace on the cross to a
guardian angel's smile. When Glasgow feels betrayed by her fiancé, Henry
Anderson (called "Harold S." in the text), the image, unutterably hideous
and malignant, appears again. In despair, she takes an overdose of sleeping
pills. Dreaming of her mother, sister, and nurse, she returns to the comforting maternal world of love and ritual the apparition had cast in shadow.

Instead of the horrifying surrender or extinction of identity originally
associated with the vision, Glasgow experiences an "enlargement and complete illumination of being" with "the Unknown Everything or with Nothing . . . or with God" (*Woman* 290, 289). The once malevolent apparition,
having been feminized, now wears a countenance inclusive of all humanity.
No longer fearful, she surrenders to process, welcoming the dissolution of
boundaries between self and other that forms, in her mind, the "universal"
or "catholic" basis of art: the path "to greatness leads beyond manner,"
she writes, "beyond method, beyond movement, to some ultimate dominion of spirit" (*Certain* 148). In this way, Glasgow redefines the terms of
the epigram, "Calvinism is Catholicism without the glory of God" (Notebook). Her version of Calvinism is a kind of secularized humanism that

"rememories" (to borrow Toni Morrison's word from *Beloved*) the face at the window. Janus-like, its features reflect the androgynous ideal that Virginia Woolf called man-womanly or woman-manly (*Room* 108).

Glasgow's account of her life story—one of victimization, conflict, and isolation—paradoxically ends, as do so many Puritan spiritual autobiographies, with a communion or symbolic bonding between reader and writer (Edkins 41). This conclusion, however, does not exclude the modernist assumption that solitude nurtures creativity (Storr). Perhaps in no age would Glasgow have felt anything other than "an exile and a stranger"; nevertheless, she finds a home in art where the grace achieved comes from having "done the work [she] wished to do for the sake of that work alone" (*Woman* 279, 296). Unlike her father or her Presbyterian forebears, Glasgow lives in a world of her own, not God's, making.

The Woman Within and the woman herself are modernist mosaics. The child who saw the face at the window becomes the artist who calls her coherent and assimilable self-portrait into question. Warning the reader to question her earliest memory, to which meaning is "attached, long afterward," she ironically asks, "Doesn't all experience crumble in the end to mere literary material?" (*Woman* 3, 226). The reader, having seen Francis Glasgow's "rock-ribbed" Calvinism transformed into a literary conceit, might answer, "yes."

III

In *A Certain Measure*, Ellen Glasgow, the theorist, argued that any "living" book "contains the essence, or an extension, of a distinct identity," yet the "biographer of life" also knew that she did her best work once emotion had passed (264, 94). Then the untiring critic could have "winnowed, reassessed, and disposed" of idiosyncratic material (199). *Barren Ground* illustrates how the personal becomes political in its message and scope. The novel's heroine is as alone and besieged as Glasgow is in *The Woman Within*. Seduced and abandoned, Dorinda Oakley plows her hatred of her former lover into the land, finding in the process the philosophy of humane stoicism Glasgow thought sufficient for life and for death. Dorinda's story exists within the larger one Glasgow associated with Calvinism and its effect on American civilization (*Certain* 155). Just two generations of the Oakleys encompass the change, their pioneering spirit of adventure having disintegrated into a philosophy either of heroic defeat or of moral inertia. The novel's title comments on Dorinda Oakley's literal and spiritual inheritance. Writing about a region and a people bound by a rigid caste system, Glasgow emphasizes a moral, not a mannered, order.

Like her author, Dorinda has always lived with Calvinism, either as an ethical principle, represented by her grandfather, John Calvin Abernethy, or as a nervous malady, personified in her mother. Fashioned after Francis Glasgow, Abernethy is a retired missionary who embodies what Max Weber called "the Protestant ethic and the spirit of capitalism." The same uneasy alliance that fueled the Tredegar Iron Works during the Civil War allows him to view slavery—one of "the strange gestures of divine grace"—as a preordained form of submission to legitimate authority. The doctrines of election and predestination absolve the individual of personal responsibility. As Hogg's antihero argues, we *must* do whatever is preordained, "and none of these things will be laid to our charge" (115). The fifty slaves, on which Abernethy founds his fortune, if not his "estate," constitute "a nice point in theology." His conscience finds ease in the material success that indicates probable election. Later he sees no irony in selling "black flesh" to redeem "black souls in the Congo" (*Barren* 7–8).[7]

The doctrine of social, cultural, and sexual predestination entitles Abernethy, in his roles of patriarch and minister, to colonize natives in Africa and women at home. Glasgow's equation of slavery and marriage condemns Calvinism's not-so-benevolent paternalism. Dorinda has as little place in this tradition as Glasgow had in the tradition of southern plantation novels or, for that matter, legendary southern belles. The face that Glasgow first saw at the window now wears Abernethy's specific features. In the memoir, Glasgow finds refuge from the unknown in self-irony. In the novel, she directs the deflating irony at an express power: Calvinist patriarchy.

Mrs. Oakley's uncongenial marriage with its resulting neurasthenia recalls that of Glasgow's mother, Anne. She too inherits an adventurous and romantic spirit but no agency. With the death of her missionary fiancé, Mrs. Oakley's visions of the Congo and exotic heathens center on Joshua Oakley, a born failure who looks like John the Baptist in profile. He is as much her Other as the natives she longed to save: "the gulf between the dominant Scotch-Irish stock of the Valley and the mongrel breed of 'poor white' which produced Joshua was as wide as the abyss between alien races" (*Barren* 44)—or between Francis and Anne Gholson Glasgow.

Mrs. Oakley's thwarted ambition finds shape in neurotic dreams of "blue skies and golden sands, of palm trees on a river's bank, and of black babies thrown to crocodiles" (*Barren* 44). Her dream, both sexual and maternal, remains in truth little different from her father's reality in foreign countries, or for that matter, Pedlar's Mill, Virginia, where he peddled black flesh. Obsessed with the threat of eternal damnation, she madly perpetuates a system injurious to all women. Mrs. Oakley serves as Glasgow's warning against internalizing the law of the father. She would like Dorinda to worship a Calvinist God and practice a domestic ideal that Glasgow sees as women's ancient antagonists.

Glasgow finds little difference between a Calvinism nurtured on moral principle and one nurtured on nervous malady. Extrapolating from her father's example, she decides that religion and sentimentality make people cruelly "blind to what happened" (*Woman* 104). She does, however, have more sympathy for Mrs. Oakley's religious mania because it allows her, however poorly, to survive an unsatisfactory reality. Glasgow connects "this dark and secret river of her dream," flowing "silently beneath the commonplace crust of experience" (*Barren* 121), with creativity. The artist, as she writes in *The Woman Within*, is also "immersed in some dark stream of identity, stronger and deeper and more relentless than the external movement of living" (41). Mrs. Oakley's recurrent bouts of madness, which emanate from her frustrated creativity, seem to comment—as does Charlotte Perkins Gilman's story "The Yellow Wallpaper" (1892)—on the imprisoned female imagination. She cannot mother more babies or, like her author, give birth to books, because she cannot violate or revise traditions, such as Calvinism or paternalism, that Glasgow knew to be damaging, even insane.

Although Dorinda realizes that religion, sex, and duty have—to paraphrase Calvin—despoiled her mother of freedom and subjected her to miserable slavery, she still dreams the same quixotic dream. The Oakleys "might as well be living in the house, she sometimes thought with the doctrine of predestination; and like the doctrine of predestination, there was nothing to be done about it" (*Barren* 53). Her dream centers on Jason Greylock, a weak young doctor, whose submission to his father's "iron will" evokes the memory of Glasgow's suicidal brother, Frank. Jason wants to convert the "natives" to modern methods of farming, but they unrepentantly continue to deplete the land.

Barren Ground details what Glasgow called "the blissful tranquillity" of "falling out of love" (*Woman* 244). The outline of Dorinda's plot—an awakening to self, nature, and artistry (landscaping the wideness)—parallels that of *The Woman Within* and effects in fiction what Glasgow, who took twenty-one years to recover from her experience with Harold S., found more difficult in life. Glasgow purposefully conflates and then condemns the dreams of mother and daughter. Jason's image, which Dorinda imagines on millions and millions of "prickly purple thistles" (*Barren* 239–40), represents the last vestiges of her faith in romantic/sexual love. Her tie to Jason has always been a form of egotism, a kind of pride stronger than love or even happiness, and with the symbolic marriage of her farm and his, bought at auction, it eventually lessens. Glasgow compares Dorinda's faith in love to her mother's belief in the Calvinism that "sprang up and blossomed like a Scotch thistle in barren ground" (*Barren* 44). Religious or romantic, each woman's faith thrives on the evasive idealism that Glasgow held responsible for the corruption of American art, politics, and character (*Certain* 155). Both women's dreams prove "barren": Dorinda loses her baby, and Mrs. Oakley sacrifices her eternal soul by providing an alibi for a son guilty of manslaughter.

Lacking a sense of original sin or outraged virtue, Dorinda stands as Glasgow's critique of mid-Victorian heroines, whose minds "resemble a page of the more depressing theology" (*Barren* 198). She refuses to take what God wills. By choosing celibacy, she ensures a future free from any form of social-sexual predestination. Her instinct for survival, like Glasgow's own, owes "less to the attribute of courage than . . . to an innate capacity to exist without living, to endure without enjoying" (*Certain* 156). Glasgow presents Dorinda's choice as necessary, admirable, and to the extent that it is a form of repression, abnormal. Nothing shields her from the realization that she is ultimately alone. The terrible knowledge that Dorinda attains is not of evil, but of the void, "that unconquerable vastness in which nothing is everything" (*Certain* 159). Call the snake in the garden "god" or "love" or "evasive idealism," it thrives on self-illusion. There may be no meaning, as Dorinda suspects, in "coral strands and palm trees and naked black babies" although the very question—"What was the meaning of it?" (*Barren* 170)—prompts speculation.

Trying to fill the void, Dorinda finds meaning in work. Her affinity for nature and the female world it represents most distinguishes the plot of *Barren Ground* from that of *The Woman Within* and the teachings of Calvin. Torn, as Glasgow was, between the law of the father, represented by Abernethy, and the natural world of the mother, represented by Aunt Mehitable Green, a black midwife and conjurer modeled after her mother's nurse, Rhoda Kibble, and her own, Lizzie Jones, she clearly chooses the maternal. Aunt Mehitable's ministering to babies, the lovesick, and the infirm ties her to the cycles of nature. With Aunt Mehitable and her granddaughter, Fluvanna, Dorinda shares an affection "as strong and elastic as the bond that holds relatives together" (*Barren* 340). The women's collaborative effort to restore Old Farm highlights the exploitive and hierarchal quality of Grandfather Abernethy's Calvinist system financed by the selling of human flesh and sustained by the endless drudgery of Dorinda's mother.

Dorinda sculpts the land and in turn nourishes a series of her evolving selves. Unlike her Calvinist forefathers, she neither eroticizes the wilderness of Old Farm (Kolodny 3–14) nor sees it as a psychic territory that must be crossed to reach the promised land (D. Williams 12). Her relation-

ship with Nature is as personal and self-reflective as Alexandra Bergson's
in Willa Cather's *O Pioneers!* (1913):

Kinship with the land was filtering through her blood into her brain; and she knew
that this transfigured instinct was blended of pity, memory, and passion. Dimly she
felt that only through this emotion could she attain permanent liberation of spirit.
(*Barren* 299)

This mysterious unity with the land becomes the guiding principle of the
novel. Through the labors of her surrogate son, John Abner, Dorinda will
achieve a form of immanence in "the immutable landscape" (*Barren* 336).
Glasgow isolated the dominant elements of *Barren Ground* as space and
time and made her heroine part of the "eternal sequence" (*Certain* 158,
159), captured for her in Thomas Hardy's *The Dynasts*. When she visited
Hardy in 1914, he was moved by her recitation of his own lines: "O Immanence, that reasonest not / In putting forth all things begot, / Thou build'st
Thy house in space—for what?" (*Woman* 197). Eleven years later, Dorinda
gives the existential answer: " 'I think, I feel, I am.' The only thing that
mattered was her triumph over circumstances" (*Certain* 160).

Dorinda's state of mind and her responses to circumstances are analogous to Glasgow's after her mother's death. In the first draft of *The Woman
Within*, Glasgow notes that she prevailed by turning "with an almost physical aversion from the material symbols of the sacrificial lamb and of the
redemption through blood" to the writings of Marcus Aurelius Antonius
(manuscript). Having adopted a version of Aurelius's "humane stoicism,"
she felt that she "could bear what [she] had to bear, but [she] could not pre-
tend it away" (*Woman* 138–39). "I will not be broken," Dorinda similarly
vows: "The vein of iron which had supported her through adversity was
merely the instinct older than herself, stronger than circumstances, deeper
than the shifting surface of emotion" (*Barren* 460). The passage anticipates Glasgow's more conciliatory attitude toward Calvinism, embodied
in the motherly figure of Grandmother Fincastle in *Vein of Iron* (1935) or
the enduring ones of Asa and Roy Timberlake in both *In This Our Life*
(1941) and *Beyond Defeat* (1966).

Embracing her grandfather's personal tenets (divorced from their religious context) of "integrity, firmness, and frugality" (*Barren* 8), Dorinda
grows to resemble Glasgow in *The Woman Within* and foreshadows John
Fincastle, the protagonist of *Vein of Iron*, whose "inner life alone . . . was
vital and intimate and secure" (*Vein* 50). Discovering "the secret ecstacy
at the heart of experience" (*Barren* 27) also makes him an exile, separated
forever from those he most loves. Like an artist who inherits the religious
habit of mind without the religious heart (*Barren* 410), Dorinda creates an

interior space that exists remote, inviolate, and self-sufficient; nothing disturbs it: "not joy, not pain, not love, not passion, not sorrow, not loss, not
life at its sharpest edge, nothing" (*Vein* 111). Ironically, her perseverance
leads, as Calvinism teaches and *The Woman Within* elucidates, to a kind of
election. Dorinda's "deep instinct for survival" becomes "a dynamic force"
(*Certain* 160)—indicated by the section titles "Broomsedge," "Pine," and
"Life-Everlasting"—that transforms, as does art itself, barren ground into
Elysian fields. She comes to grace or experiences, in secular terms, to what
Calvin termed a "quickening." By recovering herself, she begins the jour-
ney that ends for Glasgow in a vision of Everything or Nothing or God.

IV

Barren Ground and *The Woman Within* insist that the life of the mind contains "an antidote to experience" (*Woman* 296), that work can give one
what Henry James called "a standpoint in the universe," the something that
"holds one in one's place" (*Letters* 101). Paired, they illustrate how much
Glasgow lived both inside and outside history and myth, in selected realities and the "Reality" she thought "profounder than the depths of experience" (*Woman* 125; *Barren* 497). The Reality that Dorinda finds in Nature
was not an option for her creator, who believed that the artist, almost by
definition, mediates between the worlds of father and mother, between
realities and Reality.

"Authorizing" the personal, Glasgow found her own versions of the
"universal" and "modernism." Someone as anomalous as Glasgow—
woman, writer, feminist, and animal rights activist—had perhaps no other
place she could turn but to herself. It is not surprising that an author who
came to believe that all creative writing was, in some manner, autobiographical might have wondered, "How can one tell where . . . memory
end[s] and imagination begin[s]?" (*Woman* 281). Neither is it surprising
that her version of her career changed as she aged, the first realist in the
South becoming in retrospect the first modern. Glasgow's valuation of
subjectivity and historicity set her apart from poets, such as Pound or
Eliot, who exalted the word as language above all else. Offering herself as
both text and archetype, she revised Calvin's plot to accommodate, even
favor, her highly self-referential and lettered world. In her fiction, Calvinism becomes, historically and psychologically, marker, measure, and
foil. Glasgow's work bridges two worlds: the Calvinist, whose diarist tradition she continues in *The Woman Within*, and the modern, whose past
and present she traces in her social history. Her belief in a recoverable
and transferable history—along with her belief in words like loyalty and

honor—may distinguish her from the so-called lost generation, but it also makes her a foremother of Southern Agrarians, such as Robert Penn Warren and Stark Young, who wanted to reclaim the native humanism they saw rooted in the rural life of their particular region. Despite Glasgow's feeling that it was "easier to break with the tradition" (*Woman* 280)—whether that of True Womanhood or the sentimental histories her father enjoyed— than to endure it, *The Woman Within* and *Barren Ground* suggest, in their representations of Calvinism, not only how much the inherited realities comprise Reality but also how arbitrary such distinctions are. Only in the imagination perhaps can Calvin and Darwin sustain a kind of unholy and empowering alliance that grants a feeling of spiritual luxury.

Notes

1. For additional information about Francis Glasgow's association with the Tredegar Iron Works, see Dew 16, 168–69, 235, and 252.

2. The first myth can be summed up by Glasgow's own observation that the less a woman knew about life, the "better prepared she would be to contend with it" (*Certain* 90). A woman's charm lay in her innocence (or ignorance), her ability to suffer in silence, her piety and altruism (A. Scott 5, 7). See also J. Jones; Fox-Genovese; Clinton; Bleser; and Welter.

The second myth romanticized plantation life: "We are slaves to our slaves," many a Southerner lamented. The system prospered on silence and on women playing "their parts of unsuspecting angels to the letter" (Chesnut 163–64, 122).

3. For general information on Calvinism, I have relied on Howard; Pahl; McGrath; M. Gordon; and Duke *et al.* For discussions of modernism that pertain to this essay, see Hutchinson and Clark.

4. For an analysis of this change, see Raper, *From*.

5. Although Glasgow creates the impression that she recorded thoughts and feelings as they spontaneously occurred, the manuscript reveals that analysis did come later. The first typed draft shows many working revisions, from words and phrases to whole sections on Harold S., that have been typed over with rows of x's. Glasgow seems to have read the draft several times, making small changes, usually word substitutions, which are marked with ink and pencil. The second draft is a copy of the first with modifications in punctuation, the addition of dates, and the reordering of sentences. See Ellen Glasgow Collection, Notebook.

6. See Lacan 1–7 and 281–91. See also Eagleton 151–93 and 166; and Klein 334. Klein describes the creative writer as impelled by the desire to rediscover the mother. See also Suleiman (who quotes Klein) 357.

7. For a discussion of race and religion, see Washington 482–88.

MILTON J. BATES

Apocalypse Now *and the New England Way*

I

PERRY MILLER OBSERVED four decades ago that the English Protestants who settled in New England "established Puritanism — for better or worse — as one of the continuous factors in American life and thought." Consequently, he said, there can be no understanding of America without an understanding of Puritanism (*American* ix). By Puritanism Miller meant a coherent intellectual system, the "New England Mind" he had anatomized in two weighty volumes. Two decades later, Sacvan Bercovitch ventured a more sweeping claim for the role of New England Puritanism in American culture. "The myth of America," he maintained, "is the creation of the New England Way" (*Puritan* 143).

These are large claims for a small colony, by no means the only one in North America, located far from the centers of seventeenth-century civilization. Yet they become plausible if one adds to the Puritans' contemporary influence the preeminence conferred on them by student textbooks and a distinguished tradition of historical scholarship, a status only recently challenged in the name of multiculturalism. In every American epoch, and particularly during moments of national crisis, writers and thinkers have revisited New England Puritanism to assess the evils or achievements of their own day. One thinks of Franklin in the eighteenth century; Emerson and Hawthorne in the nineteenth; and William Carlos Williams, Arthur Miller, and Robert Lowell in the first half of the twentieth.

The Vietnam War certainly qualifies as a moment of national crisis, and it likewise prompted thoughtful Americans to search the Puritan legacy for answers to basic questions: How did we get into such a demoralizing and ultimately unsuccessful war? Why did it take us so long to get out? What did we learn from the experience? In this essay I show how one film director tried to answer these questions and, in the process, found himself tracing the myth of American back to its Puritan roots. Francis Ford Coppola's *Apocalypse Now* (1979) testifies to the continuing influence of the New England Way even as it deplores some of its consequences. To appreciate what is at stake in the film, we must first review the pertinent features of early American Puritanism.

II

What we have come to call the New England Way is a fabric of many threads, some theological, others political, economic, and cultural. So intricately are they interwoven that it is difficult to tease out a single thread without disturbing the others. To consider the New England Puritans' attitude toward the wilderness, for example, is also to consider their attitude toward the American Indian, the community, and history. But for the sake of discussion I address these separately in the following distillation of early New England history.

As Roderick Nash points out, the New England Puritans were Europeans first and foremost. As such, they were steeped in a body of myth and folklore that represented the wilderness as a place of supernatural and monstrous beings. These included the Wild Man, a naked, hairy creature who devoured children and ravished young women (10-13). He was an apt symbol of what the Puritans feared they might become were they to linger too long in the wilderness and succumb to its temptations (24, 29). Their mythology of the wilderness was further embellished by typological readings of the Bible, which figured the Old World—and particularly such centers of abomination as Rome and Canterbury—as Egypt or Babylon. The desolate landscape of the New World was the desert in which the Israelites wandered for forty years before entering the promised land of Canaan. Leaders such as Bradford and Winthrop were the equivalents of Moses, Joshua, and Nehemiah.

For the Puritans, wandering in the wilderness was the type of everyone's earthly sojourn. Thus Bunyan's *Pilgrim's Progress* opens with a reference to the "wilderness of this world" (8), a metaphor elaborated by Roger Williams in his dictionary of the Narragansett language: "the Wildernesse is a cleere resemblance of the world, where greedie and furious men persecute and devoure the harmlesse and innocent as the wilde beasts pursue and devoure the Hinds and Roes" (107). If life as a whole could be figured as a wilderness, there were phases of life for which the figure seemed especially apt. As David Williams has shown, the Puritans regarded the wilderness as primarily a place in the human spirit, a place of disorder and madness, a hellish "black hole of unknowing" that had to be negotiated during conversion and rebirth (14, 26). Since the true wilderness lay within, one could undergo a genuine "wilderness" experience without leaving London or Leyden.

Conversion was thought to be more likely, however, in physical circumstances that mirrored the inner wilderness (D. Williams 58). Regarded from this point of view, the inhospitable landscape of New England was a mixed blessing. On the one hand, it was a place of spiritual trial; on the other hand, it was a place of closeness to God and sanctuary from Old World persecutors (Nash 16, D. Williams 28). Their Canaan lay not beyond this waste land, as it did for the Israelites, but within it. Through cultivation, the "hideous and desolate wilderness" described by Bradford (17) could be transformed into a land of milk and honey.

The Puritans differed from their contemporaries in their emphasis on the wilderness aspect of the New World. The Virginia and Maryland planters more often figured the landscape as a new Eden (Bercovitch, *Puritan* 137–38), and Thomas Morton, a non-Puritan notorious for his quarrel with the Puritans, characterized New England in his *New English Canaan* as a "paradice" and "Natures Master-peece" (180). This is not to say that the Puritans were immune to the beauty of the landscape, properly cultivated. Samuel Sewall's rhapsody on Plum Island, where his parents landed in 1634, represents for Miller the moment when an English Puritan "had become an American, rooted in the American soil" (*American* 213).

Moreover, since wilderness was as much an inner as an outer phenomenon, a first-generation Puritan's view of the landscape was strongly colored by his or her sense of the human condition. The more orthodox, labeled "Arminians" by their opponents, saw themselves as sinners in need of the spiritual trial by wilderness; hence they were inclined to describe their physical surroundings as a wilderness. In contrast, those who were called "Antinomians" believed themselves to be spiritually in the land of Canaan and saw a correspondingly felicitous terrain wherever they looked (D. Williams 47–48). As a result of the labors of their parents, New Englanders of the second and third generations inherited a land that resembled Canaan more than the desert, so many assumed that a commensurate transformation of the spirit had taken place (D. Williams 63). The Halfway Covenant of 1662 implicitly supported this view. Thereafter, children of converted church members could become provisional members of the congregation without testifying that they had personally traveled the inner wilderness.

Yet the old typology lingered as a spiritual ideal. In her classic frontier captivity narrative, Mary Rowlandson confesses that during the time she lived in prosperity and comfort, she sometimes wished for trials and afflictions (365). When the Wampanoags took her captive for three months in 1675, they forced her to repeat the first generation's painful but spiritually efficacious entry into the wilderness. Rowlandson's story reflects the Puritan view not only of the wilderness but also of the community and the American Indian. By structuring her account as a series of "removes" from the community in Lancaster, Massachusetts, she endorses John Winthrop's belief that the pilgrim soul's true home is a "city upon a hill" ("Model" 91). Winthrop's city was scarcely established on its hilltop, however, when some of its citizens were lured back into the wilderness—not by the desire for conversion but by greed for land that could be purchased cheaply from the natives. The Puritan clergy and "men of note" deplored such "Indian-izing" but could do little to prevent it, beyond publicizing the occasional instance of a "backsettler" punished by an Indian attack.[1]

For Rowlandson and other New England settlers, the American Indian personified the wilderness and shared its ambiguous status in European folklore and Puritan typology. The Indian was the Wild Man of folklore, his ritual cannibalism an object of particular horror because it mirrored, diabolically, the Christian Eucharist (Slotkin 124). At the same time, his conversion was one of the ostensible purposes of the Puritan errand into the wilderness. According to one theory, American Indians were the lost tribes of Israel; according to another, they were simply heathens (Berco-vitch, *Puritan* 101; Slotkin and Folsom 61–63). In either case their con-version had a place in salvation history, for it was among the *miracula* or *magnalia* that were supposed to precede the Second Coming of Christ. Schooled in the teachings of apocalyptists like Richard Mather and John Cotton, the Puritan emigrants believed that they were living in the "last days" prefigured by Jesus' triumphant entry into Jerusalem (Matt. 21) and the Book of Revelation.

With each Indian who renounced native culture and kin to live with other converts in "praying towns," the Second Coming and the Christian millennium appeared a step closer. In the meantime, the Indian served a useful rhetorical purpose. Preachers could contrast native converts with the unregenerate English settlers and perhaps shame the latter into mend-ing their ways. Ultimately it was the conversion of their own people that mattered to most Puritans, and the Indian was regarded more as a symbol of spiritual disorder than as a soul to be saved.

It was all the easier, therefore, for the image of the American Indian to be revised according to political expediency. Unlike other European colo-nists, the New England Puritans assumed that the land belonged to them by divine decree; the Indian "Canaanites" would have to convert or be exterminated (Bercovitch, *Puritan* 141). In Virginia, the massacre of 1622 ended any hope of peaceful co-existence with the Indians (Pearce, *Savag-ism* 7). In New England, despite the Pequot War of 1637–1638, the shift to a policy of extermination did not occur until King Philip's War in 1675–1676. In his *Brief History* of that war, Increase Mather attributes the conflict in part to insufficient zeal for the conversion of the Indians (Slotkin and Folsom 84, 190). But the treachery of some "praying Indians" suggested to some witnesses, including Mary Rowlandson, that the natives were incapable of genuine and lasting conversion. After the 1670s the Indians were considered an evil to be purged from the body politic (Slotkin and Folsom 35). Warfare against them was regarded as an antitype of the Israelites' battles against the Canaanites and Amalekites and as a type of Armageddon, the great battle that would usher in the Christian millennium.

King Philip's War not only carried Puritan apocalypticism to a new height (Bercovitch, *Puritan* 103) but also called onto the stage of history an unlikely Puritan hero. Before the war, Benjamin Church lived apart from any congregation in an unsettled part of Rhode Island. There he enjoyed a close friendship—thought by some to be a romantic liaison—with a female sachem named Awashonks (Slotkin and Folsom 373). During the war he used that friendship and Indian methods of warfare to fight the natives, dismissing fears that his tactics would "Indianize" the English. Apparently motivated by a combination of compassion and pragmatic policy, he tried to halt the massacre of some 600 Narragansett men, women, and children in the Swamp Fight of 1675, characterized by Slotkin and Folsom as a "seventeenth-century My Lai" (381). He led the company of white rangers and nonpraying Indian allies that hunted down Philip and many of his lieutenants and warriors. When he captured Annawon, the military leader of the Wampanoags, the old warrior honored him with the symbolic gift of Philip's royal wampum belts.

Church fell from favor with Puritan authorities toward the end of his career when, in an action that reveals the ruthlessly pragmatic side of his personality, he ordered the execution of French prisoners while fighting the French and American Indians. That he was never fully in sympathy with the New England Way is suggested not only by his deeds but also, Slotkin and Folsom contend, by his manner of recounting them in a personal narrative published in 1716. Whereas other Puritan narratives of the war play down individual achievement and attribute success to Divine Providence, *Entertaining Passages Relating to Philip's War* betrays Church's personal pride in his accomplishments. By then, however, the fabric of the New England Way had already begun to unravel.

III

In terms of plot and characterization, Coppola's *Apocalypse Now* is most obviously indebted to *Heart of Darkness*, Joseph Conrad's novella about Belgian trade and conquest in Africa. Much as Conrad's Marlow journeys up the Congo to retrieve Kurtz, Coppola's Captain Willard (played by Martin Sheen) travels up the Nung (that is, Mekong) River into Cambodia to assassinate a Special Forces colonel (Marlon Brando) also named Kurtz. But in its treatment of wild places and wild men and in its conception of community and history, *Apocalypse Now* belongs to the tradition of American Puritanism. Apparently without conscious design, Coppola created a powerful contemporary image of the New England Way. Then, reacting to the image in much the same way that a later generation reacted to Puritanism, he devised a countermyth that also reflects American cultural history.

Though Colonel Kurtz has long since withdrawn from the city upon a hill at the beginning of Coppola's film, he is still fighting the same enemy and his methods are for the most part identical to those of the "nabobs," whom he despises.[2] Like them, he uses friendly indigenous troops (Montagnards) to fight the Viet Cong (VC) and North Vietnamese Army (NVA). Like them, he employs selective assassination, wholesale slaughter, and psychological warfare to accomplish his aims. Kurtz acknowledges the kinship between his methods and those of the military command in a radio transmission captured on tape. "What do you call it," he asks, "when the assassins accuse the assassin?"

Despite these affinities, Kurtz must be eliminated because his methods are deemed "unsound" by military and civilian intelligence. Their unsoundness lies primarily in his separation from the community and communal authority, as mediated by his superiors. Whereas Willard is an assassin under orders, Kurtz is an assassin who recognizes no authority beyond himself. He has established what Philip H. Melling calls a "bad enclave" (22), a separate base of power in a part of Indochina remote from Saigon and Nha Trang, where he exercises godlike power over his followers. Though the crew of the river patrol boat (PBR) find this blasphemous— Chef (Frederic Forrest) calls it "pagan idolatry"—they are attracted to his Indianized style of life and warfare. Lance (Sam Bottoms), the surfer from Southern California, is the first to show signs of going native as the PBR leaves civilization in its wake; once in Cambodia he paints his face and trades his fatigues for a loincloth. Chef likewise exchanges his helmet for a hat of reeds, forgetting the lesson he learned in his encounter with a tiger: "Never get off the boat."

The tiger episode prompts Willard to reflect that Kurtz had not only gotten off the boat but had also gone "all the way." As Willard travels up river, presumably retracing Kurtz's journey into the heart of darkness, he is confronted at every turn by vulgarized 1960s versions of the frontier myth. He comes upon an airmobile cavalry squadron whose commander, Colonel Kilgore (Robert Duvall), combines nostalgia for the glory days of the horse-mounted cavalry with a West Coast passion for surfing and beach parties. When the boat stops to refuel at Hau Phat, an appropriately named ("how fat") oasis of excess, Willard witnesses a USO show staged by the rock impresario Bill Graham, featuring Playboy bunnies dressed as cowboys, an American Indian woman, and a cavalry trooper Indian hybrid.

These absurd conflations of past and present visually reflect the absurdities of American policy in Vietnam. Willard hears Kilgore threatening to bomb a village "back to the stone age" for its sympathy with Viet Cong "savages." At the USO show he ponders the contrast between American sex-for-success (the show is a reward for an operation named Brutal Force) and the enemy's political commitment. At the Do Lung Bridge on the Cambodian border, he witnesses one final example of official American policy gone awry. The lost souls who wander this purgatorial landscape, or who try to escape it by plunging into the river after the PBR, have neither a leader nor any clear sense of mission beyond the daily rebuilding of the bridge.

Willard becomes increasingly annoyed at the antics of the PBR crew, ranging from Lance's water skiing to Chief's (Albert Hall) insistence that they search a sampan even though the search will delay their mission. Willard's experiences thus supply the narrative link between the young, careerist Kurtz and the man who unaccountably defied authority and got off the boat. If Kurtz is a renegade and an egotist, a Benjamin Church writ large, he is also a reformer, a Puritan separatist in flight from the American equivalents of Egypt and Babylon. He deliberately chose the Cambodian wilderness, and with it the potential for madness, as the means to some unspecified personal Canaan. The more Willard sees of the fool's paradise that Kurtz rejected, the more he admires Kurtz and looks forward to meeting him.

Is Kurtz in fact a madman, as both his detractors and admirers believe? Certainly he is a man obsessed, like many of the New England Puritans, with impending apocalypse. Shortly before Willard arrives at Kurtz's headquarters in a decaying temple, he reads a front-page newspaper account of the Tate-LaBianca murders that took place in Bel Air and Los Angeles in August 1969. After killing Rosemary LaBianca, Charles Manson's "family" printed the words *Helter Skelter* in blood on a refrigerator door. The title of a Beatles song, the phrase was the Manson family's term for Armageddon. According to one family member, "helter skelter was to be the last war on the face of the earth. It would be all the wars that have ever been fought built one on top of the other, something that no man could conceive of in his imagination" (Bugliosi and Gentry 184). Kurtz appears bent on a similar project. The words *Apocalypse Now* are crudely lettered on the temple steps, and the area is littered with corpses and severed heads. Manson-like, he has surrounded himself with devotees like Colby (Scott Glenn), a would-be assassin who defected to his side and adopted face paint, and the photojournalist (Dennis Hopper), based on the Russian in Conrad's story.

Kurtz's apocalyptism seems motivated in part by a sense of divine mission, with himself as both prophet and divinity. In biblical times Jehovah ordered King Saul to exterminate the Amalekites along with all their livestock for resisting the Israelites' incursion into the promised land (1 Sam. 15). Kurtz is determined not to repeat Saul's mistake by sparing any of the enemy, man or beast. On the taped radio transmission he is heard to say, "we must kill them, we must incinerate them, pig after pig, cow after cow, village after village, army after army." Kurtz's design may be even more comprehensive than Jehovah's, to judge from the words scrawled in red ink on the first page of a typescript found in his chamber: "DROP THE BOMB EXTERMINATE THEM ALL." The phrase "them all" may refer only to the ostensible enemy, the VC and NVA. Or, as in *Heart of Darkness*, it may include all of the indigenous people, whom Conrad's Kurtz had come to regard as "brutes" (123).[3]

Kurtz has neither bombs nor bombers at his disposal, and one cannot imagine him collaborating with the American military command even to accomplish his final solution. These practical considerations aside, however, it is clear that Kurtz has arrived at the position of the New England Puritans during King Philip's War, when exterminating the natives began to seem a more prudential policy than converting them.

Yet Kurtz's desire for Armageddon springs from more than mad genocidal fantasy. It is also the death wish of a man who has lived his life like a snail crawling along the edge of a straight razor. He reads and rereads Eliot's poem *The Hollow Men*, with its ominous epigraph ("Mistah Kurtz—he dead") and its repeated "This is the way the world ends." He does not fear the end; the lyrics of the Doors song heard at the beginning of the film echo his conviction that "the end" is his "only friend." He is determined merely that his end shall come with a bang, not a whimper. He wants to die like a soldier, as Willard puts it, not like "some poor wasted rag-assed renegade."

Kurtz therefore grooms Willard, a fellow army officer, as his executioner, a role that the younger man might otherwise be too reverent to perform. He lectures Willard on the need to befriend "horror," and to illustrate his point he tells an anecdote about the VC amputating the arms of children vaccinated by the Green Berets. Kurtz admires the courage of this ruthless deed. Willard, who showed himself capable of such ruthlessness on the river when he shot a wounded Vietnamese woman rather than jeopardize his mission, is subjected to one final test when Kurtz drops Chef's severed head in his lap. Then he is deemed ready to play the role of assassin.

Kurtz in effect orders his own execution, though Willard believes that Kurtz in turn takes his orders from the jungle. Here Coppola's Kurtz differs significantly from Conrad's. In *Heart of Darkness* Kurtz is a guilty, ruined creature whose famous dying words—"The horror. The horror"—disclose a profound awareness of moral degeneracy. Marlon Brando, though he had not read Conrad's novella, wanted to play Kurtz as a figure of American guilt in Vietnam (Marcus 54). But Coppola emphatically rejected this interpretation, presenting instead a Kurtz who passes from horror to wonder without looking back. His protagonist chooses death in obedience to a grand eschatological necessity. What the military command regards as insanity, he regards as clairvoyance and a virtuous determination not to lie. Unlike the New England Puritans, however, he has no illusions that his end will precipitate a new millennium. His apocalypse is both now and forever.

Yet there are clues that Kurtz also entertains an antiapocalyptic notion of history and personal destiny. Besides the Bible, with its linear scheme of history leading to the events predicted in the Book of Revelation, his reading includes Sir James Frazer's *Golden Bough* and Jessie L. Weston's *From Ritual to Romance*. These works inscribe biblical archetypes within a cyclical scheme of history, what Mircea Eliade has called the myth of the eternal return. According to this myth, particularly as set forth in the volume of *The Golden Bough* entitled *The Dying God*, Kurtz must die so that Willard can succeed him as the king of the Montagnards. Intercut with images of Willard slaying Kurtz with a machete are images of the Montagnards using the same implement to kill a water buffalo, perhaps as a totemic sacrifice. Thus Kurtz's death, intended by the military command to be merely a political assassination, is also the primal patricide and a potentially efficacious fertility ritual.[4]

Herein lies a contradiction that the film fails to resolve—namely, how the madman who calls for the extermination of "them all" can also be the sacrificial victim who offers himself for the well-being of the Montagnard community. The first Kurtz comes from Conrad's novella and Puritan typology, whereas the second seems to have evolved from Coppola's desperate search for a satisfactory ending to the film. In the original script written by John Milius, Kurtz and Willard engage the NVA in a climactic battle. When helicopters arrive to rescue them, Kurtz shoots them down rather than lose the opportunity for a warrior's death. Coppola disliked this ending, which he considered too "macho" and cartoonlike. As the filming dragged on and production costs vastly exceeded budget, he agonized over other conclusions.

At this juncture someone pointed out the similarity between the developing Kurtz-Willard story and the myth of the Fisher King (Marcus 55). Then Coppola's wife, Eleanor, persuaded him to witness a ritual performed by the Ifugao Indians who were playing the Montagnards in the film, and he made the connection between their ceremonial slaughter of animals and the killing of the divine King in Frazer's account. Toward the end of *Hearts of Darkness* (1991), a documentary filmed mainly by Eleanor, Coppola ruminates about the continuity of life, the cycle of death and rebirth, as mankind's oldest and profoundest insight. He apparently believed that he had gotten beyond the impasse of Puritan apocalyptism—linear history leading to the end of earthly time—by reaching further back, to a more primitive, cyclical conception of history.

Even as Coppola expounds the cyclical thesis in *Hearts of Darkness*, the Doors' "This is the end" plays incongruously in the background, a reminder that *Apocalypse Now* begins and ends in the apocalyptic mode. To succeed Kurtz as the king of the Montagnards, Willard would have to remain among them. At first it appears that he might do so. From an elevated position at the top of the temple steps he surveys the worshiping tribe. The camera catches his face in the instant of decision, balanced between replacing Kurtz as king and returning to civilization as a mere soldier. Coppola wanted the film to end here, with Willard's return implied but not yet chosen. Following test screenings, however, he acceded to the wishes of viewers who preferred the less ambiguous ending in which Willard drops his machete and descends the steps (Marcus 56). Holding Kurtz's report in one hand and leading Lance with the other, he returns to the PBR. He is "on the boat" again, reversing Kurtz's journey. The final image of his face juxtaposed with the green stone face of the Cambodian goddess is meant to recall the moment when he might have chosen otherwise.

As this image fades from the screen in the Paramount Pictures videotape version of the film, the credits roll against a black background.[5] But in the 35 mm print distributed to most theaters the credits appear against footage of the fiery destruction of Kurtz's compound. Critics disagree about the significance of the more apocalyptic coda. Frank P. Tomasulo calls it a "prowar" ending that proves "Willard has learned Kurtz's lessons so well that he *has become him*, and allowed the colonel's last wish to be fulfilled" (155). Tomasulo therefore assumes that Willard answers the radio call from "Almighty," his connection with military headquarters, and calls in the map coordinates for an air strike. According to this scenario he ruthlessly destroys the Montagnards along with Colby and the photojournalist.

John Hellmann argues, to the contrary, that the coda is Willard's "mental enactment" of Kurtz's desire, a consummation Willard himself rejects (233). I find Hellmann's interpretation more persuasive, inasmuch as "Almighty's" call goes unanswered in the film. The bombing is represented outside the film's narrative frame and without the usual realistic markers; it takes place soundlessly in an infrared light. Coppola himself maintained that it is "fantasy" (qtd. in Marcus 52). As such, it serves as a symmetric frame to a film that begins with a fiery yet surreal napalm strike. In that prologue the transition from burning palm trees and helicopter rotor blades to the ceiling fan in Willard's room in Saigon suggests that the opening footage likewise belongs to the realm of dream.

For a sophisticated New England Puritan, a mentally enacted apocalypse would have been nonetheless real. As Frank Kermode remarks, apocalypse can be disconfirmed without being discredited (*Sense* 8). When the end fails to arrive on schedule, the apocalyptic timetable can be revised. Or apocalypse can be reconstrued as immanent spiritual experience rather than imminent temporal end (26–27, 30). Like wilderness, apocalypse then becomes an individual spiritual experience—in this case the experience of crisis—rather than a historical event.

I doubt that Willard tries to realize Kurtz's genocidal fantasies by calling in an air strike. But neither am I persuaded that he rejects Kurtz's vision of the end. Willard is temperamentally a Puritan even before he meets Kurtz. He enters the terrifying wilderness of self in his Saigon hotel room and behaves like a man profoundly aware of inner disturbance and guilt. "What are the charges?" he asks the military police who come to take him to Nha Trang. There he accepts the mission as punishment for what he calls his "sins" and is coached to regard his errand into the physical wilderness as part of a metaphysical conflict between good and evil, rationality and irrationality. Though he no longer sees the world in terms of such dichotomies by the end of his journey, he remains sufficiently the Puritan to reject any pagan myth of eternal recurrence. Willard's mental enactment of apocalypse therefore reflects his spiritual kinship with Kurtz.

Like Marlow in Conrad's novella and other narrators of the genre Kenneth Bruffee has named elegiac romance, Willard is a sympathetic apologist for his heroic alter ego. Unlike them, however, he shows no sign of resolving his ambivalence toward Kurtz. As Bruffee has shown, the narrators of elegiac romance typically come to terms with loss by telling their stories; they are then able to get on with their lives (50–51). Willard, by contrast, appears to have reached a spiritual dead end. He can only savor the irony of returning bodily to the boat while remaining spiritually a castaway. "They were gonna make me a major for this," he reflected on his way to kill Kurtz, "and I wasn't even in their fuckin' army anymore." *Apocalypse Now* thus conforms more closely to the structure of tragedy, as defined by Kermode, than to romance: "tragedy assumes the figurations of apocalypse, of death and judgment, heaven and hell; but the world goes forward in the hands of exhausted survivors" (82).

IV

To refigure apocalypse as immanent rather than imminent event is to move it from the end of the *saeculum* or historical time to the middle. Apocalypse became "secular" in this sense of the word even before the dissolution of the New England Way in the early eighteenth century. During the late secular crisis of the Vietnam War, *Apocalypse Now* suggests, the American myth that derives from Puritanism became a form of cultural suicide. Although the Montagnard (Ifugao) ritual offers a way out of this dead end, Willard elects not to take it. But what if he were to choose otherwise? In the alternative scenario, he would accept the mantle of power from Kurtz and live for a time among the Montagnards. Then, perhaps, he would return to Saigon, and eventually to America, imbued with an antiapocalyptic sense of history.

In *Apocalypse Now* this peripeteia or reversal of plot is ascribed to an exotic, primitive culture. Yet it also has an American genealogy dating back to the twilight of the New England Way. Richard Slotkin calls this reversal "regeneration through violence" and finds an intimation of it in Church's *Entertaining Passages*. It reaches full articulation, however, in John Filson's story of Daniel Boone, entitled *The Discovery, Settlement and Present State of Kentucke* (1784). Prior to the publication of *Kentucke* it was assumed that any white person who lived among the American Indians would become a savage himself. The settler could dally in the wilderness only as the passive (and usually female) captive of Indians or as the bloody (and usually male) avenger of Indian aggression (Slotkin 145). Boone was twice captured by the Shawnee and lived for a while as their adopted son. In Filson's version of the story he nevertheless remained a civilized Christian and a willing instrument for the conversion of wilderness into an agrarian Eden.

History and legend record another Boone who was notoriously wary of encroachment by other white settlers (H. Smith 53–58). But Filson's mythic Boone has become a quintessential American type, an evolutionary link between the Puritan era and our own. Henry Nash Smith has traced Boone's literary sons from Cooper's Leatherstocking down to the heroes of modern pulp fiction. It should surprise no one, then, to find versions of the Boone myth in literary and cinematic responses to the Vietnam War. Along with vestiges of Puritan ideology, it appears in a film released shortly before *Apocalypse Now*, Michael Cimino's *The Deer Hunter* (1978). Although this is not the place for a detailed analysis of such a complex film, it can be usefully compared with *Apocalypse Now* in broad outline.

Michael Vronsky (played by Robert DeNiro), the deer hunter of the title, resembles Cooper's Deerslayer in several respects. He is versed in the

American Indian signs that forecast a successful hunt and values the discipline of the one-shot kill, as though his rifle were a muzzle-loader rather
than a semiautomatic. Like Leatherstocking, Kurtz, and Willard, he is
more at home in a world without women. At a wedding reception he flirts
with Linda (Meryl Streep), the fiancée of his housemate Nick (Christopher
Walken), until he learns that the bride is pregnant by someone other than
the groom. In puritanical protest against both her prurience and his own,
Michael runs naked through the darkened streets of Clairton. Figuratively
speaking, he runs all the way to Vietnam, where he shows himself capable
of Kurtz and Willard's ruthlessness and ability to befriend horror. He sets
an NVA soldier afire with a flamethrower and coolly plots an escape from
enemy captivity while his comrades are paralyzed by terror or fatalism.

On his return from Vietnam, Michael dodges a "welcome home" party.
His evasion of community suggests that he has gotten "off the boat," like
the antisocial Green Beret sergeant whom he meets earlier in the American Legion hall. But he embraces the peripeteia rejected by Willard in
Apocalypse Now. As he is assimilated by Clairton, he begins to nurture communal feeling in others. He persuades one buddy, confined to a wheelchair,
to leave the veterans hospital and return to his wife and son. He tries but
fails to persuade Nick to abandon his suicidal addiction to drugs and Russian roulette in Vietnam. The change in Michael's outlook is dramatized
in the second of the two deer hunts, where he deliberately fires over the
head of a majestic stag and cures a fellow hunter of the macho posturing
in which he himself once indulged.

Like Filson's Boone, Michael returns from the wilderness and helps to
rebuild the community, though his community resembles Winthrop's city
upon a hill (Clairton means "bright town") rather than Filson's agrarian
Eden. After Michael and his friends bury Nick, they adjourn to a tavern
for breakfast, gradually shedding their awkwardness in the domestic rituals
of pouring coffee and scrambling eggs. Having opened with one communal moment, a wedding, the film closes with another, as the party joins in
singing "God Bless America" and toasting Nick's memory. Though sad,
the song is far from being the "mournful dirge" described by one critic
(Martin 116). It affirms a social bond that has survived great loss.

The peripeteia in *The Deer Hunter*, the reversal that allies the film
with the Boone myth rather than Puritan apocalypticism, warrants closer
scrutiny. Is it violence per se that triggers Michael's regeneration? Certainly his hunterly acceptance of violence is more conducive to surviving
the war than Nick's sentimental appreciation of nature ("the way the trees
are"). In Michael's case, however, the ruthlessness needs to be tempered by
love. It is in Linda's company that he takes his first steps toward reintegra-
tion into the community, and she gives him a reason to remain in Clairton.

By itself, love might not be enough to effect regeneration. Nick, too, had been in love with Linda. But the combination of love and violence is portrayed as redemptive.

As an alternative to Puritan apocalyptism, Cimino's regenerative vision in *The Deer Hunter* has much to offer. Most criticism of the film has focused on a residue of the New England Way, the controversial scenes in which the VC appear as sadistic brutes who force their captives to play Russian roulette. Whether Cimino personally shared this view of the Vietnamese, a view that some critics consider racist, is beside the point.[6] The camera shows the enemy whom Michael hates, and he has little opportunity — perhaps also little inclination — to change his opinion of them after his regeneration. However troubling this negative stereotype may be, it is probably less insidious than another message endemic to the Boone myth, namely, that the end (regeneration) confers legitimacy on the means (violence).

Michael Herr's deservedly admired *Dispatches* legitimizes violence in much the same way. Herr invokes the Puritan myth of the wilderness when he traces the Vietnam War to "the proto-Gringos who found the New England woods too raw and empty for their peace and filled them up with their own imported devils" (49). Later in the same chapter, alluding to Filson's revision of the Puritan myth, he describes a Western (*Nevada Smith*, with Steve McQueen) in which the hero comes through a blood bath "burned clean but somehow empty and old too, like he'd lost his margin for regeneration through violence" (60). Herr concedes that his own margin became perilously slim at times, yet he recalls the year fondly, asserting that "Vietnam was what we had instead of happy childhoods" (244). Pushing Herr's logic to its absurd conclusion, one might argue that a nation should wage constant war. Why deprive any generation of a second chance at childhood happiness?

Though *The Deer Hunter* and *Dispatches* are not overtly political works, they have proven most offensive to viewers and readers who opposed the war. It is an indication of the Boone myth's flexibility, however, that it was also adopted by antiwar writers, who modified it to suit their purposes. Long before Coppola undertook *Apocalypse Now*, Susan Sontag, Gary Snyder, and Robert Bly represented Vietnam as a "Puritan" war of extermination against the "Indians" of Southeast Asia. As an antidote to this pathological impulse in American culture, each prescribed some form of "Indianizing."[7] Their advice accorded with several facets of the 1960s counterculture: environmentalism, the rejection of puritanical sexual mores, sympathy for American Indian activism, and a fondness for "Indian" modes of dress (headbands, beads, and so forth). The violent corollary of their regeneration remained largely out of sight or masked by love ("All you need is love," sang the Beatles), though it surfaced occasionally in the more militant demonstrations, the hazing of soldiers, environmental "monkey wrenching," self-destructive drug trips, and—notoriously—in a knifing death at the Altamont Rock Music Festival in 1969.

The Boone myth appealed to people from opposite ends of the political spectrum because it seemed to promise the moral regeneration (however defined) of the individual and the social regeneration of the community. The establishment and the counterculture could agree on the regenerative pattern if not on the specific means. The New England Way may have shaped the myth of America, as Bercovitch claims (*Puritan*), but it had little popular appeal after the seventeenth century. *Apocalypse Now* suggests why this was so, at least during the Vietnam War. Kurtz's zeal for killing America's enemies might please the establishment, but not his separatist strategy. His defiance of authority might delight the counterculture, but not his compulsion to exterminate the native people. Depending on one's politics, one could blame Kurtz—or the values that Kurtz embodies—for starting the war or for losing it. Furthermore, since Kurtz is a Puritan in a secular age, he can offer no comforting vision of the future, no Christian millennium, to compensate for these drawbacks. His apocalypticism is at best tragic, at worst insane.

This is not to say that we have nothing to learn from Coppola's Kurtz. Hawthorne made a literary career of telling stories that recover the hard truths of New England Puritanism. Coppola does the same in *Apocalypse Now*, almost despite himself. Even as Kurtz arranges for Willard to succeed him as king, he seems to realize that the younger man will decline the role and thereby frustrate his plan (and Coppola's nostalgia) for regeneration. So he assigns Willard an alternative mission—to explain to his son the rationale behind his apparently insane project. In the patriarchal world of *Apocalypse Now*, Kurtz's son replaces the "Intended" of Conrad's novel.[8] We in turn replace the son as the inheritors of Kurtz's apocalyptic vision, since the son never appears on camera and we are already privy to everything Willard would tell him. Kurtz's vision constitutes one of the difficult lessons of the Vietnam War, one that was also fundamental to the New England Way. Whatever Vietnam may teach us about American hubris or misguided foreign policy, it also teaches us that we must choose our historical and political narratives carefully, for some plots are irreversible.

Notes

1. Increase Mather uses the example of a man named Wakely, who was killed along with most of his family during King Philip's War, to teach this lesson in *A Brief History of the Warr with the Indians in New-England* (Slotkin and Folsom 99).

2. Here I disagree with Melling, who represents Kurtz as in every respect the antithesis of those who order his assassination (176–77).

3. The more inclusive reference recalls a graffito occasionally seen in Vietnam and still printed on T-shirts available from military supply stores: "Kill them all — let God sort them out." An oft-repeated joke made the same point: How do we end the Vietnam War? Evacuate the friendlies by boat and bomb the country. Then sink the boats.

4. Freud derives totemic sacrifice from a primal patricide in *Totem* (141–42).

5. The 70 mm version shown in some theaters likewise ended with the image of Willard's face. The credits to this version were printed on playbills and distributed to viewers (Marcus 52).

6. Just, for example, characterized the film as a "racist muddle" (65). "I am puzzled and appalled," he went on to say, "at the need for inventing a metaphor for the Vietnam War; I mean an invention with no basis whatever in fact." Actually, the metaphor may have had some basis in fact. Pfc. Robert Garwood, who was convicted of collaborating with the enemy while a prisoner in North Vietnam, tells of two South Vietnamese army soldiers who were blindfolded and compelled to play Russian roulette until one was killed (Groom and Spencer 54–55).

7. Sontag compared American foreign policy in the 1960s to the Indian wars in "What's Happening in America," then idealized the North Vietnamese as noble savages in "Trip to Hanoi" (193–274). Snyder represented the war as the establishment's way of exorcising the ghosts of massacred Indians, even as the youth counterculture was recovering Indian values (103–16). Bly likewise compared the Vietnamese to massacred Indians in "Hatred of Men with Black Hair" (*Light* 36) during the 1960s, then urged men to get in touch with the Wild Man within themselves in the 1980s (*Iron*).

8. As my colleague Carol Sklenicka pointed out to me, *Apocalypse Now* also lacks any equivalent of the magnificent jungle queen in *Heart of Darkness*, unless one counts the silent Montagnard girl glimpsed outside Kurtz's chamber. By the same token, the film lacks any equivalent of Awashonks in Benjamin Church's narrative.

PART THREE

"Nothing Fit Us"
Writers Who Claim Their Own Traditions

JONATHAN N. BARRON

New Jerusalems
Contemporary Jewish American Poets and the Puritan Tradition

WHEN SIGMUND FREUD named his son after Oliver Cromwell, he linked the world of the modern Jew to the world of the seventeenth-century Puritan. I have always been taken by that fact, but only recently have I realized that the name "Oliver Freud" can be read as a poem expressing the condition of the contemporary Jewish poet. Interpreted as a poem, this name explains the strategies and techniques Jewish poets employ in order both to express their own vexed relationship to the countries they inhabit and to express certain important aspects of the dominant literary traditions of those same countries, such as the American millennial tradition.

For example, Sigmund Freud thought of himself as Viennese, not as Jewish. It was the Germans who insisted he be labeled a Jew. Fortunately for Freud, England enabled him to be Viennese once more, albeit a Viennese in exile. Nearly three hundred years earlier, Oliver Cromwell had also welcomed the Jews to England (from which they had been forcibly expelled in 1290).[1] We normally view Oliver Cromwell as a prig, but this name, "Oliver Freud," when read as a poem, refuses to let the reader see the usual context. Generally, when one considers the Puritans, one reads them either as rebels or as prigs. Usually they are discussed as the victims of intolerance or the figures espousing an ideology of intolerance. But "Oliver Freud" reminds us of the historical fact that for the Jew the Puritan can be read as a kind neighbor, a figure of both tolerance and respect.

In Jewish exegisis of the Bible and other sacred writings, the reader's task is to find the gap or missing element in the scripture in order to expose that gap so that it can finally be bridged. Read as a poem, the name "Oliver Cromwell" exposes the issue of tolerance and so points to tolerance as a gap in most of the stories that concern the Puritans. Only when it is exposed can the issue be discussed. Let us say, then, that "Oliver Freud" does force us to discuss the issue of tolerance with reference to the Puritans.

To the Jew, this is a particularly troubling discussion because the respect offered by the Puritans came with a price.

Cromwell incorporated the Other, the Jew, into his political, theocratic state precisely because he knew that the Other would eventually be incorporated into the Same. According to the English Puritans, the Jew would, by divine fiat, one day convert. The expected millennial New Jerusalem and the second coming of Jesus himself depended on the conversion of the Jews. In seventeenth-century America, as well as in seventeenth-century England, such ministers as Cotton and Increase Mather awaited "the conversion of the Jews, [as] an aspect of the millennial promise that was regarded to be a crucial prerequisite by which the advent of the last things might be identified" (Lowance 135). The Puritans were benign only in that they would not force the Jews to convert; they felt God would find His own way of converting them so long as the Puritans gathered them all in one place. The Jew is welcomed only when Jews themselves are part of an already Christian teleology.[2]

In the Jewish exegetical tradition, every reading, every interpretation gives rise to a response. If we imagine that the name "Oliver Freud" was written by a rabbi, then, that name can be read as an exegetical commentary, a midrash. As a midrash, it raises a few questions about Puritan tolerance. It asks, what price must Freud pay to Oliver? In return, this question gives rise to more questions: Is the price paid for tolerance—loss of one's identity—worth paying? Is it ethical? This discussion would then give rise to still more questions all in an attempt to reconcile the Oliver to the Freud.

Let the name "Oliver Freud," then, be a poetic parable for the situation of the Jewish American poet. Just as my invented rabbis read that name out of the usual context of priggishness, intolerance, and rebellion and into a new context of tolerance, so too the Jewish American poet brings to light those hidden gaps and fissures that lie in our national literary tradition of millennialism. As scholars from Perry Miller to Sacvan Bercovitch have said, writers from the Puritan Edward Johnson to such twentieth-century poets as Delmore Schwartz have read America as a biblical type.

One example of a Puritan who found such millennial types in his own contemporary experience is Edward Johnson. Jesper Rosenmeier explains:

Johnson's poems . . . are significant because they show us that a century after Luther, the principle of finding Christ's presence in Biblical realities—the types—had now been extended to make even contemporary, historical presences into prophetic, type-like figures. Johnson was the first historian and poet in New England who sought to create a past by converting the dead among the first generation Puritans into memories that could support the living generations on their march to the New Jerusalem. (170)[3]

Rosenmeier explains that the work of Edwards, Thoreau, and Whitman follows from Johnson in that they, too, read America as a biblical type. Puritan typology, Rosenmeir tells us, enabled Emerson to "see the prophetic memory of the New Jerusalem, Christ's bride, in the starlit sky over New England" (173). Johnson, like so many Puritans, conflates a nationalist dream with a religious one.[4]

Ironically, the Jewish American poet Delmore Schwartz also read America in terms of the Christian millennial dream, which, even in the late 1950s, continued to exert a strong hold on American literature. In a 1958 essay he explains that, in the Atomic Age, the triumph of Stalinism, combined with the "poverty and helplessness of Western Europe" could only mean that "America, not Europe, is now the sanctuary of culture; civilization's very existence depends upon America, upon the actuality of American life. . . . No matter what may be wrong with American life, it is nothing compared to the police state, barbarism, and annihilation" (46). Although this does not appear to be Christian, the very idea that America will be the location for a New Jerusalem is a specifically Christian, Puritan idea. Schwartz's essay tells us just what happens when a Jewish American poet enters the dominant American tradition.

Not all Jewish American poets feel compelled to accept the Christian millennialism espoused by Schwartz. Some find a way to write in that tradition without joining it. They do so by using the Jewish exegetical tradition itself. In the Jewish tradition, the commentary on sacred texts is gathered in both the Talmud and the Midrash; the Midrash are those books that collectively comment on and interpret the Jewish biblical canon. One student of such exegesis explains the task of biblical commentary or midrash as follows: "The Torah, owing to its own intertextuality, is a severely gapped text, and the gaps are there to be filled by strong readers, which in this case does not mean readers fighting for originality, but readers fighting to find what they must in the holy text" (Boyarin 16).[5] Rather than resort to the varieties of *figura* and to typology common among the Puritans, the rabbis find the gaps, contradictions, and lacunae in the Torah (the "Old" Testament and other works of the Jewish Bible) precisely so that they can fill them. The various interpretations, therefore, are a series of attempts to connect what might appear at first to be disconnected. This process, moreover, is endless because it is bound in time; "the text makes its meaning in history" (17). In other words, insofar as one generation notices or fails to notice a gap, a later generation will offer a corrective "filling," or point to another fissure that requires a bridge.

Like the rabbis who comment on the Bible in the Midrash, Jewish American poets read the central passages from the poetic scripture of the American millennial tradition and reveal in them the gaps and fissures that demand to be filled and bridged. This seemingly more secular American poetic canon is a "canon" that requires a particularly Jewish commentary. Such commentary will seek to recontextualize and refocus the reader's gaze away from one context and into another, and it will do so by noting the gaps that arise in the central American texts. Jewish American poets are particularly interested in recontextualizing the canon in this way because its millennial tropes are decidedly Christian. To understand what some Jewish American poets do with that canon, one must first accept the fact that it *is* a decidedly Christian poetic tradition in the first place. If we accept that premise, we can better understand why the Jewish American poet who enters into a discussion of that canon enters as a midrashic rabbi. He or she enters in order to ask questions and reveal the gaps and fissures such a monological tradition contains. The two poets I have chosen, Philip Levine and Gerald Stern, exemplify the existence of a midrashic hermeneutics in American literature by interpreting William Stafford as the rabbis interpreted Moses in the Midrash. Seeing the poem "Traveling Through the Dark" as a central canonical text, Levine and Stern, like two midrashic rabbis, reveal the gaps that arise in so decidedly Christian a story, a story that by definition excludes the Jew.[6] Few would suggest that this poem is not central. One finds it in trade paperback anthologies of contemporary American poetry, and in two standard textbook anthologies of poetry—*The Norton Anthology of Poetry* (Allison) and *The Norton Anthology of Modern Poetry* (Ellmann and O'Clair). One also finds it in at least two American literature anthologies (Prentice Hall and HarperCollins) and in a variety of textbook introductions to literature (HarperCollins, Harcourt Brace Jovanovich, Norton, and Bedford, Saint Martins).[7]

Stafford

William Stafford does not himself announce the Christian context of "Traveling Through the Dark" but readers familiar with Christianity supply that context as a matter of course. The poem's plot is straightforward: A man driving up a mountain spots a dead, pregnant doe. He stops his car and throws the doe over the riverbank. Through a series of deft rhetorical maneuvers, Stafford places this plot into a larger Christian story: an allegorical tale about a Christian soul's journey to redemption.

The title itself refers to St. John of the Cross and to all the now familiar theological journeys that take one through "the dark night of the soul." The poem states the plot with ease: "Traveling through the dark I found a deer / dead on the edge of the Wilson River road" (1-2). But the hard moral, theological questions begin with the third line: "It is usually best to roll them into the canyon" (3). One cannot help but ask, why is it best?

The poem does not say. Why does Stafford stop his car in the first place? Because "that road is narrow; to swerve might make more dead" (4). If the dead deer is not moved, then people driving by might swerve and crash. Stafford's concern is not with the dead animal but with the people who might be affected by it.

The poem achieves its parabolic status when Stafford prepares to throw the doe over the edge. As he gets closer, he discovers that she is pregnant; the fawn, "alive, still, never to be born" (11). What may have been an easy moral decision to dump the deer over the edge is now complicated by the living "unborn" fawn. Stafford says, "Beside that mountain road I hesitated" (12). The theological allegory of this poem now emerges in the term "hesitation"—one hesitates before God because one fears what one might do. Stafford tells us, "I stood in the glare of the warm exhaust turning red; / around our group I could hear the wilderness listen" (15-16). In a Christian context the "wilderness" in this line belongs to Satan. It is his domain because in the wilderness Satan listens for and awaits the sin that is about to occur. If one chooses to read "wilderness" as God's domain, then it must be read as a place that still awaits redemption, still listens for the one who will offer it salvation. However one chooses to read "wilderness," the emphasis of the poem is on the Christian who "hesitates" while the wilderness listens. The ambiguity of this line is a theological ambiguity. The wilderness listens for the word of God, the wilderness waits with no little cynicism for an epiphany that would challenge Satan. Or, the wilderness, at this point, listens for the sound of a man who is about to be converted to sin; it eagerly awaits a man who is about to join Satan's dominion. In either case, the dead animal by the road signifies God's ability to test Stafford's moral virtue, a specifically Christian moral virtue. If Stafford throws the deer over, he kills the fawn. If he does not, either the doe or the fawn (should it be "born") might cause an accident and perhaps lead to the death of a human. Stafford must choose the human over the animal.

The final stanza emphasizes this moral crisis. Whereas the first four stanzas contain four lines, the final stanza contains only two: "I thought hard for us all—my only swerving—, / then pushed her over the edge into the river" (17-18). "Us all" includes both the animals and Stafford: the entire wilderness scene, and the human community in general. The verb "swerve" at this point demands to be read in its theological context. Stafford's swerving occurs only when he thinks. It occurs when he no longer allows his deeds to be governed by faith. When he thinks, he declares a freedom from God; he begins to doubt. Stafford alone "thinking," at this point, can be read as Stafford questioning his own faith, his God. As he questions what he is about to do, the wilderness listens for the answer Stafford will have to come to on his own.

For Puritan poets "this world was God's metaphor for His communicable glories and . . . another part of their duty was to see and utter that metaphor, to use the figural value of this world to turn their attention and affections to the next" (Daly 81). The Christian journey to salvation requires Stafford on his way "up the mountain" to sacrifice a fawn. His sacrifice will aid future travelers on that same road upward toward salvation. Perhaps in another reading of the word "swerved," Stafford, like a biblical saint, "swerves" for us when he kills the fawn. His sin is our salvation.

The success of this poem in contemporary anthologies, I believe, is due to its ability to allegorize in a masked, almost secular manner, a specifically Christian theology. Stafford's poem, after all, is about a familiar trinity of themes: sacrifice, death, and redemption. These three themes are only familiar, however, if the road to the New Jerusalem requires a specifically Christian journey.

Stern

Gerald Stern, for one, does not read this journey as a specifically Christian one. As a result, he, like Sigmund Freud, who named his son Oliver, offers a new poem, a new name, that asks the reader to see the same story but in a new context. Specifically, Stern's poems "Behaving Like a Jew" and "Burying an Animal on the Way to New York" present us with the same plot: A man drives a car until he sees a dead animal. Then the man decides to remove the animal from the road. Where Stafford's poem discusses redemption in terms of death and sacrifice, Stern asks us to recontextualize the plot and read it as a story about respect. Stern's poems ask the hard question, is sacrifice ever justifiable, even in the name of a journey toward the New Jerusalem of redemption? His answer is "no." Forget redemption that requires a sacrifice, he says. We dare not ever sacrifice another life for our own, and therefore we must only encounter the dead animal on the road as an opportunity—a type—for our respect. In this way, Stern reveals the hidden and dangerous implications latent in Stafford's poem. After all, Stern suggests, once we justify the sacrifice of a fawn in the name of a man, why not justify the death of a man in the name of another man?

The means by which Stern asks these questions is particularly midrashic. He may be said to use a device known as a mashal: "The mashal is a story whose meaning by itself is perfectly clear and simple, and because of its simplicity enables one to interpret by analogy a more complex, difficult, or hermetic text" (Boyarin 106). Boyarin, contrasting the mashal to the parable as it appears in the Gospels, argues that the mashal "gives to the Torah narrative a clear ideological value, without reducing the vitality and vividness of the representation of character and event in it" (85). Stern's mashal on Stafford, "Behaving Like a Jew," exposes the gaps and fissures of Stafford's story of redemption.

Stern's mashal exposes the problems inherent in Stafford's poem by transforming Stafford's dead animal from a deer into a rodent: a dead opossum. Through this switch, Stern points to a gap in Stafford's moral logic. It is, we recall, "precisely these gaps in the text which the midrash reads" (Boyarin 94). When Stern changes the species, he exposes the link between morality and proper names.[8] A "doe and fawn" raise hard moral questions precisely because they belong to the larger cultural paradigm inhabited by the equation of deer with royalty, which suggests that a deer is somehow an exalted animal. When Stern changes the doe into an opossum, he all but asks, "Would we feel the same way about a rodent?" In this question the hierarchy that underlies Stafford's moral dilemma—humans are better than animals, and some animals are better than others—is exposed.

A mashal, however, like any midrash, exposes a gap in order to fill it. Stern's mashal is no different. He tells us that this dead opossum shot through the head by a bullet is not about the theological relationship between God, Satan, and humanity; rather, it is about the social relationship between humans, animals, and other humans: "I am going to be unappeased at the opossum's death. / I am going to behave like a Jew / and touch his face, and stare into his eyes, / and pull him off the road" (ll. 15–18). These lines explain that, for Stern, the central issue brought to light by this type, the dead animal on the road, is the issue of respect. Stern will not be appeased, nor will he hesitate.

He dare not hesitate because the very thing Stafford did to save a human life, sacrifice the fawn, has now been done for more sinister reasons. An oppossum has been shot. It has been sacrificed. Stern's poem, unlike Stafford's, does not ask or wonder why someone would shoot this rodent. Such speculation will not do anything to alter the fact: the rodent has been shot. The more difficult question is, therefore, an implied one. Why is it that people show so little respect for life? Why does Stafford assume that someone will hit the fawn, should it be born, or even hit the doe? Why should we not assume that people might have enough respect to stop for the living and for the dead? In Stern's poem, the moral obligation lay on the individual witness. Since he sees the dead animal, he must show it the respect that the man who shot it failed to show: that is, Stern suggests that the shooter should have buried the animal.

In the first six lines of his poem, Stern conflates the animal kingdom and the human community and so blurs the clear moral distinction between creatures that informs Stafford's poem. "When I got there the dead opossum looked like / an enormous baby sleeping on the road" (ll. 1–2). After noticing the bullet hole, Stern tells us that "it took me only a few seconds" (l. 3) to "get back again into my animal sorrow" (l. 6). These lines insist that death is always unacceptable. Because Stern has an "animal sorrow," a link even to the opossum, he must respect this creature as he would any creature; he must bury it. He must do what the person who shot it failed to do. He must show respect.

Stern's poem changes Stafford's plot when he excludes the figure of the "unborn" fawn. There is no potential life in Stern's poem. By excluding a baby, Stern focuses his poem's attention entirely on the issue of burial. There is no life here. Stern, in this way, asks the following question: why should a moral dilemma arise only when there is the potential for life? Even if Stafford had come across a dead doe without a fawn, he should still have had a moral obligation to think about what he must do. Stern's poem can be read as a directed analogue, a mashal, precisely because his poem suggests that the issue of pregnancy is beside the point; one's obligation before a corpse is to bury that corpse. To "roll it" into the canyon is a matter of obligation not of faith. From this perspective, Stern implies that there is never any need to hesitate. One has no need to think, no need to hesitate. Nothing could be more clear, in ethical terms, than to show respect to this abandoned dead rodent. Stern makes this point about burial and respect for the dead by first exposing the ideology that celebrates such roadside "carnage" in the first place.

> I am sick of the country, the bloodstained
> bumpers, the stiff hairs sticking out of the grilles
> the slimy highways, the heavy birds
> refusing to move;
> I am sick of the spirit of Lindbergh over everything,
> that joy in death, that philosophical
> understanding of carnage, that
> concentration on the species.
> (ll. 7-14)

These lines refer to two cultural products of the Puritan millennial tradition both of whom reveal a sinister message that that tradition might be said to broadcast. The first product is a cultural hero, Charles Lindbergh, while the second is a now critically forgotten poet, Anne Morrow Lindbergh. Both of these figures revel in "that joy in death," and both attempt to explain "carnage" with philosophy. Lindbergh the pilot was alleged to be in sympathy with Hitler in the 1930s, while Anne Morrow Lindbergh, his wife, wrote a poetry that insisted on the sentimentalization of death, a poetry that exalted the human above the animal kingdom.[9]

Anne Morrow Lindbergh's poetry, in fact, sparked quite a debate in the late 1950s. In 1957, the poet John Ciardi, literary editor of the *Satur-*

day Review of Literature, wrote a review and letter in which he condemned her latest collection for much the same reason that Stern condemns it in this poem, calling it "that sort of pernicious poetry I mean to have none of" ("Reviewer's" 54). So controversial were his views that *Time* magazine reported in its "Press" section that the reader reaction to Ciardi had "produced in the words of Editor [Norman] Cousins 'the biggest storm of reader protest in our 33-year history'" ("Critic" 45).

When Stern recalls the Lindberghs, he conjures up the pernicious aspect of the American millennial tradition. According to Stern, the *Spirit of St. Louis*, Charles Lindbergh's plane, can be read metaphorically. A metaphor, we recall, contains a vehicle (the expression) and a tenor (the thing expressed). In this case, the vehicle is a literal vehicle, the airplane. The tenor, however, located on the painted text of that plane, is the theological "spirit of St. Louis." In Stern's poem, the *Spirit of St. Louis*—the spirit of the conquistador, and of the missionary—becomes "the American spirit" itself: it will justify any sacrifice in the name of the Lord. Stern, however, in his mashal, would rather we look at who *drives* the vehicle. He would have us focus our attention on the pilot, the man Lindbergh, who drives that spirit in the sky. If there is an American spirit, Stern implies, then its type should not be Lindbergh (pilot and poet, both), because if that is the driver, then he or she will never stop for that type—the dead animal on the road—nor will they swerve; they will rather take "joy in death" and sacrifice what needs to be sacrificed.

Exposing the American love of death in these lines enables Stern to insist that hesitation before death is dangerous. When Stern describes "that joy in death, that philosophical / understanding of carnage, that / concentration on the species," he directly responds to Stafford's claim that "I thought hard for us all." He tells us that killing is *always* "carnage" and that Stafford's excessive "concentration on the species" can also justify wanton destruction of other species. The theology of Stafford's "Journey" can justify the sacrifice of anything labeled Other.

Stern's poem tells us, by analogy, that Stafford did the right thing—roll the doe into the canyon—for the wrong reasons. Stern's mashal gives better reasons by pointing to a code of respect that is not based on God but on a cross-species communion. Stern's poem will not tolerate a theology that would justify the death of one creature in order to save another. Rather than oppose Stafford's Christianity with a normative Judaism, Stern opposes it with a secular ethics. Early Judaism made use of animal sacrifice, and Stern will have no part either in that practice or in its contemporary symbolic expression. To make clear his opposition to the very idea of sacrifice, however, Stern tells the story of the dead animal on the road under the title "Behaving Like a Jew." Sacrifice is not Jewish, he implies, nor should it be American. But respect is both Jewish and American. However, there are particular Jewish rules that explain how one properly respects the dead—in this poem, Stern insists on these rules.

He insists on a traditional Jewish concentration on burial itself because he means to insist on a tradition based on respect as a duty, as an obligation, as a rule.[10] Respect is not going to make the man who buries feel better, nor will it redeem him. Rather, it will grant to that dead creature some dignity. Stern locates the source of such respect in these lines:

> I am not going to stand in a wet ditch
>
> . . . .
>
> and praise the beauty and the balance
> and lose myself in the immortal lifestream
> when my hands are still a little shaky
> from his stiffness and his bulk
> and my eyes are still weak and misty
> from his round belly and his curved fingers
> and his black whiskers and his little dancing feet.
> (19–28)

These concluding lines tell us that Stern's own animal life requires him to show respect even to an opossum. He tells us that "when my hands and my eyes" see and touch this creature, he, the one who sees and touches, is obligated by that sight and by that touch, by the connection itself, to grant the dead the respect offered through burial. Note here his *obligation* to perform this action. He is not going to be made better because he does it. This story has nothing to do with Stern and everything to do with "behaving like a Jew," which is to say, acting ethically by following rules that have little to do with the individual performing those rules and everything to do with the other creature.

In his second mashal to Stafford's poem, "Burying an Animal on the Way to New York," Stern focuses on a question raised by his earlier mashal. If we are to read the type—dead animal on the road—as involved not in a story of redemption and sacrifice but in one of respect, then who governs? Under what law are we obligated to respect and bury the dead, even a dead rodent? This second mashal can also be read as a commentary on Stafford's third line: "It is usually best to roll them into the canyon."

Stern's response to these questions is both comical and Jewish. His rules for burying an animal are derived, as all Jewish rules of conduct are derived, from the sacred text itself. In this case, the sacred text is Stafford's poem, and in that poem Stern finds the textual support for his own rules governing the proper burial of an animal. As the philosopher Emmanuel Levinas has explained, we act ethically not for ourselves but for those others whom still others might threaten and harm. A neighbor does not fear her neighbor, she fears the third party who might harm the neighbor.

In his philosophy, Levinas offers one means by which to understand Jewish ethics, which are themselves derived from the 613 commandments located in the Bible. From Levinas's perspective, these commandments ensure that others will be looked after. They do not simply make the one following the commandments a better person (although that may be their effect), they ensure that others are and will remain safe. Both the Talmud and the Midrash contain much commentary and discussion not only of those commandments but of many other rules as well. Altogether, the legal code governing Jewish life is known as "halacha." Discussion of it, too, is dependent on a series of interpretive rules. One of those rules, the "binyan av," explains how one can construct "a general principle derived from one Biblical text, or from two related texts" (Handelman 58).

Stern's second mashal, then, his "Burying an Animal," reads like a halachic text: a series of rules of behavior explaining how one is to conduct oneself. It could very well come out of the pages of either the Midrash or the Talmud, but instead it comes directly out of Stafford's poem. Using the rule of the binyan av, Stern constructs a general rule out of Stafford's specific text. But the great difference is in the tone. Stern's poem is high comedy. Stern's binyan av derived from Stafford asks us to drive right over a corpse whenever we see one. Using the technique and style of Jewish law, Stern finds the rule of conduct that will govern his behavior in Stafford's "Don't flinch when you come across a dead animal lying on the road; / you are being shown the secret of life. / Drive slowly over the brown flesh; / You are helping to bury it" (ll. 1–4). This is a general rule because Stern never specifies the species, although I read "the brown flesh" as a reference to Stafford's doe and the "Don't flinch" as a reference to Stafford's "hesitation."

Stern thus creates a halacha out of Stafford: he uses the binyan av to create a very Jewish rule of behavior—"drive slowly over the brown flesh." Why is this Stafford? Because Stafford is the first contemporary American poet to notice and codify the type on which this rule depends: the dead animal on the road. Stern constructs his code out of a specific type that Stafford noticed and that anthologists have continued to reprint.

Both "Behaving Like a Jew" and "Burying an Animal on the Way to New York" demand that we read that type in terms of respect. Sardonically, Stern appears to say, "You want to respect that corpse? Then drive right over it!" In his concluding instructions Stern tells us: "Slow down with your radio off and your window open / to hear the twittering as you go by" (ll. 11–12). These lines could be read as a reaction to Stafford's sixteenth line, which reads "around our group I could hear the wilderness listen." As a reaction to that claim, Stern's lines inform us that the wilderness is never silent: it "twitters" in the face of death. The only one who has the capacity to show respect is the human being on the way to New York.

In this way, Stern transforms the Christian allegorical meaning of wilderness as the location for Satan into a literal wilderness of the living world.

Levine

Like Gerald Stern, Philip Levine also invents a mashal in order to comment on Stafford. But Levine's mashal depends on Stern. As with the Midrash, where one rabbi's commentary invokes further commentary on the commentary itself, so, too, Levine comments on Stern's comments on Stafford. In "28," Levine follows up on Stern's insistence that the type, dead animal on the road, be read in a story of respect. Levine, like Stern, is disturbed that Stafford's story, along with any story of redemption, might justify the sacrifice of one in the name of another. But Levine is not comfortable with Stern's recontextualization. Levine is not so sure that if we read the type, dead animal on the road, as part of a story about respect anything will be different; he suspects it will lead to the same problems inherent in the redemptive context.

Like Wordsworth's "Immortality Ode," "28" is a long poem about faith. In the poem's first line, Levine explains, "At 28 I was faithless." But it soon becomes clear that Levine is not discussing faith in redemption, as Stafford does in his poem. The faith Levine describes is a faith in other people, in the existence of an ethical universe. At twenty-eight, he had no faith in "the animal sorrow" that animates Stern's universe. Levine has no faith that people will hesitate before they kill him.

Levine begins his journey to the New Secular Jerusalem with a description of the road-kill he saw on the way: "the animals / that dotted the road, the small black spots / that formed and unformed crows, the flying pieces / of slate that threatened to break through / the windshield . . . were whatever they were" (ll. 5-9). At first glance line nine—"were whatever they were"—is merely humorous. But examined more closely, it is Levine's first midrashic warning about the dangers of any interpretation based too heavily on a typology.

Levine's mashal, in this analogy, asks us not to interpret dead animals at all—he asks us to follow neither Stafford nor Stern. Levine tells us not to place *any* faith in *any* type or symbol. Types and symbols, says Levine in this poem (and in most of his poems), can always be misused. We do need to notice them, he tells us, but we dare not specifically name them. To point to them is enough. He will not say what the black spots dotting the road were. Eventually, we know that he nearly becomes one of those black spots himself. The point Levine makes here is not that the black spots are dead—that is Stern's point. What matters to Levine is that someone else killed them.

Ultimately, Levine in "28" asks Stern to consider the implications of "the deep animal sorrow" supposedly shared by all creatures. He suggests that so long as we are capable of turning any life into a type, so long as we can say a creature can have a typological meaning, we are in danger of manipulating and mistreating that creature. The poem "28" suggests that even if we read the dead animal on the road as a type for respect, we have still failed to respect the creature itself.

The first lines of "28" describe Levine's twenty-eighth year, when he took a journey alone on his motorcycle to his own New Jerusalem, his "promised land," California.[11] No sooner does he begin this story, however, than he interrupts it.[12] One of the first interrupting memories is a scene describing a motorcycle accident that occurred after his journey to California. This memory also becomes a mashal on Stafford and on Stern. He remembers when a station wagon carrying a family of five ran him off the Tollhouse Road while he was going up a mountain. Remarking on the day of his high fever when he first went to California, he says that that "was 28 years ago. Since then I have died / only twice" (ll. 12–13). He then describes one of those deaths:

> Since then I have died
> only twice, once in slow motion against
> the steel blue driver's side of a Plymouth
> station wagon. One moment before impact I said
> to myself, seriously, 'This is going to hurt.'
> The kids in the Plymouth's back seat gaped
> wildly, shouted, leaped, and the father held firm
> to the steering wheel as I slipped through the space
> that was theirs, untouched, skidding first
> on the black field of the asphalt and broken glass
> that is California 168, Tollhouse Road, and over
> the edge of the mountain, the motorcycle
> tumbling off on its own through nettles and grass
> to come to a broken rest as all bodies must.
> (ll. 12–25)

The faithless Levine responds to the impending impact: "this is going to hurt." There is no sudden transcendent moment of communion either for Levine or for the driver. Levine's driver, like Stern's driver "on the Way to New York," simply follows instructions. He "holds firm to the steering wheel" and drives on. Unlike Stafford's presumed driver who might be confronted with a fawn, and like Stern's driver, this man does not swerve. Levine, meanwhile, tumbles, like the living fawn and not like the dead doe, into the canyon. In this memory, Levine makes what had been implicit in Stern and buried in Stafford overt and visible: a man has been sacrificed so that another man might better make his journey up the metaphorical mountain.

In a haunting image, Levine explains the effect of that first death. Ever since that time, he has noticed his scars in the mirror when shaving. They are "like the delicate tracings / on a whale's fins that the sea animals carve to test his virtue" (ll. 29–31). Faithless, Levine now sees the event as a natural test of his own virtue. We return, therefore, to the original context of a test of faith that Stafford offered. Levine tells us that when he sees those "delicate tracings" on his body, "I reenter the wide blue eyes / of that family of five that passed on their way / up the mountain" (ll. 31–33). This image manages to expose the problem inherent in a theology based on justifiable sacrifice. Levine's virtue was tested not by God, not by animals as types for God, but by other people. On their journey up the metaphorical mountain, they sacrifice Levine rather than themselves. Rather than swerve, they knock him off the road. He carries the sign, the literal inscription of their lack of respect for him in his scars. But Levine interprets those scars as a test of his own virtue, not as a sign of his own worthlessness. And what virtue is he discussing? I believe it to be his own ethical sensibility. His knowledge that he would not have abandoned a person he had run off a road proves to him that he has virtue. Levine's faith in other people is made more poignant still when he invokes a Nazi type: this family is a blue-eyed type for the non-Jew. Invoking the blue-eyed type for the Aryan killer, Levine invokes the image of those who made a virtue out of the sacrifice of others. The blue-eyed Aryan has no trouble justifying his sacrifice of the Jew. In this image, Levine suggests what happens when people become nothing more than types. And, by implication, he suggests why he will not resort to types, allowing me to see the Aryan killer, but not labeling him, even though he is himself the victim. He will only point to the context surrounding a man driving his family up the mountain.

Levine, the isolated figure on the motorcycle, is cast off by the family wagon on its way up the mountain to glory. What Levine emphasizes in this memory (mashal) is the fact of abandonment. This family abandoned Levine. They knew they had hit him and they did not stop. It is this sin, this error, that Stern's halachic rules of burial are meant to combat. Levine's memory, a tale of abandonment, forces us to ask, who it is that "travels through the dark"? Who dares sacrifice on behalf of anyone else? It also exposes a gap in Stern's poems: why should one expect an animal communion across the species when even those of the same species are willing to knock each other off the road and abandon one another.

Toward the end of this poem about Levine's twenty-eighth year, he returns to the present moment of composition, interrupting his narrative of the journey to California to comment on the events transpiring outside his window, now, in New England. As he looks out that window, he sees a scene that itself interprets the earlier memory when he was knocked off the road by the family in the stationwagon:

One boy drops his lunch box
with a clatter and mysteriously leaves it there
on the pavement as a subtle rebuke
to his mother, to a father holding tight to a wheel,
to a blue Plymouth that long ago entered the heaven brooding
above Detroit.
    (ll. 57–62)

The little boy dropping his lunch box enables Levine to interpret the story of his motorcycle accident. Watching the event in the present, he discovers, by analogy, that the dead animal on the road does not belong to a story about respect (Stern), or to a story about sacrifice (Stafford); it belongs to a story of abandonment.

This realization reveals a dangerous gap still present in Gerald Stern's two poems. Levine suggests that if respect depends on an intense communion, a shared "animal sorrow," then the idea of sacrifice will continue to hold sway because too few people have the sort of "sorrow" Stern invokes. It is far more likely that people will abandon both the living and the dead. Levine seems to imply that Stern's faith is without much ground in experience.

At the conclusion of "28," when Levine stares out of his window and sees the boy drop his lunch box, he finds in that scene a midrashic mashal on his own earlier mashal describing the accident. The story of the boy and the lunch box enables Levine to understand the meaning of his motorcycle accident. This connection is made in lines 59–60 when Levine suggests that the boy's mother is the metaphorical equivalent of that father who long ago ran Levine off the road: "a subtle rebuke / to his mother, to a father holding tight to a wheel" (ll. 59–60). The boy's mother, with the aid of a comma, is joined to that father who long ago held tight and ran directly into Levine. Watching the boy drop the lunch box, and realizing that it is a rebuke to a determined parent, Levine realizes, at last, why that man abandoned him long ago. The child is indeed father to the man for, like that small boy who abandoned his lunch box to rebuke his mother, so, he concludes, did the man rebuke his wife by abandoning Levine. When that blue-eyed family abandoned Levine, the driver must have been angry at some third party: no doubt his wife. In punishing Levine, the man was treating Levine as he would like to have treated that third party. Similarly, the little boy punishes his mother, declares his independence from her law, when he throws his lunch box on the pavement. The ugliness of the story becomes clear when we realize that a lunch box functions in exactly the same way as does the deer, the opossum, and even the human being.

Whenever a person is reduced to a thing, he or she can be used like a thing. The boy expresses his anger on an inanimate object. The man turns

the animate object, Levine, into a thing, a type, the expression of all that
he would like to sacrifice and remove, and so he runs Levine off the road.
Just as Levine is hit and abandoned, so, too, the lunch box is thrown and
abandoned, so, too, is the doe in Stafford's poem thrown and abandoned.
After all, once animals become types or symbols there is no reason to distinguish between a lunch box as moral instrument and a man.

The painful fact of this story of the dead animal is that someone drove
on—"If only they had stopped" (l. 62). Levine doesn't ask for anything
other than to have been "lifted to my feet" (l. 66). Levine suggests that
even the smallest acknowledgment is a form of respect. But the sort of
acknowledgment mockingly offered by Stern in "Burying an Animal" can
be quite sinister. Gerald Stern's poem implies that when we drive over the
corpse we fulfill a commandment: thou shalt always acknowledge the dead;
even if you have to drive over them, you are at least noting their existence,
recognizing that they are not just things. But Levine suggests that there
are those who will see such an act in the spirit of sacrifice, not in a spirit of
respect. Levine's comment on the type, dead animal on the road, is twofold. First, he questions why it should be reduced to a type, concluding
that such reductions have little positive value. Second, in the story as it is
told, someone always abandons the animal.

The only way to alter an ethical situation where the victim is reduced
to an object and then abandoned is to remove the very idea of typology
itself from the story. Ultimately, "28" refuses to interpret its types. Once
Levine humanizes, indeed becomes, the dead animal on the road, he offers
a rebuke to the very notion of animal as thing, as instrument: be it an instrument of respect or of sacrifice.[13] Levine prefers to point to those types
(icons, symbols) that exist on the way to a New Jerusalem—that ethical
realm where all differences are tolerated—without interpreting them. If he
does not interpret them, after all, he cannot be accused, as Stern accuses
Stafford, of sacrificing the Other in the name of the Same. In the conclusion to "28," for example, Levine does isolate a type—the fresh-faced
young girl—but he refuses to interpret her.

He does not have to interpret her, because she belongs to the American
social text as it has come to be written in the American canon. American
literature is full of young girls who are meant to typify the spirit of optimism, youth, and joy that one associates with a secular New Jerusalem.
Henry James's Daisy Miller is but one example. Levine, when he points at
the end of his poem to the image of an eight-year-old girl, points to a well-
established type for the spirit of respect and faith in the Other implied by
his idea of the New Jerusalem. If Stern laments "the spirit of Lindbergh,"
then Levine can praise the spirit of America as the entirely secular, optimistic faith in a benign social contract. The spirit of America is not the

little boy who throws down his lunch box; it is the fresh-faced little blond girl. Rather than erase the child as Stern erased the fawn, and rather than sacrifice the infant as Stafford does, Levine returns to the living child and suggests that her living optimism can regenerate and make immortal the dying faith of her parents. Returning to his window in the present moment of composition, Levine sees the neighborhood children come home from school.

> I could put them [these images]
> all in a poem, title it 'The Basket of Memory'
> as though each image were an Easter egg waiting to hatch
> as though I understood the present and the past or even why
> the 8 year old with a cap of blond hair
> falling to her shoulders waves to me as she darts
> between parked cars and cartwheels into the early dusk.
>
> (147-53)

We as American readers know better than to believe Levine when he says he cannot understand the present or the past. This girl is a type for a secular faith in the good will of other people. She is the incarnation of American optimism that can cartwheel right through the "darkness of the soul." She does not hesitate even as she twirls about the parked cars. Even though, at any moment, one of those cars could rumble to life and kill her, hers is the optimism of a faith in the good will of those who might drive those cars as the dusk slowly descends to night.

Levine and Stern have in effect created a page in the American midrash that continues a debate over the ethical responsibility of one person to another. In their poems, both Levine and Stern react against Stafford's reading. Stafford suggests that sacrifice is a necessary component in the journey to salvation. He must throw the doe over to save the potential lives that might be lost should they hit either doe or fawn. But Stern wonders why Stafford has so little faith in those potential drivers. Stern even wonders if it is ethical to abandon that fawn. He asks if we are correct in supposing that other travelers might not stop should they see the doe and fawn. Might they not give the doe a proper burial? Levine, by contrast, wonders why Stern has such faith in people. He reminds us that a person most likely killed that doe, and a person certainly saw fit to sacrifice the fawn. And did not all these people have quite noble reasons for their actions? According to both Levine and Stern, if we are to read the canon well, if we are to continue to respect the poems of Stafford and the millennial tradition in which he partakes, we have to learn to ask these obstinate questions and others like them. Perhaps the best way to respect that tradition is to ask, Why should one man think for us all? Why can we not think for ourselves?

Notes

1. In his own day, Freud himself depended on such tolerance from England. He referred to his exile there in specifically Jewish terms. Realizing that he would now have to continue his research in England, he told his friends that "After the destruction of the temple in Jerusalem by Titus, Rabbi Jochanan ben Zakkai asked for permission to open a school at Yavneh for the study of the Torah. We are going to do the same [in England]. We, after all, are accustomed to our history and tradition, and some of us by our personal experience, to being persecuted" (E. Jones 221). For Freud, Protestant England in the 1930s became—like Cromwell's England of the 1640s—a land of tolerance.

2. Kibbey's excellent *The Interpretation of Material Shapes in Puritanism* explains the centrality of conversion to the Puritan faith (6–41). In particular, she explains how one Puritan, John Cotton, viewed the conversion of the Jews (80–91).

3. I take this opportunity to thank my former teacher. I first saw the wonders of the invisible world as an undergraduate in Jesper's classes at Tufts University in the early 1980s. This essay is ultimately due to him.

4. See Bercovitch and Jehlen for a more complete analysis of this intersection between the ideological and the theological as it is expressed after the Puritans.

5. As the following discussion will make clear, I am indebted to Boyarin's discussion of midrashic textual strategies.

6. In the discussion that follows, I comment on the intertextuality present in these three poems. I find it especially useful to imagine their relationship to each other in terms of a midrashic paradigm. This does not mean, however, that Stern and Levine literally intended to comment directly on Stafford's poem.

7. The poem comes from Stafford's volume of the same name, which appeared in 1960 and won the National Book Award. In order to acknowledge the continuing hold this poem exerts on the national canon, I draw from its most recent appearance in that canon (Gwynn 216). But there is hardly a poetry anthology in print today that does not include this poem. For example, the following anthologies of poetry currently in print and in use in the college classroom all include it: Strand, Donald Hall (where it is the first poem), Ellmann and O'Clair, Allison, Guth and Rico, Gwynn, and Nims. This is only the tip of the anthology iceberg; further inspection would include many standard American literature, world literature, and even general introductory anthologies to literature. Among the many are Prentice Hall's *American Literature* edited by Emory Elliott and others; HarperCollins's *American Literature* edited by Donald McQuade; X.J. Kennedy and Dana Gioia's sixth edition of the HarperCollins *Literature*; Donald Hall's third edition of the Harcourt Brace Jovanovich *To Read Literature*; Carl Bain et al.'s *Norton Introduction to Literature*; and Michael Meyer's third edition of *The Bedford Introduction to Literature*.

8. Something familiar to students of Heidegger, but the subject of another discussion.

9. Anne Morrow Lindbergh argues against those who claimed that her husband was a Nazi sympathizer (see xviii in particular and the "Introduction" for her account).

10. Jewish law is clear about what one is to do with a corpse. In particular, there must be a burial, and the burial should occur within twenty-four hours of the death.

11. The title, "28," is itself a "spot of time" containing a witty play on numbers in the spirit of the Jewish technique known as Gamatriya. The poet, age fifty-six,

is twenty-eight years older than he was when the poem takes place: 1956. Fifty-six is also the age of the man whom the twenty-eight-year-old poet goes to see in California. Twenty-eight, therefore, becomes the numerical type in Levine's own personal Bible, his past, while the antitype is his age at composition, fifty-six.

12. Wordsworth's "Immortality Ode" is also interrupted with a variety of memories and meditations based on those memories. Wordsworth's poem marks the beginning of Wordsworth's own turn to the Christian faith that would dominate his late poetry. The English Christian tradition and the American millennial tradition are brought together in Levine's "28." Of necessity, I discuss only the American connection in this essay.

Also, I should say that there is no way of knowing whether Stafford's and Stern's poems do literally form the intertext of this poem, "28." I suspect they do because Levine is not only a good friend of Stern but a close reader of his work. Also, Levine's poem is written well after Stern's.

By "his own journey" I mean that the poem is reported in the first person as if it were autobiography. Whether it in fact *is* autobiography is not the issue here. Levine, like all the poets writing in the millennial tradition, crafts allegorical, typological poetry in order to discuss the New Jerusalem.

13. Kibbey explains that the Puritan war on the Pequots was part of their rhetorical imagination. The Pequot women in particular, she argues, "perpetuated the figurae of an alien race" and so had to be murdered. "To destroy *these* bodies was an attempt to destroy the mystical, threatening power of the Pequots as material objects in the most categorical way" (104).

JANE COCALIS

The "Dark and Abiding Presence" in Nathaniel Hawthorne's The Scarlet Letter and Toni Morrison's Beloved

When you read and find something you like, try to figure out why you like it, what they did, and that's how you develop your draft. Not imitation, not emulation, but just this wide range of reading. And then have that combination of respect for the language and contempt, so you can break it.
—Bessie Jones, "An Interview with Toni Morrison"

IT MIGHT SEEM odd to suggest a stronger link between Nathaniel Hawthorne, the nineteenth-century author who was fascinated with the Puritans, and Toni Morrison, the twentieth-century chronicler of the African American experience, than a common interest in America's moral history. But Morrison, in *Beloved*, in fact deliberately retraces and "corrects" Hawthorne's line of inquiry in *The Scarlet Letter*. These two novels significantly illustrate Morrison's belief, as expressed in her recent theoretical work, that there is an "Africanist presence" that informs all of American literature, including that of Hawthorne (*Playing 5*). More particularly, these two novels display what Hawthorne and Morrison perceive as a symbiotic relationship between Puritanism and slavery in America's past. Although the two novelists share an historical vantage point, they do not possess the same artistic sensibility. Their differing views of humanity result in Morrison's re-vision of Hawthorne's novel and, more particularly, of his female protagonist. By delineating the sexual and racial tensions that are merely suggested in *The Scarlet Letter*, Morrison is able, in *Beloved*, to "revise" Hawthorne's text and to assert that his heroine is remarkable *because of*, not despite, her fallen state.

Those readers who are familiar with Toni Morrison's novels will recognize her literary territory as the psychological and social toll that slavery has taken on the lives of African Americans; however, Morrison broaches a subject of even greater breadth in her recent theoretical work, *Playing in the Dark: Whiteness and the Literary Imagination.* In this series of essays, she asserts that there is, of necessity, an "Africanist presence" in American literature,

a dark and abiding presence, there for the literary imagination as both a visible and an invisible mediating force. Even, and especially, when American texts are not "about" Africanist presences or characters or narrative or idiom, the shadow hovers in implication, in sign, in line of demarcation. (46–47)

Morrison explores at length her belief that slavery permeates the aesthetic imagination to the extent that it is a necessary feature of America's literary landscape. But while Morrison's theoretical agenda is clear, is it fair to apply her theory retrospectively? Is it possible, for example, to equate her elaboration of the "dark . . . presence" in American literature with Hawthorne's symbolic use of blackness in *The Scarlet Letter*? I believe it is.

Two kinds of evidence present themselves. First, there is textual evidence that Hawthorne relies on what Morrison refers to as "some of the common linguistic strategies employed in fiction to engage the serious consequences of blacks" (*Playing* 67). These include, for instance, what Morrison calls "metonymic displacement," in which "color coding and other physical traits become metonyms that displace rather than signify the Africanist character" (*Playing* 68). An example of metonymic displacement in *The Scarlet Letter* would be the characters' reference to Satan as "the Black Man" or Hawthorne's constant trope of light as good and shadow as evil. As Morrison notes, such usage, by "demonizing" and "reifying" blackness, offers a means of projecting such intertwined feelings as desire and fear (*Playing* 7), and I hope to illustrate that *The Scarlet Letter* reveals Hawthorne's deep struggle with these very emotions.

Further evidence of Hawthorne's comprehension of the Africanist presence is found in one of Hawthorne's essays, in which he comments on the "portentous" link he believes exists between America's Puritan and slaveholding past. In this piece, which he wrote after traveling through the South during the Civil War, Hawthorne remarks:

There is an historical circumstance, known to few, that connects the children of the Puritans with these Africans of Virginia in a very singular way. They are our brethren as being lineal descendants from the Mayflower, the womb of which, in her first voyage, sent forth a brood of Pilgrims on Plymouth Rock, and, in a subsequent one, spawned slaves upon the Southern soil,—a monstrous birth, but with which we have an instinctive sense of kindred, and so are stirred by an irresistible impulse to attempt their rescue, even at the cost of blood and ruin. The character of our sacred ship, I fear, may suffer a little by this revelation; but we must let her white progeny offset her dark one,—and two such portents never sprang from an identical source before. ("Chiefly" 319)

This brief passage, which exists as almost an aside within a lengthy essay, reveals Hawthorne's concern with the "Africanist presence." His conscious association of America's Puritan legacy with its history of slavery is certainly evident here, but what is perhaps more significant is his attitude toward the Mayflower's conflicted past. He hardly seems enthusiastic when he discusses the Puritans. They are described as a "brood" of pilgrims, a term suggesting a basic urge to reproduce and, given the least pejorative interpretation, thus multiply and populate the New World. It also carries the less-than-flattering connotations of a moody attitude toward life and a primary concern for group cohesiveness at the expense of the individual's needs. Hawthorne invests a few words with a good deal of meaning, and signals here what is visible elsewhere in his writings: his continued allegiance to, yet great frustration with, his forebears and the result of their peculiar stewardship of the "new Eden."

Among the sins of the fathers is the moral crime of allowing slavery to be introduced in the New World, which resulted in the horrendous "penalty" of the Civil War. As Sacvan Bercovitch remarks in *The Office of* The Scarlet Letter, the impending Civil War was much on Hawthorne's mind and serves as the "latent context" for *The Scarlet Letter*. Bercovitch explains that a "rhetoric of liberty" existed in Hawthorne's time that allowed the term *slavery* to be construed as any type of bondage, "private or public, civil or political, including (for Margaret Fuller and other feminists) the bond slavery of women to men" (91). I believe this observation speaks directly to Hawthorne's principal concern in *The Scarlet Letter* and is one that I return to in what follows.

Bercovitch moves on from his point concerning the rhetoric of slavery to a conclusion that I find tenuous, however: he views Hester Prynne as the embodiment of the idea of political "accommodation." In Bercovitch's opinion, Hawthorne utilizes Hester's character to argue that the most efficacious stance the American citizenry might adopt would be one that encouraged "dissenters" to rejoin the community and serve as "herald[s] of progress" in times of political or social upheaval (92, 159). But I would quite differently infer that, rather than expressing the conscious and coherent "worldview" that Bercovitch suggests is implicit in Hawthorne's writings, Hawthorne engages in something akin to an intellectual wringing of hands. For example, although he notes an "irresistible impulse" to aid the slaves in "Chiefly About War Matters," irresistible impulses typically have not been a positive sign in Hawthorne's work; rather, they lead to the downfall of one or more of his characters. Instances that come to mind are Hester's sexual liaison with Arthur Dimmesdale, Aylmer's obsession with alchemy in "The Birthmark," and Young Goodman Brown's nighttime journey.

Second, Hawthorne's closing comment in the passage cited above, that "two such portents never sprang from an identical source before," while cryptic, does not suggest an optimistic outcome, especially not the future of political accommodation that Bercovitch believes Hester's return at the end of *The Scarlet Letter* symbolizes. In fact, any attempt to prove that a coherent sociopolitical structure exists as the framework for Hester's trials diverts attention from Hawthorne's central concern, that is, the working out of an individual's response to "sin" as that person's immediate society defines it.

If we examine the way in which Hawthorne employs Puritanism in *The Scarlet Letter*, we can reach some conclusions about the way in which he utilizes social and political issues as well. As Joseph Schwartz has noted, Puritanism should not be thought of only as the American branch of Calvinism but also as a distinctive way of life (36), and it is in fact this latter, more encompassing view that Hawthorne expresses in his fiction, rather than the strict theological one. About his personal religious beliefs, Agnes Donohue remarks that "Hawthorne was suspicious of all doctrines or sects (he thought of himself as a Christian but never went to church)" (1). Schwartz concurs, based upon Hawthorne's body of work and the commentary of Hawthorne's son, that Hawthorne rejected theological Puritanism as a "lump of lead" (37).

Of course, Hawthorne's personal connection to the New England Puritans is well known. An ancestor was a judge at the Salem witch trials; his notebooks indicate his fascination with the story of a "sinful" woman who was forced to wear an "A" upon her breast; and historical records show that two of his Manning ancestors were put on public display for incestuous behavior while their brother hid out in the woods. Although Hawthorne is a prime example of the artist who uses autobiographical material as the basis for his works, it is axiomatic not to assume too close a correlation between the historical and the literary rendering of an event. Hawthorne's interest in Puritanism and slavery did not lead him to make a coherent political statement in *The Scarlet Letter* any more than it caused him to develop a consistent theological doctrine. Rather, his interest in these subjects was due to their suitability as a foundation for his moral investigations. A religion so provocative, one that insisted upon the utter depravity of human beings yet held them responsible for their actions, offered the perfect field of action for his ethical inquiry. And considering the fact that the United States was approaching civil war in what was supposed to be the new Eden, it is not difficult to see why the issue of slavery comes together with America's Puritan history to serve as the basis for narrative action in *The Scarlet Letter*.

While I do not think Hawthorne offers a politics of accommodation through his characterization of Hester, I do believe Hester's portrayal has much to tell us about another kind of politics, those having to do with the demands the community made upon the individual and particularly upon women in antebellum America. And it is this aspect of his work that informs Toni Morrison's novel *Beloved*. It would be helpful to return now to Bercovitch's point concerning the rhetoric of liberty extant in Hawthorne's time and the way slavery might connote, in addition to the enslavement of the Africans, the bond slavery of women to men. This issue, which weighed heavily on Hawthorne's mind, is central to his selection of the subject matter in his most important novel and makes him an influential literary precursor to Toni Morrison.

Hawthorne was highly conscious of the "woman issue," as it was characterized in his day. His biographical sketches include a revealing piece on Anne Hutchinson and her role as the leading feminist in the Puritan colony. This sketch manages to convey the same sense of disturbance that we find in his discussion of the Puritans and slavery in "Chiefly About War Matters." Once again, he warns the reader that there are "portentous indications" of a latent threat to the American republic, but in this instance the threat takes the form of the unwomanly woman. She is the one who assumes her intellect and morality to be on the same high plane as a man's. In Hutchinson's case, this misjudgment has resulted in her beginning "to promulgate strange and dangerous opinions"; therefore, she has to be expelled from the community (217).

Hawthorne's disapproval of Hutchinson seems clear up to this point; however, he suddenly shifts from a factual account to a fictive re-creation of Hutchinson's life. This second mode of narration, which combines historical material with an imaginative fleshing out of scene and dialogue, is akin to what we know as the "new journalism" in the late twentieth century. In this section of the sketch, Hutchinson is seen confronting the Church fathers with her unsettling ideas, or "antinomianism," which directly undercuts their authority, as it assumes that the individual's intuitive grasp of God's plan supersedes any dicta the Church might deliver to the community. For a moment, when the narrator comments that some members of the "priesthood . . . [strove] to beat her down with brows of wrinkled iron" (222), we sense that Hutchinson has, if not Hawthorne's approval, at least his sympathy.

In the next passage, however, Hawthorne resumes his essayistic style and comes down on the side of patriarchal authority when the narrator states that Hutchinson's was a case "in which religious freedom was wholly inconsistent with public safety" (222). Hawthorne then returns to his fictional mode of telling and describes the civil and religious trials that resulted in Hutchinson's expulsion from the community. In this final portion of the sketch, the prototype for Hester Prynne emerges. Here we are told that Hutchinson is a woman who stands "loftily before her judges with a determined brow; and unknown to herself, there is a flash of carnal pride half hidden in her eye" (224). The inner assurance and sensuality she radiates here later become essential features of Hester Prynne's character.

Because Hawthorne employs this dual mode of narration, we come away from this sketch wondering whether his sentiments reside with Anne Hutchinson or with the Puritans who cast her out of the colony. The net effect seems to be that the first authorial voice, the essayistic one that signals approval of the Puritans' indictment of Hutchinson, cancels out the second, or fictive, voice. So why does Hawthorne employ two modes of telling, especially in such a brief piece? Such a technique generally allows the narrator to remain a disinterested observer. But the overall structure and rhetoric Hawthorne employs are those used by a teller of moral tales, so readers come away confused as to Hawthorne's position regarding the issues he puts before us.

Larzer Ziff accounts for the ambiguity of tone by suggesting that the "young Hawthorne" who wrote the biographical sketch was "unsympathetic" to Hutchinson's dilemma but that "years later his Hester Prynne was to bear a strong resemblance" to the woman who is referred to in *The Scarlet Letter* as the *sainted* Anne Hutchinson. Ziff believes that Hawthorne exhibits sympathy for Hester yet states that her "career show[s] what Anne Hutchinson stood for was still untenable" ("Artist" 263). As with Bercovitch's theory of a politics of accommodation, I find that Ziff's reading of Hester's character—one allowing Hawthorne to convey sympathy for, yet brand as unworkable, the "strong" woman's position—grants Hawthorne a more consciously thought-out and philosophically consistent position than the text actually exhibits.

Instead of taking any firm position, I believe Hawthorne's "new journalistic" rendering of Hutchinson's life and his shaping of Hester Prynne's character reveal his fear of, yet desire for, the strong woman who confronts the male-dominated community. His fascination with this personality is illustrated by his attention to such women in his works, including the prominent feminist Margaret Fuller, who served as the model for the character of Zenobia in *The Blithedale Romance*. Yet his fear of such individuals, which would include the "damned mob of scribbling women" against whom he competed daily in order to make a living, causes his stance in relation to his characters to remain ambiguous—and far less conscious than some critics believe. As Henry James once remarked, Hawthorne "innocently exercised" his artistry "because with that delightful unconscious genius it remained . . . inconclusive to the end" (*Theory* 300). James did not wish to demean Hawthorne's work. But he did want to point out that Hawthorne was relatively unconscious (relative to James's heightened perceptions, one presumes) of the deeper meanings his work offers, not only concerning its immediate subject but also regarding the author's view of the world.

In *Playing in the Dark*, Toni Morrison makes a comment similar to James's when she explains that authors are not necessarily wholly conscious of the issues they "limn out" in their works, but they "always know, at some level," what is "blanketed in their text" (4). It is often said that what is best in Hawthorne's work is his careful positing of a narrative circumstance that will morally challenge his central characters and his subsequent playing out of their responses to that ethical dilemma. Beyond that, I would suggest that we can also find "blanketed" in *The Scarlet Letter* an anxious attention to the "strong" woman, to Hester Prynne as the challenger, the disrupter, the pariah of the community. And in this sense, Hester serves as the dark presence that Morrison locates in all "white" texts. Speaking of American romance in particular, Morrison notes that this genre allows its authors to explore "quite specific, understandably human, fears" such as:

Americans' fear of being outcast, of failing, of powerlessness; their fear of bound-arylessness, of Nature unbridled and crouched for attack; their fear of the absence of so-called civilization; their fear of loneliness, of aggression both external and internal. (*Playing* 37)

By refusing to acknowledge the supremacy of Puritan doctrine over her intuitive sense of right and wrong, Hester serves as the lightning rod for the community's fears, as do such women as Anne Hutchinson, Margaret Fuller, and Sethe Suggs in Morrison's *Beloved*. These women threaten the established religious and social order and, in doing so, symbolize the troubled self—and the community as a whole—when it wrestles with the discrepancy between what it is and what it hopes to be. Although the community resists such dark knowledge of itself, Morrison explains that "images of blackness can be evil *and* protective, rebellious *and* forgiving, fearful *and* desirable,—all of the[se] self-contradictory features. . . . Whiteness, alone, is mute" (*Playing* 59). Morrison insists that the dark presence is an essential part of mortal being; however, this idea is not readily accepted by the Puritan colony, which views itself as ever-vigilant against the influence of Satan.

Society tends to view life quite literally in black-and-white terms, and it brands such women as Anne Hutchinson, Hester Prynne, and Sethe Suggs as outlaws or, as Morrison puts it, as "metaphysically black" and "danger-ously female" ("Unspeakable" 223). Hawthorne, who is drawn to such figures, allows Hester to gain our respect by ignoring the Calvinist doctrine of salvation only through God's grace and redeeming herself through good works (Donohue 52). This exercise of the "covenant of grace," of a direct intuition of God's caring as opposed to the orthodox belief in obedience to the Church, explicitly refers to the teachings of Anne Hutchinson, who, like Grandma Baby Suggs in *Beloved*, is a "natural" rather than an institutionally sanctioned preacher.

Up to a point, there is nothing new in this presentation of the pariah, or scapegoat, which has existed as a type throughout the history of literature and religion. Hawthorne offers us something more, however, when he presents a woman as pariah *and* redeemer. In the concluding chapter of *The Scarlet Letter*, which is surprisingly brief, Hester chooses to return to Salem and takes up what Donohue notes is her "once enforced and now elected alienation" (50). It may be argued that Hawthorne does not wish us to view Hester's outcome as positive; after all, the short chapter almost seems tacked on to the main narrative. Yet Hawthorne's protagonist undermines authorial intention here and her actions strike the reader much differently than Hawthorne might have wished.

We are told that Hester has returned as a penitent and will lead a quiet life offering counsel to troubled women in the community. Although she had hoped earlier that she might be "the destined prophetess" of Heaven's "new truth," the narrator states firmly that "the angel and apostle of the coming revelation must be a woman, indeed, but lofty, pure, and beautiful; and wise, moreover, not through dusky grief, but the ethereal medium of joy . . ." (344–45). What the narrator *tells* us falls short of what the text *shows* us, however. As with Tolstoy's Anna Karenina, we find a far more heroic figure in Hester than was anticipated by her author. As I mentioned earlier, Hawthorne's genius lies in putting his characters to the test, so while his narrator might speak of searching for the ideal woman to inspire humanity, readers generally have been far more interested in characters such as Hester who remain flawed yet exhibit extreme fortitude in the face of moral and social conflict. The reader's continued fascination with Hester Prynne has more to do with how she regards herself and what she is able to accomplish given her circumstances—and the scope of her accomplishments changes drastically once we have read the few short pages Hawthorne allots to the conclusion of her story. Hester's posture is what Morrison finds valuable in Hawthorne's novel as well. As Deborah McDowell remarks concerning Morrison's (and other black women writers') works, these narratives dramatize "not what was *done* to . . . women, but what they *did* with what was done to them" (146). Hawthorne is well aware of the latter narrative strategy as he employs it himself, but he offers the reader more, I think, in *The Scarlet Letter* than was his conscious intention.

By returning Hester to the community that has spurned her in those last few pages of the novel, Hawthorne adds a formidable dimension to her character. Rather than remaining part of a larger narrative that considers the moral fiber of several key characters, she becomes the focal point and only visible survivor of these trials and, moreover, opens the door for the possible redemption of her community. It is because she is a pariah *and* redeemer that Hester continues to fascinate us after the climactic moment in the narrative has passed, and it is as pariah and redeemer that Hester prefigures many of Toni Morrison's female protagonists, including Sethe Suggs in *Beloved*.

Sethe, who is bound to her community in an equally difficult manner, appears to represent all that is evil, or at least unfortunate, in humanity. She has been forced to make a choice between returning her children to slavery or killing them and has committed what the community perceives to be a heinous crime. Her sin causes her to become ostracized by the black community, which is itself on the margins of the dominant, white society. In this manner, Morrison quite consciously places Sethe in a position where she is twice removed from the privileged society and thus is brutally alienated, physically and socially. By making Sethe the scapegoat of both the black and white communities, Morrison is better able to convey the painful isolation of the African American community to white readers. At the same time, she establishes Sethe as a pariah/redeemer figure for the black community. Although Sethe has committed the worst sin imaginable, she will also cause her community to exorcise its awful past, which is made manifest in the daughter who has returned from the grave.

As Barbara Hill Rigney notes, Morrison's "wilderness characters" take on the burdensome role of pariah with "their purpose ultimately [being the] purification of [the] community" (52). Like other marginalized people, the African Americans depicted in *Beloved* have come to fault themselves for their predicament. Their shame and frustration fuels their hatred of the dominant, white segment of society and, simultaneously, causes their desire to become part of that group because it is the privileged one. To relieve the group of these paradoxical emotions, someone must denounce the societal codes that bind the minority group to its confused self-image. However inadvertently, Hawthorne suggests that this is Hester's role at the conclusion of his novel.

In *Beloved*, this role is initially filled by Baby Suggs but is ultimately taken up by Sethe and Denver. After Halle buys his mother out of slavery and Baby Suggs rides to Ohio and freedom with Mr. Garner, she literally and figuratively finds herself: "suddenly she saw her hands and thought with a clarity as simple as it was dazzling, 'These hands belong to me. These *my* hands'" (141). Now she is able to piece together a new identity, first by rejecting the name "Jenny," which the Garners have called her, and then by choosing to be called "Baby," her husband's term of endearment for her, and "Suggs," her married name. In essence, on her short, yet highly symbolic journey from Kentucky to Ohio, this former slave transforms herself into a free woman. After throwing off the remnants of her destitute self-image, she assumes one that is self-empowering and that also nourishes her community. Thus she comes to be known to her people as "Baby Suggs holy."

Baby Suggs is able to keep her faith alive until schoolteacher comes to reclaim Sethe and her children. But when Sethe kills Beloved, Baby Suggs realizes that evil continues to flourish in the world; she had merely moved it to the periphery of her mind. She decides she has been guilty of preaching a false lesson to her people and this new knowledge—of the durability of slavery, of Sethe's capacity for infanticide, in short, of the depth of mortal sin—kills her.

The turns which Baby Suggs's life takes, as well as the shape of Sethe and Denver's narratives, reveal Morrison's central statement about the lives of African American women in slavery and (relative) freedom. It is not mere chance that Morrison's redeemer figures are women, or that they comprise three generations of the same family. Matriarchal lineage is an important and empowering feature of Morrison's novels. For most of her life, Baby Suggs has been enslaved; although free at the end of her life, she is still psychologically unable to conquer slavery. Sethe, who represents the next generation, has no greater promise than the simple possibility of living out her life—*if* she is able to keep the past in check. Denver is the "charmed child," however, and as such, she has the greatest probability of reaching her full potential. She has a young man by her side, a teacher-mentor to guide her, and the possibility of going to Oberlin College in her future. It is in Denver that the promise of Baby Suggs's spiritual guidance and Sethe's inner strength on behalf of her children, which has cost her her own well-being, may finally be fulfilled.

Morrison offers her readers only the *promise* of the future at the end of the novel, however. I believe that she is cautiously optimistic here because she does not wish to distract our attention from the horrifying nature of the slaves' lives, which she has worked so painstakingly to portray. Yet the end of the novel makes a clear statement in and of itself: it is the women who conjure up the power to banish the ghost baby from the community, and it is through the strength and endurance of women such as Ella and Denver that there will be a future for that community. Once Denver forces herself to leave the porch of 124 to seek help, she causes the women of the community to resume their neighborly duty toward the Suggs family. Ella then leads the other women to 124 to drive off the spirit of the dead baby, and when Sethe steps outside and sees them,

it was as though the Clearing had come to her . . . the voices of women searched for the right combination, the key, the code, the sound that broke the back of words.

Building voice upon voice until they found it, and when they did. . . . It broke over
Sethe and she trembled like the baptized in its wash. (*Beloved* 261)

In Morrison's world, the women heal and redeem.

Committed to her vision of the female pariah/redeemer's role in society,
Morrison feels the need to challenge the assumptions that underlie portrayals of female characters such as Hester. Hawthorne's suggestion of the
generative spirit of women at the end of *The Scarlet Letter* offers one point
at which Morrison hopes to "correct" Hawthorne in *Beloved*. When Hester
returns to Salem, the women of the community seek her out; presumably,
these are the same women who castigated her when she emerged from the
prison. By requesting her counsel, they will not only aid her return to the
community but perhaps, in time, offer her a way to play a significant role
in it. But where Hawthorne stops short of signaling Hester's complete re-
integration into Salem, Morrison offers assurances that the Suggs women
will regain their place in their community.

Despite Hawthorne's declaration in *The Scarlet Letter* that some purer
soul that knows less of "dusky grief" must serve as the redeemer figure,
Morrison believes that there is no place for a heavenly messenger in the fictional worlds that she and Hawthorne have created. The redemptive power
must come from within the community itself—or not come at all. Baby
Suggs holy, tells her people in the Clearing that "the only grace they could
have was the grace they could imagine. That if they could not see it, they
would not have it" (*Beloved* 88). In other words, there will be no fortuitous
rescue from above; however, as long as human beings exercise their power
to imagine grace, it will be immanent.

But in Hawthorne's world the possibility of grace remains questionable.
As Terry Otten remarks, Morrison's pariah/redeemer figures must rebel
"against a morally deficient system" to show that "evil can be redemptive
and goodness can be enslaving" (4). Hawthorne is able to show us quite
vividly how the institutionalization of God's grace, that is, the practice
of Calvinism in the New World, has stifled the faculty for self-renewal
in all but a few outcasts, who are women. Hawthorne admits that spiritual leadership by women is feasible and even appropriate; but he cannot
reconcile his conception of the ideal woman who should serve in this capacity with those "madwomen" who have attempted to fill it, such as Anne
Hutchinson, Margaret Fuller—or Hester Prynne.

The vision that Hawthorne cannot fathom is readily understood by
Morrison and other feminist writers and critics, however. Alicia Ostriker,
for example, discusses the power of "revisionist myth-making" whereby
the woman's voice, more human and therefore more "personal or confessional," alters the dominant, male mythmaking tradition. These feminist
myths, Ostriker tells us, "are corrections, they are representations of what

women find divine and demonic in themselves; they are retrieved images of what women have collectively and historically suffered; in some cases they are instructions for survival" (215). Similarly, Michael Awkward, discussing Morrison's and other black women writers' mythmaking, comments on their ability to revise the Western genre of the novel by making the language their own by "populating it" with their "own intention" (8). In this vein, Morrison's adaptation of Hawthorne might well be described as her heightening of some aspects of the work at which Hawthorne has only hinted.

Morrison's direct appropriation of Hawthorne's "language" is most apparent in the scenes that take place in the Clearing. This symbolic setting, which is a re-visioning of Hawthorne's forest setting in *The Scarlet Letter*, makes evident Morrison's "respect for and contempt of" Hawthorne's work (B. Jones 151). Many of the character triads in Hawthorne's novel — for example, Hester, Arthur Dimmesdale, and Pearl; or Hester, Dimmesdale, and Roger Chillingworth — are echoed in *Beloved* but to a different end. Hester fails to reconcile with either one of her "spouses," or to feel unconditional love for Pearl as a result of their encounters in the forest. But Sethe is able to come to terms in the Clearing with her personal past, which concerns her husband, Halle, and her lover, Paul D. Then, with Denver, she takes on the challenge of Beloved, who poses a great threat to the psychological well-being of the community as she represents the collective ills of a society burdened with the sin of slavery.

In both novels the Clearing exists outside of the "civilized" world and thus is an unsanctioned place that evokes the "boundary" fears delineated by Morrison. Individuals who abide by society's code will not go there willingly; yet the pariahs of the community know it to be a place of refuge and individual freedom. The wise elder, Baby Suggs holy, knows that the "divine and demonic" cohabit there; yet she is confident that the divine can dominate the demonic if one only imagines such a state of grace. And it is in the Clearing that Sethe and Denver get their first hint that they must follow Baby Suggs's life-giving vision or lose themselves in the seductive demands of Beloved.

In the Clearing when Beloved repeatedly kisses her mother's throat, Sethe finally realizes that the dead ghost baby has come back to take revenge upon her by tempting her with an all-consuming love. Morrison's scene echoes the brookside chapter in *The Scarlet Letter* in which Hester entreats Pearl to come to her. Only after Hester picks up the scarlet letter and pins it back on her breast will Pearl do as she is told. She kisses her mother on the brow and the narrator remarks that "by a kind of necessity that always impelled this child to alloy whatever comfort she might chance to give with a throb of anguish — Pearl put up her mouth and kissed the scarlet letter too!" (301).

The perversion of a child's love for her mother, so brilliantly illustrated here by Hawthorne, is reworked by Morrison in *Beloved* to foreground the sexual and racial tensions that are deeply embedded in Hawthorne's text. Specifically, having chosen to make explicit the societal causes of that perversity—ones that Hawthorne presents at a metaphorical distance—Morrison is able to work toward ameliorating the very real and very painful problems she has exposed. Morrison's redeemer figure, Sethe, must overcome her tremendous guilt and reject her ghost baby to save her own life and safeguard the community from further harm. But it will take a combined effort of Denver, Ella, and the other women of the community to allow her to do so.

While Hawthorne leaves Hester marginalized by insisting that she cannot be fully reintegrated into her community, Morrison takes a more positive stance by asserting in *Beloved* that changes can be made, that society can learn not to fear the unfamiliar and to confront what is morally abhorrent. She indicates that it is never too late to acknowledge the pariah as the redeemer and thus subdue the darkness that is always present in the mortal world. As William Blake observed a century before her, one need only locate the song that can break the back of institutionalized thinking and allow the regenerative spirit to flourish.

In *The Scarlet Letter*, Hawthorne illustrates the dangers of Puritanism as practiced in colonial New England. The overzealous piety of the nation's forefathers stifled, and in some cases destroyed, the individual spirit. It is ironic, yet typical in Hawthorne's fictive world, that the Reverend Mr. Dimmesdale is undone by his own religious fervor. Hester Prynne appears to do little more than survive her ordeal. Yet a close look at the novel's ending reveals that her vitality is not subdued; Hester simply finds a less confrontational means of expressing it. In naming her as counselor and nurse to the women of Salem, Hawthorne suggests that Hester now "ministers" to the community.

Where Hawthorne only hints at Hester Prynne's role as pariah and redeemer, Toni Morrison insists that saint and sinner are two aspects of the same psyche. Therefore, it is sophistic to proclaim that there are an elect few and to damn the rest of humanity. Interweaving Hawthorne's disturbing vision of the New World theocracy with her belief that slavery emanates from that source, Morrison calls upon us to turn away from the failed myth of our nation's founding. In *Beloved*, she explores the idea that women, who understand that human nature is flawed yet contains the seeds of grace, have the potential to redeem the New World. In this manner, Morrison transforms Hawthorne's hints and suggestions into an opportunity for America to realize and cast off its true demons.

MICHAEL TOMASEK MANSON

Poetry and Masculinity on the Anglo/Chicano Border
Gary Soto, Robert Frost, and Robert Hass

The guy who pinned
Me was named Bloodworth, a meaningful name.
That night I asked Mom what our name meant in Spanish.
She stirred crackling papas and said it meant Mexican.
—Gary Soto, "The Wrestler's Heart"

IN THIS SCENE from his autobiographical sequence *Home Course in Religion* (1991), the adolescent Gary Soto wrestles not only with an Anglo empowered by a "meaningful name" but also with his manhood as he tries to make sense out of his defeat. He finds he must—like so many young men in U.S. literature—turn his defeat into a victory if he wants to become a man. And yet Soto's path to manhood is unfamiliar, even, we might say, un-American. As traditionally understood, U.S. literature is expected to depict a "pure American self divorced from specific social circumstances" confronting "the promise offered by the idea of America" (Baym, "Melodramas" 71). That promise, furthermore, is supposed to be threatened "with particular urgency" by "the figure of one or more women" (72). Soto, however, not only turns to his mother for succor but asks her for a heritage. He thus refuses to enter the New World naked and forge a new, self-reliant manhood. He rejects the role of Adam that so many critics have defined as the essence of the Americanness of U.S. literature. We inherited the role of Adam, of course, from the Puritans who saw the continent as an opportunity for the individual to forge an unmediated relationship with God. By turning away from this opportunity and concerning himself instead with heritage—with what different "bloods" are "worth"—Soto breaks what critics have valued as the "continuity of American poetry" with Puritanism.[1] This break means either that Soto's poetry does not measure up to our best literature or that we will need new ways of describing our literary history.

We might begin with the notion that the term "U.S. literature" is larger and more inclusive than "*American* literature," which is centered by its writers and critics alike around a Puritan origin that posits the "American self as the embodiment of a prophetic universal design" (Bercovitch, *Puritan* 136).[2] This model of *American* literature reproduces the distinction first made by the Puritans between their City on a Hill and a surrounding wilderness populated by savages, a distinction I will call *boundary*, by which I mean to suggest both a perception of difference and a will to conquer.[3] Boundaries are created by leaps or bounds into the unknown or that which is different, and those leaps—like the Puritan leap into the Americas or the sudden jump of the U.S. boundary in 1848 across the northern half of Mexico—stretch across wilderness that must be filled in or conquered. For an alternative to boundary, we might turn to Gloria Anzaldúa, who describes the *border* as the place where "two or more cultures edge each other, . . . where the space between two individuals shrinks with intimacy" (3). Etymologically, border signifies a "cut" across a landscape, thus suggesting both difference and similarity, the difference arising from some prior, historical act of violence. To think in terms of borders, then, is to be aware of the differences that exist on either side, to know their historical causes, and to look for opportunities to cross those borders, letting difference "shrink with intimacy."

With this border model in mind, we can reread Gary Soto's wrestling scene not as a failure to produce *American* self-reliance but as an attempt to resist it. *Home Course in Religion*, I will argue, tells the story of Soto's growth into manhood, describing his replacement of boundaries with borders as he gradually extricates himself from the domination of the *American* self. Empowering this reconception of the self and of masculinity is a Chicano Catholic understanding of the border as mediator rather than boundary.[4] That Soto's conception of mediation is Chicano Catholic rather than simply Catholic becomes clear when we compare it to Robert Hass's use of mediation, which is Catholic but also *American*. My desire, however, to replace an *American* literary history centered around Puritanism with a border one focused on cultural exchange also requires that we begin to see even the most *American* literature as a border product reflecting the plural origins of the United States, and toward that end, I begin by briefly considering a third California poet, Robert Frost.

I

The most popular of all the major modernists, Robert Frost is also the most *American*, frequently promoting a history of the United States based on boundaries. The most dramatic example is the poem he read at John F. Kennedy's inauguration, "The Gift Outright." Right away, the first line—"The land was ours before we were the land's"—suggests a boundary, as the British leap onto this continent is seen as manifest destiny. The settlers must only fill in the boundaries preordained for them.

There is, however, a deeper understanding of boundary here. Although the poem is explicitly concerned with the conquest of the continent in the seventeenth, eighteenth, and nineteenth centuries, its assumptions belong instead to the dawn of the twentieth century and the 1898 war with Spain. In a 1934 interview, one year before he wrote "The Gift Outright," Frost claimed that one of his ten favorite books and "surely one of the very best of our modern best-sellers" was the historical romance *The Prisoner of Zenda* (*Collected* 738), which was published in 1894, just two years after Frost graduated from high school. As Amy Kaplan explains, historical romances of the 1890s like *The Prisoner of Zenda* created a new form of masculinity more appropriate to the overseas empire gained after the Spanish-American War.

This new overseas empire required a fresh understanding of boundary both for the nation and the masculine body. During the earlier, continental expansion, U.S. writers compared the nation to a body that must expand or die, but the new overseas empire was "informal," economic rather than territorial.[5] Rejecting an older European-style colonialism, the United States concentrated on controlling trade routes and establishing military bases in former Spanish possessions like Cuba and the Philippines, while leaving these countries varying degrees of putative political independence. Because expansion was now disembodied, Kaplan argues, the United States required a "double discourse" that depicted the nation and the masculine body as "spectacles" that must be continually re-presented. Andrew Jackson, Indian-fighter, was replaced as masculine model by Teddy Roosevelt, who was seen simulating, doubling, his masculinity in photographs and in "authentic" costumes constructed in New York (Kaplan 655). While Jackson was simply vigorous, Roosevelt's spectacular masculinity was a technological feat. Roosevelt's virility was as disembodied, as "informal," as the empire he represented.

A product of this new double discourse of imperialism, "The Gift Outright" emphasizes not manly vigor but its doubling. The one reference to physical conflict takes place in a parenthesis, while the rest of the poem emphasizes the disembodied, spectacular nature of manifest destiny:

> Such as we were we gave ourselves outright
> (The deed of gift was many deeds of war)
> To the land vaguely realizing westward,
> But still unstoried, artless, unenhanced,

The "unstoried, artless, unenhanced" land is, of course, the Puritans' wilderness. What is new is the "land vaguely realizing westward," as if the land only became real—tangible, embodied, em-boundaried—as *Americans* took possession of it. More importantly, the conquest of the continent requires the mastery of the self, since Frost emphasizes not the hardihood of the frontiersman but his confusion and lack of self-knowledge. "We were England's," he tells us, "still colonials," and because of that, we were "weak." Ultimately, we possessed the land only when we "found salvation in surrender" and stopped "withholding . . . ourselves." Significantly, the "we" here applies specifically to white, English settlers and to any readers who can identify with their position, not to those already inhabiting the land. In fact, part of Frost's evidence that *Americans* have failed to "story" the land is that they have named their lands "Virginia" and "Massachusetts," after the English queen who sent them here and the Native Americans they conquered, not after *themselves*. Although "The Gift Outright" acknowledges as "deeds of war" the border conflicts with Mexico in 1846 and Spain in 1898, Frost's understanding of "story" represses full knowledge of these conflicts in favor of an emboundaried notion of national and racial mission. He cannot face squarely the Spanish-American War that necessitated a spectacular masculinity and informal empire. "The Gift Outright" thus represents a modern doubling of Puritan boundaries.

A border history of our literature, however, should look not only for its Puritan roots (the boundaries that have been drawn) but also for the borders that have been crossed. We might remember, first of all, that Frost was born in California because his New England father had lit out for the territories in 1873, wanting to be part of the "settlement" of the West, which of course had already been settled by Mexicans and Native Americans.[6] After his father's death, the eleven-year-old Frost moved to New England with his mother and sister, making him both foreign and native to New England. His experience moving back from the frontier thus revealed an inner border between New Englanders and Californians.

The crossing of this border, in fact, made possible his birth as a poet. John Walsh's biography has shown that the poet who, according to legend, struggled for twenty years unnoticed by an outdated literary establishment was instead a mediocre poet struggling to find his "voice." Frost only discovered his voice, Walsh tells us, when he stopped writing poetry in 1908 and started imitating the vocal mannerisms of his farmer neighbors (63). After two years, this tutelage inspired a writing process that ultimately resulted in the brilliant dialogues of *North of Boston* (1914). The origin of Frost's poetry is thus plural: he became a poet when he learned the language of his New England neighbors, letting "difference shrink with intimacy" as Anzaldúa says it must on the border.

Frost's border-crossing created not only his distinctive use of language but also the theme for much of his early work, particularly in *North of Boston* where two versions of *American* boundary frequently conflict. These dialogues have generally been seen as typical of regionalism's depiction of conflicts between rural folk and sophisticated urbanites.[7] "Mending Wall," for example, presents a confrontation between a New England farmer and the poem's speaker, who, like Frost, is knowledgeable about New England ways though perhaps not a New Englander himself. Instead of seeing a country-city conflict here, we might see the farmer as a Puritan who expresses the purity of his faith by adhering to tradition—"He will not go behind his father's saying." His father's belief that "Good fences make good neighbors" itself descends from the Puritans, who fled Europe in part because European society threatened to corrupt them. The Atlantic thus formed a "fence" between the New World and the Old, a different kind of boundary than the one we have been discussing but a boundary nonetheless. Emerson echoes and develops this distrust of neighbors when he claims in "Self-Reliance" that "Society everywhere is in conspiracy against the manhood of every one of its members" (2:49). The farmer acts on this advice when he "wall[s] out" neighbors' threats to his rootedness in tradition.

The speaker, meanwhile, rebels against tradition. Like a frontiersman, he cannot abide fences that carve up the land, robbing him of space in which to remake himself. And it is reinvention that motivates the speaker, the possibility that the "something" that "doesn't love a wall" is a mischief inherent in us that defies and goes "behind" every "father's saying." The speaker's antinomianism is an inheritance every bit as Puritan as the farmer's, but their roles in filling in *American* boundaries have put them at odds.

"Mending Wall" intends, however, to bring the two *American* perspectives together even though no simple healing is possible. The speaker may begin the poem proposing that the gaps in the wall are so large that "even two can pass abreast," but he ultimately imagines, as Puritans do, that the Other is an "old stone *savage* armed" (emphasis added). Healing thus comes not from the characters, who remain locked in conflict, but from us, the readers. Frost's note at the beginning of *North of Boston* tells us that "*Mend-*

ing Wall takes up the theme where *A Tuft of Flowers* in *A Boy's Will* laid it down," and in "The Tuft of Flowers," we learn that "Men work together . . . / Whether they work together or apart" only when they focus on the work itself, letting community come in visionary moments. In "Mending Wall," that community is never realized by the speaker, but it can be there for the reader as we watch the characters work together and "mend wall" despite their disagreements. As Frost later said, we must lift such conflicts to a "higher plane of *regard*" ("Comments"). From this viewpoint, the differences between the two men "shrink with intimacy." Frost is a border poet when he crosses the division between these two different kinds of *American*, and he can do so partly because his childhood on the border has made him aware of the differences that lie within our boundaries.

On rarer occasions, as in "America Is Hard to See" (1951), Frost can step outside our boundaries and create a true border poetry. This poem revises the first one he ever wrote, "La Noche Triste," an account of Cortez's defeat of the Aztecs inspired by Frost's adolescent reading of William Hickling Prescott's famous *History of the Conquest of Mexico* (1843). In "La Noche Triste," as in Prescott's history, the defeat of the Native Americans is romanticized. The Native Americans are no longer "savage" in the Puritan sense, but the inevitability of European victory testifies to the superiority of "civilization," thus retaining the manifest destiny of Puritan historiography. Revising this poem, Frost extricates himself from its racist imperial history to understand that the destiny of the United States has never been manifest. Ending with Cortez's raid on the Aztecs, Frost spends much of the poem demythologizing Columbus's discovery of the Americas. Columbus was a bad mariner ("He wasn't off a mere degree / His reckoning was off a sea"), and his motives were suspect: "Not just for scientific news / Had the Queen backed him to a cruise."

As Frost suggests, the promise of *America* has frequently been pecuniary, but he is more disturbed by the Puritan claims for the continent as a New World, "The race's future trial place, / A fresh start for the human race." Strikingly, he admits,

> I was deceived by what he did.
> If I had had the chance when young
> I should have had Columbus sung
> As a god who had given us
> A more than Moses' exodus.

> But all he did was spread the room
> Of our enacting out the doom
> Of being in each other's way,
> And so put off the weary day
> When we would have to put our mind
> On how to crowd but still be kind.

Frost's history is still flawed—the continent was not wilderness but was already "crowded" with Native Americans and, later, with Mexicans and Mexican Americans—but he has still crossed a border. Reflecting on the history of Mexico he read as an adolescent, he realizes that the myth of American exceptionalism has prevented the United States from learning how to live on the border Anzaldúa describes, a place where peoples meet and "crowd" but can still be "kind." In his most perceptive poetry, Frost sometimes finds himself living on just such a border.

II

As a border poet, Gary Soto does not find his roots in Puritanism; he finds instead that Puritan roots threaten his growth. To thrive, he must struggle against the Puritan desire to make boundaries, and *Home Course in Religion* recounts his effort to create a masculinity liberated from the *American* self that dominates so much of Frost's poetry. This reconception is made possible when Soto sees the border as mediation rather than boundary. Before tracing Soto's reconstruction of a border masculinity based on mediation, however, we will need to explain how Soto's use of mediation is both Chicano and Catholic.

Unlike Calvinism, Catholicism emphasizes mediation. While Calvinism sees nothing between God and the self, Catholicism believes that the Church can both intercede with God on the self's behalf and represent God to the self (Bercovitch, *Puritan* 22). By "Church," Catholics mean not only the institutional body of priests, nuns, bishops, and so on, but the entire community of the faithful, both the living and the dead. The Church can mediate between God and the self because as the "body of Christ" it embodies the divine while remaining human. Justus Lawler uses this corollary, *analogia entis*, to distinguish between Catholicism and Protestantism: Professing *analogia entis*, Catholics believe that "the contingent self is paradoxically merged with the absolute, while . . . nevertheless remaining contingent." Protestants, however, believe that "the finite is so imprisoned . . . that it cannot become the infinite; . . . it can only be breathed upon, as one would breathe upon a piece of metal to polish it" (95). Frost represents this Protestant view when he speaks of poetry as a "momentary stay against confusion": Just for a moment, he suggests, the divine breath makes the soul's metal shine, but confusion tarnishes it quickly, requiring the soul's constant renewal.

Robert Hass, on the other hand, represents the Catholic view in "Meditation at Lagunitas" (*Praise* 1979). In this poem, Hass reflects on the continuity of recent philosophy with Plato—"All the new thinking is about loss. / In this it resembles all the old thinking"—and decides that although desire is indeed "full / of endless distances," still "There are moments when the body is as numinous / as words." Hass's "moments" differ from Frost's "momentary stays" because Hass follows the doctrine of *analogia entis* in believing that such moments occur when we experience "wonder at . . . presence," the numinous within the body, within words—in Lawler's terms, the infinite merged with the finite. Frost's work is marked by whimsy and caprice: one can never tell when God's breath will stay our confusion. For Hass, however, wonder is always available in the presence of the body, just as it is always available at the Catholic Eucharist.

Despite his Catholicism, however, Hass remains *American* (and there-fore Puritan) in his attitude toward the land. This attitude can be traced back to Stevens and, behind him, to Emerson, whose vision of a "new man in a paradisiacal New World" Bercovitch has traced to Jonathan Edwards and Cotton Mather (*Puritan* 157). Stevens ends "Sunday Morning" with this promise:

> Deer walk on our mountains, and quail whistle
> About us their spontaneous cries,
> Sweet berries ripen in the wilderness

Retaining the Puritan sense of boundary, of the encircling "wilderness," Stevens points with pride to "our" mountains, the frontier again repre-senting for *Americans* the chance to rejuvenate the self. *America*, he im-plies without irony, is the chosen world for supreme fictions; no place is better suited since no place is, as Frost says in "The Gift Outright," so "unstoried, artless, unenhanced." Inheriting much of Stevens's thought and imagery, Hass concludes "Meditation at Lagunitas" by remembering "Sunday Morning" 's ripening berries:

> There are moments when the body is as numinous
> as words, days that are the good flesh continuing.
> Such tenderness, those afternoons and evenings,
> saying *blackberry, blackberry, blackberry*.

If the first line is Catholic, then the rest are *American*, investing the land—as Stevens, Emerson, and the Puritans do—with redemptive promise. Only our attention to this *American* land, to its berries and bodies, Hass sug-gests, will help us recover our millennial mission.[8]

More even than Hass, Soto is convinced of *analogia entis*, but he looks not to an individual and visionary relation to the land as Hass, Stevens, and the Puritans do. Their repeated desire for transcendence is replaced by Soto's desire to learn how to be "nice," to build healthy relationships with others—this is what he means by "holiness." Hass's patronym is no more English than Soto's, but Hass's people belong to those Europeans who were eventually accepted economically, socially, and institutionally, racism turning into prejudice and finally acceptance. Because of that shift, Hass can be "Anglo" and his poetry *American*, despite his Catholicism. For Soto, however, people are more important than the land because they mediate between God and other humans. Living in an "occupied America," Soto lacks the classic immigrant's faith in the land's promise, knowing instead that the boundary of the United States crossed his people in 1848.[9] Soto thus places his hopes in community, expecting to find himself and God through the mediations of others.

We can see both Soto's Catholic similarity to Hass and his Chicano difference by reading "A Sunday" with "Meditation at Lagunitas" in mind. Soto's poem begins where Hass's leaves off: "There are moments when the body is as numinous / as words, days that are the good flesh continuing" becomes

> That the flesh should go on now seems to matter.
> And goodness in the meantime. I'm trying
> To be like others in the church. Katie
> Says it's possible, even at this corner,
> Leavenworth and Bush, drab men in three sweaters,
> Bum on his beat between a boarded-up grocery
> And hell.
> (70)

Soto is silent about what happened at church to make the "flesh continuing" "seem to matter," but Hass focuses precisely on that moment—the visionary transcendence achieved when the "flesh continuing" is simply "good," as the land *America* is simply good when Emerson steps onto the common to become a transparent eyeball. Soto is silent about his epiphany perhaps because Sunday Mass is supposed to remind one of the goodness of the flesh, of the miracle of the Incarnation. In fact, we might notice here that Hass functions as Matthew Arnold believed poets should, performing the role religion once did. In the United States, this understanding of the poet dovetailed nicely with Emerson's belief that the poet should create a sacred yet secular *America*. But Soto stands outside these traditions since, for him, the visions and consolations sought by Emerson, Arnold, and Hass occur at every Sunday Mass, where it "matter[s]" that "the flesh should go on now." Soto can thus turn his attention in the poem from transcendence to the kind of "goodness" that happens "in the meantime," between Sundays as we work as God's intermediaries for others. Katie reminds Soto of just that point when she explains that "God is someone who is with you, / Like now" (71). The double meaning of "someone" (God or Katie) implies that Katie mediates between God and Soto just as Soto mediates between God and Katie.

This Chicano Catholic emphasis on mediation—on the border where God and humanity meet—distinguishes Soto from the more Puritan or *American* Hass. Soto tries "To be like others in the church" while Hass transcends the "endless distances" between people in order to discover their individuality, "the way her hands dismantled bread, / the thing her father said that hurt her." Soto tries to be "nice" by finding a road or mediation between his own mean streak and others' sensibilities while Hass jumps, *bounds*, from "distance" to "tenderness." What moves "A Sunday" forward is not the possibility of transcendence that is so palpably in the offing in every line of Hass's "Meditation" but the many borders across which niceness must travel. Katie reminds Soto that he "should know better" than to watch her "running water / In the bathroom sink" (71), and he ends the Sunday evening by reminding himself not to look at his students' underwear when they uncross their legs (74). In between, he realizes that playing backgammon with Katie differs from playing chess with his daughter because Katie "wants my company" while "Mariko wants my money" (72), thus understanding that games require different kinds of niceness from him. With Mariko he is a "kind fool with dead bishops" (72), while he and Katie "smile at our losses / And stare out the windows" (71). Each Hass poem, like each Frost poem—like each day for the Puritan—represents a new, determined effort to achieve transcendence, bounding the distance between finite and infinite. But each Soto poem crosses—mediates between—borders, seeking the community that is found when we recognize not only the differences between us but also the commonalities.

III

"A Sunday" appears late in *Home Course in Religion*, representing a self that is learning how to "be like others" and be "good," to mediate "holiness." But much of the volume is devoted to describing how that growth was made possible only after Soto learned to understand masculinity outside the bounds of an *American* self. Properly understood, the masculinity Soto exhibits in the later poems is *machismo*, the masculinity of a strong and loving husband and father, not its degraded form, a violent misogyny born of poverty and oppression (Anzaldúa 83). Although Catholicism both helped and hindered Soto's growth from a degraded to a virtuous form of *machismo*, both the process and the product of his growth lie outside the bounds of *American* poetry and its corresponding Calvinism and masculinity.

The key to *machismo*, to either form of it, is that it is mediated, taught, Soto suggests, by others. He learns it first as "meanness," the invasion of the sensibilities of others. In "Apple," a retelling of the Fall, Soto places his "first temptation" to steal (14) in the context of looking into the family album and remembering the mean tricks to which his family subjected him: his brother telling him that "Captain Kangaroo / Lives in that house" or that "That kid said you were black"; his uncle asking him to help start the car—"I pulled / From the front fender and was dragged up the alley, / The engine whirring warm air into my face." "I didn't catch on right away," he tells us in a characteristic understatement, "That meanness was part of the family" (12). Soto retains responsibility for his Fall (his mature *machismo* will allow nothing less), but his awareness that the Fall was a border he crossed means he also realizes the role of mediation. Falling was taught to him. Although Soto blames no single person for this culture of meanness, he does focus on his tyrannical stepfather, Jim, who liked to claim that the young Soto was having the "Best years of your life" even while he presided over a home in which "Everyone was scared . . . even Mom." Jim's claim makes the young Soto remember more meanness:

> The best years,
> He said, and I thought of my brother and David,
> How earlier they had pinned me to the ground.
> And let Pinkie, David's homing pigeon,
> Perch on my forehead, weight like a warm stone.
> ("Best Years" 19)

Although Jim is not directly responsible for this violence, he creates the conditions for it, thus mediating a degraded *machismo*.

U.S. literature is littered with abusive fathers, but ever mindful of the border, Soto implies that Jim's meanness results from *American* boundaries, the Puritan desire to conquer the wilderness. Drunk and watching a Western on TV, Jim rages about Pearl Harbor while his three stepchildren look on:

> We were scared,
> The three of us, and when he said Nips
> Should be dead, a TV Indian tumbled
> From a cliff with a fist of smoke in his back.
> (20)

Soto's imagery is precise and allusive: the putatively treacherous Indian is shot in the back while Jim describes Japanese treachery at Pearl Harbor, the "fist" of smoke communicating the personal hatred that belies the un-reality of the TV image. Jim embraces the simplicity of TV, reproducing its emphasis on the boundaries between "white" and "red," *American* and

"Nip." Crossing the border, Soto is aware of both the Anglo and Chicano origins of the meanness that dominated his youth.[10] To read Soto as a border poet thus means we must abandon quests for the continuity of U.S. poetry and articulate instead the struggle of some of our writers to forge selves out of non-Puritan origins.

Soto resisted the culture of meanness represented by Jim, not by being self-reliant as a Calvinist and *American* must, but by opening himself to mediations that represented other ways of living. First of all, Catholicism gave him pride in his difference from his Anglo neighbors ("Palm-leaf crosses withered in the kitchen window / For our Okie [11] neighbors to look at in awe"), and then in church a "good priest . . . stared holiness / Into my body," creating a new set of values:

> Now I'm quiet,
> The telephone is quiet, my family
> And the people I like best are quiet.
> The nuns would be proud of me . . .
> ("Pink Hands" 7–8)

Soto's self-presentation here may seem tame, even small in its solicitation of the nuns who taught him in grade school, to readers trained to appreciate the grand ambitions of Whitman and the ironies of Frost—the drama of the isolate self struggling to fulfill the promise of *America*. But Soto cares about a rather different drama—the question of how to build healthy communities—and thus he focuses here on how the example of particular priests and nuns provided an alternative to his own meanness, his brother's and uncle's cruelty, and his stepfather's reproduction of *American* boundaries.

Because Soto's resistance to a culture of meanness that is both Chicano and *American* originates in mediation rather than in self-reliance, the process of his transformation takes an unconventional shape. Much Anglo men's literature combines rejection of the father with some form of repatriation, some reestablishment of the patriarchy in another name. Either the son/quester experiences transcendence, thus discovering patriarchal power in the self; or he declares himself a figurative orphan and finds a new man to father him, as Robin does in "My Kinsman, Major Molineaux"; or he displaces blame onto women and seeks escape from their feminine and feminizing world, as Rip Van Winkle does (Fetterley 3).

As many feminist critics have argued, the first two forms of repatriation rely on the third in some way, but through mediation, Soto remakes masculinity without blaming women or placing them outside any bounds. For example, he experiences transcendence as a healthy response to pain but not as a satisfactory way of living. In "Best Years," he tells us that

Sometimes you don't want to get up after
A brother has slapped you around,
But look skyward between branches of sycamore—
The pinpricks of stars, planes, end-of-the-world colors.

(19)

Despite the efficacy of this "skyward" vision, transcendence is finally too apocalyptic, too "end-of-the-world" and dependent on extreme duress for Soto, who wants to live in a community in which people can treat each other well. For this purpose, the solitude of transcendence, even the transcendent solitude of Hass's lovers, is simply not enough. Furthermore, instead of scapegoating women or finding a mythic father, Soto discovers the father through a woman: "That night I asked Mom what our name meant in Spanish. / She stirred crackling *papas* and said it meant Mexican." In this telling phrase, which is his only use of Spanish in the volume, Soto suggests that his father—his papa—is the potato his mother fries, a cultural legacy larger and more communal, if less glamorous, than any patronym.[12] The young Anglo who pinned Soto has the "meaningful name" Bloodworth and can point to a private legacy that descends only through his father's side or "blood," but Soto can point to a culture that gives him worth ("The Wrestler's Heart" 36). He is repatriated into a community, not a self.

This communal legacy means that, if the father is bad, Soto can find other mediators—a central theme in *Home Course*. The volume portrays Soto as both resisting and participating in the culture of meanness for which his stepfather mediates. While the Church first provides Soto the motive for resistance to this culture, at adolescence Soto turns to masculinity. Again, unlike many other coming-of-age stories, the achievement of masculinity enables, not the creation of a single, isolate self, transcendent in its separation, but a place in a growing community. Soto learns about that place through his relationship with "Scott, a real friend," whose father is also dead ("Fall and Spring" 34).

Soto's friendship with Scott is a border meeting between the self and other selves. They share their secrets: their feelings about their dead fathers, the girl Scott "liked in seventh grade" (34), and Soto's conviction that "I have lived before" and may be "Chinese" (33). But perhaps the most important element in their friendship is their decency. Although they share a degraded *machismo*—they siphon gas, destroy abandoned houses, and flirt with self-destruction—and despite the fact that "Neither one of us / Believed in hell, and neither believed / In good grades,"

We both agreed that Mrs. Tuttle
Was a nice person, and, Scott first,

Said that we were sorry for parking in front of her house
And thinking weird thoughts about her La-Z-Boy recliner.
                                    ("School Night" 39)

Catholicism has lost its hold on such doctrinal issues as hell, but it impresses on the young men a respect for "nice" people. They show true *machismo* when, "Scott first," they confess their sin against Mrs. Tuttle. The moment recalls our first knowledge of Soto's Catholicism. In "Pink Hands," he tells us that "I never understood / The Trinity, and still have doubts" (7), but in "The Dictionaries," he says he thought the Trinity "was something like / People inside each other / And was somehow like manners" (11). We see here Soto's consistent doctrinal uncertainty as well as his consistent valorization of "manners" and "niceness," those social and cultural forms that mediate or cross borders between people. However degraded his *machismo* becomes, Soto retains this Chicano Catholic belief, building community as he resists the culture of meanness.[13]

Resistance becomes an open break with the patriarchy that underwrites this meanness when Soto learns that *machismo* goes beyond men's fraternity to a community with women. To achieve this community he must eradicate the misogyny from both his Catholicism and his early *machismo*. The volume's title poem describes Soto's frustration with studying religion in college. Quoting several books, he comments on the relative clarity of each one, stating that even the intelligible ones made him sleepy, using up "the good air in my brain" (49). After the seventh book, "I woke only when / My girlfriend came over with a bag of oranges" (52), and after she leaves, he reads the Bible's description of Doubting Thomas, who touched Jesus's wounds. The poem ends,

> I began to feel ashamed because my left hand
> Turning the pages was the hand that had snapped
> Her panties closed. I got up from the couch
> And washed that hand, stinky trout that I took to bed.
> It was then, on a night of
> More Top Ramen and a cat-and-dog storm,
> That I realized I might be in the wrong line of belief.
>   (52)

From now on, Soto suggests, he will base both his theology and his sexuality on something other than misogyny.

The "wrong line of belief" is not only the notion that sex—particularly women's sexuality—is dirty, but also the idea that women are only sexual objects. Soto's relationship with his girlfriend is not nearly as healthy as the one he shares with Scott:

> She said that she was lonely
> When I wasn't around. I said that people feel

> Like that because they don't know themselves.
> I said just be mellow, just think of
> Yourself as a flower, etc.
> When I placed my hand on her thigh, she opened her legs
> Just a little. . . .
> (52)

Instead of entering her emotion as he did Scott's, Soto responds with the language of boundaries, of self-reliance (just know yourself, he tells her), and moves immediately to a formulaic attempt at seduction ("think of / Yourself as a flower, etc."), taking no heed of her reluctance as she opens her legs "just a little." There is no meeting at this border. By the end of the poem, Soto realizes that the *machismo* that brought him so close to Scott has failed to create true intimacy between the sexes.

Soto does not describe the road that led him across the border from this realization to his mature relationship with women, but the evidence of that maturity lies all about the second section of *Home Course in Religion*. In "The Asking," displaying true *machismo*, he gives his wife and daughter respect, treats them well, and works with his wife to provide for their family and to perform household chores:

> Carolyn is tired. She went to work,
> Cooked. After dinner she'll want to be by herself.
> To smoke and run a garden hose in our pond.
> Mariko and I talk while we eat.
> . . . .
> I do the dishes. . . .
> (60)

This picture contrasts sharply with Soto's stepfather, who ruled the house from his armchair and gave his wife and children no psychological space.

The maturity of Soto's new *machismo* is clearest when he addresses his failures. Returning to "A Sunday," which features Soto's growing understanding that "God is someone who is with you," we also see an occasional inability to cross borders. When Soto returns from Mass, first his wife, Carolyn, jokes with him and then she shows him "where an arbor should go":

> I look at the ground and try to find
> Something to say. I want my wife to like me.
> I look up to a homing pigeon cooing
> On the neighbor's fence. We call Mariko,
> Our daughter, who comes out of the house
> With a book in her hand. That's a homing pigeon,
> I point. You see the band on its leg?
> We forget about the arbor. We go inside.
> (72)

Soto's response begins with a profound awareness of a failed border cross-ing—he has nothing to say about the arbor even though Carolyn has asked for a comment. He wants to be "nice," for her to "like" him, but apparently he cannot, at least not in the way she would like. Instead of giving up and allowing a boundary to form—what Hass calls in "Meditation" an "endless distance," or in "Heroic Simile" the "limits to imagination" found in the "silence of separate fidelities" between two people—Soto turns to another kind of mediation. By being nice to his daughter, Mariko, Soto communi-cates his love for Carolyn. They can now "forget about the arbor." There is loss here, a confession of his ineffectiveness that reminds us of his earlier acknowledgment that Carolyn's friends at her Japanese Methodist church "are nicer than me" and "that I would never be / As nice as they" ("The Family in Spring" 65). But he partially makes up for his inability to discover anything nice to say about the arbor by creating an eloquent reminder of his love. When he and Carolyn call Mariko out of the house to see the "band" on a homing pigeon, the poem picks up an important image from "The Family in Spring"—the wedding band, which he once never wore but now does because it "says you're married" and makes him feel like "I was in the right place" (64). Soto cannot be as nice as he wants to be, but he can still make his love felt. His love of and through his daughter brings him and Carolyn "inside." Mariko becomes Soto's pigeon, carrying him home to wife and family. The homing pigeon with which his brother had tormented him in "Best Years" now has a finer purpose as Soto replaces the culture of meanness with a love of border crossings.

Finally, this mature *machismo* transforms Soto's understanding of his own masculine physicality as he replaces his teenage violence and self-destructiveness with karate. He realizes that karate's physicality is an at-tempt to deal with the past—"Finger pokes / Can blind a stepfather" and "You admit / You're a playground kid who never had enough" ("The His-tory of Karate" 57)—but he again applies masculinity to the end of build-ing community. He teaches karate to "dirty angels in dirty *gis*" at the Boys' Club (55), giving these boys, who are growing up much as he did, a mature father figure. He understands that

> They need love, Christ but not Christ,
> A father with unexpected gifts in one hand,
> A glove in the other.
> ("The Asking" 60)

These children do not need dogma; they need a mediator who can em-body Christ's healing grace, like a father who can bring "unexpected gifts" as well as a constructive discipline like karate. Soto himself had no such father—unless we realize that fathers can also be found in the good father staring holiness into him and in his mother stirring crackling *papas*.

Living on the border has meant for Soto a transformation of the self as profound as any in U.S. literature, though it cannot properly be called *American*: Soto faces no wilderness either within or without; his manhood is neither "beset" nor "spectacular"; transcendence is only useful when he has been decked; and people draw the best out of him more than the land does. Soto was born only a year after Frost realized that we must learn how to "crowd but still be kind," but for Soto that is what living in the United States has always meant. Perhaps this is what our literary history can mean as well once we think of Puritanism not as the origin of our boundaries but as just one edge along our many, crowded borders. If the modern era must accomplish something, it is surely a new understanding of our world that recognizes, in the words of poet Jay Wright, that the "multi-cultural is the fundamental process of human history" (14).

Notes

I am grateful to Anne Macmaster, Marianne Noble, Carol J. Singley, Timothy Spurgin, and Kathryn Manson Tomasek for their assistance on this essay.

1. Lewis's *American Adam* and Pearce's *Continuity of American Poetry* have helped define *American* literary history around these themes. Although Bercovitch is critical of Puritanism, he too finds it central to American identity in works like *The Puritan Origins of the American Self*. In "Melodramas of Beset Manhood," Baym explains how these literary histories are masculine and therefore partial at best, and TuSmith extends Baym's argument to U.S. ethnic literatures, describing their emphasis on community. I will contrast a community similar to those TuSmith describes with Bercovitch's description of the individualistic American self instituted by Puritanism.

2. For the purposes of this essay, "Anglo," "America," and "American" will represent the hegemonic discourse of the United States that limits its history and literary criticism to Puritan and English origins. From this perspective, assimilated Germans, Italians, and other European immigrants can be seen as "Anglo" and "American" insofar as they subscribe to a specific ideology described by Bercovitch (*Puritan*), Takaki, and others: the belief that the U.S. has a special destiny, inherited through and most fully embodied by those of English descent. For a fuller explanation of this dynamic, see also Marinaccio's essay in the present volume.

3. For a history of this distinction between civilization and savagery, see Takaki 24–50. Takaki explains that settlers in the Virginia colony viewed Native Americans as ignorant but educable heathens, while the Puritans demonized them as devilish savages. Ultimately, Puritan ideology won out, setting "a course for the making of a national identity in America for centuries to come" (44). I call this construction of a difference that must be conquered "boundary."

4. Chabram notes a recent shift from studies that describe a "uniform response to mainstream practices and literary assumptions" by marginalized social groups to studies that "unearth their heterogeneous—and oftentimes contradictory—responses" (141). I hope to indicate some of this heterogeneity by describing

Soto's perspective through a multiple adjective—Chicano Catholic. Many Chicano writers, for example, from Alurista to Anzaldúa, have criticized the role of Catholicism in oppressing their people. A fuller study would describe Soto's position as a middle-class writer while remaining sensitive to the changed meaning of middle-class in this context. Pérez-Torres touches on class in contrasting Soto and Ana Castillo (268), while Sánchez demonstrates what a more detailed analysis would require.

5. The term "informal empire" is LaFeber's.

6. For the Puritans and the *American* ideology they instituted, land was "wilderness" and required "settlement" if its denizens were "savages" (Takaki 39). For a description of how these attitudes carried over into the conquest of Northern Mexico in the 1830s and 1840s, see Takaki 171.

7. See, for example, Kemp's fine study.

8. Raised Catholic, Hass has rejected his childhood faith for a "mystical" one that yet shows a debt to both Puritan ideology and Catholicism. First, in essays on Lowell and Wright, Hass opposes Calvinism—the "evangelical side of American culture," with its "hatred of intelligence" (*Twentieth* 39), "stylized violence" (42), and contribution to the "annihilative rage of capitalism" (20)—to the "unborn myth which American poetry was making" (19). As his language shows, however, this *unborn* myth still participates in Puritan ideology in its jeremiad-like rhetoric. Second, although Hass wants to replace Catholic "sacramental mediation" with a "contemplative peace beyond any manifestation in the flesh," he still calls his "mystical" apprehension of God an "*embodiment* of what can't be embodied" (22, emphasis added). He thus develops a secular American mysticism through a partial rejection and refinement of a Catholic apprehension of *analogia entis*. In this sense only is he a Catholic writer.

9. See Acuña's landmark history, *Occupied America*.

10. Although racism means that "most / Of us wouldn't get good jobs, some / Would die," Soto also suggests in "The Levee" that "We deserved this life" because television has been internalized, "wreathed in dollies / And the glow-in-the-night Christ on the windowsill" (38).

11. Literally, Okies are the impoverished Oklahomans who moved West after the Dust Bowl of the 1930s.

12. In the Americas, *papa* means "potato," which in Spain is called *patata*. *Papa* can also refer to the Pope, thus combining the themes of religion, culture, and masculinity. *Soto*, meanwhile, means "grove" or "thicket," the wilderness Puritans hope to conquer, making very apt Soto's mother's quip that the name means "Mexican."

13. Soto reaches a low point when he imitates Jim's prejudices. In the last two poems of the first section, Soto carefully juxtaposes his teenage prejudices— "Fuckin' queers" ("Drinking in the Sixties" 43)—with his stepfather's—"He had words for blacks, / Stalin, the yellow race that could jump up and down / And destroy us all" ("Spelling Words at the Table" 45). The phrase "had words" recalls the poem that introduced Jim ("our stepfather had words / For men with long hair" ["The Music at Home" 17]), thus giving us one origin for Soto's early homophobia. Soto will become a poet when he no longer possesses or "has" words but travels across their borders.

ROCCO MARINACCIO

"Communism Is Twentieth-Century Americanism"
Proletarian Poetry and the Puritan Tradition

IN HIS 1936 Presidential campaign, Earl Browder, head of the Communist Party U.S.A., urged voters to reject Roosevelt's empty promises of progress and to choose the genuine progress promised by the Communist ticket. Knowing that commitment to progress traditionally defines the American character, Browder represented the Communist as the true American dedicated to the nation's work along its historic course. His motto, "Communism Is Twentieth-Century Americanism," equates the millenarian promise of Marxist radicalism with American idealism and, in so doing, characterizes the national mission as inherently revolutionary. Despite Browder's self-proclaimed radicalism, then, his rhetoric illustrates a continued faith in the Puritan narrative of American history and, as a result, reinscribes the secularized reinterpretation of the Puritan errand that has dominated constructions of national identity since the early nineteenth century.

Browder's motto exemplifies a legitimation strategy common not only to practical Party politics but also to the radical or, as it was more generally called, proletarian writing of the twenties and thirties. Like Browder, proletarian writers often identified the American mission as a revolutionary one, and they consequently valued the literary text in terms of its usefulness to that mission. Such a valuation is, however ironically, the distinctive mark of the national tradition. As Sacvan Bercovitch argues in *The American Jeremiad*, "What distinguishes the American writer is his commitment to the national covenant" (181). Indeed, proletarian literature often demonstrates a tenacious belief in the dominant historical narrative. So powerful is the promise of America that the proletarian's work frequently affirms rather than subverts the political status quo and, in so affirming, reveals the significance of Puritan constructions of the national identity and mission

even to some of the most aesthetically and politically oppositional literature of the modern era.

This habit of affirmation illuminates not only the aesthetic pressures
but also the ultimately domesticating and coopting function of the jeremiad discourse, which intervenes in the most frequently anthologized proletarian texts and in the movement's most self-consciously literary under-
takings. Such an intervention suggests the centrality of this discourse to
dominant constructions of literary value. In addition, the containment of
such a potentially radical alternative as Marxism demonstrates the conservative cultural work of the jeremiad. Within the generally marginalized
field of proletarian literature, I will distinguish between "mainstream" and
"marginal" proletarian texts in order to demonstrate that the proletarian poetry most widely disseminated and validated as literary both inside
and outside the proletarian movement is that which is most thoroughly
constructed by the discourse of mission. Two collections of proletarian
poetry from the mid-thirties typify this mainstream production: Granville Hicks's *Proletarian Literature in the United States: An Anthology* (1935)
and the "Social Poets" number of *Poetry* (May 1936). Both volumes were
auspiciously launched by the proletarian movement's major figures, whose
work has held some measure of literary status. Similar literary status has
long eluded marginal figures such as H. H. Lewis (1901–1985). A Missouri
farmer, nicknamed "the Plowboy Poet," Lewis generally worked outside
the proletarian literary establishment. He rejects the traditional discourse
of mission, successfully displacing the dominant tradition. Lewis's work
thus departs from mainstream proletarian literature, and his long-standing
relegation to the margins of proletarian literary production indicts the
critical Puritanism that has governed readers, writers, and critics of proletarian literature from his time forward.

From the movement's inception, proletarian writers sought to contex-
tualize their work within a radicalized American tradition. Mike Gold's
"Towards Proletarian Art" (1921), the first major call for proletarian literature in America, situates contemporary proletarian writing in a tradition
typified by Walt Whitman. Gold identifies Whitman as "[t]he heroic spiritual grandfather" of the contemporary proletarian writer (67), praising his
attention to the masses and his class consciousness: "his individuals were
those great, simple farmers and mechanics and ditch-diggers who are to be
found everywhere among the masses . . . [and] whose self-sufficiency comes
from their sense of solidarity, not from any sense of solitariness" (68).
John Dos Passos, in a 1932 *Modern Quarterly* forum entitled "Whither the
American Writer: (A Questionnaire)," calls for the proletarian writer to

"Marxianize the American tradition" rather than "junk" it (11–12). Finally, in 1939, Alan Calmer's "Portrait of the Artist as a Proletarian" lauds the proletarian who would "assert and deepen the native quality of American writing" by recognizing that "a mature literature could not be created solely out of the immediate plans and activities of a party but must be cut out of the whole grain and fibre of national existence" (14).

Their assertions of the revolutionary quality of the national mission and of the national literature notwithstanding, many proletarian writers in fact perpetuate an ideology characteristic of the American writer. Sacvan Bercovitch (*American Jeremiad*) locates the origin of this ideology in the Puritan jeremiad. He identifies this "political sermon" as the source of American literary discourse, which established the discursive practices and the cultural function of the literary text. As a mode of social critique, the jeremiad contrasts a description of contemporary social ills with the millenarian vision of the national destiny. Delineating the distance between present and future and, thereby, the cultural progress yet to be achieved, the jeremiad creates consensus and encourages social action. Within the secular literary tradition rooted in the Puritan jeremiad, each author becomes a new Jeremiah, explaining America to its people and creating a community of reader/citizens dedicated to maintaining that identity. Every text thus reinscribes the national identity, reasserting the American commitment to progress in pursuit of its millennial destiny.

It is precisely this designation of progress as a definitive cultural value that undermines genuinely radical expression. Since the national mission is defined in terms of progress, to be "radical" is to be "American" and to call for cultural reform is simply to do the work of the national mission. The discourse of mission thus contains radical expression, discouraging opposition in the face of its seemingly radical promise and incorporating alternative ideologies into the status quo. Bercovitch observes that social critique is typically contextualized within the dominant discourse of mission so that "in every case, the defiant act that might have posed fundamental social alternatives bec[omes] instead a fundamental force against social change" (204). Each new Jeremiah assumes the rhetorical purpose of the earliest Puritan to celebrate the nation in its pursuit of its destiny and to situate any call for cultural change within the ideology of progress. In the end, the "radical energies" of the social critic ultimately "serve to sustain the culture, because the same ideal that released those energies transform[s] radicalism into a mode of cultural cohesion and continuity" (205).

Bercovitch's analysis of the secular jeremiad tradition attends to those figures he calls our "classic" writers: Hawthorne, Emerson, Thoreau, Melville, Whitman. But the particular power of this tradition to seduce avowedly Marxist writers has yet to be examined. That power, I argue, partly

lies in both the underlying similarity of the American and Marxist historical myths as narratives of millenarian promise and in their corresponding
prescriptions for literary practice. Within both the American and Marxist
millennial narratives, literary discourse assumes a prophetic cast. Both the
new Jeremiah and the proletarian writer analyze the culture in terms of its
progress on its historical errand. Hicks praises the proletarian writers of
the day for continuing to express their millenarian vision, characterizing
them as "prophet[s] . . . hoping for and believing in a splendid future for
America" (25). This specific attention to historical analysis is a significant
component of socialist realism, the "Party-approved" literary discourse
that profoundly influenced proletarian writing. In Edwin Seaver's influential definition of socialist realism, he notes that it demands

that the author realize all the contradictions, the contrarieties and the complexities of the world in crisis; which demands that the artist not only see things as they
are—statically, but where they are going—dynamically; and which demands not
only that the author see where things are going, but himself take a conscious part
in leading the reader through the maze of history toward Socialism and the class-
less society. (23–24)

The proletarian socialist realist here assumes the same task as the new
Jeremiah: he must situate the present moment within the larger historical
narrative. Both do so by contrasting present and future. For both the new
Jeremiah and the proletarian writer, then, the delineation of current social
conditions performs an affirmative function. In Puritan ideology, affliction
is a sign of election; thus, cultural critique reminds readers of their historic
destiny and inspires reformist zeal. Similarly, the proletarian writer's revelation of contemporary ills works, as Seaver's definition suggests, to affirm
historical destiny and to urge renewed commitment to achieving it. Leading the reader "through the maze of history toward Socialism and the class-
less society," the proletarian writer must assert the inevitability of the revolutionary future, pointing to contemporary evidence of historical progress.
Positioned between current reality and the ideal future, the new Jeremiah
and the proletarian writer function both as chronicler and prophet. By
making clear the gap between the present and the future, they also make
clear the implications of the current social order for the promised ideal.

Finally, both the new Jeremiah and the proletarian writer intend to craft
a coherent cultural identity among the audience. Bercovitch posits this
function as central to the jeremiad's cultural work. In its ability to direct
the American people on their collective mission, he writes, the discourse
of "the Puritan errand was well-suited to the process of Americanization"
(*American Jeremiad* 26); the jeremiad, then, serves as a "ritual of socializa-
tion" (194). Proletarian poetry similarly attempts to develop a collective

identity, here grounded in class consciousness. It does so not only through persuasive political rhetoric and cultural analysis but also through the form of the literary subject. Debating the political efficacy of modernist literary discourse, many proletarian writers emphasized "collective" subject forms. Isidor Schneider, in his address on proletarian poetry at the First American Writers' Congress in 1935, argued that, given poetry's origins in song and ballad, it is "primarily a social art" (114). Only "under capitalism" did it begin "to attempt individualistic forms, especially the lyric" (117). Many proletarian writers argued that the often remote and fragmented modernist subject failed to illuminate the revolutionary potential inherent in the social order and thereby to move the reader in the revolutionary direction. Thus, as the twenties progress, proletarian writers increasingly experiment with the collective-voiced poem, which attempts to represent the voice of the people, drawing the poet out of his or her own alienated subjectivity and affirming for poet and reader the collective identity of the masses.

The proletarian writer was, however, lured by more than the seeming compatibility of Marxist and American millennialism. The conventions of any tradition, as culturally valued discursive practices, confer cultural legitimacy; the conventions of the American tradition, as indicators of individual commitment to the national mission, do so even more profoundly. The immigrant status of many proletarian writers particularly intensified this desire for cultural legitimacy, since, for the immigrant, commitment to the national mission underlies an American identity: to believe in the promise of America is to become an American. Immigrant literature thus often affirms that promise, and immigrant writers often assume the role of the new Jeremiah. In so doing, their work seeks to uncover the various social ills of the time in order to remind their fellow Americans of the distance between the dreams that impelled the immigrants to the shores of the new nation and the reality they found there.

Such a commitment to the national mission seems particularly marked among the proletarian writers of Jewish heritage. Importantly, many of the leading writers, critics, publishers, and editors, whose ideological agenda powerfully influenced all phases of literary production, share Jewish ancestry: Mike Gold, Joseph Freeman, Alexander Trachtenberg, Isidor Schneider. Sam B. Girgus, in *The New Covenant: Jewish Writers and the American Idea*, discusses the particular susceptibility of the Jewish writer to the jeremiad tradition and its corresponding vision of America. Characterized as the "new Puritans" (12), these writers are particularly committed to the idea of America as the Promised Land. In so doing, they "not only sustain . . . in their stories the rhetoric of the jeremiad but also . . . transform . . . the mythic sermon narrative to a modern setting that expresses the condition and dilemma of the modern American" (13). The primary

form of this modern jeremiad, Girgus suggests, is the blend of Marx and
the American tradition so compelling to the proletarian writer. Noting
that "[a]n important measure of the power of the American Way upon
Jewish writers and thinkers can be found in the numbers of leading Jewish
radicals who adopted the American idea while continuing to believe in one
form or another of socialism" (3), he states that, in the end, "radicalism
simply could not compete with the attraction of the ideology of America"
(4). For the immigrant proletarian writers, the consequences of genuinely
radical belief are immense; to give up the American dream would be not
only to reject their new identities as Americans but also to accept the failure of their journey to the new nation.

The habitual effort to unify American idealism and Marxist radicalism
characterizes both *Proletarian Literature in the United States* and the "Social
Poets" number of *Poetry*. Among the most highly visible collections of
proletarian poetry of the time, they appeared in the heyday of proletarian literature, when those in the movement felt it was on the verge of
widespread popularity.[1] These texts represent the most ambitious attempts
of the movement's most powerful figures to gain literary legitimacy. The
Proletarian Literature anthology was edited by, among others, Joseph Freeman, Isidor Schneider, Granville Hicks, and Mike Gold and was published
by International Publishers, the New York–based firm that was for many
years a major publisher of left literature in the nation. The "Social Poets"
number of *Poetry* was guest edited by Horace Gregory. Such attention to
proletarian writing by this politically and aesthetically mainstream journal could have occurred only during proletarian literature's brief flirtation
with literary respectability. Both volumes collect the work of writers most
closely associated with the movement, drawing from the major journals of
proletarian poetry: *New Masses*, *The Partisan Review*, and *Dynamo: A Journal of Revolutionary Verse*.

Both volumes foreground their engagement with the American literary tradition. In his introduction to the *Proletarian Literature* anthology,
Joseph Freeman characterizes its contents as "the beginnings of an American literature, one which will grow in insight and power with the growth of
the American working class now beginning to tread its historic path toward
the new world." At the same time, he takes care to remind us that "the
contents of [the] volume are a continuation of an older literary tradition"
(28). The critical essays that close the *Poetry* volume make similar claims.
William Phillips and Philip Rahv argue that the verse is "a revolt within
the tradition of poetry rather than against it" (104). Horace Gregory adds
Marx to the list of European thinkers that Americans, in their "enthusi-

asm," have "combined" with the national tradition in order to respond "to the need of the hour," and he sees the topical focus and the instrumental nature of proletarian literature as solidly in the American tradition (93–94).

The proletarian movement's commitment to the national tradition and, in particular, its continuing valuation of the discursive practices of the jeremiad are explicitly illustrated by Alfred Kreymborg's sonnet "American Jeremiad," from the *Proletarian Literature* anthology. The poem calls for the American writer to write a jeremiad for the times.[2] In it, Kreymborg traces his own decision to become a new Jeremiah and characterizes the cultural work of the literary text in terms of the jeremiad tradition:

> It's pretty hard to sing of moonlight now,
> Of benches in the park and lovers' lanes.
> I'd like to if I could, but here somehow
> Are shadows, beggars, shadows, and the rain's
> A dripping, soppy, clammy winding-sheet
> Indifferent to the tragedies of men,
> Indifferent as the many passing feet
> That make the beggars rise and drop again.
>
> What shall a lover sing when half the land
> Is driven cold and lives on dank despair?
> As long as inhumanity's in the hand
> That runs the race and whips the poor apart,
> Lovers must all embrace a bloody air
> And strangle men who starve the human heart.

As a new Jeremiah, Kreymborg opposes individual and expressive uses of poetry to communal and critical ones. He would like to sing of love, but he cannot ignore "the tragedies of men." His duty is clear: as long as the nation falls short of its promised ideal, he will sing out against those forces that prevent it from fulfilling its historic mission. Offering up his own conversion narrative as a model for "[l]overs . . . all," Kreymborg defines the role of the poet in the social crisis, a definition that accords with the literary tradition explicitly evoked by the poem's title.

Underlying the poem's critique of the social order is an awareness of America's millennial promise. Kreymborg moves to inspire the reader/citizen by contrasting the present, revealed in the portrait of the homeless and unemployed, with the better life of an implicitly guaranteed future: songs of protest are necessary only "*As long as* inhumanity's in the hand / That runs the race and whips the poor apart" (my emphasis). To further inspire cultural change, Kreymborg seeks to create a collective consciousness on the part of the reader. Not only does the poet offer the example of himself abandoning his private concerns to address the "tragedies of men," but he also appeals to the reader to join in his song: "Lovers all must embrace a bloody air." "Lover" is a particularly open subject position most readers could and would choose to assume; so addressing its readers, the poem speaks to the masses as a collective entity, urging them to social action.

The poem's social concerns are thus clear, but hardly revolutionary. As such, "American Jeremiad" illustrates not only the incongruence between American idealism and Marxist radicalism but also the proletarian writer's consistent failure to acknowledge that incongruence. The millennial narrative Kreymborg evokes remains in its American context. Rather than call for radical action, the poet calls for a rededication to traditional values. The poem lacks any specifically Marxist analysis of the current social crisis: it demonstrates no clear class consciousness, no systemic critique of capitalism, and no rearticulation of the national mission. Kreymborg's traditional sensibilities are further illustrated by his nostalgia; he would "like to" sing about love and presumably will *go back to* such songs when the current social crisis ends. Moreover, while Kreymborg's refusal to be "[i]ndifferent to the tragedies of men" proceeds from an admirable empathy for his suffering fellow citizens, his motivation for social protest seems limited to that empathy and lacking in any broadly theorized ideological assumptions. Ultimately, "American Jeremiad" simply calls for cultural renewal, invoking the idealized national destiny as an incentive to communal action in the way that American writers have since the Puritans.[3]

Edwin Rolfe's "Before the Hour," which opens the *Poetry* "Social Poets" number, exemplifies the jeremiad Kreymborg calls for. In addition, Rolfe's explicitly traditional imagery demonstrates the continuing power of the discourse of the jeremiad to contain any alternative interpretations of the social order. Both sections of the poem — "The Ship" and "Night-World" — condemn the corrupt social order in the context of the poet's reassuring repetition of prophecy. They posit the speaker sometime "before the hour" of the fulfillment of that prophecy: "The way / to certainty is charted now" (ll. 35–36). The poem's second section characterizes the millennial future as does Kreymborg, without any specific class consciousness, and marked instead by an admirable but nonetheless simple and nonrevolutionary empathy for the speaker's countrymen:

> I see all friends
> wonderfully perfect, and the earth changed
> to match the works, desires of my days;
> loving all men and mankind.
>   (ll. 24–27)

The central image of each of the poem's two parts metaphorizes the historical narrative in terms typical to the jeremiad tradition, thus solidifying

Rolfe's investment in canonical discursive practices. Part one characterizes the progress to the millennium as a pilgrimage aboard a great ship, while part two does so as the inevitable movement out of darkness into a new dawn. Part one, its metaphor of shipboard pilgrimage rooted in the Great Migration, especially well illustrates the poem's investment in the Puritan construction of the national mission:

> We shall watch its final plunge from afar,
> keeping sinews strong and our minds free
> of its sea-soaked rot. We shall be everywhere
> when faces turn, fresh-eyed, to the wind:
> not here, where decay is constant, but on shores
> that beckon as this antique vessel dies.
>
> I do not mean we will desert,
> but no ship, sinking, is worth salvaging
> in seas where masts are numerous and men are
> enough to board them, steer them to port.
> We shall be here only to save the living cargo,
> carry it untouched to greener shores.
>
> (ll. 1–12)

Like Kreymborg, Rolfe calls for a rededication to traditional values rather than for radical action. While he anticipates abandoning the rotten "antique vessel," he does so only in order to board *another ship*. His commitment to the metaphor of shipboard pilgrimage indicates his commitment to traditional constructions of the national mission. Critical of the current social order, he nonetheless holds faith in the American promise: "I do not mean we will desert." The imagery of the millennial future Rolfe posits is thus devoid of any radical connotations. The image of the "greener shores," rooted in the Puritan characterization of America as the new Eden, portrays the national destiny in wholly traditional terms.

In short, "American Jeremiad" and "Before the Hour" both fail to rearticulate the nation's historical progress in radical terms. Despite their vehement critique of the present social order, Kreymborg and Rolfe construct no alternative vision of the national destiny; indeed, both poets seem to lack the very language with which to do so. Kreymborg only vaguely alludes to a better future he cannot characterize. His rendering of the Depression scene is, by contrast, vivid and concrete; such a contrast makes his vagueness about the future appear less a matter of choice than a result of some conceptual block or imaginative failure. Rolfe, on the other hand, imagines his future more concretely, yet he is wholly invested in conventional metaphors that reinscribe the dominant historical narrative. As a result, he, like Kreymborg, is silent where he should speak loudest, and their texts lack any fully articulated radical vision.

Such absences typify American literature of social protest. The inability of the American writer to construct alternative historical narratives results from the jeremiad's characteristic substitution of symbolic for social analysis. Bercovitch defines social analysis as "secular, relativistic, and therefore open to a consideration of radically different systems of thought and action." Symbolic analysis, on the contrary, "confines us to the alternatives generated by the symbol itself . . . within a fixed, bipolar system. Since every symbol system unites opposites, . . . we can understand what is being represented only by measuring it against its opposite. . . . Thus the search for meaning is at once endless and self-enclosed" (*American Jeremiad* 178). Within the symbolic discourse of mission, then, alternative historical narratives are generated only in binary relation to the dominant narrative and, furthermore, are meaningful only in negative relation to that dominant narrative. As a result, any alternative narratives appear as absence, as a state of unfulfillment. What Bercovitch calls the "symbol of America" thus incorporates only the millennial narrative and its negation—America fulfilled and America failed. No positive alternative narratives are possible. Consequently, cultural critique has two "literary" modes: faith or despair. The American writer, analogously, has two culturally prescribed roles, both of which reinscribe the dominant mission narrative: the new Jeremiah, maintaining a commitment to America's millenarian promise, or the anti-Jeremiah, bemoaning a disillusion at America's failure to achieve its vaunted destiny. Either way, the mission narrative retains its definitive cultural status.

The canonical practice of symbolic analysis thus inhibits radical social protest by specifically marginalizing the social analysis that might lead to alternative constructions of the national mission. As a result, we must go outside the mainstream political and literary circles of the proletarian movement to find poets, uninterested in courting literary legitimacy, who reject the symbolic rhetoric of the jeremiad for an alternative rhetoric of social analysis. One such poet is H. H. Lewis. His work appears in *Poetry* and *New Masses*, but also in a wide variety of less prominent journals, such as *The Left* and *The Rebel Poet*, published outside of New York. Four volumes of his work were published by a fellow farmer, B. C. Hagglund of Holt, Minnesota, and were available through the mail by the poet himself: *Red Renaissance* (1930), *Thinking of Russia* (1932), *Salvation* (1934), and *The Road to Utterly* (1935). During his poetic career, he made only intermittent trips from his Missouri farmhouse. After a trip to New York in 1942, he remained on his farm, living in obscurity and poverty until his death.

Lewis typifies the proletarian writer whose rough-hewn verse and vitriolic political sensibilities have consistently alienated readers and critics. Even to many within the proletarian movement, Lewis was an embarrassment because, it was believed, he undermined its claims to literary legiti-macy. This sensitivity is typified by Alan Calmer's "Portrait of the Artist as a Proletarian." Calmer's critique specifically opposes "utilitarian" and "enduring" literary values, mockingly characterizing the young proletar-ian writer as a lower-middle-class "bohemian," whose background has left him "entirely shut off from cultural currents" (3). Such critical Puritan-ism continues to characterize analyses of proletarian poetry. The *Prole-tarian Literature* anthology is a touchstone for the study of thirties prole-tarian poetry; in general, the writers represented within it and the *Poetry* "Social Poets" number have dominated the limited critical attention paid to the movement. Lewis's presence in these volumes is minimal: he is absent from the *Poetry* number and has two relatively mild poems, "Un-holy Roller" and a short version of "I'll Say," in the *Proletarian Literature* anthology.

Lewis's poetry has gone virtually unnoticed by contemporary scholars because of its distinctly "unliterary" nature. Explaining Lewis's erasure from modern literary history, Cary Nelson calls Lewis "the academic's nightmare of the political" (44–48) and locates the source of Lewis's dis-repute in his fiery satirical rhetoric. His work is unashamedly opinionated, fiercely critical, and scabrously humorous. He tends toward simple rhymes and meters, and he enjoys puns and exaggerated sound and word play. In-deed, Lewis's work is hardly consistent with twentieth-century notions of literary discourse; his polemical rhetoric generally lacks "the surface indecision and ambivalence that many critics since the 1950s have deemed a transcendent, unquestionable literary and cultural value" (Nelson 44).

However, Lewis's relegation to the margins of an already marginal lit-erary movement is rooted in something more than his violation of postwar critical sensibilities. He moves, in fact, against much more deeply ingrained literary values. Rejecting symbolic for social analysis, he displaces the dis-course of mission that has since the Puritan era signified the "literary" text. The key to Lewis's radical social analysis lies in the title to his sec-ond collection, *Thinking of Russia*. As he says in the title poem, "I'm always thinking of Russia, / I can't keep her out of my head. / I don't give a damn for Uncle Sham, / I'm a left-wing radical Red" (ll. 1–4). The revolutionary progress of Soviet Russia, "[w]here the masses are fully in power, / As free as the flag is Red" ("Example-Song," *Road* ll. 39–40), provides a positive alternative to the dominant mission narrative and, thus, offers an alterna-tive framework within which to analyze American society. As a postrevo-lutionary, non-Western, and nonsymbolic alternative, the historical reality of Soviet Russia disrupts the binary symbol of America and provides Lewis entrance into the discourse of social analysis. Lewis thus escapes the ideo-logical boundaries that entrap more "literary" proletarian writers. Writing from outside the American millennial narrative, he can explore rhetorical alternatives to the jeremiad and offer a radical analysis of the social order.

Lewis's *The Road to Utterly* exemplifies a strain of proletarian literature that critics and writers both inside and outside the proletarian movement have worked to erase from the literary landscape.[4] Its epigraph indicates the significance of Soviet Russia to Lewis's radical social analysis: "Written by a Missouri Farmhand and Dedicated to Soviet Russia." While Kreymborg and Rolfe remain committed to the symbolic discourse of mission, Lewis challenges the interpretive privilege of this discourse. Thus, he examines the Depression misery chronicled in much of his poetry not solely within the context of the American mission narrative but also within an explicitly Marxist framework. Unlike the symbolic analysis of the new Jeremiah, then, Lewis's social analysis incorporates alternative interpretations of the cultural crisis. Lewis is, of course, a committed Marxist whose sympathies are never in doubt, but he nonetheless presents competing historical narratives as particular products of different ideological perspectives. As a result, Marxist radicalism and American idealism exist not as thesis and antithesis but as a pair of distinct alternatives, and Lewis's freedom to choose Marxism releases him from the self-enclosed binary symbol of America.

For instance, in "Example-Song," the personified "Hunger" wreaks misery on the depressed American countryside:

> Then through the worsened far and wide
> Grim Hunger goes personified,
> Playing amid confusion,—
> Till navel, back to bone inside,
> D-r-u-m-s the Revolution.
>
> (ll. 5-9)

Lewis's vivid portrait of Depression America is marked by the harsh criticism of the jeremiad: the people are oppressed, starving, disillusioned. Within the symbolic analysis typical of that form, the speaker's response to such conditions is limited to renewed faith or bitter despair. Lewis's practice of social analysis, however, offers him alternative interpretive possibilities, and he is able to move outside the ideological and rhetorical constraints of the jeremiad. Lewis sees not simply America's continuing and perhaps eternal failure to fulfill its original promise, but, in addition, its progress along the revolutionary path of Russia. Situating the social crisis in the context of Marxist revolutionary history, he can rearticulate the historical significance of that crisis, so that hungry, rumbling stomachs announce both the failure of capitalism and the imminence of revolution.

Lewis specifically invokes the American mission narrative in the title poem of *The Road to Utterly*. The journey along the road to the fictional town of Utterly is a metaphor for the teleological narrative of American history. The trip to "Utterly" suggests the passage to a completed, unqualified state of fulfillment, yet the speaker seems to see only misery and decay:

> Such a dismal lot to see
> On the road to Utterly.
>
> Hill erosion-ruined by Spoil
> With deluging sweat of Toil.
> . . . .
> Now Depression's added pall
> Glooming over hill and all;
> Sown the bad and reaped the worse
> By the evolving Mammon-curse.
>
> (ll. 1-4, 9-12)

The speaker's dismal disillusion exposes the empty promise of America. In his early passage along the road the speaker is fueled by the American dream: born at the "century's hopeful morn" (l. 47), he is carried along by "dreamings of SUCCESS" (l. 53), but, like all other common folk, he is "mocked" by his dream (l. 56). On the road is visible nothing but decay; it is a journey through a wasteland of eroded soil, weeds, empty homes.

In a passage that specifically overturns the Puritan myth of the city on the hill created out of the savage wilderness, the speaker alludes to the fertile land and the harmony with nature of the Indian civilizations, whose dim past is suggested by the triple parenthesis:

> On the ridge that grayly runs
> Through the South of Native Sons,
> Past the cotton-minded ones,
> Toward the town of Utterly.
>
> (((Where, beyond the eye and ear,
> Indians prospered, even here)))
>
> (ll. 19-24)

Until this moment, the poem appears to be an antijeremiad. The speaker sees only that America's promise has not been kept; he is left, it seems, with a meaningless existence. But his responsiveness to Native American culture saves him from the despair of the anti-Jeremiah. His reference to their oppression (following a reference to slavery) not only exposes the culture of racism but also posits Native American society as a distinct alternative to contemporary America. In so doing, the poem begins to reveal itself as something more than an antijeremiad.

This responsiveness to alternative social formations is more fully revealed in the poem's striking final moment. The speaker describes the road to Utterly as a

Course that blindly forward wends,
While another Hope impends,
Through the worst to be;
Trending as a river trends,
Even with the backward bends,
Toward the sea;
Till the profit system ends, —
That's the road to Utterly.
(ll. 66–73)

Here the speaker rearticulates the metaphoric narrative he has employed throughout. In so doing, he demonstrates the relative interpretive freedom of social analysis. Freed from the conventions of symbolic analysis, the speaker imagines a positive alternative to the mission narrative. The road to Utterly may indicate the dissolution of the American covenant and the failure of the national mission, but it also signifies the end of capitalist oppression and the progress toward the revolutionary future.

As a result of his faith in the revolutionary future, Lewis's analysis of contemporary events is often celebratory. "Song of the Moment," which opens *The Road to Utterly*, demonstrates the joyous exclamation that is unavailable to the traditional American writer of social protest, for whom millennial fulfillment is constantly deferred if not wholly in doubt. Lewis, his confidence in a revolutionary future bolstered by events in the Soviet Union, asserts that he would prefer to be a member of the oppressed masses in his own historical moment than to be a man of privilege from the past. The poem ends with rejoicing:

Now while the underling rises
All over the anguished earth;
Now at the parturient crisis
For civilization's birth;
Now—as the Bolsheviks din it,
When the Nazi's turn Red, kerpow;
Oh I'm glad to be living this minute,
Now—at this moment—now!
(ll. 41–48)

Writing from outside the American millennial narrative, Lewis abandons the anxiety and the disillusion that characterize both the jeremiad's resolute commitment to the national mission and the antijeremiad's totalizing despair.

Moreover, Lewis's rejection of symbolic for social analysis provides him with a concrete, radical prophetic imagery that Kreymborg and Rolfe lack. Because the revolutionary progress of Soviet Russia exists as a positive alternative to the dominant American narrative, Lewis can concretely illustrate a new and different future distinct from the vague allusions of his proletarian colleagues. Russia is "America's loud EXAMPLE-SONG" ("Example-Song" ll. 31), the "socialist outcome fully fed" (l. 12). The Soviet present—"That unified one sovereign throng" (l. 28)—becomes the American future. Moreover, Lewis frequently rearticulates traditional imagery, turning it on its head for his radical purposes. For instance, "One Bright Star" portrays a metaphoric journey similar to that in Rolfe's "Before the Hour," employing the familiar American imagery of pilgrimage. However, Lewis's pilgrimage intends to arrive at something more unambiguously revolutionary than a "greener shore," as the ship heads for

> One bright Star
> Agleam in the black,
> Through negative-war
> Through clouded attack;
> Lo, yonder assured,
> Not ever obscured,—
> One bright Star
> Of paeans unmoored.
> (ll. 10–17)

Here, the destination is clearly the postrevolutionary state already achieved by Soviet Russia, victimized by propaganda and symbolized by the single star in its flag.

The poetry of Kreymborg, Rolfe, and Lewis quoted in this essay is likely the first by these authors many readers have ever encountered. Their work is not widely available, they have received little critical attention, and they are seldom taught. Continued inattention to their work will only maintain the sanitized, largely depoliticized portrait of modern American literature that characterizes canonical narratives of literary history. Introducing proletarian poetry into these narratives and reading the great diversity of the movement's writers in dialogue with each other and with canonized modernist writers will, on the other hand, reveal much about the political complexities of modern literature, not the least of which is the ongoing cultural work of the Puritan jeremiad. Since the operations of cultural norms are often most powerfully evident on the margins of a culture, the study of proletarian literature can tell us much about the conservative political function of canonical discursive practices rooted in the jeremiad. Moreover, the critical fault lines separating mainstream and marginal proletarian literature can expose the extent to which critical Puritanism has governed and continues to govern American readers and critics. Reading writers like Lewis helps us to understand more completely the nature of that critical Puritanism and the voices it silences. That such Puritanism still dominates public dialogue about progress and change is attested to by our current president, who characterizes his agenda for change as "the New Covenant." Clinton's commitment to Puritan formulations of the revolutionary national mission should remind us of Earl Browder's willingness to equate cultural change with cultural renewal. Restoring writers like Lewis to our literary history will open up our cultural dialogue to voices that reject such formulations. In so doing, we will then be able both to acknowledge and to disrupt discursive practices that have determined the production and reception of social critique from the Puritan era to our own.

Notes

1. The mid-thirties, in addition to the publication of these two notable volumes, also saw the increased publication of proletarian novels; the occasion of the First American Writers' Congress in April 1935; the formation of the Book Union, a proletarian version of the Book-of-the-Month Club in October 1935; the first-time listing of "Proletarian Literature" as a distinct category in *The Year Book Review Digest* for 1935; the second edition of Hicks's *The Great Tradition*, with its new chapter on contemporary proletarian literature, in 1935; and the twenty-fifth anniversary number of *New Masses*, with its highest press run ever (100,000 copies), in December 1936.

2. In my analyses of the poetry quoted in this essay, I will generally identify the speaker as the poet. Such an identification is common to readings of explicitly political verse, especially that which is relatively polemical. I will distinguish between poet and speaker only in those poems with obviously metaphorical narrative structures. While I do not doubt that the political sympathies expressed in these poems are as personal as those of the former group, it seems nonetheless awkward to identify the speaker of a clearly fictional narrative as the poet.

3. Engel makes a similar observation. Surveying the three *Unrest* anthologies (1929–1931), which collected poems from the radical presses for each calendar year, he asserts that many "radical poets were carrying on . . . the tradition, stemming from the more idealistic of the Puritans, that America should be different and better" (46) and, further, that any "alleged radicalism" is simply "empathy with the individual as one's fellow sufferer" (45).

4. Given the potential power of Soviet Russia to disrupt the privileged symbol of America, critics such as Calmer sought to trivialize (not to mention stereotype) proletarian poetry as "a minor body of verse, dealing chiefly with the struggles of the working class abroad rather than on the native scene" (4). As a result of the inextricable relationship between the national mission and canonical discursive practices, the *Proletarian Literature* anthology—which Calmer co-edited—and the "Social Poets" number virtually ignore events in Russia, obscuring the wide range of poetry about that nation found in limited-circulation journals and the work of smaller presses.

Works Cited

Acton, William. *The Functions and Disorders of the Reproductive Organs in Childhood, Youth, Adult Age, and Advanced Life.* 4th Am. ed. Philadelphia: Lindsay and Blakiston, 1875.

Acuña, Rodolfo. *Occupied America: A History of Chicanos.* 2nd ed. New York: Harper, 1981.

Alexander, Michael. *The Poetic Achievement of Ezra Pound.* Berkeley: U of California P, 1979.

Allison, Alexander, et al. *The Norton Anthology of Poetry.* 3rd ed. New York: Norton, 1983.

Ammons, Elizabeth. *Edith Wharton's Argument with America.* Athens: U of Georgia P, 1980.

Anzaldúa, Gloria. *Borderlands/La Frontera: The New Mestiza.* San Francisco: Aunt Lute, 1987.

Apocalypse Now. Dir. Francis Ford Coppola. United Artists, 1979. Videotape: Paramount, 1987.

Auerbach, Erich. "*Figura.*" Trans. Ralph Manheim. *Scenes from the Drama of European Literature: Six Essays.* Minneapolis: U of Minnesota P, 1984, 11–76.

———. *Mimesis.* Trans. William R. Trask. Princeton: Princeton UP, 1974.

Awkward, Michael. *Inspiriting Influences: Tradition, Revision and Afro-American Women's Novels.* New York: Columbia UP, 1989.

Baker, Bruce P. "Before the Cruciform Tree: The Failure of Evangelical Protestantism." *Literature and Belief* 8 (1988): 14–26.

Baker, Carlos. *Ernest Hemingway: A Life Story.* New York: Scribner's, 1969.

Barker-Benfield, G. J. *The Horrors of the Half-Known Life: Male Attitudes Toward Women and Sexuality in Nineteenth-Century America.* New York: Harper, 1976.

Barton, Bruce. *The Man Nobody Knows: A Discovery of the Real Jesus.* Indianapolis: Bobbs-Merrill, 1925.

———. Rev. of *The Sun Also Rises* by Ernest Hemingway. *Atlantic Monthly* 139 (Apr. 1927): 12, 14.

Barton, William E. *The Autobiography of William E. Barton.* Introd. Bruce Barton. Indianapolis: Bobbs-Merrill, 1932.

Bauer, Dale Marie, and Andrew M. Lakritz. "*The Awakening* and the Woman Question." Koloski 47–52.

Baym, Nina. "Melodramas of Beset Manhood: How Theories of American Fiction Exclude Women Authors." *American Quarterly* 33 (1981): 123–39.

———. "Passion and Authority in *The Scarlett Letter.*" *New England Quarterly* 43 (1970): 209–30.

Bensick, Carol. "Preaching to the Choir: Some Achievements and Shortcomings of Taylor's *God's Determinations.*" *Early American Literature* 28.2 (1993): 133–47.

Benstock, Shari. *Women of the Left Bank: Paris, 1900–1940*. Austin: U of Texas P, 1986.

Bercovitch, Sacvan, ed. *The American Jeremiad*. Madison: U of Wisconsin P, 1978.

———. Introduction. *The American Puritan Imagination: Essays in Reevaluation*. New York: Cambridge UP, 1974, 1–16.

———. "The Ends of American Puritan Rhetoric." *The Ends of Rhetoric: History, Theory, Practice*. Ed. John Bender and David E. Wellbery. Stanford: Stanford UP, 1990. 171–90.

———. *The Office of* The Scarlet Letter. Baltimore: Johns Hopkins UP, 1991.

———. *The Puritan Origins of the American Self*. New Haven: Yale UP, 1975.

Bercovitch, Sacvan, and Myra Jehlen, eds. *Ideology and Classic American Literature*. New York: Cambridge UP, 1986.

Bernstein, Michael. *The Tale of the Tribe: Ezra Pound and the Modern Verse Epic*. Princeton: Princeton UP, 1980.

Berryman, John. "Changes." *Poets on Poetry*. Ed. Howard Nemerov. New York: Basic, 1966. 94–103.

———. *Homage to Mistress Bradstreet*. New York: Farrar, 1956.

———. "An Interview." *Harvard Advocate* 103 (Spring 1969): 5–9.

Berthoff, Warner. *The Example of Melville*. Princeton: Princeton UP, 1962.

Bishop, Elizabeth. *The Complete Poems, 1927–1979*. New York: Farrar, 1983.

Blackall, Jean. "Edith Wharton's Art of Ellipsis." *Journal of Narrative Technique* 17 (1987): 145–62.

Blasing, Mutlu Konuk. *American Poetry: The Rhetoric of Its Forms*. New Haven: Yale UP, 1987.

Bleser, Carol, ed. *In Joy and in Sorrow: Women, Family, and Marriage in the Victorian South, 1830–1900*. New York: Oxford UP, 1990.

Bloom, Harold. *Poetry and Repression: Revisionism from Blake to Stevens*. New Haven: Yale UP, 1976.

Bly, Robert. *Iron John: A Book About Men*. Reading, Mass.: Addison-Wesley, 1990.

———. *The Light Around the Body*. New York: Harper, 1967.

"Book Notices." *Bachelor of Arts* 2 (Mar. 1896): 570–72.

Book of Common Prayer. Oxford: Oxford UP, n.d.

Bordo, Susan R. *The Flight to Objectivity: Essays on Cartesianism and Culture*. Albany: State U of New York P, 1987.

Bourne, Randolph. "The Puritan's Will to Power." *History of a Literary Radical and Other Essays*. New York: Huebsch, 1920. 176–87.

Boyarin, Daniel. *Intertextuality and the Reading of Midrash*. Bloomington: Indiana UP, 1990.

Boyd, Lois A. "Shall Women Speak?" *The Journal of Presbyterian History* 56.4 (Winter 1978): 281–94.

Boyd, Lois A., and Douglas Brackenridge. *Presbyterian Women in America: Two Centuries of a Quest for Status*. Westport, Conn.: Greenwood, 1983.

Bradbury, Malcolm, and James McFarlane, eds. *Modernism: 1890–1930*. New York: Penguin, 1976.

Bradford, William. "Of Plymouth Plantation." P. Miller, *American* 5–20.

Bradstreet, Anne. *The Works of Anne Bradstreet*. Ed. and introd. by Jeannine Hensley. Cambridge: Harvard UP, 1967.

Breen, T. H. *Puritans and Adventurers: Change and Persistence in Early America*. New York: Oxford UP, 1980.

Breitwieser, Mitchell Robert. *Cotton Mather and Benjamin Franklin: The Price of Representative Personality*. New York: Cambridge UP, 1984.

Brennan, Joseph X. "*Ethan Frome*: Structure and Metaphor." *Modern Fiction Studies* 7 (1961–1962): 347–56.

Brooker, Jewel Spears. "Substitutes for Religion in the Early Poetry of T. S. Eliot." *The Placing of T. S. Eliot*. Ed. Jewel Spears Brooker. Columbia: U of Missouri P, 1991. 11–26.

Brooks, Cleanth. *The Hidden God: Studies in Hemingway, Faulkner, Yeats, Eliot, and Warren*. New Haven: Yale UP, 1963.

Brooks, Van Wyck. *The Wine of the Puritans: A Study of Present Day America*. London: Sisley's, 1908. New York: Mitchell Kennerley, 1909.

Bruffee, Kenneth A. *Elegiac Romance: Cultural Change and Loss of the Hero in Modern Fiction*. Ithaca: Cornell UP, 1983.

Brumm, Ursula. *American Thought and Religious Typology*. New Brunswick, N.J.: Rutgers UP, 1970.

Bugliosi, Vincent, and Curt Gentry. *Helter Skelter: The True Story of the Manson Murders*. New York: Norton, 1974.

Burke, Kenneth. *A Grammar of Motives*. Berkeley: U of California P, 1969.

———. *The Rhetoric of Religion*. Berkeley: U of California P, 1970.

Bush, Ronald. *T. S. Eliot: A Study in Character and Style*. New York: Oxford UP, 1985.

Calderón, Héctor, and José David Saldívar, eds. *Criticism in the Borderlands: Studies in Chicano Literature, Culture and Ideology*. Durham: Duke UP, 1991.

Calder, Angus. *T. S. Eliot*. Atlantic Heights, N.J.: Harvester, 1987.

Calmer, Alan. "Portrait of the Artist as a Proletarian." *Saturday Review of Literature* 31 (July 1937): 3–4, 14.

Calvin, John. *Institutes of the Christian Religion*. vol. 1. Trans. Henry Beveridge. Grand Rapids, Mich.: Eerdmans, 1983. 2 vols.

Canaday, John. *Mainstreams of Modern Art*. 2nd ed. New York: Holt, 1981.

Cather, Willa. *On Writing*. New York: Knopf, 1949.

———. *The Professor's House*. New York: Vintage, 1973.

———. *The World and the Parish: Willa Cather's Articles and Reviews, 1893–1902*. Ed. William H. Curtin. 2 vols. Lincoln: U of Nebraska P, 1970.

Chabram, Angie. "Conceptualizing Chicano Critical Discourse." Calderón and Saldívar 127–48.

Chapman, John Jay. "Emerson, Sixty Years After." *Atlantic Monthly* Jan. 1897: 27–41; Feb. 1897:222–40. Rpt in *Emerson and Other Essays*. New York: Scribner's, 1898.

Chase, Richard. *The American Novel and Its Tradition*. Garden City, N.Y.: Doubleday, 1957.

Chesnut, Mary Boykin. *A Diary from Dixie*. Ed. Ben Ames Williams. Cambridge: Harvard UP, 1980.

Chodorow, Nancy. *Feminism and Psychoanalytic Theory*. New Haven: Yale UP, 1989.

Chopin, Kate. *The Awakening: Case Studies in Contemporary Criticism*. Ed. Nancy A. Walker. New York: St. Martin's, 1993.

Church, Benjamin. *Entertaining Passages Relating to Philip's War*. Boston: B. Green, 1716.

Ciardi, John. "A Close Look at the Unicorn." *Saturday Review of Literature* 12 Jan. 1957: 54–57.

———. "The Reviewer's Duty to Damn: A Letter to an Avalanche." *Saturday Review of Literature* 16 Feb. 1957: 24–25, 54–55.

Clark, Suzanne. *Sentimental Modernism: Women Writers and the Revolution of the Word.* Bloomington: Indiana UP, 1991.

Clinton, Catherine. *The Plantation Mistress: Woman's World in the Old South.* New York: Pantheon, 1982.

Coale, Samuel Chase. *In Hawthorne's Shadow: American Romance from Melville to Mailer.* Lexington: UP of Kentucky, 1985.

Conrad, Joseph. *Heart of Darkness and The Secret Sharer.* New York: Signet, 1950.

Cookson, William. *A Guide to the Cantos of Ezra Pound.* New York: Persea, 1985.

Cousins, Norman. "Critic Under Fire." *Time Magazine* 18 Feb. 1957: 44–45.

Crowley, John. *The Mask of Fiction: Essays on W. D. Howells.* Amherst: U of Massachusetts P, 1989.

Culley, Margo, ed. *The Awakening.* 2nd ed. New York: Norton, 1994.

Daly, Robert. *God's Altar: The World and the Flesh in Puritan Poetry.* Berkeley: U of California P, 1978.

The Deer Hunter. Dir. Michael Cimino. EMI/Columbia/Warner, 1978.

Degler, Carl N. *At Odds: Women and the Family in America from the Revolution to the Present.* New York: Oxford UP, 1980.

Delbanco, Andrew. *The Puritan Ordeal.* Cambridge: Harvard UP, 1989.

DeShazer, Mary K. *Inspiring Women: Reimagining the Muse.* New York: Pergamon, 1986.

Dew, Charles B. *Ironmaker to the Confederacy: Joseph R. Anderson and the Tredegar Iron Works.* New Haven: Yale UP, 1966.

Dickinson, Emily. *The Poems of Emily Dickinson.* Ed. Thomas H. Johnson. 3 vols. Cambridge: Harvard UP, 1955.

———. *The Letters of Emily Dickinson.* Ed. Thomas H. Johnson and Theodora Ward. 3 vols. Cambridge: Harvard UP, 1958.

Dillard, Annie. *Pilgrim at Tinker Creek.* New York: Harper, 1988.

Donohue, Agnes. *Hawthorne: Calvin's Ironic Stepchild.* Kent, Ohio: Kent State UP, 1985.

Dos Passos, John. "Whither the American Writer: (A Questionnaire)." *Modern Quarterly* 6 (Summer 1932): 11–12.

Douglas, Ann. *The Feminization of American Culture.* New York: Avon, 1977.

Duke, Alastair, Gilliam Lewis, and Andrew Pettegree, eds. and trans. *Calvinism in Europe, 1540–1610: A Collection of Documents.* New York: St. Martin's, 1992.

Eagleton, Terry. *Literary Theory: An Introduction.* Minneapolis: U of Minnesota P, 1983.

Eakin, Paul John. *The New England Girl: Cultural Ideals in Hawthorne, Stowe, Howells and James.* Athens: U of Georgia P, 1976.

Edel, Leon. *Stuff of Sleep and Dreams: Experiments in Literary Psychology.* New York: Harper, 1982.

Edkins, Carol. "Quest for Community: Spiritual Autobiographies of Eighteenth-Century Quaker and Puritan Women in America." *Women's Autobiography: Essays in Criticism.* Ed. Estelle C. Jelinke. Bloomington: Indiana UP, 1980. 39–52.

Edwards, Jonathan. *Selected Writings of Jonathan Edwards.* Ed. Harold P. Simonson. New York: Ungar, 1970.

———. *The Works of Jonathan Edwards.* Ed. Perry Miller et al. 13 vols. to date. New Haven: Yale UP, 1957– .

Eggenschwiler, David. "The Ordered Disorder of *Ethan Frome.*" *Studies in the Novel* 9 (1977): 237–46.

Eliade, Mircea. *The Myth of the Eternal Return.* 1949. Trans. Willard R. Trask. New York: Pantheon, 1954.

Eliot, T. S. *After Strange Gods.* New York: Harcourt, 1934.

———. *The Complete Poems and Plays, 1909–1950.* New York: Harcourt, 1952.

———. "A Commentary." *Criterion* 2.7 (Apr. 1924): 231–35.

———. "A Commentary." *Criterion* 10.39 (Jan. 1931): 306–10.

———. "A Commentary." *Criterion* 6.2 (Aug. 1927): 97–100.

———. "A Commentary." *Criterion* 6.3 (Sept. 1927): 193–96.

———. "The Function of Criticism." *Criterion* 2.5 (Oct. 1923): 31–42.

———. "The Idea of a Literary Review." *Criterion* 4.1 (Jan. 1926): 1–6.

———. *The Letters of T. S. Eliot.* Ed. Valerie Eliot. Vol. 1. London: Faber, 1988. 1 vol. to date.

———. "Literature, Science, and Dogma." *The Dial* 82.3 (Mar. 1927): 239–43.

———. *For Launcelot Andrewes.* New York: Forum, 1928.

———. *Murder in the Cathedral.* New York: Harcourt, 1963.

———. *On Poetry and Poets.* London: Faber, 1957.

———. *The Sacred Wood.* London: Methuen, 1972.

———. *Selected Essays.* New York: Harcourt, 1964.

———. *Selected Prose of T. S. Eliot.* Ed. Frank Kermode. London: Faber, 1980.

———. *The Use of Poetry and the Use of Criticism.* Cambridge: Harvard UP, 1964.

Elliott, Emory, ed. *Puritan Influences in American Literature.* Chicago: U of Illinois P, 1979.

Ellmann, Richard, and Robert O'Clair, eds. *The Norton Anthology of Modern Poetry.* 2nd ed. New York: Norton, 1988.

Emerson, Ralph Waldo. *The Complete Works of Ralph Waldo Emerson.* Centenary ed. Ed. Edward Waldo Emerson. Boston: Houghton, 1903–30. 12 vols.

Engel, Bernard F. "The 'Unclassed' Rebel Poet." *Midwestern Miscellany* 17 (1989): 45–53.

Fetterley, Judith. *The Resisting Reader: A Feminist Approach to American Fiction.* Bloomington: Indiana UP, 1978.

Fiedler, Leslie. *Love and Death in the American Novel.* New York: Stein and Day, 1948.

Filson, John. *The Discovery, Settlement and Present State of Kentucke.* 1784. Rpt. as *The Discovery and Settlement of Kentucke.* Ann Arbor: University Microfilms, 1966.

Fitzgerald, F. Scott. *The Notebooks of F. Scott Fitzgerald.* Ed. Matthew J. Bruccoli. New York: Harcourt, 1978.

Forrer, Richard. *Theodices in Conflict: A Dilemma in Puritan Ethics and Nineteenth-Century American Literature.* New York: Greenwood, 1986.

Foucault, Michel. *Discipline and Punish: The Birth of the Prison.* 1975. New York: Vintage-Random, 1979.

Fox-Genovese, Elizabeth. *Within the Plantation Household: Black and White Women of the Old South.* Chapel Hill: U of North Carolina P, 1988.

Frazer, Sir James George. *The Golden Bough: A Study in Magic and Religion.* 3rd ed. 12 vols. New York: Macmillan, 1935.

Freeman, Joseph. Introduction. G. Hicks, et al. 9–28.

Friedman, Susan Stanford. "Creativity and the Childbirth Metaphor: Gender Difference in Literary Discourse." *Feminist Studies* 13.1 (1987): 49–82. Rpt. in *Speaking of Gender.* Ed. Elaine Showalter. New York: Routledge, 1989. 73–100.

Frost, Robert. *Collected Poems, Prose, and Plays*. Library of America Ser. New York: Penguin, 1995.

———. [Comments after "Desert Places."] *Robert Frost Reads His Poetry*. Caedmon, TC 1060, 1956.

Gelpi, Albert. *The Tenth Muse: The Psyche of the American Poet*. Cambridge: Harvard UP, 1975.

George, E. Laurie. "Women's Language in *The Awakening*." Koloski 53–59.

Gerstner, John A. *Jonathan Edwards: A Mini-Theology*. Wheaton, Ill.: Tyndale, 1987.

Gilbert, Sandra M. "The Second Coming of Aphrodite: Kate Chopin's Fantasy of Desire." *Kenyon Review* 5 (Summer 1983): 42–66.

Gilbert, Sandra M., and Susan Gubar. *The War of the Words*. New Haven: Yale UP, 1988. Vol. 1 of *No Man's Land: The Place of the Woman Writer in the Twentieth Century*. 3 vols.

Gilligan, Carol. *In a Different Voice: Psychological Theory and Women's Development*. Cambridge: Harvard UP, 1982.

Girgus, Sam B. *The New Covenant: Jewish Writers and the American Idea*. Chapel Hill: U of North Carolina P, 1984.

Glasgow, Ellen. *Barren Ground*. New York: Doubleday, 1925.

———. *The Battle-Ground*. New York: Doubleday, 1902.

———. *A Certain Measure: An Interpretation of Prose Fiction*. New York: Harcourt, 1943.

———. *The Descendant*. New York: Arno, 1977.

———. Ellen Glasgow Collection. Accession number 5060. Alderman Library, U. of Virginia, Charlottesville.

———. "'Evasive Idealism' in Literature: An Interview with Joyce Kilmer." Raper, *Ellen*, 122–28.

———. *In This Our Life*. New York: Harcourt, 1941.

———. Notebook 3. Ms., box 6. Ellen Glasgow Collection.

———. "The Novel in the South." Raper, *Ellen*, 68–83.

———. *They Stooped to Folly*. New York: Doubleday, 1929.

———. *Vein of Iron*. New York: Harcourt, 1935.

———. *Virginia*. New York: Doubleday, 1913.

———. *The Woman Within*. New York: Harcourt, 1954.

———. *The Woman Within*. Ms., boxes 5, 74. Ellen Glasgow Collection.

Godbold, E. Stanly, Jr. *Ellen Glasgow and the Woman Within*. Baton Rouge: Louisiana State UP, 1972.

Gold, Mike. "Towards Proletarian Art." *Mike Gold: A Literary Anthology*. Ed. Michael Folsom. New York: International, 1972, 62–70.

Goldensohn, Lori. *Elizabeth Bishop: The Biography of a Poetry*. New York: Columbia UP, 1992.

Goodman, Debra Joy. "The Scapegoat Motif in the Novels of Edith Wharton." Diss. U of New Hampshire. 1976.

Gordon, Lyndall. *Eliot's Early Years*. New York: Noonday, 1977.

———. *Eliot's New Life*. New York: Noonday, 1989.

Gordon, Marshall. *Presbyteries and Profits: Calvinism and the Development of Capitalism in Scotland, 1560–1707*. New York: Oxford UP, 1980.

Green, Robert W., ed. *Protestantism and Capitalism*. Boston: Heath, 1959.

Greenblatt, Stephen J. *Sir Walter Raleigh: The Renaissance Man and His Roles*. New Haven: Yale UP, 1973.

Gregory, Horace. "Prologue as Epilogue." *Poetry* 48.2 (1936): 92–98.

Greven, Philip. *The Protestant Temperament: Patterns of Child-Rearing, Religious Experience, and the Self in Early America*. New York: Knopf, 1977.

Griffin, Peter. *Along with Youth: Hemingway, the Early Years*. New York: Oxford UP, 1985.

Grimes, Larry E. *The Religious Design of Hemingway's Early Fiction*. Ann Arbor, Mich.: University Microfilms, 1985.

Groom, Winston, and Duncan Spencer. *Conversations with the Enemy: The Story of PFC Robert Garwood*. New York: Putnam, 1983.

Gura, Philip F. *A Glimpse of Sion's Glory: Puritan Radicalism in New England, 1620–1660*. Middletown, Conn.: Wesleyan UP, 1984.

Gusdorf, Georges. "Conditions and Limits of Autobiography." *Autobiography: Essays Theoretical and Critical*. Ed. James Olney. Princeton: Princeton UP, 1980. 28–48.

Guth, Hans, and Gabriele Rico, eds. *Discovering Poetry*. New York: Prentice-Hall, 1993.

Gwynn, A. S., ed. *Poetry: A HarperCollins Pocket Anthology*. New York: HarperCollins, 1993.

Haffenden, John. *John Berryman: A Critical Commentary*. New York: New York UP, 1980.

Haight, Roger. *The Experience and Language of Grace*. New York: Paulist, 1979.

Hall, David D. "Understanding the Puritans." *Essays in Politics and Social Development: Colonial America*. Ed. Stanley Katz. Boston: Little Brown, 1971. 32–50.

Hall, Donald, ed. *Contemporary American Poetry*. 2nd ed. New York: Penguin, 1972.

Haller, William. *The Rise of Puritanism*. New York: Harper, 1957.

Hamblen, Abigail Ann. "Edith Wharton in New England." *The New England Quarterly* 38 (1965): 239–44.

Handelman, Susan. *The Slayers of Moses: The Emergence of Rabbinic Interpretation in Literary Theory*. Albany: State U of New York P, 1982.

Hanneman, Audre. *Ernest Hemingway: A Comprehensive Bibliography*. Princeton: Princeton UP, 1967.

Hardon, John A. *Modern Catholic Dictionary*. Garden City, N.Y.: Doubleday, 1980.

Hardy, Thomas. *The Dynasts*. New York: St. Martin's, 1965.

Hass, Robert. *Praise*. New York: Ecco, 1979.

———. *Twentieth Century Pleasures: Prose on Poetry*. New York: Ecco, 1984.

Hawthorne, Nathaniel. "Anne Hutchinson." *Complete* 217–26.

———. "Chiefly About War Matters." *Complete* 299–345.

———. *The Complete Works of Nathaniel Hawthorne*. Vol. 12. Ed. George Parsons Lathrop. Boston: Houghton, 1882–1883. 13 vols.

———. *The Scarlet Letter*. Library of America Ser. New York: Literary Classics, 1990.

Hays, Peter L. "First and Last in *Ethan Frome*." *NMAL: Notes on Modern American Literature* 1 (1977): Item 15.

Hearts of Darkness: A Filmmaker's Apocalypse. Dir. Eleanor Coppola. Showtime, 1991.

Heimert, Alan, and Andrew Delbanco, eds. *The Puritans in America: A Narrative Anthology*. Cambridge: Harvard UP, 1985.

Hellmann, John. *American Myth and the Legacy of Vietnam*. New York: Columbia UP, 1986.

Hemingway, Ernest. *Across the River and Into the Trees*. New York: Scribner's, 1950.

———. *The Complete Short Stories of Ernest Hemingway*. Finca Vigía ed. New York: Scribner's, 1987.

———. *88 Poems*. Ed. Nicholas Georgiannis. New York: Harcourt, 1979.

———. *The Old Man and the Sea*. New York: Scribner's, 1952.

———. "Preface." *A Moveable Feast*. New York: Bantam, 1964. n. pag.

———. *Selected Letters, 1917–1961*. Ed. Carlos Baker. New York: Scribner's, 1981.

Herbert, George. "The Flower." *The Complete English Poems*. Ed. John Tobin. New York: Penguin, 1991. 156–57.

Herr, Michael. *Dispatches*. 1977. New York: Random-Vintage, 1991.

Hicks, Granville. *The Great Tradition: An Interpretation of American Literature Since the Civil War*. New York: Macmillan, 1933.

———, et al., eds. *Proletarian Literature in the United States: An Anthology*. New York: International, 1935.

Hoffman, Frederick J. *The Twenties: American Writing in the Postwar Decade*. 1955. New York: Free P, 1965.

Hogg, James. *The Private Memoirs and Confessions of a Justified Sinner*. 1824. London: Cresset, 1964.

Holden, Alan. "Anne Bradstreet Resurrected." *Concerning Poetry* 2 (1969): 11–18.

Hollander, John. "Observations on Moore's Syllabic Scheme." *Marianne Moore: The Art of a Modernist*. Ed. Joseph Parisi. Ann Arbor: University Microfilms, 1990. 83–102.

Homans, Margaret. *Women Writers and Poetic Identity: Dorothy Wordsworth, Emily Brontë, and Emily Dickinson*. Princeton: Princeton UP, 1980.

Hooker, Thomas. "The Application for Redemption." Heimert and Delbanco 177–78.

———. "The Soul's Preparation for Christ." Heimert and Delbanco 24–26.

Howard, Victor B. *Conscience and Slavery: The Evangelist Calvinist Domestic Missions, 1837–1861*. Kent, Ohio: Kent State UP, 1990.

Howe, Susan. *My Emily Dickinson*. Berkeley: North Atlantic, 1985.

Howells, William Dean. *April Hopes*. Introd. Kermit Vanderbilt. Bloomington: Indiana UP, 1974.

———. *Dr. Breen's Practice*. Boston: Osgood, 1881.

———. "Editor's Study." *Harper's Magazine* 72 (1886): 972–76; 73 (1886): 475–80; 75 (1887): 476–80; 77 (1888): 476–80; 79 (1889): 314–19.

———. *Heroines of Fiction*. 2 vols. New York: Harper, 1901.

———. *An Imperative Duty*. Introd. Martha Banta. Bloomington: Indiana UP, 1970.

———. *The Lady of the Aroostook*. Boston: Houghton, 1879.

———. *Literary Friends and Acquaintance: A Personal Retrospect of American Authorship*. Ed. David F. Hiatt and Edwin H. Cady. Bloomington: Indiana UP, 1968.

———. *The Minister's Charge, or the Apprenticeship of Lemuel Barker*. Introd. Howard M. Munford. Bloomington: Indiana UP, 1978.

———. *A Modern Instance*. Introd. George N. Bennett. Bloomington: Indiana UP, 1977.

———. *My Literary Passions*. 1895. New York: Kraus, 1968.

———. "A Psychological Counter-current in Recent Fiction." *North American Review* 173 (1901): 872–88.

———. "Puritanism in American Fiction." *Literature and Life*. New York: Harper, 1902. 278–83.

———. *The Quality of Mercy*. Introd. James P. Elliot. Bloomington: Indiana UP, 1979.

———. Rev. of *A Compendious History of New England*, by J. G. Palfrey. Vols. 3, 4. *Atlantic Monthly* 30 (1872): 621–24; 31 (1873): 743–46.

———. *The Rise of Silas Lapham*. Introd. Martha Banta. Bloomington: Indiana UP, 1971.

———. *The Shadow of a Dream*. Introd. Martha Banta. Bloomington: Indiana UP, 1970.

———. *The Son of Royal Langbrith*. Introd. David Burrows. Bloomington: Indiana UP, 1969.

———. *Through the Eye of the Needle. Altrurian Romances*. Introd. Clara Kirk and Rudolf Kirk. Bloomington: Indiana UP, 1968.

———. *The Vacation of the Kelwyns: An Idyll of the Middle Eighteen-Seventies*. New York: Harper, 1920.

Hughes, Walter. " 'Meat Out of the Eater': Panic and Desire in American Puritan Poetry." *Engendering Men: The Question of Male Feminist Criticism*. Ed. Joseph A. Boone and Michael Cadden. New York: Routledge, 1990. 102–21.

Hutchinson, William R. *The Modernist Impulse in American Protestantism*. Cambridge: Harvard UP, 1976.

Isabelle, Julanne. *Hemingway's Religious Experience*. New York: Vantage, 1964.

James, Henry. *The Letters of Henry James*. Ed. Percy Lubbock. Vol. 1. New York: Scribner's, 1920. 100–102. 2 vols.

———. *Theory of Fiction*. Ed. James E. Miller, Jr. Lincoln: U of Nebraska P, 1972.

James, William. *The Varieties of Religious Experience: A Study in Human Nature*. New York: Modern Library, 1902.

Jardine, Alice. *Gynesis: Configurations of Woman and Modernity*. Ithaca: Cornell UP, 1985.

Johnson, Barbara. *A World of Difference*. Baltimore: Johns Hopkins UP, 1987.

Johnson, Carol. "John Berryman and Mistress Bradstreet: A Relation of Reason." *Essays in Criticism* 14 (1964): 338–96.

Johnston, Kenneth. "Hemingway's Search for Story Titles." *Hemingway Review* 6 (1987): 34–37.

Jones, Bessie W. "An Interview with Toni Morrison." *The World of Toni Morrison*. Ed. Bessie W. Jones and Audrey L. Vinson. Dubuque, Ia.: Randall/Hunt, 1985. 127–51.

Jones, Ernest. *The Life and Work of Sigmund Freud*. Vol. 3. New York: Basic, 1953.

Jones, Jacqueline. *Labor of Love, Labor of Sorrow: Black Women, Work, and the Family from Slavery to Present*. New York: Basic, 1985.

Just, Ward. "Vietnam: The Camera Lies." *Atlantic Monthly* Dec. 1979: 63–65.

Kalstone, David. *Becoming a Poet: Elizabeth Bishop with Marianne Moore and Robert Lowell*. Ed. Robert Hemenway. Afterword James Merrill. New York: Farrar, 1989.

Kaplan, Amy. "Romancing the Empire: The Embodiment of American Masculinity in the Popular Historical Novel of the 1890's." *American Literary History* 2 (1990): 659–90.

Kappel, Andrew J. "Notes on the Presbyterian Poetry of Marianne Moore." *Marianne Moore: Woman and Poet*. Ed. Patricia C. Willis. Orono, Me.: National Poetry Foundation, 1990. 39–51.

Karlsen, Carol F. *The Devil in the Shape of a Woman: Witchcraft in Colonial New England*. New York: Norton, 1987.

Keefer, Michael H. "Accommodation and Synecdoche: Calvin's God in *King Lear*." *Shakespeare Studies: An Annual Gathering of Research, Criticism, and Reviews.* Vol. 20. Ed. J. Leeds Barroll. 23 vols. to date. New York: Franklin, 1988. 147–68. 1965– .

Keller, Karl. *The Only Kangaroo Among the Beauty: Emily Dickinson and America.* Baltimore: Johns Hopkins UP, 1979.

Kemp, John C. *Robert Frost and New England: The Poet as Regionalist.* Princeton: Princeton UP, 1979.

Kenner, Hugh. *A Homemade World: The American Modernist Writers.* New York: Morrow, 1975.

———. *The Pound Era.* Berkeley: U of California P, 1971.

Kermode, Frank. *The Genesis of Secrecy: On the Interpretation of Narrative.* Cambridge: Harvard UP, 1979.

———. *The Sense of an Ending: Studies in the Theory of Fiction.* New York: Oxford UP, 1967.

Kibbey, Ann. *The Interpretation of Material Shapes in Puritanism.* New York: Cambridge UP, 1986.

Kierkegaard, Søren. *The Concept of Dread.* Trans., introd., and notes by Walter Lowrie. Princeton: Princeton UP, 1941.

Klein, Melanie. *Love, Guilt, and Reparation and Other Works, 1921–1945.* New York: Doubleday, 1977.

Kolodny, Annette. *The Land Before Her: Fantasy and Experience of the American Frontiers, 1630–1860.* Chapel Hill: U of North Carolina P, 1984.

Koloski, Bernard, ed. *Approaches to Teaching Chopin's* The Awakening. New York: Modern Language Association, 1988.

Kouidis, Virginia M. "Prison into Prism: Emerson's 'Many-Colored Lenses' and the Woman Writer of Early Modernism." *The Green American Tradition: Essays and Poems for Sherman Paul.* Ed. H. Daniel Peck. Baton Rouge: Louisiana State UP, 1989, 115–34.

Kreymborg, Alfred. "American Jeremiad." Hicks et al. 171.

Lacan, Jacques. *Écrits: A Selection.* Trans. Alan Sheridan. New York: Norton, 1977.

LaFeber, Walter. *The New Empire: An Interpretation of American Expansion, 1860–1898.* Ithaca: Cornell UP, 1963.

LaHaye, Beverly. *The Spirit-Controlled Woman.* Eugene, Ore.: Harvest, 1976.

Laing, R. D. *The Politics of the Family and Other Essays.* New York: Pantheon, 1969.

———. *Self and Others.* Harmondsworth, England: Penguin, 1971.

Lanham, Richard A. *A Handlist of Rhetorical Terms.* Berkeley: U of California P, 1968.

Lang, Amy Schrager. *Prophetic Woman: Anne Hutchinson and the Problem of Dissent in the Literature of New England.* Berkeley: U of California P, 1987.

Lawler, Justus George. *Celestial Pantomime: Poetic Structures of Transcendence.* New Haven: Yale UP, 1979.

Leach, Nancy R. "New England in the Stories of Edith Wharton." *The New England Quarterly* 30 (1957): 90–98.

Lears, T. J. Jackson. *No Place of Grace: Antimodernism and the Transformation of American Culture, 1880–1920.* New York: Pantheon, 1981.

Levinas, Emmanuel. *Difficult Freedom: Essays on Judaism.* Baltimore: Johns Hopkins UP, 1990.

Levine, Philip. *A Walk With Tom Jefferson: Poems.* New York: Knopf, 1988.

Lewis, H. H. *The Road to Utterly.* Holt, Minn.: Hagglund, 1932.

———. *Thinking of Russia*. Holt, Minn.: Hagglund, 1932.

Lewis, R. W. B. *The American Adam: Innocence, Tragedy, and Tradition in the Nineteenth Century*. Chicago: U of Chicago P, 1955.

———. *Edith Wharton: A Biography*. New York: Random, 1975.

Lindbergh, Anne Morrow. *War Within and Without: Diaries and Letters of Anne Morrow Lindbergh, 1939–1944*. New York: Harcourt, 1980.

Lowance, Mason I., Jr. *The Language of Canaan: Metaphor and Symbol in New England from the Puritans to the Transcendentalists*. Cambridge: Harvard UP, 1980.

Lukács, Georg. *The Theory of the Novel*. Trans. Anna Bostock. Cambridge: Massachusetts Institute of Technology P, 1971.

Lynn, Kenneth S. *Hemingway*. New York: Simon and Schuster, 1987.

Mancini, Joseph, Jr. "John Berryman's Couvade Consciousness: An Approach to His Aesthetics." *Recovering Berryman: Essays on a Poet*. Ed. Richard J. Kelly and Allan K. Lathrop. Ann Arbor: U of Michigan P, 1993. 169–78.

Marcus, Greil. "Journey Up the River: An Interview with Francis Ford Coppola." *Rolling Stone* 1 Nov. 1979: 51–57.

Marti-Ibañez, Felix. *Centaur: Essays on the History of Medical Ideas*. New York: MD Publications, 1958.

Martin, Wendy. *An American Triptych: Anne Bradstreet, Emily Dickinson, Adrienne Rich*. Chapel Hill: U of North Carolina P, 1984.

Mason, Mary Grimley. Introduction. *Journeys: Autobiographical Writings by Women*. Ed. Mary Grimley Mason and Carol Hurd Green. Boston: Hall, 1979. xiii–xv.

May, Henry Farnham. *Ideas, Faiths, and Feelings: Essays on American Intellectual and Religious History*. New York: Oxford UP, 1964.

Mazzaro, Jerome. *Postmodern American Poetry*. Urbana: U of Illinois P, 1980.

McDowell, Deborah E. "Negotiating Between Tenses: Witnessing Slavery After Freedom—*Dessa Rose*." *Slavery and the Literary Imagination*. Ed. Deborah E. McDowell and Arnold Rampersad. Baltimore: Johns Hopkins UP, 1989. 144–63.

McGrath, Alister E. *A Life of John Calvin: A Study in the Shaping of Western Culture*. Oxford: Blackwell, 1990.

Melling, Philip H. *Vietnam in American Literature*. Boston: Twayne, 1992.

Mellow, James R. *Hemingway: Life Without Consequences*. Boston: Houghton, 1992.

Mencken, H. L. "Puritanism as a Literary Force." *A Book of Prefaces*. New York: Knopf, 1917.

Merrin, Jeredith. *An Enabling Humility: Marianne Moore, Elizabeth Bishop, and the Uses of Tradition*. New Brunswick, N.J.: Rutgers UP, 1990.

Meyers, Jeffrey. *Hemingway: A Biography*. New York: Harper, 1985.

Miller, Perry, ed. *The American Puritans: Their Prose and Poetry*. Garden City, N.Y.: Anchor, 1956.

———. *Errand into the Wilderness*. Cambridge: Harvard UP, 1956.

———. *Jonathan Edwards*. New York: William Sloane, 1949.

———. *The Life of the Mind in America: From the Revolution to the Civil War*. New York: Harcourt, 1965.

———. *The New England Mind: From Colony to Province*. 1953. Boston: Beacon, 1961.

———. *The New England Mind: The Seventeenth Century*. New York: Macmillan, 1939.

———, ed. *The Transcendentalists: An Anthology*. Cambridge: Harvard UP, 1950.

Miller, Perry, and Thomas H. Johnson, eds. Introduction. *The Puritans*. Rev. ed. Vol. 1. New York: Harper, 1963. 1–79. 2 vols.

Millier, Brett C. *Elizabeth Bishop: Life and the Memory of It*. Berkeley: University of California P, 1993.

Milton, John. *The Complete Poetry of John Milton*. Ed. John T. Shawcross. Garden City, NY: Anchor, 1971.

Modleski, Tania. *Feminism Without Women: Culture and Criticism in a "Post-Feminist" Age*. New York: Routledge, 1991.

Molesworth, Charles. *Marianne Moore: A Literary Life*. New York: Athenaeum, 1990.

Monteiro, George. "Ernest Hemingway, Psalmist." *Journal of Modern Literature* 14 (Summer 1987): 83–95.

———. "Hemingway's Christmas Carol." *Fitzgerald/Hemingway Annual, 1972*. Ed. Matthew J. Bruccoli and C. E. Frazer Clark, Jr. Englewood, Colo.: NCR Microcard, 1973–1976. 207–13.

———. "Santiago, DiMaggio, and Hemingway: The Aging Professionals of *The Old Man and the Sea*," *Fitzgerald/Hemingway Annual, 1975*. Ed. Matthew J. Bruccoli and C. E. Frazer Clark, Jr. Englewood, Colo.: NCR Microcard, 1976. 273–80.

Montgomery, Edrene S. "Bruce Barton's *The Man Nobody Knows*: A Popular Advertising Illusion." *Journal of Popular Culture* 19 (Winter 1985): 21–34.

Moore, Marianne. *The Complete Poems of Marianne Moore*. New York: Viking, 1981.

———. *The Complete Prose of Marianne Moore*. Ed. Patricia C. Willis. New York: Viking Penguin, 1986.

———. *Moore Family Letters*. The Rosenbach Museum & Library. VI:11b:10.

Moore, Mary Warner. [copied note]. *The Marianne Moore Newsletter* 4.1 (Spring 1980): 13.

Morgan, Edmund S. *The Puritan Family: Religion and Domestic Relations in Seventeenth-Century New England*. New York: Harper, 1965.

———. *Visible Saints: The History of a Puritan Idea*. Ithaca: Cornell UP, 1965.

Morrison, Toni. *Beloved*. New York: Plume, 1987.

———. *Playing in the Dark: Whiteness and the Literary Imagination*. Cambridge: Harvard UP, 1992.

———. "Unspeakable Things Unspoken: The Afro-American Presence in American Literature." *Michigan Quarterly Review* 28 (1989): 9–34. Rpt. in *Toni Morrison*. Ed. Harold Bloom. Modern Critical Views. New York: Chelsea, 1990. 201–30.

Morton, Thomas. *New English Canaan*. 1637. Ed. Charles Francis Adams, Jr. 1883. Burt Franklin Research and Source Works Ser. 131. New York: Burt Franklin, 1967.

Mulvey, Laura. *Visual and Other Pleasures*. Bloomington: Indiana UP, 1989.

Murad, Orlene. "Edith Wharton and *Ethan Frome*." *Modern Language Studies* 13 (1983): 90–103.

Nash, Roderick. *Wilderness and the American Mind*. 3rd ed. New Haven: Yale UP, 1982.

Nelson, Cary. *Repression and Recovery: Modern American Poetry and the Politics of Cultural Memory, 1910–1945*. Madison: U of Wisconsin P, 1989.

New, Elisa. *The Regenerate Lyric: Theology and Innovation in American Poetry*. New York: Cambridge UP, 1993.

Nims, John Frederick, ed. *Western Wind: An Introduction to Poetry*. 3rd ed. New York: McGraw, 1992.

Norton, John. *Abel Being Dead Yet Speaketh*. Heimert and Delbanco 211–17.

Olney, James. "The Ontology of Autobiography." *Autobiography: Essays Theoretical and Critical.* Ed. James Olney. Princeton: Princeton UP, 1980. 236-67.

Ong, Walter J. *In the Human Grain: Further Explorations of Contemporary Culture,* New York: Macmillan, 1967.

Ostriker, Alicia Suskin. *Stealing the Language: The Emergence of Women's Poetry in America.* Boston: Beacon, 1986.

Otten, Terry. *The Crime of Innocence in the Fiction of Toni Morrison.* Columbia: U of Missouri P, 1989.

Pahl, Jon. *Paradox Lost: Free Will and Political Liberty in American Culture, 1630-1970.* Baltimore: Johns Hopkins UP, 1992.

Parker, Dorothy. "A Book of Great Short Stories." *New Yorker* 29 Oct. 1927: 92-94.

Patterson, David. Introduction. *My Confession.* By Leo Tolstoy. New York: Norton, 1983. 5-9.

Pearce, Roy Harvey. *The Continuity of American Poetry.* Princeton: Princeton UP, 1961.

———. *Savagism and Civilization: A Study of the Indian and the American Mind.* 1965. Baltimore: Johns Hopkins UP, 1967.

Pelikan, Jaroslav. *Reformation of Church and Dogma (1300-1700).* Chicago: U of Chicago P, 1984.

Pérez-Torres, Raphael. *Movements in Chicano Poetry: Against Myths, Against Margins.* New York: Cambridge UP, 1995.

Penfield, Janet Harbinson. "Women in the Presbyterian Church-an Historical Overview." *Journal of Presbyterian History* 55 (Summer 1977): 107-24.

Pettit, Norman. *The Heart Prepared: Grace and Conversion in Puritan Spiritual Life.* 1966. Middletown, Conn.: Wesleyan UP, 1989.

Phillips, William and Philip Rahv. "Private Experience and Public Philosophy." *Poetry* 48.2 (1936): 98-105.

Porter, David. "Emily Dickinson: The Poetics of Doubt." *Emerson Society Quarterly* 60 (Summer 1970): 86-93.

Pound, Ezra. *ABC of Reading.* New York: New Directions, 1960.

———. *The Cantos.* New York: New Directions, 1981.

———. *Collected Early Poems of Ezra Pound.* Ed. Michael John King. New York: New Directions, 1976.

———. *Gaudier-Brzeska: A Memoir.* New York: New Directions, 1970.

———. *Guide to Kulchur.* New York: New Directions, 1970.

———. *Literary Essays.* Ed. T. S. Eliot. New York: New Directions, 1968.

———. *Make It New: Essays.* London: Faber, 1934.

———. *Selected Letters of Ezra Pound, 1907-1941.* Ed. D. D. Paige. New York: New Directions, 1971.

———. *Selected Prose, 1909-1965.* Ed. William Cookson. New York: New Directions, 1975.

Prioleau, Elizabeth Stevens. *The Circle of Eros: Sexuality in the Work of William Dean Howells.* Durham: Duke UP, 1983.

Provost, Sarah. "Erato's Fool and Bitter Sister: Two Aspects of John Berryman." *Twentieth Century Literature* 30 (Spring 1984): 69-79.

Rahner, Karl. "Man as the Event of God's Free and Forgiving Self-Communication." *Foundations of Christian Faith: An Introduction to the Idea of Christianity.* Trans. William V. Dych. New York: Seabury, 1989. 116-37.

Ransom, John Crowe. "Characters and Character: A Note on Fiction." *American Review* 6 (1936): 271-88.

Raper, Julius Rowan, ed. *Ellen Glasgow's Reasonable Doubts: A Collection of Her Writings*. Baton Rouge: Louisiana State UP, 1988.

———. *From the Sunken Garden: The Fiction of Ellen Glasgow, 1916–1945*. Baton Rouge: Louisiana State UP, 1980.

Read, Herbert, ed. and introd. "Notes on Language and Style." By T. E. Hulme. *Criterion*. 3.12 (July 1925): 485.

Reising, Russell. *The Unusable Past: Theory and the Study of American Literature*. New York: Methuen, 1986.

Reynolds, David S. *Beneath the American Renaissance: The Subversive Imagination in the Age of Emerson and Melville*. Cambridge: Harvard UP, 1989.

Reynolds, Michael S. *The Young Hemingway*. Oxford: Basil Blackwell, 1986.

Rich, Adrienne. "Anne Bradstreet and Her Poetry." Bradstreet ix–xxi.

Rigney, Barbara Hill. *The Voices of Toni Morrison*. Columbus: Ohio State UP, 1991.

Robinson, Douglas. *The Translator's Turn*. Baltimore: Johns Hopkins UP, 1991.

Rolfe, Edwin. "Before the Hour." *Poetry* 48.2 (1936): 61–63.

Rose, Alan Henry. " 'Such Depths of Sad Initiation': Edith Wharton and New England." *The New England Quarterly* 50 (1977): 423–39.

Rose, Phyllis. "Modernism: The Case of Willa Cather." *Modernism Reconsidered*. Ed. Robert Kiely. Cambridge: Harvard UP, 1983. 123–45.

Rosen, David. *The Changing Fictions of Masculinity*. Urbana: U of Illinois P, 1993.

Rosenmeier, Jesper. "To Keep in Memory: The Poetry of Edward Johnson." P. White 158–74.

Rosenwald, Lawrence. "*Voces Clamantium in Deserto*: Latin Verse of the Puritans." P. White 303–17.

Rothenberg, Jerome, ed. *Technicians of the Sacred: A Range of Poetries from Africa, America, Asia, and Oceania*. Garden City, N.Y.: Anchor, 1969.

Rothman, Ellen K. *Hands and Hearts: A History of Courtship in America*. New York: Basic, 1984.

Rotundo, E. Anthony. *Manhood: Transformations of Masculinity from the Revolution to the Modern Era*. New York: Basic, 1993.

Rowe, Karen E. "Prophetic Visions: Typology and Colonial American Poetry." P. White 47–66.

———. *Saint and Singer: Edward Taylor's Typology and the Poetics of Meditation*. New York: Cambridge UP, 1986.

Rowlandson, Mary. "A Narrative of the Captivity and Restoration of Mary Rowlandson." Slotkin and Folsom. 315–69.

Rutman, Darrett B. *American Puritanism: Faith and Practice*. New York: Norton, 1970.

Sánchez, Rosaura. "Ideological Discourses in Arturo Islas's *The Rain God*." Calderón and Saldívar 14–26.

Santayana, George. "The Genteel Tradition in American Philosophy." *University of California Chronicle* 13 (1911): 357–80. Rpt. in *Winds of Doctrine: Studies in Contemporary Opinion*. 1913. New York: Scribner's, 1926. 186–215.

Scheick, William J. *Design in Puritan American Literature*. Lexington: UP of Kentucky, 1992.

Schneidau, Herbert N. *Ezra Pound: The Image and the Real*. Baton Rouge: Louisiana State UP, 1969.

Schneider, Daniel J. *Symbolism: The Manichean Vision: A Study in the Art of James, Conrad, Woolf, and Stevens*. Lincoln: U of Nebraska P, 1975.

Schneider, Isidor. "Proletarian Poetry." *American Writers' Congress*. Ed. Henry Hart. New York: International, 1935.

Schroeter, James. "Willa Cather and *The Professor's House.*" *Willa Cather and Her Critics.* Ed. James Schroeter. Ithaca: Cornell UP, 1967. 363–81.

Schwartz, Delmore. "The Present State of Poetry." *The Selected Essays of Delmore Schwartz.* Ed. Donald A. Dike and David H. Zucker. Chicago: U of Chicago P, 1977. 30–50.

Schwartz, Joseph. "Three Aspects of Hawthorne's Puritanism." *New England Quarterly* 36 (June 1963): 192–208. Rpt. in *Twentieth-Century Interpretations of* The Scarlet Letter. Ed. John C. Gerber. Englewood Cliffs, N.J.: Prentice-Hall, 1968. 34–47.

Schweik, Susan M. *A Gulf So Deeply Cut: American Women Poets and the Second World War.* Madison: U of Wisconsin P, 1991.

Schweitzer, Ivy. "Maternal Discourse and the Romance of Self-Possession in Kate Chopin's *The Awakening.*" *Boundary* 2.17 (Spring 1990): 158–86.

———. *The Work of Self-Representation: Lyric Poetry in Colonial New England.* Chapel Hill: U of North Carolina P, 1991.

Scott, Anne Firor. *The Southern Lady from Pedestal to Politics, 1830–1930.* Chicago: U of Chicago P, 1970.

Scott, R. B. Y., ed. and trans. *Proverbs and Ecclesiastes.* Vol. 18 of *The Anchor Bible.* Garden City, N.Y.: Doubleday, 1979.

Seaver, Edwin. "Socialist Realism." *New Masses* 23 (Oct. 1935): 23–24.

Sergeant, Elizabeth Shepley. "Idealized New England." *New Republic* 8 May 1915: 20–21.

Showalter, Elaine. "Tradition and the Female Talent: *The Awakening* as a Solitary Book." Chopin 169–89.

Shurr, William H. *Rappaccini's Children: American Writers in a Calvinist World.* Lexington: UP of Kentucky, 1981.

Simpson, Eileen. *Poets in Their Youth.* New York: Random, 1982.

Singley, Carol J. *Edith Wharton: Matters of Mind and Spirit.* New York: Cambridge UP, 1995.

Singley, Carol J. and Susan Elizabeth Sweeney. "Forbidden Reading and Ghostly Writing: Anxious Power in Wharton's 'Pomegranate Seed.'" *Women's Studies* 20 (1991): 177–203. Rpt. in *Anxious Power: Reading, Writing, and Ambivalence in Narrative by Women.* Ed. Carol J. Singley and Susan Elizabeth Sweeney. Albany: State U of New York P, 1993. 197–217.

Slotkin, Richard. *Regeneration Through Violence: The Mythology of the American Frontier, 1600–1860.* Middletown, Conn.: Wesleyan UP, 1973.

Slotkin, Richard, and James K. Folsom, eds. *So Dreadfull a Judgment: Puritan Responses to King Philip's War, 1676–1677.* Middletown, Conn.: Wesleyan UP, 1978.

Smith, Allan Gardner. "Edith Wharton and the Ghost Story." *Gender and Literary Voice.* Ed. Janet Todd. Women and Literature New Ser. 1. New York: Holmes, 1980. 149–59.

Smith, Chard Powers. *Yankees and God.* New York: Hermitage, 1954.

Smith, Henry Nash. *Virgin Land: The American West as Symbol and Myth.* Rev. ed. Cambridge: Harvard UP, 1970.

Smith, Paul. *A Reader's Guide to the Short Stories of Ernest Hemingway.* Boston: Hall, 1989.

Smith-Rosenberg, Carroll. *Disorderly Conduct: Visions of Gender in Victorian America.* New York: Knopf, 1985.

———. "The Female World of Love and Ritual: Relations Between Women in

Nineteenth-Century America." *Signs: Journal of Women in Culture and Society* 1 (1975): 1–29.

Snyder, Gary. *Earth House Hold: Technical Notes and Queries to Fellow Dharma Revolutionaries.* New York: New Directions, 1969.

Sontag, Susan. *Styles of Radical Will.* 1969. New York: Farrar, 1987.

Soto, Gary. *Home Course in Religion: New Poems.* San Francisco: Chronicle, 1991.

Spangler, George. "The Shadow of a Dream: Howell's Homosexual Tragedy." *American Quarterly* 23 (1971): 110–19.

Spenser, Luke. "Mistress Bradstreet and Mr. Berryman: The Ultimate Seduction." *American Literature* 66 (June 1994): 353–66.

Spivak, Gayatri Chakravorty. "Displacement and the Discourse of Woman." *Displacement: Derrida and After.* Ed. Mark Krupnick. Bloomington: Indiana UP, 1983. 169–96.

St. Armand, Barton Levi. *Emily Dickinson and Her Culture: The Soul's Society.* New York: Cambridge UP, 1984.

Stafford, William. *Traveling Through the Dark.* New York: Harper, 1962.

Stead, C. K. *Pound, Yeats, Eliot and the Modernist Movement.* New Brunswick, N.J.: Rutgers UP, 1986.

Steele, David N., and Curtis C. Thomas. *The Five Points of Calvinism Defined, Defended, Documented.* Philadelphia: Presbyterian and Reformed, 1975.

Stephens, Robert O., ed. *Ernest Hemingway: The Critical Reception.* New York: Burt Franklin, 1977.

Stern, Gerald. *Lucky Life.* Boston: Houghton, 1977.

Stevens, Wallace. *The Palm at the End of the Mind: Selected Poems and a Play.* Ed. Holly Stevens. New York: Vintage, 1972.

Stewart, Randall. *American Literature and Christian Doctrine.* Baton Rouge: Louisiana State UP, 1958.

Stitt, Peter A. "The Art of Poetry XVI." *Paris Review* 53 (1972): 177–207.

Storr, Anthony. *Solitude: A Return to the Self.* New York: Free, 1988.

Stouck, David. "Willa Cather and the Russians." *Cather Studies 1.* Ed. Susan J. Rosowski. Lincoln: U of Nebraska P, 1990. 1–20.

Strand, Mark, ed. *The Contemporary American Poets: American Poetry Since 1940.* New York: Mentor, 1971.

Straumann, Heinrich. *American Literature in the Twentieth Century.* 3rd ed. New York: Harper, 1965.

Suleiman, Susan. "Writing and Motherhood." *The (M)other Tongue: Essays in Feminist Psychoanalytic Interpretation.* Ed. Shirley Nelson Garner, Claire Kahane, and Madelon Sprengnether. Ithaca: Cornell UP, 1985. 352–77.

Susman, Warren I. *Culture as History: The Transformation of American Society in the Twentieth Century.* New York: Pantheon, 1984.

Takaki, Ronald. *A Different Mirror: A History of Multicultural America.* Boston: Little, 1993.

Tawney, H. R. Introduction. Weber 1–11.

Taylor, Edward. *The Poems of Edward Taylor.* Ed. Donald S. Stanford. New Haven: Yale UP, 1960.

Teresa of Avila. *Interior Castle.* Trans. E. Allison Peers. Garden City, N.Y.: Doubleday, 1961.

Thickstun, Margaret Olofson. *Fictions of the Feminine: Puritan Doctrine and the Representation of Women.* Ithaca: Cornell UP, 1988.

Tichi, Cecelia. *Shifting Gears: Technology, Literature, Culture in Modernist America.* Chapel Hill: U of North Carolina P, 1987.

Tolstoy, Leo N. *My Confession* Ed. Nathan H. Dole. *Complete Works of Lyof N. Tolstoi.* Vol. 9. New York: Wheeler, 1898. 24 vols.

Tomasulo, Frank P. "The Politics of Ambivalence: *Apocalypse Now* as Prowar and Antiwar Film." *From Hanoi to Hollywood: The Vietnam War in American Film.* Ed. Linda Dittmar and Gene Michaud. New Brunswick, N.J.: Rutgers UP, 1990. 140–58.

Tompkins, Jane. *Sensational Designs: The Cultural Work of American Fiction, 1790–1860.* New York: Oxford UP, 1985.

Trench, Richard Chenevix. *Notes on the Parables of Our Lord.* New York: Appleton, 1855.

Turner, James. *Without God, Without Creed: The Origins of Unbelief in America.* Baltimore: Johns Hopkins UP, 1985.

TuSmith, Bonnie. *All My Relatives: Community in Contemporary American Ethnic Literature.* Ann Arbor: U of Michigan P, 1993.

Tyler, William Royall. Personal interview. 25 April 1990.

Urgo, Joseph R. "A Prologue to Rebellion: *The Awakening* and the Habit of Self-Expression." *SLQ* 20 (1987/88): 22–32.

Vendler, Helen. "Marianne Moore." *A Part of Nature A Part of Us: Modern American Poets.* Cambridge: Harvard UP, 1980. Rpt. in *Marianne Moore.* Ed. Harold Bloom. Modern Critical Views. New York: Chelsea, 1987. 73–88.

Waggoner, Hyatt. *American Poets from the Puritans to the Present.* Boston: Houghton, 1968.

Wagner-Martin, Linda. *Ellen Glasgow: Beyond Convention.* Austin: U of Texas P, 1982.

Walsh, John Evangelist. *Into My Own: The English Years of Robert Frost, 1912–1915.* New York: Grove, 1988.

Washington, Joseph R., Jr. *Anti-Blackness in English Religion, 1500–1800.* New York: Edwin Mellen, 1984.

Watts, Emily Stipes. " 'The posy UNITY': Anne Bradstreet's Search for Order." *Puritan Influences in American Literature.* Ed. Emory Elliott. Urbana: U of Illinois P, 1979. 23–37.

Weber, Max. *The Protestant Ethic and the Spirit of Capitalism.* Trans. Talcott Parsons. Introd. R. H. Tawney. New York: Scribner's, 1958.

Welter, Barbara. "The Cult of True Womanhood: 1820–1860." *American Quarterly* 18 (Summer 1966): 151–74.

Westbrook, Perry. *Acres of Flint: Writers of Rural New England, 1870–1900.* Washington, D.C.: Scarecrow, 1951.

Weston, Jesse L. *From Ritual to Romance.* 1920. New York: Peter Smith, 1941.

Wharton, Edith. *A Backward Glance.* New York: Scribner's, 1933.

———. *The Collected Short Stories of Edith Wharton.* Ed. R. W. B. Lewis. Vol. 1. New York: Scribner's 1968. 2 vols.

———. *Ethan Frome.* 1911. New York: Scribner's, 1970.

———. *French Ways and Their Meaning.* New York: Appleton, 1919.

———. *The Letters of Edith Wharton.* Ed. R. W. B. Lewis and Nancy Lewis. New York: Scribner's, 1988.

———. Letters to Sara Norton. Edith Wharton Papers. Houghton Library, Harvard University, Cambridge, Mass.

———. "Life and I." *Novellas and Other Writings.* Ed. Cynthia Griffin Wolff. Library of America Ser. New York: Literary Classics, 1990. 1069–96.

White, Elizabeth Wade. *Anne Bradstreet: "The Tenth Muse."* New York: Oxford UP, 1971.

White, Peter, ed. *Puritan Poets and Poetics. Seventeenth-Century American Poetry in Theory and Practice*. University Park: Pennsylvania State UP, 1985.

Whitfield, Sarah. *Magritte*. London: South Bank, 1992.

Wigglesworth, Michael. "God's Controversy with New England." *Early American Poetry: Selections from Bradstreet, Taylor, Dwight, Freneau, and Bryant*. Ed. Jane Donahue Eberwein. Madison: U of Wisconsin P, 1978. 323–38.

Williams, David R. *Wilderness Lost: The Religious Origins of the American Mind*. Selinsgrove, Penna.: Susquehanna UP, 1987.

Williams, Raymond. *The Politics of Modernism*. Ed. Tony Pinkney. London: Verso, 1989.

Williams, Roger. *A Key into the Language of America*. 1643. Ed. R. C. Alston. English Linguistics, 1500–1800: A Collection of Facsimile Rpts. 299. Menston, England: Scholar, 1971.

Williams, William Carlos. "Marianne Moore." *Marianne Moore: A Collection of Critical Essays*. Ed. Charles Tomlinson. Englewood Cliffs, N.J.: Prentice-Hall, 1969. 85–90.

Willis, Patricia C. *Marianne Moore: Vision into Verse*. Philadelphia: Rosenbach Museum & Library, 1987.

Wilson, Edmund. "Justice to Edith Wharton." *Edith Wharton: A Collection of Critical Essays*. Ed. Irving Howe. Englewood Cliffs, N.J.: Prentice-Hall, 1962. 19–31.

Winters, Yvor. *Maule's Curse: Seven Studies in the History of American Obscurantism*. Norfolk, Conn.: New Directions, 1938.

Winthrop, John. "A Model of Christian Charity." Heimert and Delbanco 82–92.

———. "Speech to the General Court." Miller, *American* 90–93.

———. *Winthrop's Journal: "History of New England" 1630–1649*. Ed. James Kendall Hosmer. Vol. 2. New York: Scribner's Sons, 1908. 2 Vols.

Wolff, Cynthia Griffin. *Emily Dickinson*. New York: Knopf, 1986.

———. *A Feast of Words: The Triumph of Edith Wharton*. New York: Oxford UP, 1977.

———. "Literary Reflections of the Puritan Character." *Journal of the History of Ideas* 19.1 (Jan.–Mar. 1968): 13–32.

———. *Samuel Richardson and the Eighteenth-Century Puritan Character*. Camden, Conn.: Archon, 1972.

———. "Thanatos and Eros: Kate Chopin's *The Awakening*." *American Quarterly* 25 (1973): 449–71. Rpt. in Chopin 233–58.

Woolf, Virginia. *A Room of One's Own*. New York: Harcourt, 1957.

———. *A Writer's Diary: Extracts from the Diary of Virginia Woolf*. Ed. Leonard Woolf. New York: Harcourt, 1954.

Wright, Jay. " 'The Unraveling of the Egg': An Interview with Jay Wright." *Callaloo* 6.3 (1983): 3–15.

Yaeger, Patricia S. " 'A Language Which Nobody Understood': Emancipatory Strategies in *The Awakening*." *Novel: A Forum on Fiction* 20 (1987): 197–219. Rpt. in Chopin 270–96.

Ziff, Larzer. "The Artist and Puritanism." *Hawthorne Centenary Essays*. Ed. Roy Harvey Pearce. Columbus: Ohio State UP, 1964. 245–69.

———. *Puritanism in America: New Culture in a New World*. New York: Viking, 1973.

Contributors

ALIKI BARNSTONE is Assistant Professor of English at Bucknell University. She is the author of the critical study *A Changing Rapture: The Development of Emily Dickinson's Poetry*. She is co-editor of *A Book of Women Poets from Antiquity to Now* (Schocken/Random House, 1980, 2nd. ed. 1992). She has published critical articles on Emily Dickinson, Emilia Lanier, Mary Wilkins Freeman, Andrew Marvell, and Ruth Stone. At present she is working on an annotated edition of H.D.'s *Trilogy* (New Directions, forthcoming 1998) and is editing an anthology, *Voices of Light: Spiritual Poetry by Women from Around the World* (Shambhala Books, forthcoming 1998). Her book of poems, *Madly in Love*, was published by Carnegie Mellon University Press in 1997.

JONATHAN BARRON is Assistant Professor of English at the University of Southern Mississippi. His publications include "Robert Frost and a New Tradition" in *His "Incalculable" Influence on Others: Essays on Robert Frost in Our Time*, edited by Earl Wilcox (University of Victoria, 1994), and, coauthored with Jenneth Johnson, " 'A Power to Virtue Friendly': The Peddlar's Guilt in Wordsworth's 'The Ruined Cottage' " in *Romantic Revisions*, edited by Robert Brinkley and Keith Hanley (Cambridge University Press). He is writing a book about the state of contemporary poetry.

MILTON J. BATES is Professor of English at Marquette University. His publications include *Wallace Stevens: A Mythology of Self* and *The Wars We Took to Vietnam: Cultural Conflict and Storytelling*.

MUTLU KONUK BLASING is Professor of English at Brown University. Most recently she has published *American Poetry: The Rhetoric of Its Forms* (Yale University Press, 1987), and *Politics and Form in Postmodern Poetry: O'Hara, Bishop, Ashbery and Merrill* (Cambridge University Press, 1995).

JANE COCALIS teaches American literature at Webster University in St. Louis, Missouri. Her research interests include modernist literature and American women's poetry. She continues to work on revisionary myths in literature.

SUSAN GOODMAN is Associate Professor of English at the University of Delaware and has recently published *Edith Wharton's Inner Circle*, which is a companion to *Edith Wharton's Women: Friends and Rivals* (University Press of New England). She has also edited, with Daniel Royot, a collection of essays, *Femmes de Conscience: Aspects du Feminisme Americain, 1848–1875* (Sorbonne University Press). She is currently writing a biography of Ellen Glasgow.

MICHAEL TOMASEK MANSON teaches English at Wheaton College in Norton, Massachusetts. He has published essays on Lorine Niedecker, Sterling Brown, and Jay Wright, and is currently working on a book entitled *The Politics of Poetic Form: Modernism, Proletarian Poetry, and the Black Renaissance*.

ROCCO MARINACCIO received his Ph.D. in English from the University of Wisconsin and is now an Assistant Professor at Manhattan College in New York City. He is working on a book on the Objectivist poets and their relation to proletarian literature in the 1920s and 1930s.

JEREDITH MERRIN is Associate Professor of English at Ohio State University. She is the author of *An Enabling Humility: Mariane Moore, Elizabeth Bishop, and the Uses of Tradition*. She has also written articles and chapters featuring these two poets, including a chapter on Moore and Bishop for the *Columbia History of American Poetry*. Her book of poetry, *Shift*, was published in 1996 by the University of Chicago Press (Phoenix Poets Series).

LORIS MIRELLA received his Ph.D. from Duke University in 1991. He has taught as a lecturer at the University of Pennsylvania in the departments of English and Comparative Literature. His main areas of interest include modernism and postmodernism, literary theory, and film studies. His most recently published articles examine English modernist poetry in relation to the Spanish Civil War and, in a co-authored work, connections between magical realism and North American cultural identity.

GEORGE MONTEIRO is Professor of English at Brown University. Among his recent publications are *Robert Frost and the New England Renaissance* (1988), *A Man Smiles at Death with Half a Face* (a translation) (1991), *The Correspondence of Henry James and Henry Adams* (1992), and *The Presence of Camões* (1996).

JOHN J. MURPHY, Professor of English at Brigham Young University and a leading Cather scholar, has edited two major volumes on Cather: *Critical Essays on Willa Cather* (1984) and *Willa Cather: Family, Community, and History* (1990). He also edited the Penguin edition of *My Antonia* (1994) and is currently preparing the scholarly edition of *Death Comes for the Archbishop* for University of Nebraska Press. He has contributed dozens of essays on Cather's fiction to periodicals and critical collections; his *My Antonia: The Road Home* (1989) remains the only book-length study of a single Cather text. Murphy serves as editor of the *Cather Newsletter* and *Literature and Belief*.

ELSA NETTELS is Professor of English at The College of William and Mary, where she has taught since 1967. Her publications include *James and Conrad* (1977, SAMLA Studies Award for 1975); *Language, Race, and Social Class in Howells's America* (1988), and *Language and Gender in American Realist Fiction: Howells, James, Wharton, and Cather* (1997). She has been the recipient of a year-long fellowship from the National Endowment for the Humanities.

ELISA NEW is Associate Professor of English at the University of Pennsylvania, where she teaches American Literature with an emphasis on American poetry, American religion, and especially the literature of New England. She is author of *The Regenerate Lyric* (Cambridge, 1993) and articles on Bradstreet, Taylor, Dickinson, and Edwards, as well as on modern Jewish culture. Her works in progress include *The Line's Eye: Poetic Experience, American Site*, to be published by Harvard University Press in 1997.

CAROL J. SINGLEY is Associate Professor of English at Rutgers University, Camden, where she teaches American literature and culture and feminist theory. She is the author of *Edith Wharton: Matters of Mind and Spirit* (Cambridge University Press, 1995) and co-editor of *Anxious Power: Reading, Writing, and Ambivalence in Narrative by Women* (State University of New York Press, 1993). Her essays on nineteenth- and twentieth-century American writers, including Catharine Maria Sedgwick, Emily Dickinson, Sarah Orne Jewett, and Edith Wharton, have appeared in various journals and collections.

IVY SCHWEITZER, Associate Professor of English and American Literature, lives in Vermont and teaches at Dartmouth College in the departments of English, Women's Studies, and Comparative Literature. Her first book, *The Work of Self-Representation: Lyric Poetry in Colonial New England* (1991) explores the construction of gender in Puritan culture. She is currently working on a study of women's interracial friendships as they are represented in U.S. cultural texts from 1830 to 1990.

CYNTHIA GRIFFIN WOLFF received her undergraduate and graduate degrees from Harvard University. She has taught at Boston University, Queens College, Manhattanville College, and the University of Massachusetts at Amherst; currently, she is Class of 1922 Professor of Humanities at the Massachusetts Institute of Technology. She has written three books: *Samuel Richardson and the Eighteenth-Century Puritan Character*, *A Feast of Words: The Triumph of Edith Wharton*, and *Emily Dickinson*. She has edited more than a dozen books, and has authored several dozen essays, most recently examinations of mid-nineteenth-century slave and abolitionist narratives. Currently, she is conducting research for a critical biography of Willa Cather.

M8175-T4
71